Luminos is the open access monograph publishing program from UC Press. Luminos provides a framework for preserving and reinvigorating monograph publishing for the future and increases the reach and visibility of important scholarly work. Titles published in the UC Press Luminos model are published with the same high standards for selection, peer review, production, and marketing as those in our traditional program. www.luminosoa.org

Precarious Creativity

Precarious Creativity

Global Media, Local Labor

Edited by

Michael Curtin and Kevin Sanson

UNIVERSITY OF CALIFORNIA PRESS

University of California Press, one of the most distinguished university presses in the United States, enriches lives around the world by advancing scholarship in the humanities, social sciences, and natural sciences. Its activities are supported by the UC Press Foundation and by philanthropic contributions from individuals and institutions. For more information, visit www.ucpress.edu.

University of California Press
Oakland, California

Suggested citation: Curtin, Michael and Sanson, Kevin (eds.). *Precarious Creativity: Global Media, Local Labor*. Oakland, University of California Press, 2016. doi: http://dx.doi.org/10.1525/luminos.10

Library of Congress Cataloging-in-Publication Data

Names: Curtin, Michael, editor. | Sanson, Kevin, 1980- editor.
Title: Precarious creativity : global media, local labor / edited by Michael Curtin and Kevin Sanson.
Description: Oakland, California : University of California Press, [2016] | "2016 | Includes bibliographical references and index.
Identifiers: LCCN 2015038834| ISBN 9780520290853 (pbk. : alk. paper) | ISBN 9780520964808 (e-edition)
Subjects: LCSH: Labor and globalization. | Mass media and globalization. | Mass media–Employees. | Cultural industries–Employees. | Precarious employment–Social aspects.
Classification: LCC HD9999.C9472 P74 2016 | DDC 331.7/6130223–dc23
LC record available at http://lccn.loc.gov/2015038834

CONTENTS

ILLUSTRATIONS

FIGURES

TABLES

Carsey-Wolf

Mellichamp

University of California
Santa Barbara

ACKNOWLEDGMENTS

Precarious Creativity grew out of a multiyear project on the globalization of labor in the film and television industries, a venture that has been generously supported by the Mellichamp Global Dynamics Initiative and the Carsey-Wolf Center at the University of California, Santa Barbara. This anthology is but one beneficiary of the generous and visionary philanthropy of Marcy Carsey, Dick Wolf, and Duncan and Suzanne Mellichamp.

We also wish to thank our sterling team of authors, who pitched in at every turn, making superb contributions, enduring numerous rounds of revision, and performing with a professionalism and timeliness that made this an intellectually rewarding experience for both of us.

We furthermore want to thank the Carsey-Wolf Center staff—Sheila Sullivan, Natalie Fawcett, and Alyson Aaris—for their critical assistance in organizing the enormously successful conference that launched this endeavor. The conference benefited as well from the participation and support of motion picture workers and organizers, most prominently Mariana Acuña Acosta, Steve Kaplan, and Daniel Lay. A shout-out as well to Jennifer Holt and Karen Petruska, our co-conspirators at the Media Industries Project, and to John Vanderhoef and Juan Llamas-Rodriguez, who provided indispensable research assistance on all aspects of this project. We also wish to thank David Marshall, Melvin Oliver, John Majewski, Constance Penley, and Ronald E. Rice for the administrative and moral support they have leant to the Carsey-Wolf Center over the years.

We are grateful as well for the sage and enthusiastic editorial guidance of Mary Francis. She deserves credit for encouraging us to publish this volume as an open access title through the Luminos program at the University of California

Press. We are proud to note that *Precarious Creativity* is the first anthology offered through Luminos, a distinction made possible through financial support from the libraries of the University of California, Santa Barbara and Queensland University of Technology. We truly appreciate this opportunity, believing these essays should be widely read and critically debated, since they examine some of the most pressing concerns of our global era. Read freely, reflect deeply, and act accordingly.

Precarious Creativity

Global Media, Local Labor

Michael Curtin and Kevin Sanson

In most parts of the world, screen media workers—actors, directors, gaffers, and makeup artists—consider Hollywood to be glamorous and aspirational. If given the opportunity to work on a major studio lot, many would make the move, believing the standards of professionalism are high and the history of accomplishment is renowned. Moreover, as a global leader, Hollywood offers the chance to rub shoulders with talented counterparts and network with an elite labor force that earns top-tier pay and benefits. Yet despite this reputation, veterans say the view from inside isn't so rosy, that working conditions have been deteriorating since the 1990s if not earlier. This grim outlook is supported by industry statistics that show the number of good jobs has been shrinking as studios outsource production to Atlanta, London, and Budapest, among others.

No longer is Hollywood the default setting for major film and television productions. California faces stiff competition from both domestic and international locations. New York, Georgia, and Louisiana have all emerged as major production centers, often jostling with Canada and the United Kingdom for the top spots on yearly production reports. In fact, the most recent study from FilmL.A. concludes (somewhat hastily): "While these jurisdictions may trade yearly rank positions for total project count, budget value and production spending, there are no jurisdictions immediately poised to dethrone them."[1] Yet studio bosses and producers have made it clear that they intend to keep scouring the globe for lower labor rates and less regulated environs. Right-to-work states are especially attractive, as are overseas locations where unions have little or no clout. In many places, governments offer tax breaks and subsidies as further inducements, sending a message to rivals that no single production center enjoys uncontestable pre-eminence.

Consequently, producers have grown ever more fleet footed, playing off one place against another in a never-ending quest to secure the most favorable conditions for their bottom lines. Today's increasingly mobile and globally dispersed mode of production thrives (indeed, depends) on interregional competition, driving down pay rates, benefits, and job satisfaction for media workers around the world. Producers say corporate financial imperatives compel them to contain costs, especially labor costs. Consequently, workdays are growing longer, productivity pressures are more intense, and creative autonomy is diminishing. Overall, this has put severe financial, physical, and emotional strain on workers and their families and further threatens the many independent businesses that service the major studios.

At the 2013 Academy Awards, evidence of this trend gained wider currency when the Oscar-winning visual effects team from *Life of Pi* used part of its acceptance speech to express solidarity with demonstrators outside the Dolby Theater who were protesting Hollywood's "race to the bottom." Like most studio features, the film earned widespread critical acclaim and more than $600 million at the global box office by relying heavily on visual effects. Yet the very artists who created those effects were outraged by the fact that their Oscar-winning company, Rhythm & Hues, had been driven into bankruptcy only days before the awards ceremony. The news sent ripples of outrage through the effects community, since it was seen as a telling indicator of the precarious conditions under which even the best companies and their employees currently operate.[2] Fierce global competition for studio contracts forces shops into an aggressive bidding process that ultimately undermines the welfare of employees. Throughout the VFX sector as a whole, workers suffer from low pay, long hours, and uncertain job security. Much of this is attributable to the fact that digital effects artists lack union representation, but unionized workers are also feeling the crunch.

In 2007, the Writers Guild of America went on strike against the Hollywood studios to claim their share of the growing revenue stream from digital media, such as Blu-ray, Netflix, and Hulu. Although royalties and benefits were at the core of the dispute, writers also complained about growing pressure to produce ancillary content for web sites and social media in addition to the work they put into film and television scripts. This unpaid "second shift" is part of a growing pattern of employers using worker concerns over job security to raise productivity.[3] Sometimes producers specifically demand additional off-the-clock labor. Other times these expectations are conveyed more subtly as logical extensions of, for example, a TV showrunner's marketing and promotional obligations. Successful shows now require supplemental multiplatform publicity, such as personal tweets, blogs, and behind-the-scenes footage exclusively produced for online distribution. WGA members also expressed frustration about the encroachment of corporate sponsors into sacred spaces like the writers' room.[4] These concerns fueled a bitter three-month showdown between the guild's 12,000 members and the Alliance of

Motion Picture and Television Producers, representing the major studios. With support from other craft and talent unions, the WGA strike brought Hollywood to a standstill but in the end made only modest progress on key issues. Furthermore, in a cruel epilogue, writers now find studios using the (questionable) financial losses associated with the work stoppage as justification for offering less-than-favorable compensation packages in the poststrike era.[5]

Hollywood has a tradition of labor activism that stretches back to the 1930s, with unions and guilds today representing a wide spectrum of artistic, craft, and industrial employees. Although the history of labor representation has been fraught with tensions and controversies, screen workers have at times been capable of mounting campaigns to resist managerial pressures and agitate for better conditions. By comparison, Louisiana, Georgia, and Florida—all now seen as viable locations for motion picture production—are right-to-work states where local laws undermine the prospect of unionization, making the workforce more pliable. Moreover, outside the United States, in cities like Prague, where there are no creative or craft unions, day rates for talent and crew are a small fraction of what U.S. and U.K. crew members earn. In other locations, such as Vancouver and London, unions have offered significant concessions to attract Hollywood productions, cutting wages and revising work rules to satisfy U.S. producers. And in China, the world's second-largest theatrical market and therefore a desirable partner for coproductions like *Transformers 4*, unions are an arm of the Communist Party, representing the interests of ruling elites rather than workers.

When Hollywood producers select a distant locale, they are often welcomed as a fresh source of skilled jobs in a glamorous industry, but the jobs they create tend to be temporary, and the workplace pressures are often more intense than in Southern California. Safety issues are perhaps indicative. On February 20, 2014, tragedy struck on a railroad bridge in rural Georgia where a film crew had set up a hospital bed in order to shoot a dream sequence for *Midnight Rider,* an independent, low-budget picture about the Allman Brothers rock band. Working outside the bounds of the regular production schedule and hoping to "steal" a memorable shot, the crew, which included Oscar-winning actor William Hurt, suddenly found itself in the path of a fast-moving freight train. As they frantically scattered, twenty-seven-year-old Sarah Jones, the second assistant camera operator and the youngest crew member, tenaciously adhered to the protocol of her craft by struggling to protect the equipment, a fatal misjudgment that cost her life. Her death sent shock waves through the industry. Web sites and social media lit up with expressions of outrage. T-shirts, umbrellas, and improvised signage on motion picture sets around the globe enunciated a sentiment widely shared in the world's most glamorous industry: "We are all Sarah Jones."

According to the Occupational Safety and Health Administration, at least ten other on-set fatalities occurred in the United States during the decade leading up to Jones's death. Although no reliable figures exist for accidents outside the States, workers were quick to recall fatalities during the filming of *The Dark Knight Rises* in the United Kingdom in 2008,[6] *The Expendables 2* in Bulgaria in 2011,[7] and *XXX* in the Czech Republic in 2012.[8] Said one camera operator, "You can probably ask any film production technician who's been on the job ten years, and they can probably give you half a dozen incidences where they should have been killed or injured, and just by the grace of God they weren't."[9] Another noted that most crew members, especially young and inexperienced ones, are afraid to speak up about safety concerns for fear of jeopardizing their chances at future jobs.

Mobile production outside the purview of strong union oversight isn't the only factor inciting concern about the increasing personal risk. In 2006, Oscar-winning cinematographer Haskell Wexler produced *Who Needs Sleep?* a searing documentary inspired by the death of an assistant camera operator in a car crash after falling asleep at the wheel on his way home from an eighteen-hour workday. For Wexler, then in his early eighties, the tragedy was representative of a growing trend toward excessively long work shifts, which are often scheduled back-to-back with little turnaround time. The film documents personal and family stress engendered by early calls, late nights, and long weeks. As part of a broader movement called "12on12off," the documentary advocates industry-wide reform to rein in such abuses. Although supported by a wide spectrum of craft workers, talent, and even producers, many were unwilling to speak on camera for fear of being quietly blacklisted in a town where jobs are growing ever more scarce. Even union leaders were skittish about the campaign, many of them afraid to antagonize studio bosses and spur the ongoing migration of production jobs out of California. With so many individuals resigned to suffering in silence, it undermines the potential for collective action and institutional reform.

And yet what is perhaps most remarkable about these precarious labor conditions is that the pattern repeats itself in many parts of the world. In October 2008, the Federation of Western India Cine Employees, an alliance of twenty-two unions representing below-the-line workers ranging from dancers and extras to editors and carpenters called a citywide strike in Mumbai, the entertainment capital of South Asia. More than 147,000 workers participated in the labor action, and topline talent, including Shah Rukh Khan and Amitabh Bachchan, walked out in sympathy, shutting down film and TV production on the eve of a busy holiday season.

At the time, the average filmworker was making $9.75 a day, and the average television employee a little more than $8 a day. Unions representing craft workers and service employees began agitating for higher wages around 2005, pointing to the burgeoning prosperity of Bollywood, which was then generating over $3 billion a year in revenues and paying its marquee talent more than a million dollars for each film. In 2007, unions and producers signed a memorandum of understanding that would raise wages by as much as 15 percent. Eighteen months later, workers walked out after extended haggling about broken promises, claiming more than $10 million in unpaid wages, with many workers saying they hadn't seen a paycheck in months. In addition to wages, the strike raised concerns about long work hours that in some cases involved thirty-hour shifts. On-the-job safety and meal breaks were other points of contention.

Facing a massive labor action that drew public support from Bollywood's biggest stars, producers quickly relented, agreeing to raise wages in line with the original memorandum, arbitrate claims for unpaid wages, and establish a twelve-hour cap on work shifts.[10] Despite this quick victory, union leaders expressed deeper concerns about what they say are concerted attempts to undermine organized labor by hiring nonunion workers and relocating production outside of Mumbai, especially to overseas locations like Scotland and Australia. Closer to home, officials criticized a system of subcontracting that helps producers circumvent union agreements. Most notoriously, some subcontractors delayed paychecks for months or even refused to pay at all. Union leaders have complained that workers are more vulnerable than ever and that hard-earned gains from the past are being challenged at every turn.

The Bombay motion picture industry was until recently renowned as a familial system of employment that was at turns discreetly exploitative and touchingly paternalistic. Since the 1990s, the commercialization of television and the corporatization of the movie business have transformed a national media economy into a multimedia global juggernaut with skyrocketing revenues and blockbuster production budgets. Consequently, the relations of production have grown more formal and contractual. They have also been transformed by management logics that are remarkably reminiscent of those being practiced by the major Hollywood media conglomerates.

Of course very significant differences remain, and as we will see in the chapters that follow, similarities in labor trends around the world are marked by enduring and profound differences as well. Chapters about the radical alterity of the Nigerian videofilm industry and tumultuous conditions of creativity in the Arab world make this point only too well. Yet our essays converge around the issue of precarity, a term that points to a broader set of concerns about relations of production and the quality of social life worldwide. Andrew Ross drew these connections in *Nice Work If You Can Get It,* arguing that "no one, not even those in the traditional professions, can any longer expect a fixed pattern of employment in the course of their lifetime, and they are under more and more pressure to anticipate, and prepare for, a future in which they still will be able to compete in a changing marketplace."[11] Ross characterizes precariousness as a common condition for workers all over the world, from the low-end service sector in developing nations to white-collar elites in centers of capital. No longer can individual workers expect a single career; instead they must ready themselves for iterative change and persistent contingency as standard employment and its associated entitlements become artifacts of a bygone industrial era. Precarious livelihoods are indicative of a new world order of social and economic instability.

Although film and television workers are often characterized as highly trained industrial elites, they share similar concerns, which have been fueled by the growth of media conglomerates and the globalization of production. Beginning in the 1980s, deregulation and privatization rippled around the world, transforming national economies and profoundly affecting media industries. Pressed by commercial interests, most governments relinquished long-standing public service policies, opening the door to transnational investment and unleashing a torrent of technological innovation that spurred the development of new media delivery services through satellite, cable, Internet, and mobile communication channels.

Some effects have been positive, but others have proven quite troubling. Today both private and public media systems around the world are driven by market imperatives that foster intense competition between transnational services and local providers. Media sovereignty, previously a foundational principle of national regulation, has been trumped by discourses of consumer sovereignty and market competition. With national borders eroding and services multiplying, media companies have responded by merging into vast multiplatform global conglomerates, including Hollywood's Time Warner, Bollywood's Reliance Media, Brazil's Grupo Globo, and the pan-Arab Rotana Group.

Leading media companies today are larger and more complicated than ever before. They are also more closely attuned to financial imperatives than they are to the subtleties of creative endeavor or the nuances of audience taste. Media CEOs spend most of their time wooing investors and crafting quarterly reports rather than thinking about content or creativity. This in turn insulates corporate decision makers from creative practice, privileging content that is relentlessly market-tested at all stages of production, resulting in a creative process that begins and ends with competitive positioning. In the fields of narrative film and television, this has encouraged a fixation on marquee talent and presold brands that can be parlayed into blockbuster media franchises. In the minds of many executives, marketable content is king, which means they are willing to bid astronomical sums for the services of Shah Rukh Khan or the rights to Harry Potter.

Pressed by the rising costs of franchise rights and top talent, conglomerates seek to contain production expenses by trimming budgets in other areas, especially below-the-line labor. As suggested above, this logic is manifested in new power plays aimed at increasing productivity and diminishing the wages of craft and service workers. Moreover, producers and executives outsource jobs to independent contractors, resist input from union officials, and undermine the creative authority of skilled artisans. New technologies have furthermore allowed employers to knit together transnational production teams so that workers often find themselves collaborating or competing with lower-paid counterparts in such places as Hengdian and Hyderabad. This respatialization of media labor exerts persistent pressure on workers and labor organizations, offering employers novel forms of leverage.

Yet the shifting geographies of media production have also opened the door to opportunities for screen media workers. Government policymakers in many parts of the world initially expressed reservations about deregulation and globalization, but they ultimately welcomed the chance to collaborate with transnational media conglomerates, embracing a set of commercial practices that have increasingly become the norm. During the 1990s, policymakers began to position their countries as hotspots of the "creative economy," reasoning that intellectual and cultural output had become distinguishing features of the world's wealthiest societies. Sophisticated financial services and biotech research are emblematic of this global postindustrial hierarchy, but the most charismatic sector is popular culture, which many believe is the signature component of creative economies. An oft-repeated anecdote of the era pointed to a 1994 presidential advisory report in South Korea that compared the total revenues from Steven Spielberg's *Jurassic Park* to the export earnings from 1.5 million Hyundai automobiles. This striking comparison instigated a greater allocation of government resources to the media sector, contributing to the renowned "Korean Wave" of pop cultural exports that subsequently swept across East Asia.[12]

The policy discourse on creative economies has fueled competition among such cities as London, Vancouver, Beijing, and Dubai, all aspiring to become media capitals renowned for their talented workforces. Many governments offer subsidized facilities, tax incentives, and labor concessions that are designed to nurture local capacity and lure producers away from other locales, especially Hollywood, where real estate and labor costs are substantially higher. Yet these cities now face competition as well, fueling a race to the bottom as conglomerates hopscotch the globe, playing each place against the others, in large part by exacting concessions from workers.

Arresting this race to the bottom will require greater awareness by all parties. Public policy research has explored ways to nurture a creative economy, but little has been written about the declining labor conditions within those economies. Much has been made of the challenges posed by media conglomeration, but little of it addresses the impact on creative employees and workplace practices. And while researchers have detailed the causes and effects of "runaway production," little of this work is framed by a global perspective, nor does it examine possibilities for building transnational labor alliances or regulatory frameworks that will be essential if conditions are to improve.

Shortcomings in current research are largely caused by institutional constraints. Executives generally focus on market research and cost containment strategies that have the potential to improve their quarterly reports.[13] Government leaders seek policy recommendations that will help them grow their economies.[14] University administrators privilege media management studies to further embed their institutions within prevailing funding structures. And labor organizations support research that has immediate relevance to their existing members.[15] No organization has the motivation to build a balanced and comprehensive portrayal of the trends, conditions, and concerns of screen media workers during an era of unprecedented challenges and opportunities.

As for scholarly research, media globalization has garnered significant attention, but there remains a relative paucity of research on labor issues.[16] A notable exception is *Global Hollywood,* which provides a critical framework for understanding the play of power between major media conglomerates and their increasingly globalized workforce.[17] Like many political economies of media, the authors argue that Hollywood uses both commercial and political strategies to ensure its cultural dominance around the world.[18] Uniquely, however, the authors also analyze the changing conditions of creative labor in the film and television industries, contending that studio operations have become increasingly mobile, allowing producers to pursue cost advantages and government subsidies worldwide. Moreover, by threatening to move their operations to the most amenable location, studios exploit the advantages of a global labor market *and* exact concessions from Hollywood unions at home. In a groundbreaking argument, the authors show how the New International Division of Cultural Labor (NICL) is driving down wages and working conditions globally. Yet the analysis operates largely at the level of metatheory and talks little about conditions on the ground or the specific middle-range dynamics of this race to the bottom.[19] Susan Christopherson offers a similarly expansive perspective on runaway production in the film and television industries, noting that government incentive programs and flexible modes of production have made it easier for transnational media firms to outsource labor.[20]

Among the forces driving these changes are local and national economic development policies that are informed by the work of scholars such as Richard Florida, who contends that globalization has unleashed a growing competition among cities to attract creative talent in order to enhance their service and information industries, which he considers the most prosperous sectors of the global economy.[21] Likewise, John Howkins suggests that mature industrialized countries must invest in the "creative economy" if they are to cope with challenges posed by the flight of manufacturing overseas. Howkins contends that deindustrialization can best be addressed by enhancing the human capital that a country has to offer. This approach has been embraced by policymakers in many parts of the world as a justification for subsidies, infrastructural investments, and training programs in media, computer, and design industries, among others.[22] Although these policies are often controversial,[23] some scholars have nevertheless embraced them, realizing that failure to take action could doom the prospects of local media institutions and further strengthen Hollywood's global grip. At the same time, though, they are attentive to the challenges and compromises that such policies entail.[24]

Interestingly both the political economy and economic development approaches tend to gloss over localized effects of globalization on the actual labor practices at cultural and creative work sites. By comparison, researchers in the sociology of work tradition offer empirically rich inquiries into the personal and professional lives of creative workers in advertising, fashion, design, music, new media, and the arts.[25] Their work reveals recurrent concerns about a largely flexible, itinerant workforce. Hired on a contractual basis, these workers suffer intensifying productivity demands that intrude on their personal and family lives. They furthermore confront creative and compensatory risks that make them vulnerable to swings in demand and in turn make them willing to accept less than desirable assignments. This scholarship also examines gender, racial, and global inequalities. Such issues resonate with many of our own preoccupations with the quality of screen media labor, especially in an era when digital technologies are reshaping the contours of work and industry organization. Yet we worry that literature on the sociology of work tends to find latent creative potential anywhere, in anyone, and from anything. This diffuse conception of cultural work does not do justice to the specificities of screen media's industrial mode of production and pays scant attention to the particular qualities of its highly specialized and detailed division of labor.

A more nuanced and richly textured approach can be found in the work of John Caldwell and his colleagues, who explore both the stylistic implications of screen media labor routines and the ways workers understand, represent, and theorize their labor.[26] Inspired by ethnographic and discourse analysis, "production studies" use specific instances to analyze broader trends and relations of power, but they tend to stop short of linking their analysis to a global political economy, preferring instead to offer specific claims about the internal dynamics of media industries and workplaces. They also tend to be suspicious of totalizing frameworks, preferring to see power as multivalent and capillary rather than centrally anchored by the logic of capital. Again, this scholarship is path-breaking and highly innovative, but it rarely—with the exception of Mayer[27]—extends its frame of analysis to account for global dynamics.

The approaches outlined above are sometimes pitted against each other, but recent developments suggest the necessity of adopting an integrative approach to address the relentless and pervasive class warfare being waged against creative workers around the world. We are deeply concerned by the rapid transformation of screen media, noting the growing convergence of visual and narrative styles, the ascendancy of commercial values at all levels of practice, and the increasing interconnection of media institutions within a global regime of accumulation. We do not see these trends as indicative of a "once-and-for-all victory" by a capitalist cabal but rather as specific aspects of an ongoing war of position distinguished at once by adversity and opportunity for the labor movement. In fact, this tension—between adversity and opportunity, between gains and losses, between hope and despair—remains a structuring concern across the collection as a whole. In what follows, we invited contributors from around the world to offer insight into the changing nature of film, television, and digital media work in diverse locations: Hyderabad, Lagos, Prague, New Orleans, Miami, the Middle East, and of course, Hollywood. Case studies address the growing pressures on creative workers in these cities and regions as well as the opportunities made available by the increasingly global nature of media production. Debates also touch on issues of advocacy and negotiation—identifying what resources are (or are not) available to address some of the challenges that confront workers in the screen media industries. The collection therefore maps out what we see as a significant terrain of scholarly inquiry into the multiple and specific ways that local labor practices engage with and contest processes of media globalization.

Perceptive readers will notice a range of agendas and perspectives across the chapters. They will also detect a shared commitment to untangling the nuances of precarious creativity across different industry sites and scales, and in spaces where those sites and scales converge as part of larger global projects. Our ultimate intervention not only considers the struggles taking place within the spatially dispersed operations of the world's largest media conglomerates but also brings these approaches into conversation with research that expands scholarly inquiry into working conditions and labor organizing efforts around the world. In doing so, we hope the collection constitutes a scale-making project of its own by transgressing disciplinary, methodological, and geographic boundaries in its engagement with current debates on creative labor.

Labor relations are a historical phenomenon—over time they inevitably adapt and transform.[28] But the contributors to this collection approach the contemporary moment as a particularly critical historical juncture, a point in time when corporate consolidation, digital technologies, and the globalization of production have so altered the structural forms and everyday practices of screen media production that our object of study risks appearing much more amorphous. This in turn raises urgent questions about how we even conceive of labor in the first place when meaningful opportunities for creative endeavor now appear ubiquitous to those who champion the shady boundaries between producers and consumers, professionals and amateurs, work and fun. This point is made most forcefully in Toby Miller's opening critique of the popular and critical enthusiasm for digital media's emancipatory potential, a contemporary zeitgeist, he argues, that constitutes a detrimental blind spot in our scholarly attempts to wrangle with the dark and damning risks technophilia poses to the environment and organized labor. For Miller, we are so enamored with (digital) disruption, transformation, and transcendence that old media and its associated critiques, like political economy, have become passé. So too are concerns about the everyday lives of professional media workers, now that everything from political activism to creative production has succumbed to the open and participatory allure of digital technologies and social media networks. John Caldwell also cautions against overly enthusiastic readings of the digital era by drawing attention to the increasingly core creative and economic value of what he calls "spec work," a reiterative process of brainstorming, calculated guesswork, and creative presumption that has become pervasive among above- and below-the-line workers. Think public pitch fests, beta-tested web series, freely circulating demo reels, or online self-promotion. Like Miller, Caldwell doesn't champion this development as the function of a more open, democratic, and participatory capitalist system but regards it as the opposite: an unregulated, unruly, and uncompensated practice that undermines labor value by giving away much intellectual property for little in return.

Marking labor as more diffuse and dispersed shares some conceptual similarity with the notion of the social factory most closely linked to autonomist Marxism, a school of thought that rejects the industrial factory as the sole site of labor relations and instead posits a more decentralized perspective wherein "the whole society is placed at the disposal of profit."[29] Shanti Kumar explicitly engages with this concept in his essay on the proliferation of "film city" proposals across a number of major cities in India. By building buzz and excitement about their urban environs, film city promoters attempt to brand locations as hotbeds for creative activity and innovation; in doing so, they mobilize urban life as a whole in the pursuit of capital. By this logic, individuals are not alienated objects employed as pawns in a game for global competitive advantage but rather eager contributors to a city's creative momentum because of the affective allure of participating in that process. Vicki Mayer similarly explores the economic and affective registers of urban labor relations in her discussion of the HBO production *Treme*, which was filmed in New Orleans in the 2010s. Mayer turns to the "moral economy" of local labor to better understand how the show's producers encouraged the city's residents to take up unpaid or underpaid work as background extras on the series. She describes the strategy as "the odd pairing of the ethically right and instrumentally efficient," a form of exploitation necessary to resolve bottom-line financial pressures but nevertheless embraced by locals because their labor was framed a part of a larger moral commitment to the city's post-Katrina recovery.

Violaine Roussel engages in similar debates about transformations of the creative apparatus but shifts the focus away from the motivations of screen media workers to consider how media concentration and globalization have transformed the practice of "agenting" in Hollywood. Here she connects the diversified activities and worldwide operations of talent agencies to the increasingly complex division of labor among talent agents, who now work in teams designed to provide multimedia coverage for major clients, a dramatic change from the personalized relationships of the past. This bureaucratization of agency practice has diminished the creative aspects of the job and undermined interpersonal relations between agents and talent. Petr Szczepanik also considers the shifting nature of job functions, career trajectories, and creative collaboration by focusing on production culture in Prague. He examines local technicians who make up the vast majority of below-the-line crew on large-scale international productions. These craft workers crew up for foreign producers and department heads and thus operate in a professional world distinct from laborers who work on domestic film and television projects. Although international productions offer local technicians better pay, more stability, and opportunities for knowledge and skills exchange, these assignments rarely offer a sense of creative engagement or opportunities for upward mobility.

An even more complicated set of dynamics is at work in regional media industries, as explained by our contributors Matt Sienkiewicz, Tejaswini Ganti, and Juan Piñon. Taking issue with reductive criticisms of Western assistance to nascent media operations in Kabul, Afghanistan, Sienkiewicz paints a much more nuanced picture of the trade-offs and tensions at work when global institutions helped foster the development of Afghanistan's first cadre of female television professionals. His analysis highlights the limited yet notable success of female producers whose newfound career opportunities are nevertheless marked by a disproportionate sense of precariousness when compared to local male colleagues and media workers in other parts of the world. Turning from gender to class dynamics, Ganti chronicles what she describes as a curious paradox in the production of Bollywood films, where English has become the lingua franca among the core creative and financial decision makers. Significantly, she explains this linguistic hierarchy as a concrete manifestation of the increasingly international and commercial orientation of Hindi cinema. In short, English proficiency functions as a sign of the industry's ongoing globalization, rationalization, and professionalization, while onscreen dialects help distinguish individual films in an increasingly crowded marketplace both at home and abroad. This in turn leads to a stratified work world in which language competency serves as a marker of power and authority. Global–local dynamics also figure in Piñon's analysis of Latin American television productions. He notes that a wave of corporate consolidation, privatization, and deregulation has opened local and national television markets to the incursion of transnational media conglomerates. By navigating around national media monopolies, global companies have made pacts with local independent television producers to suture global corporate interests to local tastes and cultures. While these collaborations open space for more innovative narratives and formats, they also construct asymmetrical relationships in which local creative labor is at once necessary and ultimately dispensable.

Each of these case studies underscores the ways particular cultural and political histories and economic policies shape working conditions, cultural values, and personal/professional networks in local production cultures in New Orleans, Prague, Kabul, Mumbai, and Latin America. Yet even outside the formal circuits of capital, screen media workers are finding themselves integrated into larger global networks. Jade Miller's contribution on the Nigerian videofilm industry enumerates the ways Nollywood's fragmented exclusion from capitalist modernity engenders a high degree of informality that structures all stages of creative production—from development to distribution. This makes trust-based relationships a necessary but fraught tactic to navigate an industry with few formal governance structures, established training schemes, or labor protections. In Nollywood, power is concentrated in the hands of "marketers," the lucky few who use their knowledge of an informal, opaque marketplace to enshrine their control over the industry.

In the discussions thus far, we can see how the spatial exploitation of film and television labor draws on an ever-expanding pool of participants. Struggles for authority, legitimacy, and inclusion continue to confront screen media workers in these locations and others, and thus underscore the need to consider the strategies and tactics workers employ to circumvent the formal and informal constraints of the social division of labor. Heather Berg and Constance Penley call the responses to these challenges "creative precarity" in their examination of the ways performers in the adult film industry survive and sometimes thrive despite formidable challenges, which include rampant piracy, diminished opportunities, and depressed wages. Drawing attention to this often overlooked site of screen media labor is a critical intervention precisely because pornography workers have long developed strategies of coping and resistance that might be adapted to other screen media work sites. Kristen Warner makes a similar historical point in her essay on casting directors and the strategies that racial and ethnic minority performers employ to circumvent exclusionary professional networks and hiring practices in the film and television industries. For Warner, the circumstances so many scholars characterize as novel developments have been an ever-present condition for minority performers in Hollywood. Yet because common industrial logic refuses to see the lack of diversity as a persistent problem, performers forgo political solidarity or collective resistance to embrace whatever strategies will improve their individual chances of getting a job. This makes meaningful social change elusive.

Possibilities for "actionable reform" figure prominently in John Banks and Stuart Cunningham's chapter about the Australian digital games industry. With the global financial crisis prompting major publishers to withdraw from the Australian market, game developers have struggled to adapt to a new industrial landscape. For some, this has been difficult, while for others it has fostered newfound creative autonomy that encourages them to produce original intellectual property.

As with the porn industry in Southern California, Banks and Cunningham find the precarious conditions of game developers in Australia not an inevitable condition but a product of government policies and industry regulations. Thus any efforts at reform must target policy and governance as mechanisms to increase certainty and stability in the sector.

Turning to East Asia, Anthony Fung and Michael Keane parse out alternative approaches to creative labor based on the particular circumstances of their respective case studies. For Keane, precarious creativity is too conceptually entwined with Western contexts, where concern is directed at the material conditions of the workforce. That is, workers who enjoy creative opportunities often make sacrifices in terms of benefits, compensation, and work hours. In China, however, creativity promises to improve the material conditions of the workforce because it opens the door to professional mobility and higher wages. Of course, there's still a dark side to creative work, but less in the realm of the material and more in the realm of imagination, where workers risk the wrath of state censorship. Fung similarly explores the contours of creative practice in East and Southeast Asia, where workers differently engage with the global digital games industry. Fung argues that the distinctive socio-political contexts of Seoul, Singapore, and Beijing shape how employees come to understand and value their own work and workaday lives. Both Fung and Keane encourage us to think otherwise about the very meaning of creativity within the diverse contexts of Asian cultural industries.

Marwan Kraidy pushes these concerns even farther by focusing on creative forms of dissent against the backdrop of the Arab uprisings of 2011 and 2012. Kraidy theorizes how the convergence of authoritarian regimes, activist politics, and digital technologies in the Middle East fundamentally alters our received notions of both creativity and precarity. He further distinguishes revolutionary creative labor from industrial creative labor, establishing the former as "an embodied, extremely precarious practice unfolding in a life-or-death situation, one among several kinds of labor (from physical struggle to mainstream media production) that challenge authoritarian leaders." Kraidy's intervention, then, not only makes visible different forms and qualities of precarious creativity but also extends the parameters of debate about creative labor, reframing core concerns about global visibility, creative autonomy, and subjectivity.

Kraidy's contribution shares much with earlier entries that highlighted the different registers—economic, affective, and political—of urban labor relations, while also theorizing a particular mode of production with a distinctive global orientation. Similarly his chapter recalls the strategies and tactics of other marginalized media workers when he enumerates the modes of resistance revolutionary artists employ in the face of extreme circumstances.

It's fitting to conclude this collection, then, with an extended discussion of the future prospects for collective action: what can traditional unions and advocacy groups do to ensure safe working conditions and quality of life in such tumultuous times? Herman Gray responds with ruminations on the larger assumptions that structure research and policy regarding the industry's diversity problems. In particular, Gray traces how coupling on-screen representation and off-screen demography has come to shape so much critical debate about racial parity and progress, and how the site of media production has served as the default target for state, industry, and academic interventions. Most interventions not only have failed but have become predictable institutional exercises with little tangible value. Given these shortcomings, Gray suggests other research possibilities for studying race and racism within the context of a dramatically shifting intermedial landscape, pointing to new forms of affect, attachment, and identification as powerful tools for pursuing social justice within the context of creative practice. Likewise, Allison Perlman establishes an alternative framework through which to study the politics of creative labor by recasting media advocacy itself as a form of media work. Focusing on the National Hispanic Media Coalition, she demonstrates the critical value of media advocacy in contexts where individual laborers lack the ability to personally agitate for collective change in the workplace. Yet this work is threatened by the precarious existence of the advocacy organizations themselves, as they increasingly (and paradoxically) rely on funding from corporate media to support their operating budgets, reliance that can compromise a group's ability to carry out its core functions on behalf of the constituencies it represents. In similar fashion, Miranda Banks and David Hesmondhalgh outline a number of pressures undermining the current effectiveness of labor unions and guilds in the entertainment industries. Marketization, digitization, and freelance labor are obvious culprits, but through an extended examination of the Writers Guild of America, the authors offer a compelling account of how a national labor organization can proactively respond to and influence global production flows and transnational labor networks. Banks and Hesmondhalgh contend that even though significant obstacles remain, the struggle to establish a global consciousness among screenwriters is perhaps a first step toward building the sorts of international alliances necessary to tackle many of the challenges described in this book.

Overall, this collection of essays attempts to expand the geographic and intellectual range of screen media studies, moving past romanticized assumptions about creative work in favor of more incisive discussions about power, equity, and collective action. Our contributors contend that we must first make visible the escalating stress and strain confronting media workers worldwide before outlining compelling alternatives or transferable solutions. *Precarious Creativity* therefore encourages readers to view these issues through a global lens in order to avoid the provincialism that has too often characterized labor and policy debates. Although well aware of the diverse conditions of screen media production, this volume offers critical reflection on the ways workers are increasingly caught up in a global production apparatus. As our contributors make clear, the central tension is not one between local laborers in different regions—a perspective that feeds too easily into the hands of producers—but is rather a struggle against the diverse yet increasingly interconnected modalities of exploitation in screen media production around the world.

NOTES

1. FilmL.A., *Feature Film Report* (Los Angeles: FilmL.A. Research, 2014), 13.

2. Michael Curtin and John Vanderhoef, "A Vanishing Piece of the Pi: The Globalization of Visual Effects Labor," *Television and New Media* 16.3 (2015): 219–239.

3. Michael Curtin, Jennifer Holt, and Kevin Sanson, eds, *Distribution Revolution: Conversations about the Digital Future of Film and Television* (Berkeley: University of California Press, 2014), 159–163.

4. Curtin, Holt, and Sanson, *Distribution Revolution*, 191–192.

5. Felicia D. Henderson, "It's Our Own Fault: How Post-strike Hollywood Continues to Punish Writers for Striking," *Popular Communication* 8.3 (2010): 232–239.

6. "The Curse of Batman: Special Effects Expert Killed while Shooting Stunt Scene on Set of Latest Film," *Mail Online*, November 4, 2008, www.dailymail.co.uk/news/article-1082689/The-Curse-Batman-Special-effects-expert-killed-shooting-stunt-scene-set-latest-film.html.

7. Nellie Andreeva, "UPDATE: Stuntmen in 'Expendables 2' Fatal Accident Identified," *Deadline*, October 31, 2011, http://deadline.com/2011/10/stuntman-dies-during-the-filming-of-the-expendables-2-188158/

8. "Stuntmen Harry O'Connor Dies during Aerial Stunts for TripleX," *Aint It Cool News*, April 7, 2002, www.aintitcool.com/node/11928

9. David S. Cohen and Ted Johnson, "'Midnight Rider' and the Fatal Flaws of Hollywood Safety," *Variety*, March 11, 2014, http://variety.com/2014/biz/news/midnight-rider-accident-leaves-the-industry-pondering-the-fatal-flaws-in-on-set-safety-1201129615/.

10. Madhur Singh, "The Bollywood Strike Hits Festival Season," *Time*, October 2, 2008, http://content.time.com/time/world/article/0,8599,1846497,00.html; "1.5 Lakh Bollywood Workers Strike: Demand Regulated Working Hours," October 1, 2008, http://articles.economictimes.indiatimes.com/2008-10-01/news/27725277_1_film-shooting-western-india-cine-employees-indefinite-strike; Randeep Ramesh, "Strike by 100,000 Film Workers Brings Bollywood to a Standstill," *Guardian*, October 2, 2008, www.theguardian.com/world/2008/oct/02/4; "Bollywood Workers Strike 'Over,'" *BBC*, October 3, 2008, http://news.bbc.co.uk/2/hi/south_asia/7651586.stm.

11. Andrew Ross, *Nice Work If You Can Get It: Life and Labor in Precarious Times* (New York. New York University Press, 2009), 2. Also see a special issue of *Theory, Culture and Society* edited by Rosalind Gil and Andy Pratt, 2008.

12. Doobo Shim, "South Korean Media Industry in the 1990s and the Economic Crisis," *Prometheus* 20.4 (2002): 337–350; Chi-Yun Shin and Julian Stringer, *New Korean Cinema* (Oxford: Oxford University Press, 2005); Beng-Huat Chua and Koichi Iwabuchi, *East Asian Pop Culture: Analysing the Korean Wave* (Hong Kong: Hong Kong University Press, 2008).

13. Media companies generate a lot of internal research that they don't make public for competitive reasons. They also contract proprietary studies from market research firms and management consultants and subscribe to independent market research services, such as Nielsen, NRG, Rentrak, as well as getting research input from talent agencies, MPA, and so on.

14. E&B Data, *The Effects of Foreign Location Shooting on Canadian Film and Television Industry* (Toronto: Department of Canadian Heritage, 2010); BaxStarr Consulting Group, *Fiscal and Economic Impact Analysis of Louisiana's Entertainment Incentives* (New Orleans: Louisiana Economic

Development Office, 2011); Screen Australia, *Playing for Keeps: Enhancing Sustainability in Australia's Interactive Entertainment Industry* (Sydney: Screen Australia, 2011); Film Policy Review Panel, *A Future for British Film* (London: Department of Culture, Media and Sport, 2012).

15. Labor unions and guilds do not disclose research they commission to protect its value during contract negotiations. The most prominent exceptions are studies on employment practices and diversity. For example, "2014 DGA Episodic Television Diversity Hiring Report," September 17, 2014, www.dga.org/News/PressReleases/2014/140917-Episodic-Director-Diversity-Report.aspx; Darnell Hunt, *Turning Missed Opportunities Into Realized Ones: 2014 Hollywood Writers Report* (Los Angeles: WGA, 2014), www.wga.org/uploadedFiles/who_we_are/HWR14.pdf; SAG AFTRA, "2007 and 2008 Casting Data Reports," www.sagaftra.org/files/sag/documents/2007–2008_CastingDataReports.pdf.

16. David Morley and Kevin Robins, *Spaces of Identity: Global Media, Electronic Landscapes and Cultural Boundaries* (New York: Routledge, 1995); Arjun Appadurai, *Modernity at Large: Cultural Dimensions of Globalization* (Minneapolis: University of Minnesota Press, 1996); John Tomlinson, *Globalization and Culture* (Chicago: University of Chicago Press, 1999); Michael Curtin, "Media Capitals: Toward the Study of Spatial Flows," *International Journal of Cultural Studies* 6.2 (2003): 202–228; Homi K. Bhabha, *The Location of Culture* (New York: Routledge, 2004); Marwan Kraidy, *Hybridity: The Cultural Logic of Globalization* (Philadelphia: Temple University Press, 2005); Terhi Rantanen, *The Media and Globalization* (Thousand Oaks, CA: Sage, 2005); Nederveen Pieterse, *Globalization and Culture: Global Melange,* 2nd ed. (Lanham, MD: Rowman & Littlefield, 2009).

17. Toby Miller, Nitin Govil, John McMurria, Richard Maxwell, and Ting Wang, *Global Hollywood 2* (London: British Film Institute, 2005).

18. Thomas H. Guback, *The International Film Industry: Western Europe and America since 1945* (Bloomington: Indiana University Press, 1969); Herbert I. Schiller, *Mass Communication and American Empire,* 2nd ed. (Boulder, CO: Westview, 1969).

19. Miller et al., *Global Hollywood 2.*

20. Susan Christopherson, "Behind the Scenes: How Transnational Firms Are Constructing a New International Division of Labor in Media Work," *Geoforum* 37 (2006): 739–751.

21. Richard Florida, *Cities and the Creative Class* (New York: Routledge, 2005).

22. John Howkins, *The Creative Economy* (New York: Penguin, 2001).

23. Louis Story, "Michigan Town Woos Hollywood, but Ends Up with a Big Part," *New York Times,* December 3, 2012, www.nytimes.com/2012/12/04/us/when-hollywood-comes-to-town.html?_r = 0.

24. Ben Goldsmith and Tom O'Regan, *The Film Studio: Film Production in the Global Economy* (Lanham, MD: Rowman & Littlefield, 2005); Terry Flew and Stuart Cunningham, "Creative Industries after the First Decade of Debate," *Information Society* 26.2 (2010); Ben Goldsmith, Susan Ward, and Tom O'Regan, *Local Hollywood: Glboal Film Production and the Gold Coast* (Brisbane: University of Queensland Press, 2010); Doris Baltruschat, *Global Media Ecologies: Networked Production in Film and Television* (New York: Routledge, 2010); Terry Flew, *The Creative Industries: Culture and Policy* (London: Sage, 2012)

25. Angela McRobbie, *British Fashion Design: Rag Trade or Image Industry?* (New York: Routledge, 1998); Rosalind Gil, "Cool Creative and Egalitarian? Exploring Gender in Project-based New Media Work in Europe," *Information, Communication and Society* 5.1 (2002): 70–89; Angela McRobbie, "From Holloway to Hollywood: Happiness at Work in the New Cultural Economy," in *Cultural Economy,* edited by Paul du Gay and Michael Pryke (New York: Sage, 2002); Andy C. Pratt, "Hot Jobs in Cool Places: The Material Cultures of New Media Production Spaces: The Case of the South of Market, San Francisco," *Information, Communication, and Society* 5.1 (2002): 27–50; Kate Oakley, "Include Us Out—Economic Development and Social Policy in the Creative Industries," *Cultural Trends* 15 (2006): 255–273; Mark Banks, *The Politics of Cultural Work* (New York: Palgrave MacMillan, 2007); 97 114; Mark Banks, Rosalind Gil, Stephanie Taylor, eds., *Theorizing Cultural Work: Labour, Continuity, and Change in the Cultural and Creative Industries* (London: Routledge, 2013).

26. John Caldwell, *Production Culture: Industrial Reflexivity and Critical Practice in Film and Television* (Durham, NC: Duke University Press, 2008); Vicki Mayer, Miranda J. Banks, and John Caldwell, *Production Studies: Cultural Studies of Media Industries* (New York: Routledge, 2009); David Hesmondhalgh and Sarah Baker, *Creative Labour: Media Work in Three Cultural Industries* (New York: Routledge, 2011).

27. Vicki Mayer, *Below the Line: Producers and Production Studies in the New Television Economy* (Durham, NC: Duke University Press, 2011).

28. Michael Curtin and Kevin Sanson, "The Division of Labor in Television," in *The Sage Handbook of Television Studies,* edited by Manuel Alvarado, Milly Buonanno, Herman Gray, and Toby Miller (Thousand Oaks, CA: Sage, 2015), 133–143.

29. Antonio Negri, *The Politics of Subversion: A Manifesto for the* Twenty-First *Century* (Cambridge: Polity, 1989), 79.

2

Cybertarian Flexibility—When Prosumers Join the Cognitariat, All That Is Scholarship Melts into Air

Toby Miller

The prevailing media credo, in domains that matter both a lot (popular, capitalist, and state discourse and action) and a little (communication, cultural, and media studies), is upheaval. The litany goes something like this: Corporate power is challenged. State authority is compromised. Avant-garde art and politics are centered. The young are masters, not victims. Technologies represent freedom, not domination. Revolutions are fomented by Twitter, not theory; by memes, not memos; by Facebook, not Foucault; by phone, not protest.

Political participation is just a click away. Tweets are the new streets and online friends the new vanguard, as 140ism displaces Maoism. Cadres are created and destroyed via BlackBerry. Teens tease technocrats. Hackers undermine hierarchy. Leakers dowse the fire of spies and illuminate the shady world of diplomats.

The endless iterations offered by digital reproduction and the immediate exchanges promised by the Internet have turned the world on its head. We are advised that the media in particular are being transformed. Tradition is rent asunder. Newspapers are metaphorically tossed aside. What was once their fate in a literal sense (when we dispensed with print in *poubelles*) is now a figure of speech that refers to their financial decline. Journalists are recycled as public relations people, and readers become the new journalists. Cinema is irrelevant, TV is on the way out, gaming is the future, telephony is timeless, and the entire panoply of scholarship on the political economy of ownership and control is of archaeological interest at best.

This technophilic vision of old and middle-aged media being shunted aside by new media is espoused by a wide variety of actors. The corporate world is signed up: Netflix proudly proclaims that "Internet TV is replacing linear TV. Apps are replacing channels, remote controls are disappearing, and screens are proliferating."[1] IBM disparages "Massive Passives . . . in the living room . . . a 'lean back' mode in which consumers do little more than flip on the remote and scan programming." By contrast, it valorizes and desires "Gadgetiers and Kool Kids" who "force radical change" because they demand "anywhere, anytime content."[2] I wish someone would pay me to come up with lines like those.

The state loves this new world too, despite the risks allegedly posed to its own essence. Let's drop in on a Pentagon web site to see it share the joy: "Take the world's most powerful sea, air and land force with you wherever you go with the new America's Navy iPhone app. Read the latest articles. See the newest pics and videos. And learn more about the Navy—from its vessels and weapons to its global activities. You can do it all right on your iPhone—and then share what you like with friends via your favorite social media venues."[3]

Civil society is also excited. The wonderfully named Progress & Freedom Foundation's "Magna Carta for the Information Age" proposes that the political-economic gains made through democratic action since the thirteenth century have been eclipsed by technological ones: "The central event of the 20th century is the overthrow of matter. In technology, economics, and the politics of nations, wealth—in the form of physical resources—has been losing value and significance. The powers of mind are everywhere ascendant over the brute force of things."[4]

The foundation has closed its doors, no doubt overtaken by pesky progress, but its discourse of liberty still rings loudly in our ears. Meanwhile, a prominent international environmental organization surveys me about its methods and appeal, asking whether I am prepared to sign petitions and embark on actions under its direction that might lead to my arrest. I prefer cozily comfortable middle-aged clicking to infantile attention-seeking incarceration, but either way, twinning the two is a telling sign of the times—as is doing so via corporate marketing techniques.

Even the bourgeois media take a certain pride in pronouncing their end of days. On the liberal left, the *Guardian* is prey to this beguiling magic: someone called "You" heads its 2013 list of the hundred most important folks in the media, with unknowns like Rupert Murdoch lagging far behind.[5] *Time* magazine exemplified just such love of a seemingly immaterial world when it chose "You" as "Person of the Year" for 2006 because "You control the Information Age. Welcome to your world."[6] For its part, the *New Statesman,* a progressive British weekly, heralds the new epoch in a nationalistic way: "Our economic and political clout wanes," but "when it comes to culture, we remain a superpower" because popular culture provides "critical tools through which Britain can market itself and its ideas to the world."[7]

Many academics love this new age too, not least because it's avowedly green: the Australian Council for the Humanities, Arts and Social Sciences informs the country's Productivity Commission that we dwell in a "post-smokestack era"[8]—a blessed world for workers, consumers, and residents, with residues of code rather than carbon.[9]

The illustrations gathered above—arbitrarily selected but emblematic of profound tendencies across theories, industries, and places—amount to a touching but maddening mythology: cybertarianism, the belief that new media technologies are obliterating geography, sovereignty, and hierarchy in an alchemy of truth and beauty. Cybertarianism promises libertarian ideals and forms of life made real and whole thanks to the innately individualistic and iconoclastic nature of the newer media.[10]

In this cybertarian world, corporate and governmental cultural gatekeepers and hegemons are allegedly undermined by innovative possibilities of creation and distribution. The comparatively cheap and easy access to making and circulating meaning afforded by Internet media and genres is thought to have eroded the one-way hold on culture that saw a small segment of the world as producers and the larger one as consumers, even as it makes for a cleaner economy that glides into an ever-greener postindustrialism. Cybertarians celebrate their belief that new technologies allow us all to become simultaneously cultural consumers and producers—no more factory conditions, no more factory emissions.[11]

Crucial to these fantasies is the idea of the prosumer. This concept was invented by Alvin Toffler, a lapsed leftist and Reaganite signatory to the Progress & Freedom Foundation's "Magna Carta." Toffler was one of a merry band of futurists who emerged in the 1970s. He coined the term *prosumer* in 1980 to describe the vanguard class of a technologized future. (Toffler had a nifty knack for knee-jerk neologisms, as we will see.)[12]

Rather than being entirely new, the prosumer partially represented a return to subsistence, to the period prior to the Industrial Revolution's division of labor—a time when we ate what we grew, built our own shelters, and gave birth without medicine. The specialization of agriculture and manufacturing and the rise of cities put an end to such autarky: the emergence of capitalism distinguished production from consumption via markets. But Toffler discerned a paradoxical latter-day blend of the two seemingly opposed eras, symbolized by the French invention and marketing of home pregnancy tests in the 1970s. These kits relied on the formal knowledge, manufacture, and distribution that typified modern life but permitted customers to make their own diagnoses, cutting out the role of doctors as expert gatekeepers between applied science and the self.

Toffler called this "production for self-use." He saw it at play elsewhere as well: in the vast array of civil society organizations that emerged at the time, the craze for "self-help," the popularity of self-serve gas stations as franchises struggled to survive after the 1973–74 oil crisis, and the proliferation of automatic teller machines as banks sought to reduce their retail labor force.

The argument Toffler made thirty-five years ago—that we are simultaneously cultural consumers and producers, that is, prosumers—is an idea whose time has come, as his fellow reactionary Victor Hugo almost put it.[13] Readers become authors. Listeners transform into speakers. Viewers emerge as stars. Fans are academics. Zine writers are screenwriters. Bloggers are copywriters. Children are columnists. Bus riders are journalists. Coca-Cola hires African Americans to drive through the inner city selling soda and playing hip-hop. AT&T pays San Francisco buskers to mention the company in their songs. Urban performance poets rhyme about Nissan cars for cash, simultaneously hawking, entertaining, and research-ing. Subway's sandwich commercials are marketed as made by teenagers. Cultural studies majors turn into designers. Graduate students in New York and Los Ange-les read scripts for producers, then pronounce on whether they tap into the zeit-geist. Internally divided—but happily so—each person is, as Foucault put it forty years ago, "a consumer on the one hand, but . . . also a producer."[14]

Along the way, all that seemed scholarly has melted into the air. Bitcoin and Baudrillard, creativity and carnival, heteroglossia and heterotopia—they're all present but simultaneously theorized and realized by screen-based activists rather than academics. Vapid victims of ideology are now credible creators of meaning, and active audiences are neither active nor audiences—their uses and gratifica-tions come from sitting back and enjoying the career of their own content, not from viewing others'. They resist authority not via aberrant decoding of texts that have been generated by professionals, but by ignoring such things in favor of mak-ing and watching their own.

Whether scholars like to attach electrodes to peoples' naughty bits to establish whether porn turns them on, or interview afternoon TV viewers to discern pro-gressive political tendencies in their interpretation of courtroom shows, they're yesterday's people. It doesn't matter if they purvey rats and stats and are consum-mate quantoids, or eschew that in favor of populist authenticity as acafans and credulous qualtoids. Their day has passed. "Media effects" describes what people do to the media, not the other way round.

People in all spheres of scholarship say "my children" enjoy this, that, or the other by way of media use. These choices are held up as predictions of the future. No one says the same about, for example, their children's food preferences, as if abjuring vegetables at age seven will be a lifetime activity. But when it comes to the media, children are mini-Tofflers, forecasters of a world they are also bringing into being.

Like Toffler all those decades ago, cybertarian discourse buys into individu-alistic fantasies of reader, audience, consumer, and player autonomy—the neo-liberal intellectual's wet dream of music, movies, television, and everything else converging under the sign of empowered and creative fans. The New Right of communication and cultural studies invests with unparalleled gusto in Schumpe-terian entrepreneurs, evolutionary economics, and creative industries. It's never seen an "app" it didn't like or a socialist idea it did. Faith in devolved media-making amounts to a secular religion, offering transcendence in the here and now via a "literature of the eighth day, the day after Genesis."[15] This is narcissog-raphy at work, with the critic's persona a guarantor of assumed audience revelry and Dionysian joy. Welcome to "Readers' Liberation Movement" media studies.[16]

So strong a utopian line about digital technologies and the Internet is appealing in its totality, its tonality, its claims, its cadres, its populism, its popularity, its happiness, and its hopefulness. But such utopianism has seen a comprehensive turn away from addressing unequal infrastructural and cultural exchange, toward an extended dalliance with new technology and its supposedly innate capacity to endow users with transcendence.[17] In 2011, the cost of broadband in the Global South was 40.3 percent of the average individual gross national income (GNI). Across the Global North, by comparison, the price was less than 5 percent of GNI per capita.[18] Within Latin America, for example, there are major disparities in pricing. One megabit a second in Mexico costs US$9, or 1 percent of average monthly income; in Bolivia, it is US$63, or 31 percent. Access is also structured unequally in terms of race, occupation, and region: indigenous people represent a third of rural workers in Latin America, and over half in some countries are essentially disconnected. The digital divide between indigenous people and the rest of the population in Mexico is 0.3, in Panama 0.7, and Venezuela 0.6.[19] Rather than seeing new communications technologies as magical agents that can produce market equilibrium and hence individual and collective happiness, we should note their continued exclusivity.

It is also worth noting that there are anticybertarian skeptics aplenty in both public intellectual and cloistered worlds and the third sector. They offer ways of thinking that differ from the dominant ones. Consider Evgeny Morozov's striking journalistic critiques, which have resonated powerfully in their refusal of technocentric claims for social change.[20] On more scholarly tracks, many authors have done ethnographic and political-economic work on the labor conditions experienced by people in the prosumer world as well as policy explorations of digital capitalism and the state.[21] Case studies of WikiLeaks, for instance, show the ambivalent and ambiguous sides to a phenomenon that has been uncritically welcomed by cybertarians, while we now know the extent of corporate surveillance enabled by their embrace of Facebook and friends.[22] Beyond the Global North, thick descriptions of technocentric, cybertarian exploitation and mystification proliferate as the reality of successive liberatory "springs" supposedly unleashed by social media networks is exposed.[23] And nongovernment organizations raise the flag against crass celebrations of new media technologies that damage workers and the environment.[24] This array of work provides a sturdy counterdiscourse to the admittedly still dominant cybertarian position.

TELEVISION AND THE ENVIRONMENT

Drawing on that more skeptical outlook, let's investigate in greater depth the claims made for these technologies with reference to television and the environment, before moving to discuss the world of work in greater depth. We'll see that for now, at least, cybertarian rhetoric in these areas fails on its own terms.

Consider the bold assertions made above by Netflix and IBM. The evidence for television's demise is as sparse and thin as the rhetoric about it is copious and thick. Historically, most new media have supplanted earlier ones as central organs of authority or pleasure: books versus speeches, films versus plays, singles versus sheet music. TV blended them. A warehouse of contemporary culture, it merged what had come before, and now it is merging with personal computers (which were modeled on it) to do the same.[25] The *New York Times* presciently announced this tendency over thirty years ago with the headline "Television Marries Computer."[26]

Television's robust resilience is especially salient when it comes to current affairs: 94 percent of the U.S. population watches TV news, which has long been its principal resource for understanding both global events and council politics. During the 2004 U.S. presidential election, 78 percent of the population followed the campaign on television, up from 70 percent in 2000.[27] Political operatives pay heed to this reality. Between the 2002 and 2006 midterm elections and across that 2004 campaign, TV expenditure on political advertising grew from $995.5 million to $1.7 billion—at a time of minimal inflation. That amounted to 80 percent of the growth in broadcasters' revenue in 2003–2004. The 2002 election saw $947 million spent on television advertising; 2004, $1.55 billion; and 2006, $1.72 billion. The correlative numbers for the Internet were $5 million in 2002; $29 million in 2004; and $40 million in 2006. The vast majority of electronic electoral campaigning takes place on local TV—95 percent in 2007.[28]

We might examine the famous Barack Obama campaign of 2008 and its much-vaunted use of the Internet. Here's the deal: Obama's organization spent the vast bulk of its energy and money on television. The Internet was there to raise funds and communicate with supporters. The U.S. presidency cycles with the summer Olympics. Few candidates commit funds to commercials in prime time during this epic of capitalist excess, where the classic homologues of competition vie for screen time—athletic contests versus corporate hype. Obama, however, took a multimillion-dollar package across the stations then owned by General Electric: NBC (Anglo broadcast), CNBC (business-leech cable), MSNBC (news cable), USA (entertainment cable), Oxygen (women's cable), and Telemundo (Spanish broadcast). TV was on the march, not in retreat: on election night 2008, CNN gained 109 percent more viewers than the equivalent evening four years earlier. The 2012 U.S. presidential election was again a televisual one. How many U.S. residents who watched the debates between Mitt Romney and Obama preferred the Internet to TV as their source? Three percent. How many watched on both TV and the Internet? Eleven percent. How many people shared their reactions online? Eight percent.[29]

In Europe as well as the United States, TV rules the roost by a long way when viewers seek news. Worldwide, owners of tablets like iPads are the keenest consumers of television news. These gadgets are adjuncts, partners, to the main source. If anything, they stimulate people to watch more television.[30]

The green qualities of new media technologies are as dubious as claims for their hegemony over TV. The Political Economy Research Institute's 2013 "Misfortune 100: Top Corporate Air Polluters in the United States" placed half a dozen media owners in the first fifty.[31] Cultural production relies on the exorbitant water use of computer technology, while making semiconductors requires hazardous chemicals, including carcinogens. At current levels, residential energy use of electronic equipment will rise to 30 percent of the overall global demand for power by 2022, and 45 percent by 2030, thanks to server farms and data centers and the increasing time people around the world spend watching and adding to screens.[32]

COGNITARIAT

And labor? The Entertainment & Leisure Software Publishers Association celebrates women and video games, ignoring women's part in their manufacture and disposal. Britain's report on harm to children from games neglects children whose forced labor makes and deconstructs them. And a study prepared for capital and the state entitled *Working in Australia's Digital Games Industry* does not refer to mining rare earth metals, making games, or handling electronic waste—all of which should fall under "working in Australia's digital games industry."[33] Such research privileges the consciousness of play and the productivity of industry. Materiality is forgotten, as if it were not part of feelings, thoughts, experiences, careers—or money, oddly. By and large, the people who actually make media technologies are therefore excluded from the dominant discourses of high technology. It is as if telecommunications, cell phones, tablets, televisions, cameras, computers, and so on sprang magically from a green meritocracy of creativity.

Then there is the question of "you," this dominant, imperialistic figure of prosumption. Audience members spy on fellow spectators in theaters to see how they respond to coming attractions. Opportunities to vote in the Eurovision Song Contest or a reality program disclose the profiles and practices of viewers, who can be monitored and wooed in the future. End-user licensing agreements ensure that online players of corporate games sign over their cultural moves and perspectives to the very companies they are paying to participate.[34]

More than that, Silicon Valley, Alley, Roundabout, and other hopeful variants speak mystically of "the Singularity." If it comes—current messianic predictions estimate between 2030 and 2045—then "you" will be rendered very secondary indeed. For the Singularity is "the last machine."[35] It will allegedly permit us "in the fairly near future [to] create or become creatures of more than human intelligence . . . ushering in a posthuman epoch . . . beyond human ken . . . intrinsically unintelligible."[36] The "us" will no longer be the masters of our technological world, no longer all-powerful prosumers, but one more cog in a wheel that is not even capitalist or socialist—a fleshy cog of HAL, the totalitarian computer from *2001* (1968).[37]

Such proletarianization is already upon us. Back in 1980, Toffler acknowledged the crucial role of corporations in constructing prosumption—they were there from the first, cutting costs and relying on labor undertaken by customers to externalize costs through what he termed "willing seduction." This was coeval with, and just as important as, the devolution of authority that would emerge from the new freedoms.[38] And most of the exciting new activities I have mentioned involve getting customers to do unpaid work, even as they purchase goods and services.

Just as Toffler imagined prosumers emerging from technological changes to the nature and interaction of consumption and production, he anticipated that these transformations would forge new relationships between proletarians and more educated workers. At the same time as he coined the term *prosumer,* Toffler introduced the idea of the "cognitariat": people undertaking casualized cultural work who have heady educational backgrounds yet live at the uncertain interstices of capital, qualifications, and government in a post-Fordist era of mass unemployment, chronic underemployment, zero-time contracts, limited-term work, interminable internships, and occupational insecurity. Drawing on his early childhood experiences with Marxism, Toffler welcomed this development as an end to alienation, reification, and exploitation, because the cognitariat held the means of production in its sinuous mind rather than its burly grasp. The former could not be owned and directed as per the latter's industrial fate.[39]

Cognitarians are sometimes complicit with these circumstances, because their identities are shrouded in autotelic modes of being: work is pleasure and vice versa; labor becomes its own reward. Dreams of autonomous identity formation find them joining a gentried poor dedicated to the life of the mind that supposedly fulfills them and may one day deliver a labor market of plenty.[40] But they also confront inevitable contradictions, "the glamour as well as the gloom of the working environment of the creative economy."[41]

From jazz musicians to street artists, cultural workers have long labored without regular compensation and security. That models the expectations we are *all* supposed to have today, rather than our parents' or grandparents' assumptions about lifelong—or at least steady—employment. Cultural production shows that all workers can move from security to insecurity, certainty to uncertainty, salary to wage, firm to project, and profession to precarity—and with smiles on their faces.[42] Contemporary business leeches love it because they crave flexibility in the people they employ, the technologies they use, the places where they do business, and the amounts they pay—and *in*flexibility of ownership and control.[43]

When I migrated to New York City in 1993, interviewers for broadcast stations' news shows would come to my apartment as a team: a full complement of sound recordist, camera operator, lighting technician, and journalist. Now they are rolled into one person. More content must be produced from fewer resources, and more and more multiskilling and multitasking are required. In my example, the journalist has taken over the other tasks. The job of the editor is also being scooped up into the new concept of the "preditor," who must perform the functions of producer and editor. And if journalists work for companies like NBC, they often write copy for several web sites *and* provide different edited versions of the original story for MSNBC, CNBC, CNBC Africa, CNBC Europe, and CNBC Asia.

This precariousness also sees new entrants to such labor markets undermining established workers' wages and conditions. Consider the advertising agency Poptent, which undercuts big competitors in sales to major clients by exploiting prosumers' labor in the name of "empowerment." That empowerment takes the following form: Poptent pays the creators of homemade commercials $7,500; it receives a management fee of $40,000; and the buyer saves about $300,000 on the usual price.[44]

Because this volume is concerned more with fictional than factual screen genres, it's worth recalling that such examples also apply wherever labor is not organized in strong unions (the cable versus broadcast TV labor process is a notorious instance). For example, thousands of small firms with unorganized workforces are dotted across the hinterland of California. They produce DVD film commentaries, music for electronic games, and reality TV shows[45] and are increasingly looking for opportunities in visual effects, animation, and video game development.[46] They might also be making programs for YouTube's hundred new channels, the fruit of Google's hundred-million-dollar production (and two-hundred-million-dollar marketing) wager that five-minute online shows will kill off TV. Explosions were routinely filmed for these channels near my late lamented loft in downtown Los Angeles. The workers blowing things up were paid $15 an hour.[47]

Clearly, cultural labor incarnates this latter-day loss of lifelong employment and relative income security among the Global North's industrial proletarian and professional-managerial classes. A rarefied if exploitative mode of work—that of the artist and artisan in the field of culture—has become a shadow-setter for conditions of labor elsewhere in the economy. Even reactionary bodies like the U.S. National Governors Association recognize the reality: "Routine tasks that once characterized middle class work have either been eliminated by technological change or are now conducted by low-wage but highly skilled workers."[48]

This new division of labor is becoming as global as the manufacturing one that preceded it. For alongside a casualization of middle-class jobs within the Global North, there is also a New International Division of Cultural Labor. By the 1980s, as culture became increasingly commodified and governmentalized and drew closer to the center of the world economy, it fell subject to the same pressures as secondary industries. Hence the success of Mindworks Global Media, a company outside New Delhi that provides Indian-based journalists and copy editors to newspapers whose reporters are supposedly in the United States and Europe. It promises 35–40 percent cost savings by contrast with workers at the outlets in question.[49]

CONCLUSION

Cybertarian mythology not only rests on a flawed, albeit touching, account of the person as a ratiocinative, atomistic individual who can exist outside politics and society. It equally assumes that the Internet—which in reality was born of warfare consultancies and "big science," has spread through large institutions, and is rapidly moving toward comprehensive corporate control—can be claimed for the wild children of geekdom. In place of this sweet-natured technophilic dreaming, activists, citizens, and scholars alike need fewer smiley faces; they must be displaced by quizzical ones that will turn their and our heads in the direction of our real material conditions of existence.

Despite the technocentric projections of both Cold War futurists and contemporary web dreamers, the wider culture industries largely remain controlled by media and communications conglomerates, which frequently seek to impose artist-like conditions on their workforces. They gobble up smaller companies that invent products and services, "recycling audio-visual cultural material created by the grassroots genius, exploiting their intellectual property and generating a standardized business sector that excludes, and even distorts, its very source of business," to quote the *Hindu*.[50] In other words, the cognitariat—interns, volunteers, contestants, and so on—creates "cool stuff" whose primary beneficiaries are corporations.[51]

There is some very competent research into the lived conditions of folks setting up alternative forms of collaborative work inside the cognitariat that have the potential for a more exciting way forward than the tired cybertarian rhetoric that so unthinkingly repeats and repeats and repeats ideas that belong to Reaganite dreamers.[52] When linked to the political-economic and ethnographic work outlined earlier, and the equally path-breaking research undertaken by nongovernment organizations, the future can be reinterpreted and remade by a realistic analytic frame that takes its inspiration from lived experience, in opposition to futuristic fantasy. Then the scholarship melting into air will have served its cybertarian time. Good riddance.

NOTES

Thanks to the editors for their helpful comments.

1. Netflix, "Netflix's View: Internate TV Is Replacing Linear TV," July 15, 2015, http://ir.netflix.com/long-term-view.cfm.

2. IBM Institute for Business Value, "The End of Television as We Know It," www-935.ibm.com/services/us/imc/pdf/ge510-6248-end-of-tv-full.pdf.

3. U.S. Navy homepage, www.navy.com.

4. Esther Dyson, George Gilder, George Keyworth, and Alvin Toffler, "Cyberspace and the American Dream: A Magna Carta for the Information Age," version 1.2 (Progress and Freedom Foundation, 1994), www.pff.org/issues-pubs/futureinsights/fi1.2magnacarta.html.

5. "1. You," *Guardian,* September 1, 2013, www.theguardian.com/media/2013/sep/01/you-them-mediaguardian-100–2013; "MediaGuardian 100," *Guardian,* September 1, 2013, www.theguardian.com/media/series/mediaguardian-100–2013–1–100.

6. Lev Grossman, *"Time*'s Person of the Year: You," *Time,* December 13, 2006, http://content.time.com/time/magazine/article/0,9171,1570810,00.html.

7. "Exporting the Doctor," *New Statesman,* August 22–28, 2014, 7.

8. CHASS, "Innovation in a Post-Smokestack Industry Era: Productivity Commission's Study on Science and Innovation," 2006, www.chass.org.au/wp-content/uploads/2015/02/SUB20060807TG.pdf.

9. An astonishing claim from a country that survives on per capita dirty-power exports that make it among the greatest polluters in history—but why spoil a good story? Simon Lauder, "Australians the 'World's Worst Polluters,'" *World Today,* September 11, 2009, www.abc.net.au/news/2009-09-11/australians-the-worlds-worst-polluters/1425986.

10. The first reference I have found to this is Toby Miller, "No More Cybertarians, Please—More Citizens, Thank You," *Television & New Media* 1.2 (2000): 131–134. But then I would say that.

11. Mark Graham, "Warped Geographies of Development: The Internet and Theories of Economic Development," *Geography Compass* 2.3 (2008): 771–789.

12. Alvin Toffler, *The Third Wave* (New York: William Morrow, 1980); George Ritzer and Nathan Jurgenson, "Production, Consumption, Prosumption: The Nature of Capitalism in the Age of the Digital 'Prosumer,'" *Journal of Consumer Culture* 10.1 (2010): 13–36.

13. Hugo wrote, "On resiste à l'invasion des armées; on ne résiste pas à l'invasion des idées," in *Histoire d'un crime: Déposition d'un témoin* (Paris: Nelson, 1907), 554, which is often rendered in English as the cliché I have just used. The next sentence is "La gloire des barbares est d'être conquis par l'humanité; la gloire des sauvages est d'être conquis par la civilization," which translates as "The glory of barbarians is to be conquered by humanity; the glory of savages is to be conquered by civilization." Thanks for sharing, Vic.

14. Michel Foucault, *The Birth of Biopolitics: Lectures at the Collège de France,* 1978–79, trans. Graham Burchell, ed. Michel Senellart (Houndmills: Palgrave Macmillan, 2008), 226.

15. James W. Carey, "Historical Pragmatism and the Internet," *New Media & Society* 7.4 (2005): 443–455.

16. Meaghan Morris, "The Banality of Cultural Studies," in *Logics of Television: Essays in Cultural Criticism,* ed. Patricia Mellencamp (Bloomington: Indiana University Press, 1990), 14–43; Terry Eagleton, "The Revolt of the Reader," *New Literary History* 13.3 (1982): 449–452.

17. Christine L. Ogan, Manaf Bashir, Lindita Camaj, Yunjuan Luo, Brian Gaddie, Rosemary Pennington, Sonia Rana, and Mohammed Salih, "Development Communication: The State of Research in an Era of ICTs and Globalization," *Gazette* 71.8 (2009): 655–670.

18. International Telecommunication Union, *Measuring the Information Society: Executive Summary* (Geneva: International Telecommunication Union, 2012), 4.

19. Matías Bianchi, "Digital Age Inequality in Latin America," *Democracia Abierta,* June 24, 2015, www.opendemocracy.net/democraciaabierta/mat%C3%ADas-bianchi/digital-age-inequality-in-latin-america.

20. Evgeny Morozov, *The Net Delusion: The Dark Side of Internet Freedom* (New York: PublicAffairs, 2011); and *To Save Everything, Click Here: The Folly of Technological Solutionism* (New York: PublicAffairs, 2013).

21. Andrew Ross, *Nice Work If You Can Get It: Life and Labor in Precarious Times* (New York: New York University Press, 2009); Mark Banks, Rosalind Gill, and Stephanie Taylor, eds., *Theorising Cultural Work: Labour, Continuity and Change in the Cultural and Creative Industries* (London: Routledge, 2013); Marisol Sandoval, *From Corporate to Social Media: Critical Perspectives on Corporate Social Responsibility in Media and Communication Industries* (London: Routledge, 2014); Christian Fuchs, *Social Media: A Critical Introduction* (Los Angeles: Sage, 2014); Geert Lovink and Miriam Rasch, eds.,

Unlike Us Reader: Social Media Monopolies and Their Alternatives (Amsterdam: Institute of Network Cultures, 2013); Dan Schiller, *Digital Depression: Information Technology and Economic Crisis* (Champaign: University of Illinois Press, 2014).

22. Christian Christensen, ed., "WikiLeaks: From Popular Culture to Political Economy," *International Journal of Communication* 8 (2014), http://ijoc.org/index.php/ijoc/issue/view/10#more4; André Jansson and Miyase Christensen, eds., *Media, Surveillance and Identity: Social Perspectives* (New York: Peter Lang, 2014).

23. Néstor García Canclini, *El mundo entero como lugar extraño* (Buenos Aires: Gedisa, 2014); Walter Armbrust, "The Revolution against Neoliberalism," *Jadaliyya*, February 2011, www.jadaliyya. com/pages/index/717/the-revolution-against-neoliberalism-; Rami Zurayk, *Food, Farming and Freedom: Sowing the Arab Spring* (Charlottesville, VA: Just World Books, 2011); Mukadder Çakir, ed. *Yeni Medyaya Eleştirel Yaklaşimlar* (İstanbul: Doğu Kitabevi, 2014).

24. Basel Action Network and Silicon Valley Toxics Coalition, *Exporting Harm: The High-Tech Trashing of Asia* (Seattle: Basel Action Network, 2002); Greenpeace, *How Clean Is Your Cloud?* (2012), www.greenpeace.org/international/en/publications/Campaign-reports/Climate-Reports/How-Clean-is-Your-Cloud/; Centro de Reflexión y Acción Laboral, *New Technology Workers: Report on Working Conditions in the Mexican Electronics Industry* (2006), http://sjsocial.org/fomento/proyectos/plantilla. php?texto=cereal_m.

25. Tom Standage, "Your Television Is Ringing," *Economist,* October 12, 2006, www.economist. com/node/7995312.

26. Howard Gardner, "When Television Marries Computer," *New York Times,* March 27, 1983, www.nytimes.com/1983/03/27/books/when-television-marries-computer-by-howard-gardner.html.

27. Lydia Saad, "TV Is Americans' Main Source of News," *Gallup,* July 8, 2013, www.gallup.com/poll/163412/americans-main-source-news.aspx; "The State of the News Media 2005," *Journalism. org,* http://stateofthemedia.org/2005/; "Trends 2005," *Pew Research Center,* January 20, 2005, www. pewresearch.org/2005/01/20/trends-2005/.

28. Katrina vanden Heuvel, "America Needs Electoral Reform," *Nation,* July 1, 2008, www.thenation. com/article/america-needs-electoral-reform; "Voters, MySpace, and YouTube," *Social Science Computer Review* 26 (Fall 2008): 288–300, http://ssc.sagepub.com/content/26/3/288.full.pdf+html; "An Analysis of 2007 and 2008 Political, Issue and Advocacy Advertising (TNS)," *Branson Agent,* October 16, 2007, http://bransonagentnewsline.blogspot.co.uk/2007/10/analysis-of-2007-and-2008-political.html; www. adweek.com/?vnu_content_id=1003658398&utm_source=feedburner&utm_medium=feed&utm_campaign=Feed%253A+Mediaweek-Tv-Radio-Stations-And-Outdoor+%2528Mediaweek+News+-+TV%252C+Radio+Stations+and+Outdoor%2529.

29. Ira Teinowitz, "Olympic Deal Sealed: Obama Makes $5 Million Buy," *Advertising Age,* July 23, 2008, http://adage.com/article/news/olympic-deal-sealed-obama-makes-5-million-buy/129853/; Paul J. Gough, "In '08, Big Headlines for Everybody," *Hollywood Reporter,* December 31, 2008, www. hollywoodreporter.com/news/08-big-headlines-everybody-124988; "One-in-Ten 'Dual-Screened' the Presidential Debate," *Pew Research Center,* October 11, 2012, /www.people-press.org/2012/10/11/one-in-ten-dual-screened-the-presidential-debate/.

30. John Eggerton, "Survey: TV Remains Top News Access Device," *Broadcasting and Cable,* March 17, 2014, www.broadcastingcable.com/news/washington/survey-tv-remains-top-news-access-device/129847; Nic Newman and David A. L. Levy, *Reuters Institute Digital News Report 2014* (Oxford: Reuters Institute, 2014), https://reutersinstitute.politics.ox.ac.uk/sites/default/files/Reuters%20Institute%20Digital%20News%20Report%202014.pdf; "BBC World News and BBC.com Release World's Largest Global Study of News Consumption Habits across Multiple Devices," *BBC News,* March 26, 2013, www.bbc.co.uk/mediacentre/worldnews/news-consumption.html.

31. Political Economy Research Institute, "Misfortune 100: Top Corporate Air Polluters in the United States" (2013), www.peri.umass.edu/toxicair_current/.

32. Jad Mouawad and Kate Galbraith, "Plugged in Age Feeds Hunger for Electricity," *New York Times*, September 20, 2009, A1; International Energy Agency, *Gadgets and Gigawatts: Policies for Energy Efficient Electronics—Executive Summary* (Paris: Organization for Economic Cooperation and Development, 2009), 5, 21; Climate Group, *Smart2020: Enabling the Low Carbon Economy in the Information Age* (London: Global Sustainability Initiative, 2008), 8–23; Simon Hancock, "Iceland New Home of Server Farms?" *BBC News*, October 10, 2009, http://news.bbc.co.uk/go/pr/fr/-/2/hi/programmes/click_online/8297237.stm; Organisation for Economic Co-Operation and Development, *Greener and Smarter: ICTs, the Environment and Climate Change* (Paris: Organisation for Economic Co-Operation and Development, 2010), 19.

33. Entertainment & Leisure Software Publishers Association, *Chicks and Joysticks: An Exploration of Women and Gaming* (London: Entertainment & Leisure Software Publishers Association, 2004); Department for Children, Schools and Families and Department for Culture, Media and Sport, *Safer Children in a Digital World: The Report of the Byron Review* (2008); Australian Research Council Centre of Excellence for Creative Industries and Innovation, Queensland University of Technology, and Games Developers' Association of Australia, *Working in Australia's Digital Games Industry: Consolidation Report* (2011).

34. Richard Maxwell and Toby Miller, "'Warm and Stuffy': The Ecological Impact of Electronic Games," in *The Video Game Industry: Formation, Present State, and Future*, ed. Peter Zackariasson and Timothy Wilson (London: Routledge, 2012), 179–197; Toby Miller, *Cultural Citizenship: Cosmopolitanism, Consumerism, and Television in a Neoliberal Age* (Philadelphia: Temple University Press, 2007).

35. Bryan Appleyard, "The New Luddites," *New Statesman*, August 22–28, 2014, 35.

36. Vernor Vinge, "Signs of the Singularity," *IEEE Spectrum*, June 1, 2008, http://spectrum.ieee.org/biomedical/ethics/signs-of-the-singularity.

37. "The Singularity," *IEEE Spectrum*, http://spectrum.ieee.org/static/singularity.

38. Toffler, *The Third Wave*, 266, 269–270, 275.

39. Alvin Toffler, *Previews and Premises* (New York: William Morrow, 1983); and *Powershift: Knowledge, Wealth, and Violence at the Edge of the Twenty-First Century* (New York: Bantam, 1990).

40. André Gorz, "Économie de la connaissance, exploitation des savoirs: Entretien réalisé par Yann Moulier Boutang and Carlo Vercellone," *Multitudes* 15 (2004), http://multitudes.samizdat.net/Economie-de-la-connaissance; Ross, *Nice Work If You Can Get It*.

41. Laikwan Pang, "The Labor Factor in the Creative Economy: A Marxist Reading," *Social Text* 99 (2009): 59.

42. Ross, *Nice Work If You Can Get It*.

43. Vincent Mosco, *To the Cloud: Big Data in a Turbulent World* (Boulder, CO: Paradigm, 2014), 155–174.

44. Dawn C. Chmielewski, "Poptent's Amateurs Sell Cheap Commercials to Big Brands," *Los Angeles Times*, May 8, 2012, http://articles.latimes.com/2012/may/08/business/la-fi-ct-poptent-20120508; www.poptent.net/.

45. Miranda Banks and Ellen Seiter, "Spoilers at the Digital Utopia Party: The WGA and Students Now," *Flow* 7.4 (2007), http://flowtv.org/2007/12/spoilers-at-the-digital-utopia-party-the-wga-and-students-now/.

46. Michael Cieply, "For Film Graduates, an Altered Job Picture," *New York Times*, July 4, 2011, C1.

47. Sam Thielman, "YouTube Commits $200 Million in Marketing Support to Channels," *AdWeek*, May 3, 2012, www.adweek.com/news/technology/youtube-commits-200-million-marketing-support-channels-140007.

48. Erin Sparks and Mary Jo Watts, *Degrees for What Jobs? Raising Expectations for Universities and Colleges in a Global Economy* (Washington: National Governors Association Center for Best Practices, 2011), 6.

49. Nandini Lakshman, "Copyediting? Ship the Work Out to India," *Business Week*, July 8, 2008, www.businessweek.com/globalbiz/content/jul2008/gb2008078_678274.htm; Mindworks web site, www.mindworksglobal.com/.

50. Sharada Ramanathan, "The Creativity Mantra," *Hindu*, October 29, 2006, www.hindu.com/mag/2006/10/29/stories/2006102900290700.htm.

51. Andrew Ross, "Nice Work If You Can Get It: The Mercurial Career of Creative Industries Policy," *Work Organisation, Labour & Globalisation* 1.1 (2006–7): 1–19; Carmen Marcus, *Future of Creative Industries: Implications for Research Policy* (Brussels: European Commission Foresight Working Documents Series, 2005).

52. García Canclini, *El mundo entero como lugar extraño.*

3

Spec World, Craft World, Brand World

John T. Caldwell

In the heady air of an MIT Transmedia conference, the "aca-pro" audience voiced appreciation as the futurist digital media consultant bragged about how nonhier-archical innovation hot spots like the one he'd created in his boutique company were poised to make old, conservative approaches to film and television produc-tion obsolete. Like dinosaurs and "Detroit," he argued, lazy, inefficient "old media" film/TV production professionals—who, like the auto industry, had lived long past their prime—could vanish and no tears would be shed. The unequivocal mes-sage: good riddance. Another panelist, an edgy new media branding consultant, sketched out some of his own recent viral marketing and stealth stunts that had successfully created "buzz" while costing the client little money. One stealth stunt involved triggering the Los Angeles Police Department, law enforcement helicop-ters, and public first responders to hover around a fake emergency. News coverage of this fake "media event" indeed spilled onto the marketer's covert goal: greater notoriety for a transmedia start-up in Hollywood. Again, the MIT audience know-ingly giggled at the sophisticated ironies in tricking tax-supported public infra-structure to unknowingly provide the "free" heavy marketing muscle required to launch a bit of edgy new intellectual property (IP). No one, however, discussed the political-economic or ethical downsides that this stunt buzz-making involved. Who were these people, both the aca-pro panelists and conference attendees, I wondered? How were *they* paid, and by *whom*, and for *what*, exactly? Cultural geography might provide the answers. Most of the visionaries were from New York or Boston (not Detroit or Los Angeles), where creative workers apparently no longer need or want to be paid, or have benefits, like the dinosaur film/TV/auto workers out west, mired as they were in the outdated heavy-industry quagmires apparently entombing them.

And why was I at this conference, given that the celebrated viral marketing "innovations" and free labor being worshipfully gossiped about here would horrify the fieldwork informants that I had been talking to: professional cinematographers, editors, directors, and grips? Of course, like some of the panelists, I had been publishing on "convergence media," "repurposing," and programming though "content migration" for some time. But my understanding of these current new media practices now seemed—from the perspective of Cambridge—to have come from some distant planet rather than the clean, cost-free world being celebrated at MIT. Then it hit me. My conference trip to Cambridge involved time travel; I'd fallen back thirty years into art school, and these capitalist marketing executives had become the new avant-garde: conceptual artists, performance artists, street artists, and provocateurs. But unlike their 1960s and 70s predecessors from the art world, these new-media conceptual artists were now handsomely paid for their faux outsiderness, unruly marketing innovations, snark, and boundary-crossing provocations—while simultaneously being lauded for their bored and studied public disinterest in matters of wages, benefits, or job security. If transmedia and viral marketing and branding consultants were the new "conceptual artists" of the twenty-first century, then my research must be clinging to dying professional communities defined by something more archaic and suspect: "craft" (also known as the innovator's "other").

Based on this encounter, I'd like to begin with three simple and very basic questions, before taking on and unpacking the three terms in my chapter title. First, why does TV labor matter to media aesthetics or TV studies? Second, how can or should we study it, given widespread and disruptive recent changes? And finally, given those same disruptions, where does TV production actually exist anymore? That is, where and how do we meaningfully *locate* production for research in the digital era? These questions are particularly acute in the American media sectors within which I operate—where government regulation and funding have withered, where neoliberal economics dominates, where traditional producing arrangements have disintegrated, where online crowdsourcing (via Kickstarter or Indiegogo) has become a legitimate option even for the unapologetic high-level industry professionals who increasingly slum there.

The last of my three questions actually complicates the first two, so I'd like to start there. Two possible answers to the question of where production is located were offered by economic geographer Allen Scott, as well as political economist Toby Miller and his coauthors.[1] Targeting Hollywood, both rebuffed the common clichés about production—that "it is a state of mind"—but did so in different ways. Scott's research on material resource agglomeration undercut the ephemerality state-of-mind cliché. His account detailed why certain film/television nexus points survive as geographical centers despite the clear economic advantages that might be gained by moving somewhere else. Miller and his coauthors, by contrast, disrupt the lie that geographic inertia or exceptionalism anchors production in any way, arguing that the real subject for production research today can be found in what they term the New International Division of Cultural Labor (NICL), which can migrate or shape-shift in response to rapid economic change.

Whereas Scott examines the regional anchoring of production and Miller the global dispersion and splintering of production through runaway production, my research leads me to suggest a third alternative. That is, our current predicament may follow from our failure to recognize that a widely dispersed *conceptualizing* process may be as central to the core of television/media production today as the industrial and *material* production of series, formats, and network programming once was (features that once garnered the lion's share of attention from critics and media scholars). I am suggesting here that hybrid forms of imaginative/economic speculation now systematically animate media production. Speculation—or "spec work," as I will call it—has become a fundamental part of the complex econo-mies of TV. Figuring out how to manage spec work from the deregulated creative labor "herd" helps provide rationality for TV industries as they seek to master (and eventually monetize) the unstable world of unruly fans, digital media, and remix and gift economies.

In saying this, I am not reverting to Scott's and Miller's target—media as "a state of mind" cliché—since the dispersed conceptualizing process I am targeting is as much a result and defining property of contemporary media labor as are the onscreen series that TV labor officially produces. TV is more than just the end product of TV production labor. I take television labor to be *anticipatory* as well—to include the endless prototyping, brainstorming, work shopping, ad hoc viral repackaging, and vocational spinning that precede and follow the shows for which TV companies officially take credit. Significantly, anticipatory spec work adds eco-nomic value to TV shows even if TV producers and executives ignore it. I am especially sensitive to Mayer and Stahl's critiques of labor "erasures."[2] My books *Televisuality* and *Production Culture* were both premised on paying greater atten-tion, even in aesthetic studies, to the cultural functions and institutional logics of physical production and creative workers—things that critical TV scholars had in many cases largely overlooked or dismissed.[3] Over the past two decades, I've also found that an entirely different work activity infuses physical production, one based on recurrent cognitive speculation about imagined, experiential, onscreen worlds of one sort or another. To clarify: I am *not* talking about the construction of "imagined narrative worlds" driven by fans in "transmedia franchises" of the sort Henry Jenkins has postulated.[4] I am, rather, talking about the commercial "labor" of habitual and calculated speculation now found in workaday, frequently unremarkable television job sites.

Significantly, spec work can be found in both below-the-line and above-the-line production sectors. Which means that conjecture about imagined worlds increasingly functions as part of lowly, run-of-the-mill trade practice. Anticipatory labor is *not* owned or triggered exclusively by the "creatives," executives, and producers, and can be found as well in the lowly technical crafts. In rejecting the exceptionalism we normally assign or reserve for the creative higher-ups in TV— the showrunner, producer, director, or executive—I am only arguing that we need to augment what we research; that we take seriously the rich terrain of cultural conjecture and anticipatory expression that now makes up the below-the-line worker's skill set. Such things now function as an integral part of the bigger system we think of as "television." Spec work is both workmanlike and ubiquitous, rather than unique in any way, and thus challenges media studies to rethink the parameters and boundaries we assume in production labor research.

Before drilling down deeper to examine spec work as a practice, I must clarify that the shift toward habitualized speculation as craft/creative work on the micro level, which I have just described, is linked to bigger changes in the macroscopic market predicament and thus transnational goals of many production companies, studios, and networks today. Specifically, success in media markets today depends less and less on the fabrication of a durable distributable entertainment object—which historically was the basis for television's core project of owning shows and syndicating series. In the old system, we thought that a production was over when we "locked" picture and soundtrack, then timed (or color-corrected) and archived a stable program master, and sold copies and versions in markets for distribution to buyers. Now the notion that our program masters are *never* done, always prone to change, goes well beyond the traditional alterations—remixing, recutting, dubbing—required for international distribution. Producers now know, upfront, that it is even possible (via corporate contracts as yet unknown) to completely recreate interior scenes through the digital imposition of new product placements, online links, and integrated sponsorship within preexisting narratives, onscreen. And this directly affects creative decisions creators make on the set. Digital renders masters completely malleable, reworkable, remakable, endlessly. These changes are not completely novel but a matter of degree, since we have always trimmed scenes for breaks to intercut ads, converted NTSC to PAL standards, panned-and-scanned or letter-boxed, and altered program masters for foreign languages when needed. What was once secondary is now primary, however, with masters now malleable not just at the level of plot or episode but at the level of the pixel, with effects layers "inside" fictional narratives and dramatic scenes as well. The growing presumption of an endlessly malleable program master means that the entire process of television production can now be imagined as an anticipatory function of postproduction, with the potential for (and goal of) an endless lucrative life on the "back end" of a project. Proliferating digital technologies mean that most forms of production can be understood as functions of postproduction—where the *cognitive work* of preproduction speculation on the "front end" has ramped up to keep pace with the *reiterative work* of digital repurposing on the "back end."

Issues of intellectual property stimulate these changes. Rather than make the durable syndicatable object the company's primary goal, spec work enterprises now obsess over the creation of potentially endless, malleable, and self-replicating IP. For clarity's sake, we can further distinguish (especially within the same corporations) between "big" self-replicating IP (the blockbuster or high-concept), and "small" self-replicating IP (reality TV and the unexceptional online consumer interactions that go with it). As we will discover, there is now a necessary economic relationship between "big IP" and "small IP" in the transnational multimedia conglomerates. That is, diversified corporations now need vast amounts of the cheaper, reality-based small IP to pay for their expensive big-IP blockbuster and prestige cinematic needs. We need to think beyond specific tactics of content migration or repurposing to consider this broader *intraconglomerate* dynamic that embeds them. That is, spreadable speculation now animates and monetizes production well before—and well after—the series or episode in question.[5] This temporal spreading of pre- and post-speculation is precisely why spec work has aligned so well with transmedia production, industry–fan interactions, and viral marketing, which mirror it.

I am arguing that spec work provides the broad conditions that facilitate linkages and synergies between the malleable digital "material" and technologies of TV production, on the one hand, and current corporate management strategies aimed at developing malleable and self-replicating IP (which ideally suits corporate reformatting, franchising, branding, and transmedia), on the other hand. Before mapping out the fuller range and logic of spec work, it is worth considering something more provisional—that is, how spec work fits within the rapidly changing industrial and economic landscape. This mediascape can be usefully understood within a three-part model of craft world, brand world, and spec world.

CRAFT WORLD, BRAND WORLD

The studio, the TV network, the director—such neat, clean, expedient categories for cinema and media studies research. Yet these categories are not innate, self-evident, unproblematic, or clearly bounded. The question of labor complicates the place and utility of each category in media production's para-industrial root system or "rhizome."[6] Rapid changes in how creative work is done and marketed provide one key to mapping the "nodes" of the studio, network, and director within a networked para-industrial system. Productive recent attempts to generalize about "digital labor" or "creative labor in the digital era" tend to overlook the fact that we are almost always dealing with *blended labor systems* in contemporary film and television—even within the same institutions (studio, network, director).

Presuming that digital technologies have cleanly eliminated old-media labor in the new media overgeneralizes and disregards how old-media labor somehow keeps adapting to new-media technologies even as new-media entrants disrupt the resulting blended media labor field. As such, media scholars are stuck with the difficult task of explaining how the same current screen form or genre might result from very different or contradictory work arrangements or organizational partnerships. This predicament—one *result, many* causes—muddies the water for anyone hoping to systematically research or isolate causal industrial factors behind a cultural form.

Head-scratching by others over my previous production studies suggests that I may be researching from a largely craft-labor orientation, while others have leapt ahead to focus on narrow new creative entrant perspectives as somehow *more* symptomatic of contemporary media and culture as a whole. Many in the transmedia industry seem less interested in the *physical work* or labor economics of professional screen workers than in the *conceptual artistry* of the newcomers from marketing-and-art, who are currently displacing the old-style craft labor. Of course, this innovation/craft split may seem commonsensical. Corporate sponsorship and academic politics—when married—make *innovation bias* apparently the only goal worth pursuing in media studies (*and* digital corporations). At the same time the stability-seeking *continuity practices* I continue to run into on a wide scale in film and TV industries have been simplistically linked—by both scholarly transmedia theorists and corporate start-ups—to the culturally outdated, the technically obsolete, and the industrially dead. Critical theorists and entrepreneurs (once considered strange bedfellows) both tend to view continuities as leaden, as intellectual and economic cul-de-sacs. This erasure of craft is shortsighted. Instead, I suggest that blended labor systems—enmeshed in different economic conditions—might be best understood according to the three-part model that scholars, media students, investors, and producers alike must now constantly negotiate: the "craft world," the "brand world," and the "spec world."

1. *Craft World.* Production studies must address one question before theorizing broadly about contemporary film and television in the digital era. To what extent does physical production matter anymore? As the first of the three dominant labor modes in the blended labor systems we now face, the craft world still generates considerable value via "quality" physical production. Yet many executives and producers disregard this, since physical production can *always* take place somewhere else, for less money—in their minds.

The characteristics of the traditional craft world are familiar. Production usually takes place in urban centers with dense agglomerations of skilled workers, physical resources, and para-industrial feeder organizations. As Allen Scott and Michael Curtin both demonstrate, this geographic resource massing (of infrastructure, finance, and creative labor) creates resilient media industrial synergies and helps

TABLE 3.1 Three Warring Paraindustrial Labor Regimes

	Craft World	Brand World	Spec World
Physical Production	Agglomerated, centralized	Outsourced, regionalized	Disaggregated, dispersed
Labor Protocol	Wage labor	Licensing	Virtual Pay
Aesthetic Goal	Durable artifact	Flexible reformatting	Brainstorming
Production Process	Building content, plantation farming	Concept-iteration, sharecropping	Concept strip-mining, gleaning, scavenging
Key	Engineering scarcity	Marketing scarcity	Excessive disclosure
Instigators, Enforcers	Guilds and unions	IP lawyers	Film schools, online tech corporations
Examples	Studio feature films, quality network TV	Reality TV, high-concept feature	UGC, Kickstarter, Vimeo, YouTube

keep film/TV corporations from decentralizing, from casually moving away.[7] Craft workers use unions and guilds to negotiate hourly or daily wage labor and work collectively to build content in concentrated physical spaces rather than distribute work and harvest it from outsiders elsewhere. This labor scheme, associated with larger-budgeted studio films and national networks, still aims to produce film/TV as a durable artifact that can be controlled and monetized through sequential distribution windows. Media corporations persist in partnering with craft labor, since this guarantees a high level of quality and predictability in production. The key to this first labor regime, the craft world, is *scarcity*. Unions and guilds manage and police scarcities in labor (through high barriers to entry) on the *input boundaries,* at the same time as studios market and police scarcity by controlling access to screen content (via exclusive exhibition rights) on the *output boundaries* (see Table 3.1).

2. *Brand World.* A second labor regime threatens but coexists with the first: the "brand world." This world—obsessed as it is with engineering corporate psychological signatures capable of animating long-term "interpersonal" synergies with fans—now dominates the warring blended labor systems *economically.* This may be because the brand world allows for considerable flexibility transnationally on both production's front end (the craft-world sector that feeds "high-concept" blockbuster films) and production's back end (the spec-world sector that monetizes user-generated content to promote reality TV). An ecumenical, counterintuitive logic drives the brand world. That is, as blockbuster budgets go higher and higher for fewer and fewer feature films, considerably more cheap screen content must be produced within the same corporate conglomerate to sustain it, buffer the risks, prop it up, and cover the conglomerate's high-stakes feature bets. Brand-world economics, that is, require fairly wide-ranging *complementary* screen practices, from expensive high-concept features, transnational coproductions, and

franchises on the big stage to cheaper, ubiquitous forms like reality TV, licensing, reformatting, merchandizing, and product placement, scattered across endless, unremarkable side stages. This is why contemporary screen content is best understood within the mixed conglomerate economics that I have detailed elsewhere.[8]

Like the craft world, the brand world cultivates and manages scarcity. Crafts associations cultivate scarcity by establishing high barriers to professional entry and by standardizing proprietary high technologies. By contrast, branding executives largely ignore traditional, restrictive labor arrangements in favor of harvesting the results of effective (and effusive) conceptual R&D. That is, rather than limiting the *physical supply* of expert labor and high-end technologies, the brand world initiates, stimulates, and then manages the scarcity of the *conceptual supply* of screen ideas, which can be policed and monetized through affiliation, contract, and litigation. If the International Alliance of Theatrical Stage Employees (IATSE) locals and studios agree to coexist in the craft world as "signatories," then transnational conglomerates and regional broadcasters agree to coexist in the brand world as "licensor-licensees" through the haggling of IP lawyers. The craft world presupposes a win-win for labor and management by constricting content pipelines and monetizing costlier production values. The brand world, by contrast, presupposes a financial win-win for IP rights holders and IP rights licensees—but simply disregards (sometimes cynically) *where* the production labor for the system of exhibition/broadcast comes from. The craft world is about durable screen content; the brand world is about creating a regionalized, quasi-indigenized variant of a common IP experience. The brand world looks agnostic and open to all possible creative labor solutions, and this is why it is so threatening to organized creative, professional, production labor. The brand world does not just stand as an alternative to craft or technical expertise. It actively works—by *deregulating* scarcity—to change the relatively rigid conditions upon which production workers once maintained their value.

One of the dark accomplishments of nineteenth-century American agriculture was that the South shifted from slavery as a dominant mode of capitalist production to its shadow world, a profitable, more "user-friendly-looking" labor arrangement and replacement to achieve the same ends: sharecropping. If film and television's craft world can be likened to a plantation system, where trained labor is kept on the farm but offered some level of protection, then the brand world can be likened to sharecropping, where employees give away protections in exchange for a small share of an unpredictable revenue stream and a life of permanent insecurity. Most creative labor in the transnational brand world today—including labor involved in reformatting—can be understood as profitable forms of sharecropping, arrangements that give film and television today a great deal of fluidity, insecurity, and impermanence. This follows from the fact that IP can travel quickly and replant itself in any country that wishes to partner in a format or high concept, while specialized craft labor is seen as inertial and leaden—a threat to quick profits.

3. *Spec World.* The third labor regime in the blended system is the spec world. From an agrarian design precedent, it can be understood not as an industrial plantation (like the craft world), or sharecropping (like the brand world), but as an agricultural process mimicking an early and late fall ritual that unfolds after the primary crops have been harvested: gleaning and scavenging. Some online practices today feel exactly like scavenging: the creation of incongruent mash-ups, filked music, and fan-vids in particular. The question arises, however, how this world of fans and free user-generated content can be viewed *economically* as a labor regime. Various scholars have noted how online users add value to corporations by inadvertently feeding rich marketing and demographic info to the proprietary corporations that give them "free" access; however, I am not focusing here on that form of "free" consumer labor. Rather, *spec world* refers to vast new cultural arenas in which *professional* participants and production aspirants alike are expected to produce creative works "on spec." Screenwriters have known a fairly benign form of this term for decades. *On spec* in television meant writing and submitting entire screenplays as "calling cards" intended to win over executives or producers—even though spec scripts were never expected to generate near-term revenues.[9] The real goal of the television spec script? To show producers and executives that writers seeking work have the chops and skills to write professionally—but on some show, series, film, or project of the studio or network *other* than the one listed in the title of the spec script. In television trade logic, spec scripts ideally open doors and get potential partners to start brainstorming imagined narratives, series, or relationships.

A diverse range of industrial habits now constitute the spec world. Consider the following examples:

- A vast underclass of low-paid "readers" writes up "script coverage" on every one of hundreds of screenplays submitted to the studio each month. This now obligatory narrative preanalysis essentially culls, preselects, and cognitively projects an idealized imagined narrative for quick comprehension in the minds of producers, agents, and network executives. Essentially the studio's ultimate onscreen narratives and scenes are preimagined and thus preproduced by underlings (this ad hoc process of calculated imaginative projection makes features into collectively imagined narrative aggregates).
- A personal assistant to an overbooked executive habitually employs a cultural caste system to prioritize which agents or producers get development meetings, thus acting as an unintended, low-paid narrative element gatekeeper for the select stories eventually told in series episodes. As Erin Hill has recently shown, no one sees clerical staff gatekeepers as preemptive, de facto story editors, but industrially they function that way.[10]
- A filmmaker asks the crew on a low- or no-budget feature production to bring their own gear in exchange for "points" from distribution income.

The newcomer-director implicitly "pays" his more experienced AC/record-ist/gaffer with greater license to fill gaps and stylize scenes. The film gets a "festival release," no crewmember gets distribution income, but the director leverages this quasi-improvisational first feature as calling card to raise real money for a second film.

· The star showrunner of a blockbuster TV series rarely sets foot in his "writers' room," where a dozen staffers and uncredited writers' assistants all contribute story elements. Yet press and fans alike hail the narrative as the showrunner's expression.

· Using the new Red digital camera and file-based recording, a director vastly overshoots each scene for his primetime episode. Unable to view all of his dailies due to this high shooting ratio, the director depends on his/her editor to pull the best takes, but there aren't enough hours in the postproduction week to even view all of the footage. This forces the editor to defer to lowly assistant editors, minimum-wage loggers, and undermotivated production assistants to informally preselect (and thus preimagine) the eventual narrative world, just to meet deadlines.

· An American studio enjoins a cross-cultural negotiator to break down the proposed narrative of a planned feature film in China. This matchmaker/bureaucrat puts considerable effort into speculating, pretelling, and project-ing the imagined story world to: 1) convince Chinese censors to imagine the scenes as benign; 2) convince Chinese governmental overseers that even the scenes with American actors are in some way authentically Chinese, thus justifying the claim that this should be "counted" not as an "American" copro-duction but as a privileged "domestic" Chinese film (giving it huge advantages in theaters under the Chinese quota system); and 3) convince Chinese venture capitalists that the narrative will fill theater seats across China.[11] At the same time, other producers from the same studio make the opposite arguments elsewhere, speculating that the unmade narrative will resonate with *American audiences* as an American film. The result: contradictory spec work, out of both sides of a studio's mouth.

These examples underscore how deep, systematic, and sometimes splintered acts of narrative imagination are to unglamorous industrial work. All of these practices make *speculation* or *brainstorming* central, core tasks in media. The final example—the fragmented "imaginative work" needed to get a Chinese–U.S. trans-national feature going—even shows how delegated *imaginative speculators* can align neatly with uneasy capitalist bedfellows: "*economic speculators.*"

Unfortunately, as these examples suggest, "on spec" ceased being the exception—limited to screenwriters—awhile back, and now arguably orients the industry as a whole. Vast amounts of creative work in film and television (outside of screenwriting, that is) are produced and circulated as unpaid speculative demonstrations of artistic competence or as blueprints of imagined worlds. As I have documented elsewhere, spec work includes many self-financed "festival films" (which "pretest" the value of indie directors and concepts before studios have to risk their own capital); short films ("calling-card films"); excessive serial pitching protocols at work; ceremonial public pitchfests staged at television trade gatherings; film production competitions, company "brainstorming" sessions, conference panels, how-to sessions, and "how'd they do that" demos and web sites. Spec work once applied only to the desperate and unqualified trying to break into the business—since who would be stupid enough to give their professional craftwork or writing away for free?

Given the extent of these practices, spec work arguably defines media production both outside and inside professional film production and network television. In effect, even pros now increasingly "give it away for free," in hopes of stiffing the considerable competition and winning new work—their own "guaranteed" Writers Guild of America (WGA) and Directors Guild of America (DGA) rates be damned! Professionals who give their work away for free typically defend this practice based on heightened barriers to entry. To succeed, that is, you can't just verbally pitch a new show idea to an executive anymore. You have to present additional prototyping materials—tape or video of sample scenes or a beta-tested web series—to demonstrate, dramatize, or pre-enact your proposed production. And of course, these ancillary media forms must be self-financed by the spec-artist. Much of moving image production therefore actually takes place well before the director calls "action" on day one of any shoot.

The spread of spec work feels inevitable to many fatalistic indies trying to produce within deregulated media markets. Such media sectors discourage long-term affiliations and deal entitlements. Yet while indies learn ever more sophisticated ways to "give it away for free," the emerging companies of the brand world have learned increasingly to move away from *internal* development of IP, in order to master what I would term *external* "spec-work harvesting."

In this corporate IP harvesting system, a screenwriter increasingly cannot expect to get paid the guild rate to write a treatment without facing considerable pressure to write successive screenplay drafts—without pay or acknowledgment. In essence, such writers are implicitly blackmailed and expected (or have learned how) to "sweeten the deal" with executives by agreeing to write up and submit full (and sometimes multiple) drafts for free—or for some hoped-for downstream payoff. In some ways TV series pilots have *always* been speculative, performing as a brief test run that allows producers, networks, and audience to interactively speculate on whether the pilot will be successful as a series. Yet even the practice of producing series pilots has shifted increasingly to the financeless logic of spec world. These days, you can't just independently produce your own pilot, as desperate as that might seem; you increasingly have to agree to fully self-finance the first half-dozen or dozen episodes of the proposed season to get a network deal for the whole package.

The genius of industry's blended labor systems comes in the ways industry deploys quasi-cultural institutions to allow the brand world to interface, harvest, and monetize the labor of the spec world. Such spaces function like refereed "contact zones," and include nonprofits, NGOs, and advocates (such as the IFP/Film Independent, the Sundance Institute) that keep the film/TV precariat on life support through enabling exercises involving group speculation. Such interface sites also function as cost-effective (sometimes bargain basement) IP markets. The slippage here between career and economics works because such zones promote themselves as therapeutic sites for spec-worker career development.

If filmmakers and producers once risked little by sharing creative ideas with a few key, well-placed individuals, they did so just to solicit lucrative long-term relationships. Now they have to keep their necks out and exposed for months, willing to eat the considerable losses that come from making professional media with no real or immediate promise of outside revenue. Studios and networks once provided upfront money to close a deal with a creator. Yet the many lesser networks and basic cable channels now increasingly appear to green-light deals without actually paying even seasoned producers for them. This alternative allows studios and networks to wait on the sidelines to pick up only the films, pilots, and series that have survived preliminary or initial runs—that is, series that have not already crashed and burned. Spec world is a pathetic and ugly world indeed, and not just for the hopeful users and unpaid prosumers gifting videos across the globe via YouTube and Vimeo, hoping against extremely long odds that they will be discovered.[12] In short, the spec world off-loads or, better, "preloads" more and more of the responsibility for actually producing and financing screen content onto the shoulders of the makers. Out of this process emerges an odd alignment: even film and TV professionals increasingly bear an uncanny resemblance to the younger, desperate aspirants who hope to take their jobs.

PRODUCTION CULTURE AS SPEC WORK

A broader question remains: how do these three interpenetrating labor regimes—and the spec world in particular—spur media industries to build para-industrial buffers and cultural fronts to survive? What specific cultural practices (chatter, written and visual expression, artifact making, habits and rituals) do these competing labor arrangements ramp up in ways that the "old" industries did not? Moments of industrial contestation and change greatly accelerate para-industrial cultural expression, chatter, and spec work. In some ways, this is a pitched battle.

TABLE 3.2 Cultural Practices of Three Paraindustrial Labor Regimes

	Craft World	Brand World	Spec World
Cultural Chatter	Self-legitimation, boundary-policing, controlling entrants	Cross-promotion, trade-incest, fake buzz, insider leaks	Sharing, discovery, self-marketing, replicating industry
Cultural Expressions	Professional/expert blogosphere, clip reels, WGC/snark	The showrunner-Twitterverse, EPKS, value-added web site	UGC, demo films, spec scripts, spec scenes, Facebook
Cultural Habits and Rituals	Open houses, bake-offs, technical demos migratory crew-org	Summits, markets, trade conventions, TCAs, upfronts	Pitchfests, shoot-outs, hailing-stunts, networking, bartering

As the model below suggests (see Table 3.2), each regime uses culture for different ends. The threatened craft world, for example, favors "self-legitimation" strategies, boundary policing of amateurs, and the rigid control of entrants via high barriers to entry. Its cultural expressions (online, offline, in-person) cultivate "professionalization" and the careful maintenance of socio-professional communities. Even so, preoccupation with technical "experts," masters, and mentors keeps even the social media and trade rituals of the craft world to a quaint, almost predigital scale (open houses, bake-offs, how-to's).

Brand world does not need to stage culture this way to sustain socio-professional craft communities. Yet it faces considerably more cultural work to bring sense or rationality to its worldwide licensing, reformatting, high-concept, and franchising schemes. Success in brand world means mastering cross-promotion among the conglomerate's platforms, systematic leaking of "insider" info, development of incestuous relations with the "trade" media, and creation of fake buzz. While this cultural chatter once worked via the press junket and the electronic press kit (EPK), the showrunner "Twitterverse" is perhaps the most effective tangible expression of current brand-world chatter.

The cultural chatter strategies of spec world are well known from social media, Twitter, and Facebook: sharing, self-marketing, networking, and bartering. Socio-professional cultural expressions here include: worker-generated content (WGC) mirroring user-generated content (UGC); stealth stunts and staged online "scenes" aimed at "hailing" the attention of higher-ups; circulating demos to facilitate one's "discovery"; "friending" for lateral movement across job classifications; and tweeting to build migratory crew networks. Professionals have learned spec-world postures—trade rationalizations, spin, hype, and dissembling—partly from online social media practices, then combining these with indigenous "sharing" traditions from their own craft histories.

SELF-DEFEATING LABOR TACTICS

I undertook this research partly because so many frustrated individuals that I talk to misperceive the labor regimes they operate within. Film school students *think* they are mastering the craft world (unaware that it is maintained by creative labor's scarcity practices), even though the same film students' file sharing, mash-ups, and online UGC gifting destroy the very scarcity-policed craft conditions under which they might once have made incomes in film and television. My nineteen-year-old film students usually get depressed when I point this out. By contrast, marginal producers glibly invoke their supposed Hollywood IDs, even while pitching and self-financing pilots according to the new ways of the brand world. The aggregate downward budget spiral this creates spurs runaway production—thus destroying the high-end craft world the same producers will desperately need if they ever hope to achieve industry "insider" or big-screen distinction. Alternately, below-the-line IATSE editors and above-the-line WGA members justify their "off-the-books," nonunion spec work as a way to get more work. This wistful posture is likely reinforced and legitimized by social media sharing practices that they've learned and adopted from the spec world. Sadly, this freely given surplus work undercuts peers, taking work (and thus screen time) away from others, further increasing craft-world precarity.

Finally, earnest unemployed and outsider aspirants (adept at social media from the spec world but living far from physical production centers) send upfront money, entrance fees, registration fees, and retainers to agents who are not agents, managers and talent scouts who are not managers and talent scouts, film festivals that are not film festivals, "master classes" that do not master anything, student loan mills posing as film schools, "industry insiders" who are not insiders of anything, and "exclusive" online short film "showcases" that no one from the industry ever bothers to watch. In large measure, this collective aspirational surge—the aggregated resources and capital from ubiquitous film/TV aspirational cultures so vast that the sun never sets on their worldwide borders—is what feeds the para-industrial beast and the industry it presumes to support. In these final cases, misrecognition of the spec-world labor regime by those within it alters both of the other two regimes but in very different ways: first, it destroys craft-world scarcity even as it feeds huge amounts of new ideas into the brand world, which large corporate conglomerates efficiently strip-mine.

With so much to lose and so much at stake for these three competing labor regimes, professional workers, aspirants, and scholars alike face complex alternatives in the dense para-industrial buffer. Navigating the buffer—which is now inseparable from the industry proper—requires considerable awareness and adroitness. This predicament means that the culture and spec work of production are now as obligatory to a worker's skill set as the physical competencies of production craft once were.

SPEC WORK, PROTOTYPES, PRETESTING, PILOTS
(BRAND AND FRANCHISE FODDER)

I research speculation work because corporate/professional apologists for free/ gifted labor provoke my long-standing interests in industrial aesthetics, production's cultural politics, multimedia branding rationality, and industrial reflexivity.[13] Those concerns resonate with many current labor practices: the spec script, the pitch aesthetic, the craft-worker's Facebook network, the technician's how-to demo, the underemployed editor's clip reel, the disgruntled crew member's theoretical deconstruction of executives, the creative producer's fan-pandering Twitterverse, and the endless proliferation of reps, agents, middlemen, "contact men," and handlers. Such mediators and facilitators complicate the para-industry. Yet they also provide scholars with many new opportunities for para-industrial research.

In some ways, the pilot is no longer just a preliminary artifact setting up more durable or primary forms of lasting screen content. Rather, the pilot now arguably defines *all* film and television production. Or, said differently, all film and television productions now ideally function as pilots, in the broad sense of the term. This is because most films and shows (even year-long series) merely stand in as *prototypes* that create the possibility of endless systematic iterations of the same concept. This posturing in turn heightens the prospects that a corporation can endlessly monetize its proprietary IP. For only through endless speculation, conceptual pretesting, work-shopping, and "piloting" can a brand or franchise succeed. Such is the spec world. The fact that much of both the material burden *and the justification* for spec, prototyping, pretesting, and piloting has been financially off-loaded onto workers means the labor will continue to persist as a nagging but important complication in media studies.

NOTES

1. Allen Scott, *On Hollywood* (Princeton, NJ: Princeton University Press, 2005); and Toby Miller, Nitin Govil, John McMurria, and Richard Maxwell, *Global Hollywood* (London: British Film Institute, 2001).

2. Vicki Mayer, *Below the Line* (Durham, NC: Duke University Press, 2011); and Matt Stahl, *Unfree Masters* (Durham, NC: Duke University Press, 2013).

3. John Thornton Caldwell, *Televisuality: Style, Crisis, and Authority in American Television* ((New Brunswick, NJ: Rutgers University Press, 1995); and John Thornton Caldwell, *Production Culture: Industrial Reflexivity and Critical Practice in Film and Television* (Durham, NC: Duke University Press, 2008).

4. Henry Jenkins, *Convergence Culture* (New York: New York University Press, 2006).

5. This is a play on Henry Jenkins, *Spreadable Media* (New York: New York University Press, 2013).

6. John Caldwell, "Para-Industry," *Cinema Journal* 52.3. (Spring 2013): 157–165.

7. Scott, *On Hollywood*; and Michael Curtin, *Playing to the World's Biggest Audience* (Berkeley: University of California Press, 2007).

8. John Caldwell, "Convergence Television: Aggregating Form and Repurposing Content in the Culture of Conglomeration," in *Television after TV*, ed. Lynn Spigel (Durham, NC: Duke University Press, 2004), 41–74.

9. By contrast, screenwriters still write spec scripts for film without promise of payment, yet continue maintaining "long-odds" hope that someone might buy script to make a movie.

10. See Erin Hill, "Women's Work: Feminized Labor in Hollywood, 1930–1948" PhD diss., UCLA, 2014.

11. One of the best explorations of cross-cultural spec-mediation is Aynne Kokas, "Shot in Shanghai: Western Film Co-Production in Post-WTO Mainland China," PhD diss., UCLA, 2012.

12. See example of crowd-sourced online-to-feature film project, *Life in a Day*. YouTube solicited thousands of user-shot videos to make its feature project. When the resulting aggregate project was screened online, then shown as a feature film in festivals, the project was boldly hyped as a "Ridley Scott Production," clearly erasing its utopian collectivity.

13. See John Caldwell, *Televisuality* (New Brunswick, NJ: Rutgers University Press, 1995); Anna Everett and John Caldwell, eds., *New Media* (New York: Routledge, 2003); and John Caldwell, *Production Culture* (Durham, NC: Duke University Press, 2008).

4

Film/City

Cinema, Affect, and Immaterial Labor in Urban India

Shanti Kumar

In this chapter, I argue that Bollywood must be understood as a vital force of immaterial labor for the affective contagion of mass creativity in urban India. I focus on the some of the many reasons why politicians, policymakers, film stars, filmmakers, and business leaders in India are turning their attention to the infrastructure of cinema as a potential resource for attracting economic capital and creative labor in urban and semiurban areas. The fusion of cinematic infrastructure with urban architecture is most evident in Indian cities and towns that have, or are planning to have, a "film city" in their master plans for urban development. Recent examples of this popular trend include the inauguration near Kolkata with much fanfare of Prayag Film City by the Bollywood superstar Shah Rukh Khan in April 2012; the announcement in August 2012 by actor Jackie Shroff of his investment in a partnership to build a mini–film city in Ahmedabad; the proposal by the Bihar chief minister, Nitish Kumar, in November 2012 to build a Film City near Patna in response to intense lobbying by actors from the Hindi and Bhojpuri film industries; plans by the Uttar Pradesh chief minister, Akhilesh Yadav, in October 2012 to create an IT/Film City in Lucknow; and much-advertised plans by the corporate powerhouse Sahara India to build the Sahara Pariwar Film City in its Aambi Valley development project near Pune.

The mobilization of the film industry and its infrastructure, including cinema halls, shooting locations, and production facilities, for generating economic development and sustaining growth in urban, semiurban, and rural areas is hardly new in India. For instance, these proposals for film cities take their inspiration from the pioneering efforts of Ramoji Film City, built near Hyderabad in 1996, and Innovative Film City near Bengaluru, which opened in 2008. Many academic studies have detailed the central role that cinema halls, film studios, cinematic narratives, and Bollywood-inspired consumer culture have played for many decades now in producing and sustaining India's nationalist visions and developmental goals. However, what is new about the recent spate of proposals for film cities is the way the immaterial infrastructure of Bollywood is being integrated into to the future designs and architectures of urban life as a whole in India.

Drawing on Nigel Thrift's concept of "affective cities," I examine how film cities—and plans for film cities—are being used in several cities and towns in India to produce and manage mass creativity by transforming urban life into social factories of immaterial labor.[1] As Maurizio Lazzarato defines it, "immaterial labor" is labor that produces the informational and cultural content of a commodity.[2] The informational aspect of immaterial labor refers to the ways digital technologies, computer networks, and cybernetic controls are becoming integral to the labor practices that workers used traditionally to perform in spaces such as the factory floor. The cultural aspect of immaterial labor involves the affect value of the practices of social life in areas such as fashion, tastes, traditions, and norms, which are usually not deemed relevant to matters of labor in the workplace. As information technologies have become central to all sorts of workplaces in recent times, immaterial labor has become more integral to practices of work and social life at large, according to Lazzarato. The result is that labor is increasingly becoming more "intellectual" in society, and the commodities created through practices of immaterial labor are not only goods made in a factory but also the products of "mass intellect" or "mass creativity" in social life.

I argue that Thrift's concept of "affective cities" is a powerful framework for analyzing how practices of immaterial labor in urban life are shifting the focus of work from capital–labor relations (in spaces such as the factory floor) to capital–life relations (in society at large). Using Thrift's concept of affective cities in relation to Lazzarato's theory of immaterial labor, I examine how cities in India are trying to tap into the immaterial labor of Bollywood by mobilizing film cities for the production and management of mass creativity in urban life as a whole. In this context, immaterial labor in Bollywood is not strictly limited to what is traditionally understood as the creative process of making a film. Instead, it is the workers and consumers at large who produce a range of immaterial goods and services through the constant exchange of communication, information, and knowledge about the film commodity in the political, economic, technological, cultural, and affective realms of social relations. The film city, I argue, is a concrete embodiment of the many ways in which the immaterial infrastructure of Bollywood is being fused with the traditional architectures of cities and towns in India to meet the growing demands of—and desires for—mediated mobilities in the twenty-first century.

BOLLYWOODIZATION, IMMATERIAL LABOR, AND
MASS CREATIVITY

The term *Bollywood* was coined in the 1970s to capture—often pejoratively—the similarities between India's national Hindi film industry based in Bombay (now Mumbai) and the globally dominant Hollywood film industry in the United States. However, as Ashish Rajadhyaksha argues, *Bollywood* in recent times has been used not just to describe Hindi films produced in Bombay but also to refer to "a more diffuse cultural conglomeration involving a range of distribution and consumption activities from websites to music cassettes, from cable to radio."[3] Therefore, Rajadhyaksha uses the term *Bollywoodization* to signify a very recent phenomenon in Indian cinema that has emerged since the 1990s as a result of the "synchronous developments of international capital and diasporic nationalism."[4]

In the dominant "national" model of Indian cinema, the relationship between production and consumption has always been clearly demarcated, dividing those who make films (directors, producers, writers, actors, and other crew members or below-the-line workers) from those who watch films (moviegoers, fans, and consumers of film-based media, memorabilia, and culture). As Derek Bose argues in *Brand Bollywood,* when hundreds of formulaic Hindi films are being mass-produced in Bombay, the process of filmmaking often resembles the assembly-line mode of industrial production on a factory floor.[5] Recounting a time in the 1990s when industry output had reached over 900 films per year and over 14,000 titles were registered with the Indian Motion Pictures Producers Association (IMPPA), Bose writes, "Actors like Govinda and Anil Kapoor were doing as many as five shifts a day and Mahesh Bhatt acquired the distinction of being India's first 'director by remote control.' At any given time, he had three or four projects on the floor and he would sit at home, instructing various assistants on telephone to can his shots. Films were thus directed by proxy, in keeping with the best traditions of assembly-line production."[6]

Many of these films were major box office hits because the assembly-line mode of mass production was sustained by a national network of financier-distributors whose monopoly over clearly demarcated distribution territories could ensure that mass audiences would always throng into theaters to watch their favorite movie stars on the big screen. The fairly standardized model of formulaic filmmaking and the national system of financing and distribution did not allow for—or did not require—much input from the mass audiences in relations of production. In an industry driven by what Tejaswini Ganti calls "the ratio of hits to flops," filmmakers considered the commercial success or failure of films "as an accurate barometer of social attitudes, norms, and sensibilities, thus providing the basis for knowledge about audiences."[7] Of course, the failure—or the fear of failure—of big-budget, big-star films was always a good reason for producers to incorporate audience feedback into the production process. But the creative power of the mass audiences to reframe cinematic narratives or to reshape filmmaking practices was limited in the national model of mass production, mass distribution and mass consumption in Indian cinema.

However, with the Bollywoodization of Indian cinema since the late 1990s and early 2000s, a more diffused, global model of cultural production has emerged where the relationship between film producers and consumers has, of necessity, become less hierarchical and more transversal. The changes in creative and industrial practices produced by the Bollywoodization of Indian cinema have been deftly analyzed by Aswin Punathambekar in *From Bombay to Bollywood: The Making of a Global Media Industry*. Contrasting the new Bollywoodized mode of production with the traditional model of filmmaking in Indian cinema, Punathambekar argues that the "ongoing changes in the domain of marketing and promotions are emblematic of broader reconfigurations of relations between capital, circuits of information and forms of knowledge . . . in Bombay's media world."[8] For instance, discussing the growing centrality of paratexts such as trailers, posters, music videos of song and dance sequences, and media events such as the *mahurat* (ritual inauguration of a new production) and promotional tours by film stars and singers, Punathambekar examines how marketing and promotion have become new sites of decision making, communication, and knowledge about the film commodity even before a film is released or produced.

Since the paratexts and media events discussed by Punathambekar are not traditionally considered integral parts of the filmmaking process or the film commodity, the labor involved in their production (including advertising, marketing, promotion, spot films, web sites, online chat sessions with fans, and games and contests for mobile devices) is what Lazzarato would define as immaterial labor. To recall Lazzarato's definition outlined earlier, immaterial labor consists of two types of work in the capitalist production of a commodity (such as a film): informational labor (such as the use of digital technologies, paratexts, media events, marketing, and promotion materials before, during, and after production) and cultural labor (the production of affective value through the circulation of the film commodity in social life—such the pleasures of producing and consuming the texts and paratexts of a film, the thrill of participating in media events, the social bonds of sharing and recommending "free" marketing and promotional materials about the film to online and offline friends, and so on). Taken together, the two types of immaterial labor—informational and cultural—produce affective value for the film commodity in all aspects of social life.

The affect of immaterial labor is, of course, difficult to track. As Thrift points out, there are many definitions of affect, and they are often "associated with words like emotion and feeling, and a consequent repertoire of terms like hatred, shame, envy, fear, disgust, anger, embarrassment, sorrow, grief, anguish, love, happiness, joy, hope, wonder."[9] However, Thrift finds that these words are not good translations of affect and therefore proposes to move away from definitions that focus on individualized emotions. Instead, Thrift favors approaches that define affect in terms of general tendencies and lines of forces. Of these approaches, Thrift highlights four: affect as embodied knowledge, affect theory associated with but differentiated from psychoanalytic conceptions of libidinal drives, the Spinozian-Deleuzian notion of affect as emergent capacities, and neo-Darwinian frameworks of affect as a universal expression of emotion. Summarizing his extensive review of the literature on these four approaches to affect, Thrift writes, "Four different notions of affect, then. Each of them depends on a sense of push in the world but the sense of push is subtly different in each case. In the case of embodied knowledge, that push is provided by the expressive armoury of the human body. In the case of affect theory it is provided by biologically differentiated positive and negative affects rather than the drives of Freudian theory. In the world of Spinoza and Deleuze, affect is the capacity of interaction that is akin to a natural force of emergence. In the neo-Darwinian universe, affect is a deep-seated physiological change involuntarily written on the face."[10]

Although affect—as general tendencies and lines of force—is a widespread and crucial element of urban life, Thrift argues that the affective register has been largely neglected in the study of cities. Defining urban life through the concept of "affective cities," Thrift argues that affects like anger, fear, joy, and hope manifest themselves in "the mundane emotional labor of the workplace, the frustrated shouts and gestures of road rage, the delighted laughter of children as they tour a theme park or the tears of a suspected felon undergoing police interrogation."[11] Equally, for Thrift, affect in urban life is evident in the "mass hysteria" surrounding major media events like the spectacular life or the death of a global superstar or the roar of a crowd celebrating a point scored by their team in a sports stadium. To Thrift's descriptions of the affective registers in urban culture, one could add, in the Indian context, the many ways Bollywood culture permeates the everyday lives of Indians in terms of fashion, clothing, style, song and dance, rituals, and so on. One can also point to the affective domain of "mass worship" of Bollywood stars and Bollywood culture along with the "mass fanaticism" of fans who flock to see their favorite film star at a shooting location or in a film city, or the masses of cinemagoers who insist on catching a new release in a cinema hall on the first day in cities and towns across India.

As Amit Rai's brilliant work on affect in India's new media assemblage demonstrates, film (in the traditional sense of movie-making and movie-going) is now only one of the many elements in a highly diffuse agglomeration of material and immaterial practices of production, distribution, and consumption in Bollywood.[12] Therefore, filmmakers have to make creative decisions about the filmmaking process in relation to a range of immaterial practices taking place—or which have already taken place—in diverse locations, such as malls, multiplexes, homes, and local marketplaces, and on multiple platforms, such as movie theaters, television channels, FM radio, online media, and cell phones. Foregrounding the affective connectivities between cinema and other media technologies along with the sensations generated among bodies, populations, and various graphical interfaces at locations such as the single-screen cinema hall, the multiplex, the mall, the television screen at home, and the mobile phone in public places, Rai redefines Bollywood as a new media assemblage that is "necessarily constellated, remediated and multiply overlapping."[13] Rai argues that through remediation of old and new media connectivities and sensations in and through Bollywood, affect plays a crucial role in the transformation of technologies, labor, and aesthetics in production and consumption practices of everyday life in India.

In many ways, affect has always been a central concern in Indian cinema and in the production of creativity in India more generally. In *Bombay before Bollywood*, Rosie Thomas argues that the spectator-subject of mainstream Hindi cinema has always been addressed and moved through film primarily by affect. Tracing the genealogy of Bollywood through the history of Bombay cinema, Thomas finds that in commercial Hindi films, the emphasis was—and still is—more on emotion and spectacle and less on the tightness of a linear narrative. Or, as Thomas puts it, the emphasis was more "on *how* things would happen rather than *what* would happen next, on a succession of modes rather than linear denouement, on familiarity and repeated viewings rather than 'originality' and novelty, on a moral disordering to be (temporarily) resolved rather than an enigma to be solved."[14] The pleasure value of repeat viewing, for instance, was recognized by filmmakers early on, and was built into film narratives by foregrounding the affective power of stars, music, spectacle, emotion, and dialogue. Thomas argues that affect was thus "structured and contained by narratives whose power and insistence derived from their very familiarity, coupled with the fact that they were deeply rooted (in the psyche and in traditional mythology)."[15]

Among the deeply rooted cultural narratives and traditions of everyday life that Thomas refers to are "Hindu caste, kinship and religious ideologies, in particular beliefs in destiny and karma [that] position a decentered, less individuated social subject"; "specific cultural traditions of performance and entertainment . . . notably the forms on which early cinema drew, from the performances of the professional storytellers and village dramatisations of the mythological epics, to the excesses of spectacle ('vulgar' and 'garish' according to contemporary critics) of the late-nineteenth- and early-twentieth-century Urdu-Parsi theatre with its indulgent adaptations of Shakespeare and Victorian melodrama"; and the rasa theory of aesthetics, which rejects "the unities of time and place and the dramatic development of narrative . . . [and] is concerned with moving the spectator through the text in an ordered succession of modes of affect (rasa), by means of highly stylized devices."[16]

Thomas claims that "all Indian classical drama, dance and music draw on this aesthetic," and argues that the traditions of rasa theory deeply inform the production practices of Indian cinema. However, she also finds that most filmmakers do not make any conscious reference to this cultural heritage. Similarly, Thomas wonders whether or not the emergence of the spectator-subject of Indian cinema—who is primarily addressed and moved by aesthetic modes of affect (rasa) in film narratives—can be related in any useful way to a more general history of the evolution of the "social audience" in India. Arguing that traditions of Bollywood cannot be used to provide neat causal explanations of contemporary Indian cinema and culture, Thomas suggests that traditions (such as rasa theory) must be seen "as a framework of terms of reference within which certain developments have been stifled, others allowed to evolve unproblematically, and which can be used to throw light on the different possibilities of forms of address which might be expected or tolerated by an Indian audience."[17]

As Rajinder Dudrah and Amit Rai remind us, the role of affect (or rasa) in Indian cinema cannot be understood simply through critiques of the political economy of the Hindi film industry (to make money, filmmakers have to produce emotional melodramas with song and dance to reach a "mass audience") or through cultural studies of the textual pleasures of moviegoing for spectator-subjects of Indian cinema (Indians like Bollywood films because emotional melodramas are part of their essential cultural traditions).[18] Highlighting the risks of reading rasa as the "essence" of Indian culture and cautioning against the dangers of embracing elitist or high-brahminical ideologies of rasa as the pinnacle of Hindu philosophy or aesthetics, Dudrah and Rai examine rasa in Bollywood as a "contact zone" of affect. In this zone of affective contagion, Bollywood is a new media assemblage "through and in which bodies, sensations, capital, sexualities, races, technologies and desires rub up against each other, producing differing and differential rhythms, speeds, juices (or rasas), intensities, technologies, combinations, codes, possibilities, and even languages."

Bollywood's affect (or rasa) thus functions as "a framework of terms of reference" at the infrastructural level of cinema and urban life for the creation of new architectures of cities and film cities in India. In the next section, I discuss how the affective value of Bollywood circulates at the infrastructural level in the immaterial production and management of mass creativity through the concept of the film city in urban India.

THE FILM CITY AND/AS THE IMMATERIAL INFRASTRUCTURE OF URBAN LIFE

In Bihar—considered to be one of the least economically developed states in India—Chief Minister Nitish Kumar announced in November 2012 that his government was seriously considering plans to build a film city near the capital city of Patna. The announcement by the chief minister was in response to intense lobbying by actors, producers, and directors from the Mumbai-based Hindi film industry and the local Bhojpuri film industry, which has in recent years witnessed an amazing growth and rise in popularity in India.[19] For more than a decade, major Bollywood stars from Bihar, including Shatrughan Sinha, Manoj Bajpai, director Prakash Jha, and Bohjpuri film star Ravi Kissen, have aggressively promoted proposals to set up a film city in their home state. A home-grown film city, they argue, would not only attract talent and resources from Bollywood and other regional film industries into Bihar but also stimulate the local Bhojpuri film industry. In 2013, the consultancy firm Grant Thornton submitted a feasibility report to the government of Bihar recommending the construction of a film city in the state. However, in 2014, the chief minister announced plans for building an IT city in Nalanda (his home district) in Bihar.[20]

Frustrated by lack of progress on a film city in Bihar, director Prakash Jha and actor Shatrughan Sinha are now trying to convince the government of Madhya Pradesh to set up a film city in Bhopal. The government of Madhya Pradesh has already set aside one thousand acres near Bhopal for a proposed film city complex. Bhopal, known as the "city of lakes," has emerged as a recent favorite of many Bollywood filmmakers, who are drawn to the scenic locations and picturesque beauty of the city's many lakes and gardens. Prakash Jha shot four films in Bhopal from 2010 to 2013. These films, *Raajneeti* (2010), *Aarakshan* (2011), *Chakravyuh* (2012), and *Satyagrah* (2013), are among some of the most popular Hindi films of the past few years.[21]

When Amitabh Bachchan—without any doubt the biggest film star in the history of Indian cinema—was in Bhopal to shoot for Jha's film *Aarakshan*, he was warmly welcomed by fans and embraced by the city as its unofficial brand ambassador-in-law because Bachchan's father-in-law had lived in Bhopal long ago (when Bachchan's wife, Jaya, was a young girl). It is important to note that Bachchan has also served as the brand ambassador for the Department of Tourism in Gujarat since 2010, and was appointed the brand ambassador for the Health Department in Andhra Pradesh in 2015. Following Bachchan's "Khushboo Gujarat Ki" (the fragrance of Gujarat) campaign for Gujarat tourism, it was reported that the number of hotel reservations in the state rose from 4,500 to 6,400 within two years. During that time, the number of tourists visiting Gujarat reportedly increased by 55 lakhs (one lakh is equal to 100,000). Vipul Mittra, secretary of tourism for the state of Gujarat, claimed that the state's efforts to promote tourism with Bachchan as its brand ambassador helped because "he has great credibility and people take him seriously."[22] While it is practically impossible to posit a causal relationship between the growth of tourism in Gujarat and Bachchan's position as the ambassador of the state's Tourism Department, the affective value of his promotion of the "fragrance" (*khushboo*) of Gujarat is undeniable.

Such is the respect and popularity that Bollywood superstars like Bachchan enjoy among fans across India, and the branding of cities through identification with film stars shows how cinema and celebrity culture are considered crucial for generating a buzz for public-private partnerships in government-sanctioned plans for urban development in India today. Following Bachchan's appointment as the brand ambassador of Gujarat, West Bengal roped in Shah Rukh Khan as its brand ambassador, and many other states soon followed suit. As Tanvi Trivedi of the *Times of India* reports, "Prachi Desai represents Goa tourism, Hema Malini is the face of Uttarakhand's *Sparsh* [clean] *Ganga* campaign, Saina Nehwal, badminton champ is the brand ambassador for Andhra Pradesh since 2010. Interestingly Haryana (where she was born) also wanted her to be the face. Preity Zinta is the only celebrity representing Himachal Pradesh, Celina Jaitly is the brand ambassador for Egypt, Mountaineer Anshu Jamsenpa who conquered the Mt Everest in 2011 is set to become the brand ambassador of North East India Tourism campaign. Reportedly Arunachal Pradesh wants Aamir Khan, Madhya Pradesh is interested in Abhishek Bachchan (mom Jaya Bachchan is from the state) and Chhattisgarh has asked Sushmita Sen to be their brand ambassadors."[23] Trivedi quotes filmmaker Aniruddha Roy Chowdhury, who directed Shah Rukh Khan's promotional films on West Bengal, as saying, "Even though a Bachchan or Shah Rukh don't [sic] have any connect with Gujarat or Bengal, their global appeal does the magic."[24]

As Nigel Thrift points out, in a crowded marketplace, the only way to make a commodity stand out from its competition is through "a series of 'magical' technologies of public intimacy."[25] Thrift argues that these "magical" technologies work through qualities such as the allure of glamour, style, and celebrity to produce intangible affective value for a commodity or a brand. For instance, describing how glamour works through and for commodities, Thrift writes, "For all its breathtaking qualities, glamour does not conjure up awe. It operates on a human scale, in the everyday, inviting just enough familiarity to engage the imagination, a glimpse of another life, utopia as tactile presence. . . . Glamour is about that special excitement and attractiveness that characterizes some objects and people. Glamour is a form of secular magic, conjured up by the commercial sphere."[26]

Nowhere is this link among the "secular magic" of Bollywood, political considerations of governance, and commercial logics of the marketplace more clearly articulated in pubic policy than in the state of Uttar Pradesh in northern India. In October 2012, Chief Minister Akhilesh Yadav declared a new master plan to create a TV/film city in Lucknow and an IT corridor in Agra (which will connect with the existing media and industrial enclaves of Noida near the nation's capital, New Delhi). It is significant that plans for the Lucknow-Agra-Noida TV-film-IT corridor also map onto the chief minister's proposal to extend the six- to eight-lane superhighway called Yamuna Expressway (which currently connects Noida to Agra) to the state's capital, Lucknow. The chief minster's plan to create the Lucknow-Agra-Noida corridor of media industries and superhighways is a clear indication of how media in general, and cinema in particular, are increasingly viewed by politicians and policymakers as keys to the rapid growth of urban infrastructure in India. In 2003, a report by Mckenzie, Crisil, and ICICI commissioned by the government of Uttar Pradesh recommended creating the "right mix of policies" to develop proper infrastructure to fast-track the state's growth rate by 2020. Although the report was commissioned by a previous government, the current chief minister, Akhilesh Yadav, has embraced the 2020 vision to promote "brand UP" by integrating film policy with industrial policy and infrastructure policy. The plans for a film city in the Yamuna Expressway corridor are considered crucial to promoting "brand UP."[27]

The merging of political and economic activities with the glamour of Bollywood celebrity and culture is engendering new forms of public intimacy in urban India. As Thrift reminds us, the aim of public intimacy in urban life is not simply to create new subjects for the global capitalist order (or other disciplinary regimes).[28] Instead, Thrift argues that these spaces are also "new forms of body with the capacity to alter us to that which was previously unable to be sensed—with the corollary that certain objects can no longer be sensed—so producing the potential to generate new kinds of charms."[29]

In addition to the above-mentioned state-supported plans for integrating the allure of Bollywood into the infrastructure of urban life, some corporate houses in India have embarked on creating private versions of public intimacy through the construction of film cities. The much advertised plans by the corporate powerhouse Sahara India to build the Sahara Pariwar Film City in its Aambi Valley development project near Pune are indicative of this popular trend (www.saharaindiapariwar.org/filmcity.html). One of the largest media conglomerates in India, Sahara India owns TV channels, film theaters, sports teams, hotels, retail outlets, and financial services. The founder of Sahara Group, Subrata Roy, was jailed in March 2014 by the Supreme Court of India on charges of financial fraud.[30] It is safe to assume that Sahara's plans for a film city may be on back burner for a while.

In August 2012, Bollywood actor Jackie Shroff announced his partnership in a project to build a mini–film city near Nal Sarovar in Ahmedabad, Gujarat. Initially, Shroff was promoted as the brand ambassador for Nal Sarovar Film City with industrialists Mihir Pandya and Kishansinh Solanki as the major financial backers. However, when Solanki decided to quit the project, Shroff joined Pandya as an investing partner in the project. According to Shroff, Solanki, and Pandya, what sets Nal Sarovar City apart from other film city projects in India is that the film city will be developed as part of an urban enclave with residential homes and resort areas.[31] In the promotional material for Nal Sarovar City, the "film" part of the city is underdeveloped, and the residential plots and resort areas are more prominently displayed, revealing how the concept of a film city is being used to develop and sell real estate in urban and semiurban areas near major cities like Ahmedabad in India.

If Sahara Film City and Nal Sarovar City are stalled projects, a more successful corporate venture is Prayag Film City, also known as Chandrakone Film City or Midnapore Film City, located in Chandrakone, West Midnapore, near Kolkata in West Bengal. Prayag Film City is being built by the Prayag Group, which has business interests in diverse areas such as real estate, hotels and resorts, biscuits and cakes, cements, bricks and tiles, tea, fruit, fishery, poultry, farming, aviation, news, and electronic media (www.prayag.co.in/filmcity.html). The Prayag Group plans to build its film city in three phases: phase 1 is a film zone; phase 2 consists of an entertainment zone; and phase 3 will include a hospitality zone. Phase 1 of Prayag Film City opened with great fanfare on April 15, 2012, with Bollywood superstar Shah Rukh Khan as its brand ambassador. It is important to note that Shah Rukh Khan is also brand ambassador for West Bengal, the state in which Prayag Film City is located.

In publicity brochures, Prayag Film City presents itself as a city unto itself: "Pesh hai ek city—Prayag Film City" (Presenting a city—Prayag Film City). The prominent status of Shah Rukh Khan as the brand ambassador—in the foreground with a caricatured model of the film city in the background—reminds readers of Prayag Film City's close connection to the Mumbai-based Bollywood on the west coast even if Kolkata is all the way on the other side of India. What makes this connection even stronger is the promise of "entertainment ka maha dose" (a big dose of entertainment) in Prayag Film City—delivered by none other than Shah Rukh Khan, arguably the biggest entertainer Bollywood has ever produced since Bachchan.

When all three phases are completed, Prayag Film City, according to publicity materials, will be the "world's largest film city." Currently, the title of the world's largest film city currently belongs to Ramoji Film City (RFC) near Hyderabad, which began operations in 1997. According to the Guinness Book of World Records, RFC has surpassed Hollywood's Universal Studios in both size and the range of media facilities offered. RFC is the dream project of Cherukuri Ramoji Rao, the owner of the Eenadu Media Group in Andhra Pradesh. The Eenadu Group is one of the largest media conglomerates in South India, and Ramoji Rao's business empire consists of several English and Telugu-language periodicals, including the widely read newspaper *Eenadu;* a multilingual satellite television network, ETV; a film distribution banner, Ushakiron Movies; and a financial services group, Margadarshi.[32]

Following the success of RFC, Innovative Film City (IFC) was launched on January 18, 2008, in Bidadi, which is about fifty kilometers from Bengaluru. IFC is part of the Innovative Group, which runs a multiplex cinema business along with media production and entertainment and leisure activities in Karnataka. IFC has a much smaller portfolio of films made in Bidadi than RFC. However, some filmmakers from Kannada cinema and television and other regional media have used the production facilities at IFC in the past few years, and Innovative Group plans to promote the film city as a tourist destination and production center on a much larger scale in the coming years.

What makes film cities unique in Indian cinema is that for the first time filmmakers from anywhere in the world can make an entire film from preproduction to postproduction in a one-stop studio that provides multiple outdoor locales and diverse indoor settings. In addition to being state-of-the-art media production centers, film cities are major tourist attractions that provide visitors access to a variety of picturesque gardens, entertainment parks and tours of film sets, and production studios.[33]

It is important to note that film cities are resource-intensive ventures and take a long time to complete (it took almost a decade each for RFC and IFC to get up and running). Given the intense competition within and across the major centers of film production in various Indian languages—including Mumbai for Hindi/Marathi cinemas, Chennai for Tamil cinema, Hyderabad for Telugu cinema, Bengaluru for Kannada cinema, and Kolkata for Bengali cinema—film cities are financially risky ventures.

In this regard, the value that a film city can generate for an urban center or a small town cannot be estimated in economic terms alone. Instead, it must be understood in terms of the affective value generated by a film city for an urban center seeking to expand its reach into regional, national, and global circuits of production and consumption. A growing number of cities in India are using proposals for film cities to generate a buzz and create a brand identity that sets them apart from similar cities. By embracing Bollywood stars as ambassadors and closely identifying with the latest Bollywood narratives, fashions, and trends, political and cultural elites in urban India are vying to brand their cities as the newest and best centers of creativity, innovation, and invention.

CONCLUSION

In this chapter, I have argued that Nigel Thrift's theory of "affective cities" can be a powerful tool for analyzing the rise and popularity of film cities in India. Drawing on Thrift's theorizations of affect, I have examined how the buzz generated by the circulation of Bollywood's glamour and star power is becoming integral to urban planning and development in India. I have tried to show how—beyond the economic value of creative clustering—the concept of a film city adds value to urban life in the affective realm due to Bollywood's immense popularity as a cultural phenomenon.

With growing media capacity—from low-cost outsourcing to high-tech film cities—in peripheral locations of Bollywood, workers in midsize cities and small towns in India are finding more options for immaterial labor through telecommuting, freelancing, flex time, and so on. But this kind of work does not provide the guarantees of traditional forms of industrial labor with union contracts or state-sponsored employment. The rising precarity of labor relations produced through the immaterial exchanges of media, information, and communication has put pressure on state authorities to provide a semblance of stability and order in the everyday lives of their citizens.

However, due to the growing interconnectedness and rapid deterritorialization of the global economy, the traditional command-and-control structures of the Indian nation-state are no longer capable of exerting—or inclined to exert—their sovereign authority over their territories and populations. Moreover, since the global economy also enhances possibilities for producers across the world to be in direct contact with each other, labor-capital relations can be remotely managed in various locations, often without recourse to the central authority of the nation-state. As the task of regulating global-local relations shifts toward state governments and regional authorities, film cities—or plans for film cities—have emerged as the blueprints of a new architecture for the capture and control of capital and the management and dissemination of creative labor by mobilizing the immaterial productions of cinema in the social life of cities in India.

NOTES

1. Nigel Thrift, *Non-Representational Theory* (New York: Routledge, 2008).

2. Maurizio Lazzarato, "Immaterial Labor," in *Radical Thought in Italy,* ed. Paolo Virno and Michael Hardt (Minneapolis: University of Minnesota Press, 1996), 133–150.

3. Ashish Rajadhyaksha, "The Bollywoodization of the Indian Cinema: Cultural Nationalism in a Global Arena," *Inter-Asia Cultural Studies* 4.1 (2003): 6.

4. Ibid.

5. Derek Bose, *Brand Bollywood: A New Global Entertainment Order* (New Delhi: Sage Publications, 2006).

6. Ibid., 21.

7. Tejaswini Ganti, *Bollywood: A Guidebook to Popular Hindi Cinema* (New York: Routledge, 2004), 62–63.

8. Aswin Punathambekar, *From Bombay to Bollywood: The Making of a Global Media Industry* (New York: New York University Press, 2013), 82.

9. Thrift, *Non-Representational Theory,* 175.

10. Ibid., 182.

11. Ibid., 171.

12. Amit S. Rai, *Untimely Bollywood: India's New Media Assemblage* (Durham, NC: Duke University Press, 2009).

13. Ibid., 70.

14. Rosie Thomas, *Bombay before Bollywood: Film City Fantasies* (Albany: State University of New York Press, 2013), 239. Emphasis in the original.

15. Ibid., 240.

16. Ibid.

17. Ibid.

18. Rajinder Dudrah and Amit Rai, "The Haptic Codes of Bollywood Cinema in New York City," *New Cinemas: Journal of Contemporary Film* 3.3 (2005): 143–158.

19. Ravi Dayal, "Film City Feasibility Report Submitted," *Times of India,* December 2, 2012, http://timesofindia.indiatimes.com/city/patna/Film-city-Feasibility-report-submitted/articleshow/17445887.cms.

20. IANS, "Bihar to Build IT City near Nalanda: Nitish Kumar," *Times of India,* February 20, 2014, http://timesofindia.indiatimes.com/tech/tech-news/Bihar-to-build-IT-city-in-Nalanda-Nitish-Kumar/articleshow/30736559.cms.

21. "Bhopal Best Place in Country for Shooting of Hindi Films: Prakash Jha," *Daily Pioneer,* April 10, 2013, www.dailypioneer.com/state-editions/bhopal/bhopal-best-place-in-country-for-shooting-of-hindi-films-prakash-jha.html.

22. Tanvi Trivedi, "After Big B-SRK, Other States Too Roped In Stars," *Times of India,* November 22, 2012. http://timesofindia.indiatimes.com/entertainment/hindi/bollywood/news/After-Big-B-SRK-other-states-too-roped-in-stars/articleshow/17309052.cms

23. Ibid.

24. Ibid.

25. Nigel Thrift, "Understanding the Material Practices of Glamor," in *The Affect Theory Reader,* ed. Melissa Gregg and Gregory J. Seigworth (Durham, NC: Duke University Press, 2010), 290–308.

26. Ibid., 297.

27. Manish Chandra Pandey, "Coming Up: A Film City in Uttar Pradesh," *Hindustan Times,* June 29, 2013. http://paper.hindustantimes.com/epaper/viewer.aspx.

28. Ibid.

29. Thrift, "Understanding the Material Practices of Glamor," 295.

30. Gardiner Harris, "Court Jails Indian Tycoon," *New York Times,* March 13, 2014, www.nytimes.com/2014/03/14/business/international/subrata-roy-of-india-under-court-scrutiny.html?_r=0.

31. India Glitz, "Ahmedabad to Get Mini Film City, Courtesy Jackie Shroff," *India Glitz,* August 13, 2012, www.indiaglitz.com/ahmedabad-to-get-mini-film-city-courtesy-jackie-shroff-hindi-news-84713.

32. Renji Kuriakose, "Down in the Clouds," *Week* (India), October 19, 1997.

33. Shanti Kumar, "Mapping Tollywood: The Cultural Geography of Ramoji Film City in Hyderabad, India," *Quarterly Review of Film and Video* 23 (2006): 129–138.

5

The Production of Extras in a Precarious Creative Economy

Vicki Mayer

Over the past twenty years, regional governments around the world and global film industry corporations have collaborated, if not colluded, to provide a steady stream of workers for film location shooting through legislated incentives. Seeking to reduce labor costs in relation to other fixed expenses, industry executives have successfully used incentives to reduce budgets. Meanwhile, regional policymakers have looked to film and television production as a panacea for anemic economic growth and declining employment indices.[1] Together, governments and industry have made labor into one of the primary fault lines in the political economy of film production.

For the former constituents, film employment may boost jobs numbers on annual reports but have not produced sustainable economic growth. As critics of film incentive policies point out, the vast majority of these film jobs have been transient, low-wage, or both.[2] At the upper end of the employment spectrum, the highest-skilled workers moved with productions. They have had the same economic impact as business elites, taking their earnings with them as they move from one fancy hotel to another. The larger proportion of film location workers, however, has not been so mobile. These workers—mostly in trades and services—have seen wages driven down. The adoption of right-to-work laws in the United States has put film unions in competition with antishop labor, especially in states that lack sufficient members to meet demand. Economic development offices frequently count service jobs, such as hotel, catering, and transportation staff, as multiplier results of the film economy, knowing that voters will not see the vast quantity of these low-wage, high-turnover jobs as quality careers. To mitigate the political fallout that film incentive policy has caused since the 2009 recession, local boosters typically promise that film jobs will attract other kinds of financial investors in the future, espousing a kind of optimism that has made the policy itself as precarious as the jobs it has generated.

For the film industry, the downward pressures for more abundant reserves of cheaper laborers have not abated. Producers have faced the stress of raising money and cutting costs. They have to weigh the money saved by producing outside Southern California or another major center against the investment in transporting resources, particularly the highest-skilled workers, to the location. Production budgets for labor are stratified, with decreasing studio investment distributed disproportionately to a few workers with star or brand name recognition. The move to reality television has marked an increasing reliance on talent that is either unpaid or underpaid. Volunteers, in the guise of endless levels of interns and assistants, have become part of the production apparatus. Producers have begun to face difficulties in stimulating a labor pool motivated to work for free. Workers have become jaded, even litigious; they now know that these exploited forms of labor rarely lead to stable career paths, particularly outside a global media and entertainment industry hub. In the face of a potential policy upheaval, the uncertainty of finding workers has to be strategized in new ways.

This chapter examines one strategy in the face of this emerging uncertainty in the current film labor regime. Specifically, it looks at the New Orleans–based production of the quality HBO television drama *Treme* (2010–2013) and its ability to create a moral economy for low-paying or unpaid film jobs. This strategy relied on a particular kind of call to work as a form of boosterism for the local economy and the culture that both sustains and emerges from it. The strategy succeeded because it fit well in the context of the current political economy as well as an imagined community of like-minded citizen-workers in the future. Based on conversations with series workers, primarily extras, this chapter provides a lesson about the labor strategy based on those workers who occupy the most precarious jobs in locational shooting.

THE *TREME* MORAL ECONOMY

In 2013, Louisiana surpassed California as the primary location for the production of major Hollywood motion pictures.[3] The state, one of the poorest in terms of the per capita poverty rate and median income, also outpaced Hollywood film shooting in other countries, including Canada and Ireland. This locational outsourcing, often derided as runaway production, has been a point of pride in Louisiana. There, media producers and policymakers alike have seized on film jobs as a cornerstone in the economic renewal of the entire Gulf Coast after a series of devastating environmental disasters, including two hurricanes and an oil spill, destabilized the political and economic infrastructure of the region. The city of New Orleans, which evacuated its entire population of nearly half a million people in 2005 after Hurricane Katrina and subsequently lost many longtime residents, has depended heavily on the growing film economy to bring new migrants and jobs. A 2012 *Forbes* article summarized the recent political economy: "Aggressive tax incentives have also been beneficial in luring new recruits, entrepreneurs, and large business to New Orleans. In 2002, a foundation for a new film industry had been established with a tax credit program for movies produced in the state. However, it wasn't until after Katrina that more production crews committed to continuing their work with Louisiana, and quickly saw the benefits of working in the region. In addition, the productions were pumping millions of dollars into the city's recovering economy, and providing jobs to those who wanted to get into the industry."[4] Ten years after the storm, the city still acknowledges the scars of Katrina—press articles still refer to the "post-K" era—while touting the power of the most generous film tax incentives in the United States to aid future recovery.

In this context, a television series that would focus on the city's unique vernacular value and cultural resilience in the post-K era drew special attention. The auteur television producers David Simon and Eric Overmyer said they had wanted to create a program about New Orleans music long before the storm, but that the disaster brought a sudden moral imperative to make a general concept into a story. "Even ordinary scenes played out against a backdrop of this city three months after the storm take on an incredibly different dynamic. An ordinary scene . . . is about something much bigger," said Simon, while waiting for the green light from the HBO network in 2009. Arguing for the symbolic importance of viewers witnessing a second-line parade in the months after the storm, Simon explained, "Just as a visual tableau, that's an incredible statement of human endeavor. And you place it in the context of all the political (news) and all the problems and all of the distopic things that have happened post-Katrina—if you can't (make) a story of that, shame on you."[5] Within weeks, Fee Nah Nee, the local production company for *Treme*, would begin the process of certifying the applicable tax credits for producing the series.

For four years, *Treme* indexed the tight imbrication between the film economy and New Orleans through a program focused on ordinary life and an extraordinary local culture. Music, food, and public performance took center stage in the weekly narrative, which broadcast via the subscriber channel for three and a half seasons. Beyond this, the program's producers were active in charity and volunteer efforts dedicated to local musicians and the musical cultures of the region. Production crews threw block parties in some of its affected shooting locations and helped host screening parties for residents who could not afford premium cable television service. Newspaper columns deciphered the careful cultural details and historical referents stitched into the story lines, and social media organized fans to participate in the interpretive community. From this base of avid viewers and admirers, *Treme* set out to hire local residents as part of its ethos. The hiring director, who had worked as a local on the Baltimore set of the earlier Simon/Overmyer collaboration, *The Wire*, told me he was always irked by film companies that shot in his hometown but hired outsiders. *Treme* would aim to hire residents, he explained, touting his efforts to support a local training clinic for film crew certification, because "it's the right thing to do."

It was also the most economical thing to do. Louisiana residents received an extra 5 percent in state tax credits, bringing their total discount to 35 percent of the budget. Locals do not have to be housed in hotels. They go home each day without a need for a per diem or transportation. On the set, the same director told me that the local hire brought added value to the decision-making process. They have "natural knowledge" that streamlines the production schedule. He said, "They know the Teamsters, and the bureaucrats, and also the residents. So they don't mind as much when you invade their neighborhood." In the battle to beat the budget, he said locals helped "win the hearts and minds" of the citizens.

This odd pairing of the ethically right and the instrumentally efficient was the labor strategy in *Treme*'s moral economy. Mark Banks sees moral economies as a counterweight to the alienating and individuating tendencies of marketplaces.[6] In them, the basis of the exchange relation is founded in a social relationship that recognizes the worker as a unique individual rather than an object for exploitation. By offering to restore a measure of recognition to workers' identities and experiences, these exchange economies seem to thrive in precarious settings that have already been ravaged by the worst excesses of neoliberal policies. In New Orleans, for example, privatization of recovery efforts shunted the responsibility for basic human services onto private corporations, which could then monetize relief and promote it as a form of corporate social responsibility.[7] Media industries since 2005 were at the forefront of using Katrina story lines to generate both advertising revenues and corporate goodwill, often based on their ability to harness and channel the free labor or charity of others. This was particularly apparent in a spate of reality television and talk show programs that frequently promised to improve the well-being of the ordinary people brought into the production.[8] These genres often claimed that their staff and crew were part of a family that left the local population better off. In the meantime, the programs were effective at cutting production costs by appropriating local settings and enrolling local residents, often in the form of volunteers. Although *Treme* followed this trajectory of corporate social responsibility, it also went beyond in imagining a more sustained investment in the lives of New Orleans's creative workers than a single television episode or promotional event.

To their call to help New Orleans through media labor, extras responded in droves.

A LITTLE EXTRA WORK FOR A LOT OF EXTRAS

In this calculus of righteous spends for the right costs, extras had a particular function in *Treme*. Extras, known by the euphemistic oxymoron "background artists," have historically been the most abundant local hires. Since the early twentieth century, studios have relied on the ever-renewable reserves of people flocking to Hollywood. They lured them with promises that they might "break in" to the industry if they worked hard and were lucky. Even today, the trade lore generated in Los Angeles describes how people working as extras gain a foothold in the industry by building a resume and a social network, which then leads to a stable career. Despite the low probability of Hollywood fulfilling these promises even in the classical age of production, labor unions have struggled to organize the waves of everyday people who work only irregularly, if at all. As a result, extras on a set have been the most plentiful but also the cheapest hires in the labor force. In New Orleans, extras may put in up to sixteen hours a day, only to receive as little as fifty or a hundred dollars, depending on the size of the production budget. Most of the labor then involves waiting for a chance to be in a scene.

In a local economy characterized by low wages and precarious employment, *Treme* set a high bar. One extra said he made $108 for only ten hours on the set; when the crew no longer needed him, he was dismissed but still got paid for a full day's work. The daily contracts were particularly attractive to workers in other cultural and service industries in the city, especially during seasonal or cyclical lags. As a freelancer in the arts scene explained, "If you make $100, that's great. You can get your groceries, and your beer, and your cigarettes and go on to the next gig." Beyond this, however, *Treme* drew on a reservoir of eager would-be extras based on the *ethical* promise of the program to the local cultural economy. Some of these extras had lived through Katrina, but many were new migrants who simply felt that they were contributing to something larger than a daily gig. Some even described doing extra work while visiting New Orleans, adding that they would do such a thing only for the love of *Treme*.

I came to these insights somewhat haphazardly in what began as separate studies of the program's production and reception, which gradually merged when I realized that in forty interviews, nearly every self-proclaimed fan of the show I spoke with, about half my sample, had worked as an extra, intended to be an extra, or had friends who were *Treme* extras. While this was a representative sample neither of all viewers nor certainly of New Orleans writ large, my research subjects opened a window into the deep feelings the program evoked and then put to work. These emotions demonstrate tensions in the moral economy of the production, illustrating the challenges of sustaining any local film economy that would recognize its most localized but least visible workers.

TO BE (AN) EXTRA

"It's the trend to work on the set, to be on the set, to be an extra, or have a friend that was an extra," said an African American student who grew up in an affluent uptown neighborhood. The excitement, he posited, came from the narrative itself.

"The show has the potential to be truthful and realistic to the city," he said. This appeal to the real and to fundamental truth-telling about the city in the post-K era was a frequent logic for joining the production. In this, extras were no different from fans in loving the show's careful attention to vernacular culture, regional musical and culinary traditions, and painstakingly accurate archive of the urban cultural geography. Moreover, extras described, in very emotional ways, the solidarity they felt with the series creators in telling the story of a city under threat of disintegration. As a recent resident, a retired professor who became an extra, explained, he felt like he became an insider to the city's trauma by watching *Treme* weekly in New Orleans with a group of Katrina survivors:

> That experience certainly changed [me and my wife's] relationship to the show both in terms of the knowledge gained but also a sympathy towards it. People talked about how, you know, in the opening credits, there's the patterns of mold, and people said, "Yeah, that one looks like the one I have in my [flooded] house." And so you get connected to the show in ways that are very unusual. But *Treme* has been and continues to be this booster for New Orleans as a city. And right after Katrina that was critical. So I was a worshipper of *Treme* at that time because I felt people had given up on New Orleans, I mean really had given up.

Here the speaker's desire to work for the show was imbued with a near spiritual investment in the city as portrayed through the program. Inevitably, the labor of being an extra could never live up to these lofty aspirations of being real, telling the truth, and satisfying souls.

The emotional solidarity with *Treme* served the labor needs of the production well. They stemmed from an imagined belonging, first, to a community of empathy with the residents of a traumatized city and, second, to a television program imbued with the agency to help in the recovery. By generating a community of empathy with New Orleans, the number of people who could imagine themselves doing extra work stretched beyond a period of residency or even the geography of city boundaries, bringing in new residents and even regular pilgrims to the city. These people could believe in New Orleans as a standpoint or a way of being expressed in a popular T-shirt: "Be A New Orleanian Wherever You Are." The motto, which recognizes the real exile of New Orleanians throughout the world, could also recognize anyone who felt the same passion as Simon and Overmyer did. One of my interviewees, commenting on a nonnative friend who regularly appeared on the program, called these extras the "super–New Orleanians," those residents who "go to everything more than the people born here. They are the ones who know the musicians. They have all the connections. They are kind of in love with something they want to embrace much more than in the natural way. . . . They can be almost arrogant about the *real* New Orleans." These extras put to work their shared dispositions toward the city precisely by being the kinds of culture bearers

and bards that the show spotlighted as authentic. The program succeeded in promoting and preserving this vision of the city and its citizenry in part because so
many people were willing to be part of the drama's background.

For extras, however, their personal experiences were in the foreground when
they considered why they would take off work or spend their leisure time working
at the bottom of the organizational hierarchy on a Hollywood production. People
spoke of how *Treme* had become part of their own traumatic stories: "I guess just
living here and having been through Katrina and coming back. The first two months
were so intense, and I think the show shows that in a really accurate way, just how
intense everything was" (female, thirty-seven, housekeeper). "The show was close
to home. There was a connection" (female, thirty, tour guide). In these quotes, the
locational shooting of *Treme* became part of their own temporal and geographic
locations: respectively, Katrina and home. This close siting of the series meant for
some people that they felt they *had to appear* on the program. Extras spoke of a
kind of doppelgänger effect, in which they already saw themselves in the story, and
thus wanted to memorialize it. A middle-aged man who lived through the storm
spoke of audibly laughing or sobbing through scenes, replaying them as he did
his own memories: "I kept expecting to see myself in the background because the
scenes were so real to me. . . . I think there's some weird thing in my brain that I
think I'm already a part of it. I think that would be really neat to be historically there
and on film, to be part of New Orleans" (male, forty-seven, barista and composer).

This emotional and psychological investment in the series spoke to a heightened
expectation for *Treme* that locals did not express for other productions around
the city, even those specifically focused on Katrina. On one hand, the investment
spoke to the role of media in memorializing tragedies. Amanda Lagerkvist, for
example, has written about how television recurrently reminds viewers of its own
heroic role not only in broadcasting the tragic events of September 11th to global
audiences but also in dealing with the traumatic aftermath in nationally specific
ways.[9] Seeing their lives unfold on the screen, *Treme* viewers wanted to be in the
program, as if to merge the lived and its representation. One interviewee, a local
musician, related her uncanny feelings about the program and her desire to work
for it to looking at a Beatles album: "You're just looking around. It's like when I saw
the big protest march in the last episode, I just keep seeing all these people from
different parts of my life. They were all there. They were all extras so I joked that it
was kinda like looking at a Sergeant Pepper album cover, you know, to see all these
people you recognize" (female, forty-seven, nonprofit worker and singer). Extras
wanted to not only "be in it because everyone else is in it," as one said, but to be
remembered as having been in it with everyone. Extras merged the politics of their
labor recognition with the politics of belonging to the city and its historical record.

Treme's labor market and strategy for so many extras thus relied on larger processes of popular memorialization, which on this particular program, championed

the "super–New Orleanian" as the authentic representative of the city's recent past. As proxies for the city's local culture, extras were tasked with being in and engaging with the city in a way that others would see as authentic. According to one tour guide who did extra work during a slow period, this aspect of the job was hardly a burden: "One of the days I did extra work I was down on Frenchmen Street, which I go to all the time, and I went to the Spotted Cat [music club] and watched the Jazz Vipers. . . . Now [in season two] a lot of my buddies have been on the show, so chances are if I do it again, I'm going to hang out with them and get paid for it." The proposition of getting paid to hang out takes a postmodern spin on the idea of labor, as if being an extra is not really working or somehow subverting real work. At the same time, it was *where* and *with whom* that imbued the extras with an exchange value in the first instance. Producers did not need the extras to do anything but hang around with others who could give credence to the authenticity claims for New Orleans as a particular kind of place, where people congregate every day in dark, musty alcoves animated by old-timey jazz riffs and refrains.

Beyond work on the set, the personal commitment on the part of avid viewers transformed extra work into a political project to do more hours and types of media labor off the set. Although production crews frequently refer to themselves as a "family," in the case of the *Treme,* the city at large was often seen as part of an extended production family. Crew members volunteered themselves and solicited others to manage charity and thank-you events in some of the neighborhoods with heavy location shooting. In an era of compulsory volunteerism at work,[10] many extras saw free labor as a way to build their social network in the film industry, while being recognized by others as a participant in *Treme*'s moral economy. Collecting Facebook likes and cheers of recognition at the bar screening consolidated the public meaningfulness of appearing on the show with a veneer of participating in the preservation of local culture. By equating being on set to hear some music with urban recovery, they could pretend that watching the show, being on the show, and then promoting the show through social networks would sustain other local circuits of cultural production.

Meanwhile, for some extras, familial tensions emerged. Not everyone could embody the kinds of authenticity sought by the program. A white university student hailing from the East Coast claimed she was picked immediately and placed prominently in the camera's view, while many people of color with less capital were turned away. Conversely, extras reported that crews excluded white extras when producers decided that the location should be African American. These occurrences led to various conversations about the politics of race in the production versus the city. Although no one would argue that there are still many segregated spaces in the city, production decisions at times clashed with extras' expectations of realism and truth-telling. Some of these conversations expressed bemusement, as if to reaffirm the extras' local knowledge contra the creators. In one instance, two white, middle-class retirees who had spent the day waiting with a crowd of hundreds for a restaging of a music festival pondered why the staff would have brought in buses of black, working-class school kids. Citing the increasingly unaffordable ticket prices and the overwhelmingly white audiences at the festival since Katrina, the interlocutors wondered privately if the decision was aspirational, a vision of how the festival *should* be populated. Other decisions about extras were more poignant, leading to hurt feelings when producers told extras that they did not belong in a restaging of a moment from their own lives.

If extras had a sense of the uncanny watching the show, they also had moments when their memories were edited for the screen. An extended example illustrates the disconnect on a production that attracted workers with a sense of connectedness. I met one of these super–New Orleanians at a public discussion on *Treme* that I led at a coffeehouse. She was a white woman in her fifties. I knew her from several moments in my own cultural repertoire in the city, and I knew that she knew much of the informal cultural economy portrayed in *Treme*. Her regular presence in the Treme neighborhood was also felt in public *Treme* screenings, which in the first season allowed non-HBO subscribers to see the program. *Treme* cast members and production personnel were known to drop in. After one powerful screening, the crew combed the crowd to enlist extras for an upcoming scene drawn from real events. The woman recalled telling the crew she was there the night Glen David Andrews was arrested. "[The producers] didn't really believe it too much, you know. They thought that was kinda strange, but [one of the mothers of the band members] came out and said she was glad I was there. That meant more to me than the money." Here the slight inflicted by the producers was recouped by another member of the crowd, a *Treme* viewer who was also a Treme resident. The incident illustrates the difficulties for extras who gave of themselves only to find that *Treme* did not reciprocate or took too much in return.

CONCLUDING FUTURES?

Despite the added compensation, both material and symbolic, that *Treme* provided its workforce, the production demanded a lot from its eager extras. In making the series speak to the worthiness of the city's recovery and renewal, producers sought extras who could speak to New Orleanians and for New Orleanians. Extras had to be highly invested in those vernacular details that made up *Treme*'s carefully crafted mise-en-scène. The moral politics of recognition as a worker depended on whether extras could act both as referents and as bards for the place known as New Orleans. These roles could involve more labor, often for no payment, but they also raised the specter of reification when a musical number took front stage, leaving the performances of the extras in the background. In its most extreme formulation, the labor of being an extra could be framed as a gift, which perhaps unavoidably led to hurt feelings when the gift was not recognized or reciprocated.

None of these aspects of extras' labor are registered in the quantitative analyses of jobs produced by film tax credit policies. They do, however, add nuance to the terms *local* and *labor*, which motivated these policies as well as provided fodder for both political consensus and critiques. The strategies that production companies, such as *Treme*'s Fee Nah Nee, use to be more moral and just while holding the bottom line may ultimately result in other costs. If the production includes only individuals with enough free time to do the work, either paid or unpaid, then the policies cannot be said to be building toward sustainable economies. In fact, it could be that the presence of so many extras with entitlement helps drive down the day rates of those who lack the time or the proper social networks to be desirable employees in the future. At the same time, the role of production companies in promoting themselves as instruments of urban economic recovery merely furthers the notion that private companies are the best managers of the public good. In an era of endless crises—political and economic—it is worth remembering that film production companies' reliance on cheap or free labor undermines the economic bases for public services that all workers need, such decent public schools, health care, and wages that bring the majority above the subsistence level. Until these needs are integrated more seamlessly into the New Orleans film economy, it will be no wonder if production companies continue to put their most marginal workers at the center of their most moral employment strategies.

NOTES

1. Susan Christopherson and Jennifer Clark, *Remaking Regional Economies: Power, Labor, and Firm Strategies in the Knowledge Economy* (New York: Routledge, 2007).

2. See, for example, Susan Christopherson, "Behind the Scenes: How Transnational Firms Are Constructing a New International Division of Labor in Media Work," in *Cross-Border Cultural Production: Economic Runaway or Globalization?*, edited by Janet Wasko (New York: Cambria Press, 2008); Tom O'Regan and Ben Goldsmith, *The Film Studio: Film Production in the Global Economy* (Lanham, MD: Rowman & Littlefield, 2005); Greg Elmer and Mike Gasher, *Contracting Out Hollywood: Runaway Productions and Foreign Location Shooting* (Lanham, MD: Rowman & Littlefield, 2005); Mike Gasher, *Hollywood North: The Feature Film Industry in British Columbia* (Seattle: University of Washington Press, 2002); Toby Miller, Nitin Govil, John McMurria, Richard Maxwell, and Ting Wang, *Global Hollywood 2* (London: British Film Institute, 2008); Michael Storper and Susan Christopherson, "Flexible Specialization and Regional Industrial Agglomeration: The Case of the U.S. Motion Picture Industry," *Annals of the Association of American Geographers* 77 (1987): 1104–1117; Janet Wasko, *How Hollywood Works* (London: Sage, 2003).

3. Mayor's Office of Cultural Economy, *2014 New Orleans Cultural Economy Snapshot*, New Orleans, LA, located at www.nola.gov/getattachment/Cultural-Economy/2014-CE-Snapshot-Electronic.pdf/.

4. Adriana Lopez, "A Look into America's Fastest Growing City," *Forbes.com*, July 26, 2012, www.forbes.com/sites/adrianalopez/2012/07/26/a-look-into-americas-fastest-growing-city/.

5. Dave Walker, "On the HBO 'Treme' Trail: David Simon, Eric Overmyer Discuss Creation of Prospective Drama," *Nola.com,* April 4, 2009, http://blog.nola.com/davewalker/2009/04/on_the_treme_trail_david_simon.html.

6. Mark Banks, "Moral Economies and Cultural Work," *Sociology* 40 (2006): 455–472.

7. Vincanne Adams, *Markets of Sorrow, Labors of Faith: New Orleans in the Wake of Katrina* (Durham, NC: Duke University Press, 2013).

8. Laurie Ouelette and James Hay, *Better Living through Reality TV: Television and Post-Welfare Citizenship* (London: Wiley, 2008).

9. Amanda Lagerkvist, "9.11 in Sweden: Commemoration at Electronic Sites of Memory," *Television & New Media* 15 (2014): 350–370.

10. See, for example, Melissa Gregg, *Work's Intimacy* (London: Polity, 2012).

6

Talent Agenting in the Age of Conglomerates

Violaine Roussel

"Now, everything in the talent agency business is different forever," commented a talent agent I interviewed after the announcement, in late 2013, of the acquisition of the sports marketing giant IMG (International Management Group) by the major agency WME (William Morris Endeavor). Indeed, in the past decade, Hollywood talent agencies have had to undergo drastic changes, for which they are also largely responsible. These changes are intrinsically connected to transformations that have simultaneously affected and been generated by the studios, who are the agencies' counterparts on the production side. This organizational mutation creates consequences in creative terms: it directly affects what "doing one's job" as an agent means and, inseparably and subsequently, how agents contribute to making cultural products and artistic careers. In a tumultuous time of rapid professional reconfiguration, work situations feel more precarious to creative workers and, inseparably, more uncertain to their agents. This chapter addresses such transformations.

Talent representatives in the United States are divided into four main types of professionals: talent agents, managers, publicists, and entertainment lawyers. Unlike managers, who have only recently developed as an organized occupation, agents are closely regulated by the state in which they work. They also hold a legal monopoly over the right to seek and procure employment for their clients, a service for which the agency receives 10 percent of the amount negotiated in the artist's contracts. Agents scout and "sign" talent (although not always in formal written form, especially in the large agencies), work at placing them in jobs, and negotiate deals with producers and studios. They are thus involved from an early stage of the film and television production process.

The agency business has evolved into two relatively autonomous systems: in "Little Hollywood,"[1] hundreds of small companies and one-man shops form the nebula of organizations representing beginner-artists and clients with modest careers. These agents mostly deal with casting directors, especially in television. By contrast, midsize and big agencies, such as WME, CAA (Creative Artists Agency), UTA (United Talent Agency), ICM (International Creative Management), and their smaller competitors (Paradigm, Gersh, Verve, and so on), belong to a different system of interrelations which links them to studios and established talent.[2] I will mostly focus on this "Big Hollywood." The existence of such large and powerful companies—WME and CAA now total thousands of employees—who represent high-end international talent and make transactions with major studios is unique to Hollywood.

Only recently has the American agency business come to be led by giant corporate entities that are simultaneously active in many sectors of the entertainment industry as well as beyond the domestic market. Parallel to this, production professionals have witnessed decisive transformations. This chapter provides a brief description of these organizational changes in order to explore what they imply for the practice of "agenting." I first outline the structural changes that have reorganized the agency business and redefined talent representation. Next I look closely at "independent film agents;" the emergence of this new expert profile within the big agencies is especially revealing of the mutations affecting both agency and production sides of the industry. It is also rearranging the balance of power between sellers and buyers. Finally, I examine the effects that these radical transformations, which agents have often experienced in the course of their own careers, have on what agents feel to be their professional identity.[3] The instability attached to the fast and substantial changes in agents' environment, working conditions, and responsibilities blurs their self-definition and creates fragile professional identities. While most talent representatives experience the uncertainty of their status and prospects going forward, some are in a position to embrace such a self-reinvention process, whereas others underline what they see as the degradation of the value of agenting entailed by this transformation. In addition, the new context with which these professionals have to deal influences, through their experience and their work, the process by which projects are selected, put together, and brought to life, as well as how artistic careers are handled.

HOW AGENCY GROWTH TRANSFORMS AGENTING

The prevalent narrative of change in the agency world attributes to Michael Ovitz, through his success in building CAA into the most powerful agency of the 1980s and 1990s, the role of shaping and leading the reconfiguration of the system linking the main agencies to the major studios. Turning an agenting style into an organizational "culture," the group of five young dissidents who left the reputable William Morris Agency to create CAA in 1975[4] ushered in new practices in the talent representation business. These new professional repertoires were attached to an organizational model: building teams of agents to attract high-end talent by exhibiting ostensible signs of power and importance (that is, notably, by staging relationships with other key players). At an organizational level, this strategy was intended to create a collaborative structure encouraging internal sharing of resources and assets, by contrast with the more individualistic and internally competitive model under which other agencies were organized. The success of their endeavor put Ovitz and his collaborators in a position to systematize "packaging" practices—that is, the assembling of key pieces that make up a project: in film, typically, assembling a star actor or a prominent director with a writer, other agencies' clients, and possibly financiers who are willing to bring complementary funding, and selling them as a package to a studio—and often, because the stars desired by the studios were massively represented by CAA, to impose their conditions on the buyers.

But the story of how CAA changed the industry is only one piece of the puzzle. In fact, a more collective and systemic mechanism was in play. The modes of action and organization that made CAA successful circulated widely in the agency world and hybridized as they were appropriated in different contexts. All of the leading agencies transformed on a relational level. The new ways of agenting born from this pervasion and hybridization process (focused on packaging, "poaching" competitors' clients, and so on) progressively became a professional norm in Big Hollywood. Veteran agents had to convert to new ways of doing the job that newcomers perceived as the norm. Those who launched new agencies in the early 1990s, UTA (1991) and Endeavor (1995) in particular, had the precedent of CAA in mind, but they had already distanced themselves from this model. The collective reorganizing of the agency business, in a favorable economic context in which studios had money to spend on hiring stars and developing projects, led to the constitution of a group of big agencies that had the critical mass of clients and agents to develop the practice of packaging. By the start of the 2000s, agents had negotiated unprecedented salaries for their star clients, and star power inseparably meant agency power. The balance of forces between studios and agencies, then in favor of the latter, was about to swing back.

At the same time, for agencies internally, growth translated into an increased division of labor—that is, both compartmentalization and specialization. Constituting new roles and areas of expertise inevitably generated institutional boundaries within the structure of the agencies: the departments by which agencies were traditionally organized—(talent or literary) motion pictures and television, music, theater, commercials, books—were subdivided or complemented by new divisions in charge of the uncharted territories. These emerged from media transformation (and the rise of new distribution platforms) and from the extension of the realm of entertainment to nonscripted/alternative television, gaming, branding, sports, and digital media. *Talent* has been redefined in the process, as agents nowadays represent reality television performers, chefs, web celebrities, as well as corporations and brands, as much as (and often more lucratively than) actors, directors, writers, or below-the-line personnel.[5] Developing such additional branches of activity not only equals increased specialization; it also implies the constitution of new areas of expertise, as new subprofessions and career paths emerge within the scope of talent representation.[6]

> It used to be a high level of specialization back in the days, in the 60s and 70s. At William Morris when I worked for them, I was in the music department, I wanted to get out of it, I wanted to move in the actor's business . . . they said no. And I left. They were specialized. Then, they were like "that's dumb because TV actors are movie actors, TV writers are movie writers! We want hyphening agents!" Now, you are in reality business or in digital business, and these things really don't cross over as much. That's interesting. That creates more specialization, but not the old. (Talent agent, big agency, 2012)

Transformations in the economy of media—especially with the development of cable television and the subsequent opportunities in number and quality of projects, and then with the supplanting of DVDs by digital outlets for distribution—take the form of organizational dilemmas in the private bureaucracies that are the agencies. Agency leaders know that they must institutionalize the necessary circulation of their artists between complementary sectors, toward what they believe to be the most promising new areas.[7] For instance, the boundary between film and television has become permeable, and the symbolic hierarchy between the two has been rearranged in favor of the latter. At the same time, however, for the individual agent, crossing an artist over to a different media or area of practice without deferring to colleagues in the concerned department remains a risky subversion of organizational order, as the agent quoted below describes: "I started as a literary agent [representing writers and directors], and then I branched into talent [representing actors]. I've always been in the motion picture business. When I started representing actors in addition to my writer-directors, people were like "you're doing *both*?!" It's like shocking, blasphemy. And now it's not so unusual. I'm called a hybrid agent, and it's what I love, I would not be happy to just be doing lit[erary] or just talent. I like both. They're both very different, but they cross-pollinate each other" (agent, big agency, 2013). Moving (and transferring one's skills) from one specialty to another is a challenge within the institutional structure of big agencies, whose functioning tends to reinforce the differentiation between departments (especially given the way agents are usually evaluated and compensated).

In sum, "being an agent" in Big Hollywood from the 2000s and thereafter takes on a different meaning. It involves practicing a highly specialized job, maintaining relationships with a small circle of predefined buyers regarding a given type of product or profile of client, in a quickly changing environment and in large corporate companies that have instituted a strict division of activity. It also means handling more clients, often over 150. Only top agents can preserve a managerial style of agenting by representing a few of the (rarefied) stars who still get very lucrative contracts from the studios. This transformation of agenting and agencies in Big Hollywood is directly related to the notable development of management companies in the past twenty years. Such changes are, in turn, consequential for artists and art-making: if agenting is a numbers game, the clients who are not generating enough revenue for the agency get forgotten; the projects into which agencies put effort and energy are also of a different type, as our next section will explain.

The development of large talent agencies into complex organizations has generated a new class of agency managers, who are at more of a distance from the practice of agenting and closer to other types of powerful business leaders, and whose professional value is no longer exclusively or primarily derived from their client list (and consequent ability to leave with star clients):

> The major companies, each does something similar and each is engaged in things that are different. I think our core businesses are similar, but our emphasis may be different. Our sizes are different. Our method of capitalization is different. We have private equity partners in this company. . . . But the businesses are run, managed, and operated by professionals, each of whom has been in the business for an excess of twenty years. So there's an experienced professional class of executives who run these firms but who are also agents. (Big agency manager, 2011)

The big agency world is a shrinking oligopoly. From the "Big 5" agencies (CAA, WMA, ICM, UTA, Endeavor), made "Big 4" by the WMA-Endeavor merger in 2009, two giants have emerged as a result of a concentration and diversification process: CAA and WME. The latter now surpasses its competitor in size, thanks to the 2.4-billion-dollar deal by which WME bought IMG, announced in December 2013. Combined, WME and IMG immediately totaled over 3,000 employees in cities around the world, compared with CAA's 1,500. But the growth of these companies is better measured when one considers that, in the mid-1990s, CAA only had approximately 500 employees. Both CAA and WME have relatively recently partnered up with a private equity investor;[8] they could soon have an IPO and become a public company. These new investments—which bring fresh money into the agency system—establish a new power configuration. It comes with consequences that agents can anticipate, and which they describe as threatening the creative dimension of their professional identity:

> If you are partially owned by an outside, nonentertainment company, they're kicking the tires to see their return on investment, and they're not always as knowledgeable as they need to be about really what's going on, aside from just what the bottom

line is. And so WME and CAA both have P&L statements that they have to really *manage*, and that means cutting clients, cutting agents, making choices not based necessarily on the artistry, but based on the bottom line. (Talent agent, big agency, 2013, her emphasis)

By contrast, the still privately owned agencies UTA and ICM work at repositioning their image as "artist-friendly" companies, while the industry press reveals that client representation was only 14 percent of WME's revenue in 2013.[9] The gap separating Little from Big Hollywood grows wider as bigger entities focus less exclusively on representing artists. At the same time, the studios have also radically changed and become part of large media corporations. This evolution directly affects the types of projects made (or dismissed) and the relevant strategies for spotting and manufacturing "talent." On the agency side, this process happens through the transformation of agenting work sometimes associated with the emergence of new types of positions.

LESSONS FROM THE RISE OF THE "INDIE FILM AGENT"

The 1990s saw the constitution of a new field of expertise in the agency world, which gradually consolidated during the 2000s : a few agents, who represented the rare foreign star directors or actors, started focusing on foreign coproduction and distribution opportunities, developing alliances with European or Australian counterparts who had access to sources of film funding. Those who built this new field in the domain of independent film packaging and financing drew on their ability to understand and navigate international markets. In practice, these agents were familiar with the local players who participated in the main international film festivals; they had developed a unique knowledge of the local rules of the game and had established relationships with the authorities who decided on the financing and the making of movies. The practice they invented went beyond the traditional work of foreign sales agents, who usually came into the mix only at the distribution phase. Their activity contributed to reshaping what an "indie film" is and how it can get made, which increasingly became inseparable from finding international investors and distributors. This case study illustrates how changes in the agency world and the institutionalization of a new area of specialization linked to transformations in studio practice affect the definition of cinematic genres (in this case, the indie film), the options that are open for artistic careers (international circulation of actors and directors especially), and the (interdependent) remodeling of domestic and foreign markets.

Here, I will very roughly sum up the elements involved in such a process. It all started with individual "entrepreneurs" acquiring distinctive skills, both in film finance and in film production, and penetrating into new territories in the agency business, as well as into neglected geographic spaces (mostly Europe and Australia at first). Their success stemmed from this happening at a specific point in time: their initiatives coincided with changes in production activities, in particular those of the studios. This new approach to agenting initially seemed like a risky strategy: its pioneers engaged in a marginal dimension of the agenting practice. They mostly faced skepticism and defiance on the part of colleagues in traditional positions, who viewed only the projects that studios backed as viable options, and discouraged their clients from getting involved in what they saw as uncertain independent/international endeavors. However, the success of a handful of movies (*Green Card, Until the End of the World,* and so on) quickly made perceptions shift in the agency world. As a result, in a business in which being one step ahead of competitors is key, "international agents" were rapidly taken seriously, increasingly so as their new role was progressively institutionalized in big agencies.

> [I] signed a lot of people, put a lot of movies together. And then, after a point in time, I ended up representing some movies where we didn't represent the client at all. . . . Because I represented the money that financed the movies, and they didn't know what to do with the movies. And so I became the person that helped them with making foreign sales decisions, with a foreign sales agent. In some cases, I even made certain deals myself, usually with France, Italy, and Germany, maybe the UK. But I developed an expertise for making U.S. domestic deals, no agents were doing that. Then, because of that becoming important, what was really funny was that, you know, agents aren't stupid, their basic antenna is always looking around to whatever they should know and do, or that guy's going to be ahead of them, you know, it's like this. So I would say, within six months to a year, all the agencies hired somebody who was their international person. (Former talent and independent film agent, big agency, 2013)

This role, which was initially defined mostly as "international arrangements and deal making" (with foreign financiers and distributors), was progressively reframed and increasingly characterized in reference to the manufacture of "independent films" as this new subfield of agenting was being organized. The conditions for this new specialization to stabilize were established and reinforced by the studios' strategy of almost completely withdrawing from the production segment of "big independent" films.[10] From around 2005 on, studios increasingly focused on making film franchises and sequels of previous box-office successes and in general developed fewer projects.[11] New "solutions" then had to be found to respond to the decrease in job offers and the desire of commercially successful artists to do more "arty" movies. An agent in charge of financing and packaging independent movies in a midsize agency here describes his changing relationships with studio divisions:

> We can be with the independent divisions of the studio, we can be with Focus of Universal, we can be with Searchlight of Fox, or Weinstein, or Lionsgate, or whatever. But Disney is not generally buying a lot of independent films. Warner Brothers is

not buying a lot of independent films. Right? The companies that have such massive overheads, you know, if they buy a four-million-dollar movie that goes off and makes ten million dollars in profit, it so doesn't even matter. The bottom line is they don't even want to waste their time. . . . They produce less. But it has changed, right? The studios in the 70s and 80s and 90s, it has all changed. It's like now all the studios are owned by conglomerates. It is all about the stock price. So they have to do things that move the stock. Financing a new movie doesn't necessarily move the stock. (2013)

From such an account, it could seem that international agents simply expanded their niche by filling a void left by the studios. In fact, they actively contributed to the collective shaping not only of a specialized "market" (for "indies") but also of the corresponding film genre and artistic categories. By building relationships with international partners in production and distribution according to their perception of a shrinking domestic market, they participated in feeding a self-reinforcing process. In turn, indie film teams gained importance in the agency business as the domestic box office revenue numbers gained more visibility compared to international numbers. The reversal of foreign and North American film revenues (respectively 70 and 30 percent,[12] when it used to be the reverse) has provoked anticipation and strategy in the industry, partly rearranging internal professional hierarchies. Consequently, in the course of a few years, entire divisions dedicated to financing and packaging independent movies became institutionalized and grew within the large and midsize agencies.[13] In addition, independent "indie film" consultants and financial advisers multiplied, contributing to the formation of a whole professional sector. Practitioners claimed legitimacy based on the definition of a specialized *competence* enabling them to represent a whole movie, not "just" the artists involved with it. "The basic job of an agent is to put the client to work. That's what you'd call a single point transaction. . . . But the thing about representing a *movie* is a whole other thing and nobody had done it, no agents had done this. And so, I even created a financial structure where we got paid a consultancy fee, because I was performing a service" (former independent film agent, big agency, 2013).

This interviewee underlines the different structure of remuneration distinguishing his job from other positions. His specific role relies on the valorization of a "unique skill"—"blending art and commerce"[14]—and on the exhibition of familiarity with and recognition from the world of film finance (and its bankers and investors). As a matter of fact, several of these specialized agents have a distinctive profile: they joined an agency late in their career after having worked in finance. The agency that hires someone with such a background is looking for both a level of technical expertise and a set of preexisting relationships with potential film funding sources, all the while expecting the new agent to approach movies as an "investment" like any other.[15] However, for the most part, the financial dimension of the practice is not what takes prevalence in these agents' self-definition.

As their job consists in assembling various eclectic pieces that make up an independent production, "indie film agents" can take pride in having both expert knowledge and creative autonomy. They indeed orchestrate the participation of diverse players—from financiers, producers, and distributors in various countries to creative personnel and their representatives (agents, unions, managers, and so on)—in a complex project. They draw symbolic power from this position of coordinator, which places them "above the crowd." But they also describe this role as a challenge: they first have to overcome the reluctance of agents who hold different positions and often have contradictory interests (primarily choosing the most secure job option for their clients). It's internally, in the agency world and often within their own company, that they fight their first battles. The precarious aspect of playing with such a composite system appears in this agent's words:

> Every agent, whether they want to admit it or not, has an agenda for their client. So, to get a movie made means you have to have a hundred different agents somehow come to the same agenda at the same time. I need this male actor, this female actor, this director, this writer, this producer, this line producer, this DP, this editor, and then the financier's agent and manager and blah-blah-blah. The most difficult thing by far is trying to get everyone on the same page at the same time. . . . So, it is going to all the agencies, convincing talent to do a movie, convincing the team that they should do the movie for the right price, convincing the financiers that they should do this. It is getting a lot of different people to agree on one thing. To align all the different pieces and all the different agendas and find the right financier who says, "You know what? I'm doing that." (Independent film agent, midsize agency, 2013)

As a result, these agents promote their area of specialization by stating that they accomplish "more than ordinary packaging," in the sense that they have the responsibility of putting together entire movies. Their overarching position preserves them from the fragmentation that usually confines agents to the preproduction phase, with little control over the film-making process as a whole; by contrast, it places these specialists closer to the position of a director or a producer: "It's not packaging, because packaging in my mind is just bringing on the director and an actor into it. If you're also organizing all of the financing, you're structuring, you're setting up the distribution; it's much more than packaging. It's executive producing without the executive producing title" (independent film agent, big agency, 2013).

The value of working on international independent coproductions and the very meaning of independence for these agents have to do precisely with this self-attributed "producerial" power, which solidly ties them to the artistic side of the industry and distances them from the image of the agent as a mere salesman. This observation goes beyond the case of indie film specialists; it reveals the prevalence of most agents' identification with creativity in their professional self-concept and also reveals the strength of symbolic hierarchies in even the most commercial sectors of Hollywood: "The producing that we do as agents, whether it is finding the money, or finding the other artists, or finding the script, or developing the script, or whatever it is: the not-just-making-the-deal-and-putting-them-in stuff, the other stuff, is rewarding and creates dimension to your service, and also separates the smarts from the clinicians" (talent agent, big agency, 2013).

At the end of the day, as successful as independent films may be both domestically and internationally, they are not as lucrative as big studio tent poles. Indie films are more unpredictable and require more energy from the agency side. In line with the rationalization of activity characterizing the largest agencies, and despite the growth of their independent film divisions, "going international" has not come to mean being central in the game. Studio production remains the priority, and packaging for studios the main focus.

THE "LOST ART" OF AGENTING?

For most agents, especially those who entered the profession before 2000, the globalization of the entertainment industry is not synonymous with geographic expansion or international circulation as much as it means the transformation of the "local" reality of Hollywood: the evolution of both studios and big agencies into complex corporate entities, institutionalized and rationalized in their organization, and whose activities go way beyond talent representation and filmmaking, has strongly affected the *experience* of agenting. Especially since, at the same time, technological changes have made agenting less a matter of face-to-face and physical interactions and have turned a primarily phone-based practice into a distant, fast-paced, e-mail-mediated activity.[16] The skills, profiles, and resources required to excel, and the models of success themselves, have also started to change. As a result of the agencies' organizational growth and the increased specialization that reorganizes them internally, agents are seeing their craft fall rapidly into obsolescence finding themselves in a weak position when mergers or acquisitions lead to staff reductions. In an environment that feels increasingly unpredictable, the requirement that an agent be a "forward thinker" who is constantly innovating— although not specific to this context but consubstantial to the professional ideology of agenting—intensifies. Adherence to this professional ideology of perpetual anticipation conflicts with the apprehension of being overtaken by change, and makes the fear even more difficult to voice and address. To this should be added the uncertainties generated by relatively short-term employment contracts (typically two or three years) and a compensation system increasingly based on bonuses (with a reduced salary base).[17]

Concentration and diversification processes have resulted in new challenges for agents, putting their professional self-definition into question. Although agents recognize sales as being an integral part of their job, most emphasize the artistic dimension as what gives worth to what they do. Thus they put forward their relationship with talent, their role in creative match-making, and their ability to initiate projects through packaging. Because the new conditions bring agenting closer to other sales jobs or corporate careers, many of the agents I interviewed deplored them as leading to "less of a creative experience." With a little nostalgia, this top agent at one of the biggest companies perfectly describes the loss of balance induced by the corporatization of Hollywood that most of his colleagues with comparable trajectories also express:

> I believe that advocacy, in the creative space, no matter what you are—a lawyer, a publicist, a manager, or an agent—has got to be an exclusive and nurturing relationship. And I find that, by definition, it has to therefore be a *contained* culture. A manageable size and scope. It's a balance between the right amount of agents in your infrastructure and in your culture, and the right amount of clients—high-end, medium, and up-and-coming—that creates a balance in the way you manage a company that needs to sign, service, and sell creative talent, partly, and in my opinion mostly, through packaging them together and with other like-minded artists that you don't represent. And that skill requires time and space, and creative collisions. And the more corporate you are, and the more of an order-taker, clinical kind of "here is the list," "here is the links for the thing" you are, just [going] back and forth in a more clinical, institutional way, the more the creative gets squeezed out. And the agents' advocacy, the premium on their advocacy, the premium on their brilliance is diminished by the system of having a voluminous client list to service and/or a voluminous agent body to manage. (Talent agent, big agency, 2013, his emphasis)

This definition of the agent as the artist's advocate reveals the ongoing shift of the profession, in its material organization as well as its symbolic hierarchies, and the coexistence of various paths and profiles currently forming the agenting profession. These different profiles partly correspond to generations that have entered the agency world at different times, and partly stem from the simultaneous presence of heterogeneous profiles intrinsically making up a profession that oscillates between a creative and a commercial pole. The economic prosperity of the industry in the 1990s attracted law and business graduates from prestigious schools to Hollywood. These cohorts of "Harvard kids" then populated the mailrooms of the big agencies, coming in with different expectations and, oftentimes, a less art-oriented self-definition. Even though they represent a minority of today's agents, some have now accessed leading positions of the top agencies.

Generally speaking and more importantly, the current socio-economic conditions transforming Hollywood are better adapted to the businessmen-agents' profile than to that of those who mostly wanted to "be in the arts." If they take on responsibilities, the former are likely to participate in bringing the agency world even further in this direction. Indeed, as the agent quoted below suggests, agency owners and managers who are running large businesses and have to report to their shareholders cannot value what this interviewee calls the "lost art" of agenting:

> I feel like I'm an artist. My art is being able to craft an argument and leverage other artists and find collaborations that will work. And then get the money. That's the job,

that's what I think is my art form. . . . I don't think that the executives today have a reason, nor are they cultivated, nor are they trained to think of it that way. And because, frankly, art does not necessarily mean commerce. I think that it's the goal of the owners to create more corporate executives and agents who are more interested in turning a buck than they are relating to talent. (Talent agent, big agency, 2010)

Nevertheless, this relationship to talent, art, and stardom remains remarkably important in defining the agents' worth and value, even in the most profitable areas of the business. It is not by chance that agents who share this interviewee's talent-oriented self-definition have often reached top positions in the agency business. In this professional world, the hierarchies ordering the artists, according to which aesthetic and professional recognition especially matters and closely combines with commercial success to make up someone's "worth," transfer to the ranking of talent representatives: their link to "their" artists defines the agents. In other words, being of "quality" distinguishes top talent and top representatives alike in these "markets of singularity."[18] Even in today's context of "corporate Hollywood," investors who put money in talent agencies—and not in a less uncertain business—manifest and reproduce the strength of symbolic capital attached to film stars and the magic of cinema. Prestige hierarchies in the industry still place motion pictures above television (nonscripted television shows for sure, and arguably scripted ones too, even though the development of cable channels has made the frontier between film and television much more permeable) as well as gaming and web products—in sum, above the most lucrative sectors of talent representation. This consubstantial interplay between sources of prestige and sources of revenue still organizes the industry.

The "business entrepreneur" agent and the new class of agency executives have not entirely supplanted more "creative types" in the agency world. Some of the latter turn to management, while others remain part of the organizational environment of large agencies. All participate in the self-reinforcing changes that are taking place "behind the scenes" in Hollywood, in the representation and production spaces, in interconnected ways: the structural changes shaping "global Hollywood" before our eyes (and making up the "digital media revolution") are not just a reaction to external factors. They are produced collectively and subject to sophisticated strategies on the part of big agency leaders, all the while being too much of a systemic process to be controlled by any one powerful industry player.

NOTES

1. Robert R. Faulkner, *Music on Demand: Composers and Careers in the Hollywood Film Industry* (New Brunswick, NJ: Transaction, 1983).

2. On the effects of the division between core and non-core agencies in terms of market segmentation and artistic careers, see William T. Bielby and Denise D. Bielby, "Organizational Mediation of Project-Based Labor Markets: Talent Agencies and the Careers of Screenwriters," *American Sociological Review* 64.1 (1999): 64–85.

3. My work is based on 112 interviews conducted in Los Angeles, mostly with agents and to a lesser extent with managers, production professionals, artists, lawyers, and publicists, as well as in situ observations at talent agencies or alongside an agent. This research received support from the European Commission (7th Framework Program, Marie Curie Fellowship).

4. Ron Meyer, William Haber, Michael Rosenfeld, and Rowland Perkins are the other four.

5. Below-the-line encompasses the technical professions working on film and television projects. See Laura Grindstaff and Vicki Mayer, "The Importance of Being Ordinary: Brokering Talent in the New-TV Era," in *Brokerage and Production in the American and French Entertainment Industries: Invisible Hands in Cultural Markets,* ed. Violaine Roussel and Denise Bielby (Lanham, MD: Lexington Books, 2015), 131–152.

6. In addition to formalized divisions, various other principles of fragmentation combine. Agents are categorized much like their clients are, according to homologous (prestige) hierarchies.

7. Positions of "crossover agent" are created in some agencies for that purpose. The question of how to institutionalize the activity of social and digital media agents, in a context where no one initially knows how to monetize digital content, also illustrates the strength of the institutional framework of the big agencies. On the way film and television professionals approach this "digital revolution," see Michael Curtin, Jennifer Holt, and Kevin Sanson, eds., *Distribution Revolution: Conversations about the Digital Future of Film and Television* (Berkeley: University of California Press, 2014).

8. In 2010, CAA formed a strategic partnership with the global private equity firm TPG Capital, which owns 35 percent of the agency. WME partnered with Silver Lake in May 2012, the private equity firm acquiring a 31 percent share in the agency.

9. *The Wrap,* April 13, 2014, www.thewrap.com/leaked-inside-details-of-two-billion-dollar-wme-img-financing.

10. "Independent" in this context makes sense in contrast with "studio movie," that is, the concentration of the activities of production, distribution, and retail under the unified umbrella of a studio. The practice of "packaging," traditionally attached to studio production, gets partly redefined and expanded to include the activity of putting together such "big indie films," with a focus on finding their financing and organizing their distribution. Small independent films made with no money outside of "Big Hollywood" do not belong to this category and do not result from the activity of the same participants.

11. Lynda Obst, *Sleepless in Hollywood: Tales from the New Abnormal in the Movie Business* (New York: Simon & Schuster, 2013); Roussel and Bielby, eds., *Brokerage and Production.*

12. In 2013. Motion Picture Association of America, *Theatrical Market Statistics, 2013,* p. 4, www.mpaa.org/wp-content/uploads/2014/03/MPAA-Theatrical-Market-Statistics-2013_032514-v2.pdf.

13. Midsize agencies practice "copackaging" with larger companies that have more star clients.

14. Indie film agent, big agency, Los Angeles, 2013.

15. "There is a bunch of things we do, not just financing movies. . . . We'll make investments in different movies that only come after the fact in North America. So it has nothing to do with me packaging a movie, it has to do with me saying, "Okay, I like that *as an investment,* let me see if one of my guys wants to put money in." We do all of the financial analysis and put them as producers on those movies" (indie film agent, midsize agency, 2013, his emphasis).

16. Such dematerialization mechanisms also generate more "spec work" for agents, to use the category forged by John Caldwell (see chapter 2).

17. This is also true of the agents who work in the countless small companies of Little Hollywood, although it takes somewhat different forms in their case: directly impacted by the precarization of labor affecting their clients and the subsequent diminution in revenue for their agency, they sometimes have to jump from one small boutique to another at the mercy of economic ups and downs that can quickly lead a small organization to close doors. Their fear of becoming "dispensable" (in one person's words) or irrelevant also stems from the experience of extensive technological changes: the new electronic

tools that equip the practice of agenting increasingly turn it into the rationalized management of massive lists of clients (whose profiles are submitted mechanically to casting professionals via online platforms that disclose the information about available jobs to all agencies at once) and devaluate the "craft of agenting" as the agents knew it (getting the information first based on personal connections within the casting community, having more time to advocate for individual clients, and so on). However, even the agents in the most vulnerable positions claim the ideal of the fearless entrepreneur-agent who thrives in tumultuous times, dissociating themselves from a critique of flexibility or from making common cause with precarized clients. For convergent observations, see Berg and Penley, as well as Mayer, chapters 4 and 11.

18. Lucien Karpik, *Valuing the Unique: The Economics of Singularities* (Princeton, NJ: Princeton University Press, 2010).

7

Transnational Crews and Postsocialist Precarity

Globalizing Screen Media Labor in Prague

Petr Szczepanik

Political economists and network theorists offer different assessments of the global relations of motion picture production. While spatially extended webs of productive labor are central to such approaches, neither explains specifically how these webs are constituted or how they operate in peripheral production ecologies. What is more, they do not consider the implications of the knowledge transfers and power hierarchies emerging from such transnational production contexts. By contrast, this chapter offers a concrete analysis of these issues in Prague's postsocialist film and television industries. It focuses on the segregation of the local work world and on barriers inhibiting transsectoral knowledge transfers, which originate from a two-tier production system split between international and domestic production, and characterized by different business models, gatekeepers, career prospects, and precariousness.

The state-socialist past of the Czech Republic still affects its screen industries. In 1991, Prague's once-monopolistic Barrandov Studios laid off most of its 2,700 staff, including all creative personnel. This step helped transform the Czech capital into a regional hub of international media production, attracting Hollywood on the prospect of a large, skilled, nonunion labor pool and, later on, a 20 percent rebate program. During the city's peak year of 2003, international operations attracted $178 million in investment, roughly twenty times more than wholly indigenous productions, which comprised some fifteen to forty feature films annually. There are three main gravity centers in this labor market: international productions, television broadcasting (with the public-service broadcaster holding a privileged position), and wholly local film productions. These represent three semipermeable economies, work cultures, and instances of globalization. Furthermore, each is characterized by a distinctive structure and hosts distinct career patterns. Questions about their development crystallize around the extent to which they will sustain themselves, collaborate, transfer knowledge, offset risk, and increase their competitiveness in the region.

This chapter concentrates on international productions, especially "service production" in film and television. This is the strongest sector economically, yet the most vulnerable. It is also the sector about which scholars have said the least. This chapter considers how the globalization of media production might be understood from the perspectives of the transnational crews working on international productions. Despite being among the best-paid members of the labor market, Czech personnel are afforded less creative control, job security, and professional upward mobility than their colleagues in other sectors. Interviews with prominent members of this production culture,[1] along with ethnographic data gathered by student interns,[2] suggest that inequality in working conditions has contributed to the dynamics of this professional community. The chapter therefore focuses on multidirectional local and translocal processes of mediation taking place within the global production networks connecting major East-Central European cities to other parts of the world. In so doing, it reconsiders globalization in the sphere of film production in a manner that counters prevailing U.S.-centric perspectives.

LOCALIZED LEARNING IN GLOBAL PRODUCTION NETWORKS

Recent discussion of international production is dominated by neo-Marxist criticism of the New International Division of Cultural Labor (NICL). This approach sees the globalization of film production as a means for Hollywood to strengthen its international hegemony. It is said that Hollywood achieved this powerful position in several ways, including sidestepping U.S. labor unions, disempowering and deskilling the global workforce, and fostering levels of uncertainty that destabilize local producers. NICL, it is argued, transforms locations into industrial sites for service providers, making them prone to dependency, underdevelopment, and disinvestment.[3]

Although it has broadened our understanding of the global political economy, neo-Marxist analysis of this kind can be criticized for its U.S.-centrism. By largely duplicating positions advanced by American screen unions, this approach arguably paints a somewhat unbalanced picture of power relations between U.S. companies and their overseas suppliers. Such an approach could also be accused, on the one hand, of focusing on the short-term project-based thinking of incoming producers, such as choosing between different levels of incentives, labor costs, and production services offered in competing locations. On the other hand, it could be accused of disregarding the long-term "location interests" that have led local companies and policymakers to embrace international production, including development of studios and film services, branding, and knowledge transfer.[4] My interview subjects tended to demand a more measured perspective on the effects of international production on creative labor. They did not lament the exploitation spotlighted by neo-Marxists. Rather than denounce overseas producers when confronted with the precariousness of their working lives, these workers spotlighted difficulties caused by local policies, coworkers, and intermediary service companies. They also compared their working lives to schooling, inasmuch as their work afforded opportunities to learn American-style practices without leaving their hometowns. They invoked a postsocialist imaginary derived from their mediated experiences of foreign production practices, restricted mobility, and limited career prospects.

From the perspective of a regional postsocialist production center, these location interests can be illuminated by the work of the Manchester School of Economic Geography.[5] Its theory of global production networks (GPNs) considers how opportunities for knowledge diffusion are opened by two parallel processes: the dispersion of the value chain across corporations and national boundaries, and integration across hierarchical layers of network participants. In contrast to neo-Marxism, this position considers local workers to be social actors rather than victims. It emphasizes the multiactor and multiscalar characteristics of transnational production, alongside societal and territorial embeddedness. Within GPNs, "global network flagships" source specialized capabilities from outside the company itself;[6] however, knowledge transfer does not guarantee effective knowledge diffusion. Rather, knowledge must be internalized and translated into capabilities, because local suppliers learn by converting explicit into tacit knowledge. Qualitative data garnered from my interviewees suggests that mutual learning, social networks, and cultural mediators play key roles in the lives of Prague's filmmakers.

In contrast to the permanent positions, standardized careers, and formalized training procedures that were central to the pre 1991 Czech production scene, today's interfirm, "boundaryless" careers demand that workers adapt rapidly to complex new tasks[7] and a shared industrial culture, which helps them rapidly form new teams with strangers. Central to the formation of these informal, variable social networks are horizontal flows of information and tacit organizational knowledge. American heads of departments, line producers, and above-the-line talent work directly with local crews, integrating them into production teams and exposing them to tacit knowledge.

Processes of externalization and internalization are particularly intense when lengthy location shoots expose crews to foreign working practices. Economic geography has shown us that learning through offshoring depends on face-to-face contact between incoming and local actors. Malmberg and Maskell identified three dimensions of "localized learning." First, a "vertical" dimension involves interaction between business partners, input/output relations, and their distinct yet complementary activities. Second, the "horizontal" dimension involves observation, benchmarking, and imitating similar activities. A third, "social" dimension involves everyday exposure to shared industry "buzz" or interpretative schemes. The long-term success of these processes is dependent on additional factors, including the degree of trust or quality of network relations that exists among interacting sites and between the initial local knowledge base and its institutional setup.[8]

Accordingly, I would like to propose three provisional hypotheses linking globalization of production with creative labor and localized learning in the postsocialist work world of Prague. First, the city's position in global production networks suggests a multidirectional version of globalization, wherein local agents react to global forces, and "location interests" and "localized learning" are preconditioned by historical and environmental specificities. Intermediaries play a key role in translocal transactions—in Prague's case, usually production services. Second, the "postsocialist precarity" of creative workers results more from an internal than international division of labor. Prague is compartmentalized due to a fragmented production sector, a lack of strong workers' organizations, and the selective involvement of the state. Politicians have focused on separating the constituent sectors of the screen media industry into an indigenously produced "national culture," which it feels needs state support, production services (perceived as a pure business), and the traditionally strong public service media that typically attracts their attention. Third, although it has improved the local infrastructure, the globalization of media production has failed to improve the quality of locally produced screen media due to barriers continuing to hamper transnational learning and career development. Innovative, internationally successful, and critically applauded works are more likely to come either from smaller production companies deeply rooted in the local environment, who are able to combine original content with smaller-scale international services, or from multinational companies like HBO, who nurture long-term relationships with local talent and understand the local market, than directly from workers and companies servicing Hollywood's big-budget runaway productions.

GLOBALIZING A POSTSOCIALIST PRODUCTION WORLD: PRODUCERS AND PRODUCTION MANAGEMENT AS CULTURAL INTERFACE

Providing services to overseas companies is nothing new for Prague's Barrandov Studios. The studio first engaged in this practice in the 1930s, and continued doing so during the Nazi occupation of Czechoslovakia and state-socialist rule. Under state socialism, Barrandov participated in myriad coproductions with, and provided production services to, partners from socialist and Western nations. Unlike coproductions, its services to Western producers were valued in economic, rather than ideological, terms, because they were lucrative ventures bringing much-needed hard currency into the country. After the studio privatized following the fall of state socialism in 1989, international production was still dominated by former executives of communist-era Barrandov's Foreign Commissions Department. At this time, Prague was underdeveloped, with most overseas producers using their own crews and sending rushes to cities like London. Moreover, overseas producers required local intermediaries to help deal with local accounting and legal systems, as well as providing access to essential resources like labor, sets, and locations. The state-socialist-era production managers who pursued these roles encountered significant difficulties in adapting to the new flexible regime. Many spoke little English, and their working habits and organizational culture were different from those of their new American partners. As former secret police agents, some struggled to come to terms with transparent negotiations and business practices.[9]

By the late 1990s, this older cohort who had focused on West European productions was being replaced by younger players. Some of this new generation came from the United States, the United Kingdom, and Germany, with Briton Matthew Stillman's company Stillking the most successful of the new setups. The thirty-year-old Californian David Minkowski came to Prague in 1995 to work on low-budget international productions. He teamed with Stillman, marking the start of a twenty-year process that made him the most influential figure in the Czech production services industry. Minkowski's career advanced at a rate impossible in Los Angeles, a city in which, by his own admission, he would have been unable to secure high-ranking executive positions on prominent projects like *Casino Royale* (2006).[10]

Prague's foreign services boom started in 1998. Foreign commissions required flexible, English-speaking workers. This development coincided with an estimated thirty thousand young Americans relocating to Prague. Having formed social networks, some of these "YAPS"—Young Americans in Prague—were hired by production service companies as managers to work alongside Czechs, most of whom had been employed by Barrandov during the communist period. The latter were reluctant to work the long hours common for Hollywood productions, and so Minkowski sourced bright, eager youngsters working in the city's hotels and restaurants. According to one account, "He would strike up conversations to test their English, and if they seemed smart enough to quickly learn a new, demanding job, he would ask if they wanted to work at Stillking. 'They always said, yes,' recalls Minkowski. 'I mean who would choose to be a waiter or receptionist instead of doing movies?'" Ten years later, most Stillking employees were under forty, and the Barrandov generation was gone.[11]

In 1998, Stillking expanded into big-budget productions, acting as a regional mediator for Hollywood studios wanting to shoot in countries like Hungary, Poland, and the Czech Republic. In a marketing campaign dubbed "Shoot Europe," Stillking invited foreign studios to "show us the scripts, we'll budget them for you, find the right locations and crew—and if you work with us you'll save between 30% and 50% compared to equivalent costs in the US."[12] By the late 1990s, Prague was earning a reputation for quality and not just inexpensive film production services. Bigger projects were drawn to the city by experienced crews, Barrandov's fourteen soundstages, and locations that could stand in for any European city or historical period. Consequently, a disproportionally large filmmaking community of five thousand professionals developed.[13]

This boom period ended in 2004, when governments in countries like Hungary started to implement new initiatives to bring overseas producers to their cities. Poised to soar in Hungary, foreign film investment fell 70 percent in Prague.[14] A second slump saw foreign spending drop another 66 percent in 2008. For the first time since 1992, income from international productions was less than from domestic productions.[15] In the city's postboom years, production service professionals suggested that the domestic film industry was dying. They insisted crews and the surrounding infrastructure could not survive in a small country like the Czech Republic without the support of overseas producers.

To bring the country into line with its competitors, the Czech government belatedly implemented a 20 percent cost rebate program in 2010. This step fueled a new wave of international productions, as income rose to $140 million by 2013. Yet the program was still characterized by short-term thinking, such as attracting international projects individually, rather than a long-term strategy designed to complement and develop local skills.[16] Since then, a relatively low rebate cap of $25 million has threatened such investments. Combined with the proportional allotment principle, this cap has caused the rebate to drop from 20 percent to 6–8 percent.[17] By contrast, Budapest has enjoyed considerable prosperity since introducing a cap-free rebate program.[18] In 2014, the Czech cap was finally raised by $14 million; Hungary responded by raising its limit from 20 percent to 30 percent, pushing competition to a new level.[19]

Since 1990, around 140 foreign feature films and TV series have been shot at Barrandov.[20] Of these, 60 were Hollywood productions, including *Mission: Impossible* (1996), *Van Helsing* (2004), and *The Chronicles of Narnia: Prince Caspian* (2008). A typical international production involves numerous crews shooting both at local studios and on location. Below the-line personnel are mostly Czech, heads of departments American or British, and above-the-line talent from the United States. For several months, talent and support personnel work for twelve hours plus, six days a week. Their face-to-face interaction can lead to misunderstandings and conflicts but permits them to observe others, imitate their practices, and learn by doing.

As studios and producers operate on an increasingly global scale, they must collaborate with personnel in a variety of locations. The key players in a Hollywood runaway production are typically the head of physical production (or vice president of production) at the studio, the producer, the line producer, the local production manager, the local studio manager, the production designer, the location scout, and the director. During shooting, the line producer is the studio's principal representative: s/he oversees the production on location. Line producers may hold little decision-making power, but American producers see them as specialists on locations and local crews, whose opinions influence whether to shoot at a particular overseas site. Local production service companies and production managers are the main partners of incoming line producers. Together they form a cultural interface between the United States and local production centers, as they pursue maximum efficiency by engineering Hollywood-style working conditions.[21] Incoming line producers and local production managers are therefore key channels of knowledge transfer, enabling both parties to learn from each other. However, by achieving this mutually beneficial symbiosis and assigning other agents distinct positions within the structure of the transnational team, they obstruct local personnel's access to higher-level positions.

As a profession, the film producer did not exist in Eastern Europe under state socialism, which instead used centralized production systems.[22] In the early 1990s, the role of the producer needed to be created from scratch. The old-style production managers previously employed by state-owned studios attempted to upgrade their skills and reinvent themselves either as independent producers or as production service companies catering to overseas clients. Adapting to Western production cultures and learning from foreign partners were particularly important skills for the owners of production service companies. Foreign producers became conduits of tacit, embedded organizational knowledge, which local players attempted to internalize through direct observation and imitation.

Later in the decade, the labor market hosted the first generation of postsocialist producers, consisting primarily of students from the relaunched production program at Prague's FAMU film school. These newcomers distinguished themselves from the older managers-turned-producers, embracing European norms of competing at international film festivals and coproducing films with Western partners.[23]

My interviews suggest that overseas producers and Czech personnel mainly transferred organizational knowledge relating to the division of labor, pacing, problem solving, work ethics, and communication. Even below-the-line talent contended they learned more managerial than technical skills. If technical knowledge was in fact mentioned, it did not concern filmmaking or technology but rather budgeting and accounting. This type of embedded organizational knowledge can be externalized during on-set interaction and internalized by local suppliers through observation and imitation. Production managers serve as cultural mediators during this kind of transfer. Minkowski identified the need to train new production managers as the greatest challenge to the current system, estimating that financial and organizational services represent 80 percent of Stillking's operations. Rather than reeducating veteran professionals, he picked young, English-speaking outsiders: "In the areas of accounting, production management, coordination, assistant directors, . . . locations, you can train people who don't have any experience and you can put them in positions of authority, and if they are the right personality and have the right internal skills, they can learn it quickly."[24] By the late 2000s, Czech production managers were self-sufficient, with Hollywood-style organizational skills firmly integrated into their daily routines.

Minkowski could not simply throw young English speakers into skilled technical fields like camera operation and lighting. Yet even in these areas, technical expertise was an important but inessential aspect of recruitment, as newcomers were assigned mentors from the older generation. He recalled the case of a gaffer who, although talented, "drank a lot [and] didn't work more than twelve hours, even if he was getting paid overtime." Although this gaffer's work ethic did not meet American standards, Minkowski felt apprentices might learn much from him: "They didn't have his cultural history, so they weren't running into the same problems," he explained.[25] Today, Minkowski added, these apprentices are the top technicians in Prague.

Rather than simply involving Czechs picking up Hollywood methods, these learning processes are bilateral. The importance of locational knowledge and mutual learning is spelled out by Tom Karnowski, a prominent line producer involved in international productions such as *Shanghai Knights* (2003) and *Everything Is Illuminated* (2005). He explained that before deciding to travel to a foreign location, Los Angeles producers look at who has completed projects of similar size or type in the location in question. They also take local production practices into account. Karnowski recalled that while working on *Everything Is Illuminated* with an American director and cast, he became convinced that they should utilize the skills of as much local personnel as possible and "make it like you would have a Czech film, . . . especially if we have a very low budget to work with."[26] He therefore posited Czech production culture as well suited to the improvisational techniques often used when shooting low-budget American films on location.

MULTIPLE GLOBALIZATIONS

We should avoid the pitfall of misrepresenting knowledge transfer (and spillover) enabled by spatial proximity, interaction, and monitoring as entirely positive or innocent. Contrary to some journalistic accounts, it doesn't come as an automatic, mechanistic, and unidirectional process.[27] Rather, it is important to recognize that effective knowledge absorption happens only when locals develop their own capabilities, that learning is usually a mutual process, even though it may be perceived in negative terms due to the adverse effects it is seen to have on the local culture. We might also recognize that unlearning can be just as important as learning, especially in a postsocialist working environment. Most of my Czech interview subjects talked about learning. An analysis of their revelations allows us to identify four potential paths of globalizing knowledge transfer as well as the barriers to such a transfer. These are centered respectively on incoming producers, production service providers, local independent producers, and the regional strategy of a multinational corporation (where offshoring and direct foreign investment can transform local production norms and practices). Given the limited scope of this chapter, I will restrict my focus to cases in which significant face-to-face interaction took place between Czech and overseas personnel. Before doing so, however, I offer a brief overview of local production practice and its limitations.

Czech film production is strongly influenced by a small, fragmented marketplace, television aesthetics, and the public broadcaster's long-standing position as the country's leading producer-distributor of indigenous feature films and documentaries over the last twenty years. In this period, Czech cinema held a strong market share of up to 30 percent; however, this has started to drop as newly digitized theaters express a preference for Hollywood fare. Czech films rely on location shooting, contemporary topics or nostalgia for the country's recent state-socialist past, and a bittersweet tone, and they are squarely aimed at families. Many of these low-budget films are considered part of the mainstream locally but travel badly. What is more, bigger-budget films and art-house pictures both tend to fare poorly at the international box office or on the festival circuit, even by the modest standards of other East-Central European nations, such as Hungary and Poland. Czech television programs have also struggled internationally, not least because broadcasters have been reticent to alienate their prime mature, conservative domestic audience with unsettling subject matter or radical aesthetics.

Outside observers and policymakers concluded that knowledge transfer would lead incoming producers to gradually transform the practices and styles of the domestic industry. Such a change would come from sharing a labor pool and infrastructure, and from interaction, observation, and imitation. This being said, overseas producers appear to have little interest in reshaping local production— by, for example, hiring local above-the-line talent or hiring Czechs as department heads. In short, there is no clear evidence of any transformation resulting from their presence. Even the BBC—which practices runaway production via its international branches, BBC Worldwide and BBC America—has not promoted its public service ethics or aesthetics during production. As the experience of Czech crews working on *The Musketeers* (2014–) suggests, the presence of the BBC is felt in its division of British and Czech workers and its safety regulations. Czech personnel did not even recognize the corporation as the producer of this series, noting no significant differences between working on a BBC venture or other Anglo-American projects.[28]

Second, it was anticipated that service providers would eventually diversify into producing Czech-language films. However, despite their claims to the contrary, none of the production service heavyweights—Stillking, Czech Anglo Productions, and Etic Films—has branched out into original feature productions. One of the few exceptions is the former Lucasfilm producer Rick McCallum, whose company Film United provides production services for projects like Canal+'s series *Borgia* (2011–), while developing its own fully local and coproduced projects, such as a story of Czech anticommunist resistance fighters, *So Far So Good* (in development). It remains to be seen whether Film United can support high-end Czech genre products.

More typical is the approach of Stillking, a company with solid knowledge of the Czech filmmaking community but evidently little interest in producing or coproducing Czech films. Minkowski, its production head, has met numerous Czech producers but never found a reason to work with them: "We know them and they know us, . . . but we just didn't find something that makes sense. I don't think we are the first stop for them to come and produce Czech movies, because we are not really Czech producers." He admits that the number of American films shot in Prague did not increase the importance of Czech films because "there is no connection there."[29] On the other hand, Minkowski claims that Stillking trains local crews who can then improve the technical quality of the local product. However, this claim relates only to certain aspects of the production process—primarily art direction, special and visual effects, stunts, and to a lesser extent, makeup, costumes, and camera operation. Stillking-affiliated production managers usually do not work on Czech productions, and Czech above-the-line talent does not work for Stillking.

The rate at which Czech personnel enjoy professional upward mobility within transnational crews differs from case to case, partially determined by the nationality, size, and organizational structure of the coproducer. The smaller and more flexible the company, the more Czechs hold positions close to first-line decision makers, and vice versa. Specializing in bigger-budget projects, Stillking employs a large workforce but typically only one Czech head of department (in production design). In these large crews with their military-like organization, locals usually work under second-line decision makers while operating in a segregated labor sphere. They are largely unaware of the creative effects of their roles. According to Minkowski, this type of segregation is typical of Barrandov's costume department, where a staff of mainly non-English-speaking women operates in a socially and spatially isolated workspace.[30]

Local independent producers represent a third potential path for globalizing knowledge transfer. They work on wholly Czech projects, coproductions, and minority coproductions with European partners, and some provide production services. Often independent producers specialize in partnerships with given countries or regions, as was the case with the Indian film *Rockstar* (2011).[31] Irregular, limited to practical services and dependent on narrow networks of contacts, such collaborations do not induce long-lasting knowledge transfers that would affect the quality of local products.

A fourth pathway involves a multinational corporation operating on the local market. In 1991, HBO Europe established central offices in the Hungarian capital of Budapest. Soon after, it set up an additional fourteen branches across Europe, all but one in postsocialist countries. Four of these—Budapest, Prague, Warsaw, and Bucharest—opened an original programming department. These were responsible for providing culturally local quality content for the company's subscription television and HBO GO online services, thus emulating its approach to the U.S. market.[32] A new two-tiered production strategy has come to the fore since HBO Europe recruited the experienced producer Antony Root as its new executive vice president for original programming and production. On the one hand, the company broadcasts low-budget licensed series to test local responses to a property. For instance, it produced adaptations of two Israeli series, *In Treatment* and *When Shall We Kiss,* helmed by renowned local directors and featuring established actors, for each of the four national markets noted above. On the other hand, it produces big-budget event miniseries, which, in Root's words, "put a stake in the ground for a certain kind of quality and values in a show and differentiate ourselves *[sic]* in the market."[33] One example of this approach is *The Burning Bush* (2013), an award-winning three-part drama about the Czech national hero and martyr Jan Palach, who immolated himself to protest the 1968 Soviet occupation of the country.

The screenplay for *The Burning Bush* was rejected by the Czech public service broadcaster before being acquired by HBO. The series was directed by Polish FAMU graduate Agnieszka Holland, who had previously worked for HBO in the United States. It was written by then-unknown Czech screenwriter Štěpán Hulík, and coproduced by newcomer Tomáš Hrubý. When *The Burning Bush* received fourteen awards from the national film academy after being released as a theatrical feature, it was apparent that a new approach, based on HBO's meticulous development process, was emerging.[34] As the company's Budapest-based head of development suggested, HBO's gradual development of local talent and adaptation of American-style project development practices were crucial albeit challenging steps to striking a good balance between maintaining the cultural specificities of local fare and increasing its general quality.[35] The success of *The Burning Bush* generated intense buzz across the Czech production sector, nowhere more than among public service television producers. Embarrassed about passing up this project, they singled out *The Burning Bush* as a new benchmark to which their own quality serial drama ought to aspire.

CAREER PATTERNS AND PRECARITY IN
TRANSNATIONAL PROJECT NETWORKS

International production has shaped the career trajectories of film profession-als in specific ways. Organizational concepts such as boundaryless careers[36] and semipermanent work groups[37] go some way to explaining how this phenomenon has taken shape; however, these are limited as explanatory frameworks because they do not take into account the transnational processes that accelerate some workers' careers while restricting others to low-level positions, particularly those specializing in major Anglo-American productions. The latter find themselves in the paradoxical position of being well-paid mobile workers, thanks in part to a lack of union regulations, but with little chance of professional upward mobility. They remain trapped in a segregated work world, deprived of either the financial incentive to work on local productions or any realistic chance of the type of career development enjoyed by the foreigners running the international productions on which they work.

American-born production managers are often fast-tracked. They typically skip arguably the two most challenging career steps: being given access to the indus-try and being socialized in aspects of it.[38] Instead, they acquire prized locational knowledge and develop marketable specializations at a rate impossible in Western media hubs like London and Los Angeles. As Minkowski put it, "I could have gone back to LA and become one of thousands fighting to work on films, or I could stay here and strike out on my own."[39] By contrast, for local production management, the collapse of the old hierarchical state-owned studios brought uncertainty and unemployment, but a rapid generational change granted some in their ranks swift access to the industry. The fortunate ones developed hybrid professional identities, claiming to "behave like Americans" without leaving their homeland.

To gain insight into the differences and mediating mechanisms that underpin communities of cultural workers, we can benefit from the self-reflexive comments of Czech personnel. Even those struggling to progress in the industry highlight the experience of learning rather than the feeling of being exploited. This senti-ment is bound up with their construction of hybrid cultural identities. Thus the Czech soundman Petr Forejt describes himself as becoming an American film-maker in Prague, distanced from the trivialities of a local industry in which wages and standards are low and improvisation and multitasking high.[40] Similarly, Milan Chadima, a camera operator who has worked on such projects as *The Brothers Grimm* (2005), spoke of American producers helping him escape the frustrations of shooting low-budget Czech films and commercials.[41]

These cases notwithstanding, it is clear that the careers of even the most suc-cessful Czech service production workers are characterized by striking limitations. Such individuals are not promoted to higher creative positions like department heads. They work in other international media hubs only when their employers move a project overseas and rarely take part in prestigious domestic projects. Coming closest to the privileged position of the department head were several Czech art directors, yet only one, Ondřej Nekvasil, has built what could reasonably be considered a career of international standing. Nekvasil switches between working on Czech art-house fare, teaching production design, and working as a production designer on international productions like *The Illusionist* (2006) and *Snowpiercer* (2013). Two factors underwrite Nekvasil's distinctive transnational career trajectory. A reputation-making Emmy for *Anne Frank: The Whole Story* (2001) brought him to the attention of American producers such as David R. Kappes, who hired him for the Sci-Fi Channel miniseries *Children of Dune* (2003). He is also fortunate to specialize in the aspect of local production services most valued by American producers—set design and construction, which, in spite of its high standards of craftsmanship, can be obtained 50 percent cheaper in Prague compared to Los Angeles. I asked Nekvasil what he felt sets him apart from those art directors who also work on medium-to-big-budget productions but have failed to match his level of professional success. Nekvasil said nothing of differences in skill, but instead suggested that they may prefer the relative calm of the art department over the greater responsibility of face-to-face interaction with foreign producers.[42]

CONCLUSION: A TWO-TIER, DEPARTMENTALIZED WORK WORLD

To gain a better understanding of the contemporary production world of Prague, we require a more balanced approach than those focusing primarily on the supposed exploitation of the global labor force, as neo-Marxism does, or on city development strategies, as creative industries and cluster theories do. Cultural intermediaries, knowledge transfers, and learning effects play major roles in a postsocialist, non-English-speaking country like the Czech Republic. As a result of historically specific experiences—communists discrediting labor unions, the interventionist yet selective cultural politics of the state—local film workers tend to contradict conclusions derived from studies of cultural imperialism or NICL. They criticize local policymakers rather than Hollywood producers and focus on learning and mobility barriers rather than exploitative working conditions. This is true even of individuals whose livelihood is threatened by Hollywood moving runaway productions to neighboring countries like Hungary. A new model of globalization is clearly needed if we are to gain deeper insight into the interplay between global forces "from above" like GPN's "flagships" and those from below, such as local workers. As economic geography has shown, we also need to understand the relationships between local and translocal transactions,[43] whose interaction allows for extralocal knowledge flows. In the case of the Prague screen industries, such an approach might involve examining mediating mechanisms and agencies like the service production sector in terms of their interaction with local and international partners and competitors. The production culture of Prague is effectively a two-tier system split between production services and domestic productions, which are characterized by different salaries, career patterns, and work practices. Recognizing it as such opens up new avenues of investigation. We might, for example, consider the extent to which this instance of multitrack globalization precipitates "departmentalized" thinking, especially in service productions. We might also wish to consider the implications of the "glass ceilings"[44] that have prevented many local workers from moving into original projects and securing high-level creative jobs.

NOTES

This chapter is based on a long-term research project focusing on the history of state-socialist and post-socialist production systems and production cultures in Prague and East-Central Europe, supported by the Czech Science Foundation (grant nr. P409/10/1361) and by the Fulbright Scholar Program. It is also based on data generated by the EU-funded FIND Project, which uses student internships in production companies to combine job shadowing with ethnographic research of production cultures (see www.projectfind.cz). The author would like to thank Richard Nowell for his editing assistance.

  1. The interviews were conducted in two phases: in 2009 and 2010 in Prague and Los Angeles, and in 2013 and 2014 in Brno, Prague, and Budapest. The questions solicited responses about the involvement of specific personnel in international productions and how working on these projects affects career trajectories. The interview subjects were: Ludmila Claussová (film commissioner, Prague); Radomír Dočekal (Barrandov studio's former president, Prague); Petr Forejt (sound recordist, Prague), Daniel Frisch (production manager, head of a production-service firm, Prague/Los Angeles), Thomas Hammel (producer, executive producer, Los Angeles); Michael Hausman (executive producer, first assistant director, New York); Tom Karnowski (production manager, producer, Los Angeles), Aleš Komárek (production manager, a head of a production-service firm, Prague); Tomáš Krejčí (head of a production-service firm, Prague/Los Angeles); Cathy Meils (former *Variety* correspondent in Prague); David Minkowski (production manager, head of a production-service firm, Prague/Los Angeles); Ondřej Nekvasil (production designer, art director, Prague); Steven North (producer, executive producer, Los Angeles); Rusty Lemorande (producer, Los Angeles); Cathy Schulman (producer, Los Angeles); Steven Lane (producer, Los Angeles); William Stuart (Barrandov Studios representative in Los Angeles); Jaromír Švarc (art director, Prague); Michelle Weller (former production manager in Prague, currently out of film business in Texas); Tomáš Hrubý (producer, Prague); Gábor Krigler (head of development, HBO, Budapest); Viktória Petrányi (producer, head of a production-service firm, Budapest); Pavel Strnad (independent producer, Prague); Petr Bílek (head of a production-service firm, Prague); Viktor Tauš (director, Prague).

  2. From mid 2012 to mid 2014, the EU-funded FIND Project (www.projectfind.cz) organized over one hundred student internships. As assistants for international film and television productions, interns conducted participant observations and kept field diaries.

  3. See Toby Miller, Nitin Govil, John McMurria, Richard Maxwell, and Ting Wang, *Global Hollywood 2* (London: British Film Institute, 2008).

  4. See Ben Goldsmith and Tom O'Regan, *The Film Studio: Film Production in the Global Economy* (Lanham, MD: Rowman & Littlefield, 2005).

5. Neil M. Coe, Peter Dicken, and Martin Hess, "Global Production Networks: Realizing the Potential," *Journal of Economic Geography* 8 (2008): 271–295. For examples of applying GPN theory to global media industries, see Neil M. Coe and Jennifer Johns, "Beyond Production Clusters: Towards a Critical Political Economy of Networks in the Film and Television Industries," in *The Cultural Industries and the Production of Culture,* ed. Dominic Power and Allen J. Scott (London: Routledge, 2004), 188–204; Hyejin Yoon and Edward J. Malecki, "Cartoon Planet: Worlds of Production and Global Production Networks in the Animation Industry," *Industrial and Corporate Change* 19.1 (2010): 239–271; Terry Flew, *Understanding Global Media* (New York: Palgrave Macmillan, 2007).

6. Dieter Ernst and Linsu Kim, "Global Production Networks, Knowledge Diffusion, and Local Capability Formation," *Research Policy* 31.8–9 (2002): 1417–1429.

7. See Candace Jones, "Careers in Project Networks: The Case of the Film Industry," in *Boundaryless Career: A New Employment Principle for a New Organizational Era,* ed. Michael Bernard Arthur and Denise M. Rousseau (New York: Oxford University Press, 1996), 58–75.

8. Anders Malmberg and Peter Maskell, "Localized Learning Revisited," *Growth and Change* 37.1 (March 2006): 1–18.

9. This claim is based on information gleaned from files at Barrandov Studios archive, the National Film Archive in Prague, a register of secret police agents, and interviews with current production managers.

10. Jonathan Kandell, "Americans in Prague: A Second Wave of Expatriates Is Now Playing a Vital Role in the Renaissance of the Czech Capital," *Smithsonian Magazine,* August 2007, www.smithsonianmag.com/people-places/americans-in-prague-160121860/?no-ist=&story=fullstory&page=1.

11. Ibid.

12. Daniel Rosenthal, "Czech Out Hollywood's New Euro Options," *Weekly Variety,* March 9, 1998.

13. See Olsberg SPI, "Economic Impact Study of the Film Industry in the Czech Republic" (London, 2006).

14. "The Hungarian Tax Credit System and the 20% Rebate Scheme," *Studies in Eastern European Cinema* 1.1 (2010): 127–130.

15. See government-sponsored reports on audiovisual industry: Olsberg SPI, "Economic Impact Study of the Film Industry in the Czech Republic"; "Strategie konkurenceschopnosti českého filmového průmyslu 2011–2016" (MK ČR, 2010).

16. Will Tizard, "Czech Republic Sees Jump in Foreign Production Spending as Incentives Grow," *Variety,* July 9, 2014, http://variety.com/2014/film/news/czech-rep-sees-jump-in-foreign-production-spend-as-incentives-hiked-1201259106; see also Goldsmith and O'Regan, *The Film Studio.*

17. Cathy Meils, "Czech Film Tax Incentives Shrink," *Filmneweurope.com,* June 24, 2013, www.filmneweurope.com/news/czech/105714-czech-film-tax-incentives-shrink/menu-id-150.

18. Leo Barraclough, "Film and TV Production Heats Up in Budapest: Flowing coin Attracts Hollywood Films," *Variety,* May 16, 2013, http://variety.com/2013/film/international/budapest-filming-locations-hbo-nbc-1200466459.

19. Alexandra Zeevalkink, "Hungary Ups Film Tax Rebate to Attract More Foreign Productions," *KFTV.com,* July 17, 2014, www.kftv.com/news/2014/07/17/hungary-ups-film-tax-rebate-to-attract-more-foreign-productions.

20. See "Barrandov Studios," www.barrandov.cz/clanek/reference-zahranicni-film.

21. Based on interviews with Cathy Schulman, October 23, 2009; Tom Karnowski, December 4, 2009; Radomír Dočekal, June 5, 2009.

22. See Petr Szczepanik, "The State-Socialist Mode of Production and the Political History of Production Culture," in *Behind the Screen: Inside European Production Cultures,* ed. P. Szczepanik and Patrick Vonderau (New York: Palgrave Macmillan, 2013), 113–134.

23. Interview with Pavel Strnad, December 7, 2012.

24. Interview with David Minkowski, May 19, 2009.

25. Ibid.

26. Interview with Tom Karnowski, December 4, 2009.

27. Spillover effects are highlighted by reports on the potential effects of the Czech incentive program commissioned by the government. See, for example, an industry report, EEIP, "Hodnocení dopadů regulace (velká RIA) k části návrhu zákona o kinematografii vztahující se k úpravě pobídek filmovému průmyslu (fiskálním stimulům)" (Prague, 2009).

28. Project FIND student intern field diaries.

29. Interview with David Minkowski, May 19, 2009.

30. Petr Szczepanik, "Globalization through the Eyes of Runners: Student Interns as Ethnographers on Runaway Productions in Prague," Media Industries Journal 1.1 (2013), www.mediaindustriesjournal. org/index.php/mij/article/view/23/67.

31. Q&As with producers Karla Stojáková (Axman), Ondřej Beránek (Punk Film), and Pavel Berčík (Evolution), 2012 and 2013.

32. See Gary R. Edgerton and Jeffrey P. Jones, The Essential HBO Reader (Lexington: University Press of Kentucky, 2008).

33. Antony Root, quoted in Gary Smitherman, "The HBO Treatment," C21Media, June 19, 2012, www.c21media.net/the-hbo-treatment/.

34. Informal interview with Tomáš Hrubý, March 10, 2014.

35. Interview with Gábor Krigler, March 28, 2014.

36. Jones, "Careers in Project Networks."

37. Helen Blair, "'You're Only as Good as Your Last Job': The Labour Process and Labour Market in the British Film Industry," Work, Employment and Society 15.1 (2001): 149–169.

38. See Jones, "Careers in Project Networks."

39. Minkowski, quoted in Kandell, "Americans in Prague."

40. Interview with Petr Forejt, June 17, 2009.

41. Quoted in Tomáš Baldýnský, "Quentin za to může!" Reflex, February 17, 2006.

42. Interview with Ondřej Nekvasil, June 11, 2009.

43. Peter Maskell, Harald Bathelt, and Anders Malmberg, "Building Global Knowledge Pipelines: The Role of Temporary Clusters," European Planning Studies 14.8 (2006): 997–1013.

44. See Martha M. Lauzen's annual reports: "The Celluloid Ceiling," http://womenintvfilm.sdsu. edu/files/2013_Celluloid_Ceiling_Report.pdf.

8

The Cost of Business

Gender Dynamics of Media Labor in Afghanistan

Matt Sienkiewicz

On September 11, 2001, Afghanistan's media sphere was one of the sparsest in the world. Few newspapers had survived the previous half-decade of Taliban rule, during which the nation devolved into a "country without news or pictures," according to Reporters Without Borders.[1] A single radio station, Radio Sharia, was in operation—the lone remnant of a bygone Soviet era marked by relatively sophisticated, if centrally controlled, broadcasting practices. According to the architects of the American-led invasion that would ultimately overthrow the Taliban regime, this lack of media was not only a symptom of totalitarianism but also a cause. Free media, argued President George W. Bush during a speech to the National Endowment for Democracy in 2003, was a central pillar of "successful societies" that rejected terrorism, engaged productively with the international system, and respected the rights of all people, especially women.[2] To "fix" Afghanistan would be, in part, to fix Afghan media.

Accordingly, America's war on terror brought an unprecedented level of media intervention into Afghanistan. As early as November 2001, just weeks after the start of the invasion, American media consultants were in Kabul, laying the groundwork for a hybridized public-private broadcasting system that would flourish, at least numerically, in the years to come. Today, Afghanistan's media market is as crowded as it was once barren. Countless television stations compete for viewer attention, ranging from the megalith Tolo TV, backed by the United States and co-owned by Newscorp, to the dozens of tiny outlets owned by local politicians, businessmen, and warlords. Bolstered by both direct American investment and a local economy supported by international aid, Afghan's media system today appears not only vibrant but in many ways progressive. Minority cultural groups and women are represented on screen in a fashion that only years ago would have seemed impossible. It is also now commonplace to find women in key production positions, a phenomenon unseen in Afghanistan in the years between the end of Soviet control and the arrival of NATO forces in 2001.

This chapter details the ways Western media intervention in Afghanistan has aimed to foster cultural and economic environments that encourage female media participation, as well as the significant costs and limitations that have come with it. Drawing upon a five-week research trip to Kabul as well as extensive documentary research and personal communications over several years, I aim to move beyond the sweeping ideological accusations of critics to understand the specific gender dynamics that have emerged in the world of Western-funded Afghan media production. In doing so, I argue that Western efforts to bolster Afghan broadcasting have resulted in a limited but identifiable success with regard to greater female participation in the mediasphere. Noting the differences in gendered media labor between the nonprofit and commercial spheres, I foreground the intersection of economics and culture that complicates these two approaches to media assistance. I argue, however, that both approaches have fostered a sense of precariousness in the lives and careers of all media workers, with particular instability affecting women.

RIGHTFUL SUSPICIONS

If any element of recent Western foreign policy ought to be eyed with suspicion, it is the unique confluence of gender rights discourse and media assistance that has occurred in Afghanistan since 2001. Although understood largely as separate issues, both relate directly to the post–September 11 moment, in which the United States desperately attempted to articulate a worldview in which military and cultural intervention in Afghanistan would offer a sense of increased American security. As early as September 20, President George W. Bush offered the American people a picture of an Afghanistan plagued by the dual cultural blind spots of patriarchy and media deficiency. Detailing the need to destroy the Taliban and its support for Al Qaeda, Bush noted that in Afghanistan "women are not allowed to attend school. You can be jailed for owning a television."[3] Unable to offer much in the way of concrete objectives for America's military intervention, Bush bolstered his moral standing by positioning the Taliban's Afghanistan as a perfectly inverted version of America's idealized neoliberal self-image.

Immediately, American politicians and media outlets began to construct a discourse in which foreign intervention was required both to avoid future terrorist attacks and to save Afghan women from Afghan men. In a striking example, CNN aired the BBC documentary *Beneath the Veil* multiple times in the months leading up to war, offering what Lynn Spigel describes as a chance for U.S. viewers "to make easy equivocations between the kind of the oppression the women of Afghanistan faced and the loss of innocent life on American soil on September 11."[4] Stabile and Kumar go farther in their analysis of American media coverage of Afghan women in the period following September 11, arguing that "women's liberation" amounted to "little more than a cynical ploy" used to "sell the war to the US public."[5] American media, in their analysis, offered a decidedly selective vision of Afghan history in which the Taliban played the role of the dark villain and the United States was portrayed as the white knight rushing to save Oriental damsels in distress. Effaced from this account is the uneven, hard-fought struggle of Afghan women's groups, such as RAWA, as well as the significant women's rights violations committed by the United States and local allies like the Northern Alliance.[6] Most provocatively, Stabile and Kumar go on to accuse the United States of using women as a tool through which to justify "imperialist domination," rendering the West just as guilty of erasing Afghan women's agency as the Taliban government against which it fought.

In a book-length study of the extensive aid aimed at improving the lives of women in postinvasion Afghanistan, Lina Abirafeh argues that willful blind spots produced by Western media had a direct impact on the sorts of programs that received funding and support in the country.[7] In particular, stereotypical images of oppressed chaddari-clad Afghan woman seem to have dominated the mindset of NGO and Western government decision makers, much as they had captivated American readers of best-selling nonfiction, such as *Zoya's Story*[8] and *My Forbidden Face*.[9] Official American voices emphasized the importance of undoing the drastic restrictions on women's liberty enforced by the Taliban beginning in 1990, with little attention paid to the diverse history of women's experiences in Afghanistan. Abirafeh identifies an overtly "top-down" orientation to women's rights programming, much of it embedded with a sense that Afghan women are "unable to empower themselves."[10] Echoing Islah Jad's work on the "NGO-isation" of global women's movements,[11] Abirafeh notes that Western feminism, with its emphasis on individual, often economic rights, blinded the Western aid apparatus to the traditional strengths of the Afghan women's movement.[12] In this sense, the NGO world can be understood as being in line with the emphasis on free agency and mobility that marks the landscape of globalized labor markets and contributes to the sense of precariousness that plagues media workers in every subfield. Perhaps most damningly, however, Abirafeh declares that in the rush to provide them with a dramatic and politically popular salvation, the West "forgot to consult Afghan women at all."[13]

Scholarly accounts of Western media assistance—defined here as the provision of Western funding and training to local media workers—to Afghanistan, though sparse, are hardly kinder than the critiques of gender aid. This pattern of suspicion follows a broader critical concern with media assistance, a field that remains steeped in the work of post-WWII modernization theorists, particularly Daniel Lerner.[14] James Miller usefully summarizes this critique, noting that media assistance is "fundamentally about universalizing the local and assuming an unjustifiably near causal relationship between media . . . and self governance."[15] Turning a blind eye to the idiosyncrasies of Western media and Western democracy, media assistance advocates tend to assume that the two are inherently good and fundamentally intertwined entities.

A more subtle assumption built into media assistance work is an emphasis on the individual journalist or producer as the fundamental unit of a successful mediasphere. Although money is certainly devoted to institutional capacity building in international media projects, the trend toward contract, mobile labor found throughout the American media industry inevitably affects the training that aid recipients encounter. Furthermore, as Rao and Wasserman note, this preoccupation with individualism serves as a linchpin between the economic logic of the media business and hegemonic Western understandings of media ethics, which downplay communal interests in evaluating media quality.[16] Miller suggests that such assumptions may be exacerbated by the well-meaning individuals on the frontlines of media assistance projects in places such as Afghanistan. The Western journalists and NGO workers who enact the on-the-ground aspects of media assistance often embrace the sort of precarious labor conditions with which this volume is concerned.[17] Moving from place to place to provide training, these individuals bring with them the sense that media work is an independent endeavor often in direct tension with geographical and financial stability. Though this ought not impugn the intentions of Western NGO workers and media trainers, it is impossible to ignore the tension that exists between the radical individualism that might encourage someone to move from a European capital to war-torn Afghanistan and the more communal goals of local institutions.

This emphasis on market-oriented, entrepreneurial media systems is fully apparent in the reality of postinvasion Afghan media. Alongside the military onslaught of late 2001 that brought down the Taliban regime in Kabul came a concerted and highly coordinated effort to supply Afghans with a new, ostensibly independent media system. In addition to commandeering the state radio system, American forces, through USAID's Office of Transition Initiatives (OTI), underwrote the production of a remarkably broad and diverse Afghan mediasphere. Within five years, a once broadcast-free rural Afghanistan was dotted with local radio stations surviving on a combination of foreign largesse and local advertising revenue. In addition to playing programming aimed at articulating the intentions of NATO forces and "rural transition teams," these stations offered a mix of locally produced shows and foreign-funded public service material.

Kabul quickly emerged as a true media capital, as the vacuum produced by the Taliban's near-total elimination of broadcasting gave way to a chaotic landscape in which outlets run by NGOs, warlords, and entrepreneurs competed for economic footholds and political influence. Security circumstances aligned with the "logic of accumulation" identified by Curtin in the development process of media capitals, bringing thousands of young aspiring professionals home to Kabul after years of exile in Iran, Pakistan, and the West.[18] The first great success in this new environment was Arman FM, a purely commercial radio station that nonetheless received a large initial investment from USAID's OTI. The relationship between USAID and Arman's owners, the Australian-Afghan Mohseni brothers, would continue and grow, with the United States eventually providing over $2 million in grants to Mohseni's Tolo TV, a commercial station that now dominates the crowded field of Afghan television through a mix of programming tilted heavily toward Western-style game shows and dramas. Perhaps predictably, in popular accounts of Afghan's new mediasphere, Tolo president Saad Mohseni is positioned as the protagonist of a story that emphasizes the individual entrepreneur over the realities of communal and government cooperation that make his station possible.

The unabashedly capitalist orientation of this project has drawn the ire of numerous critics, most notably Mark J. Barker, who argues that the newly oligarchic orientation of the Afghan mediasphere confirms American desires to foster a friendly "polyarchy" in the country, as opposed to a true democracy geared toward expressing the will of the people. To Barker, such a tactic emerges from the same strategy that led to the overtly deceitful content produced by the American-run Iraq Media Network in the wake of the fall of Baghdad. In each case, he argues, the United States took the steps it deemed necessary to ensure friendly leadership in occupied spaces, always at the expense of democracy and social justice.[19] The Mohseni family, in this telling, represents an oligarchic regime that the United States supports due to its willingness to engage fully in the system of global capitalism. The local NGO elites favored by America play a similar rule, inculcating Western conventional thinking and contributing to the production of a mediasphere that embraces the values underpinning the neoliberal order. I will not evaluate this broader claim here. It does, however, offer a useful starting point from which to inquire into the relationship between media assistance and egalitarianism at the level of gender in Afghanistan.

CASE BY CASE: WOMEN IN FOR-PROFIT TV

The post-Taliban period by no means represents the first time women held prominent positions in the Afghan mediasphere. The period of Soviet influence and control from the 1960s to 1989 brought a number of women into the field of journalism, as a select class of urban elites prospered while others across the country faced tremendous violence and persecution.[20] Today, older Afghan media institutions, such as the state-run *Kabul Times* newspaper and Radio Afghanistan, employ a small but significant number of veteran female journalists, most of whom left as refugees during the Taliban years and returned after NATO and the Northern Alliance took control of Kabul. Like all Afghan media workers of this era, however, these Soviet-trained individuals are routinely dismissed as "unprofessional" by younger figures in the field. In addition to lacking training in contemporary media technology, they also, according to multiple sources interviewed for this study, are believed to lack the audience-focused approach to production required to succeed in contemporary Afghanistan. Whereas in other environments wartime experience might be a source of cultural capital, in contemporary Afghanistan the wholesale remaking of the local media system on primarily capitalist principles has largely marginalized the older professionals whose experiences are tainted by the communist era.[21]

The vast majority of media producers in Afghanistan, male or female, have thus emerged over the past decade, as the country moved from a single radio broadcaster to a loosely organized system in which hundreds of outlets compete for creative talent, spectrum space, and audience attention. As a result, the overwhelming majority of television producers in Afghanistan are comfortably under the age of thirty, with radio workers skewing only somewhat older. Top-rated television programs such as Tolo's *Afghan Star* and *On the Road,* for example, are both lead-produced by men under twenty-five.

The rapid ascent of the Afghan mediasphere offers a unique set of obstacles to female participation. As was emphasized in American discourse surrounding Afghanistan in the preinvasion period, formal education for women was virtually annihilated in the country during the Taliban's reign. Thus the desire to quickly craft a robust media system in the postwar period left little time to train and recruit young women who could balance the gender aspect of Afghan media labor. Instead, labor needs were filled largely by a combination of returning refugees from Iran and Pakistan and local men with basic educational backgrounds. As Barker points out, subsidies for new stations, both local and national, were granted overwhelmingly to politically connected, well-resourced individuals identified by Americans as entrepreneurial enough to thrive in a commercial environment.[22] Such individuals, by local definition, had to be males able to curry favor either with urban political elites or rural community leaders with religious legitimacy. A combination of local resistance to female participation in the public sphere and foreign demands to quickly establish a commercially viable system left little opportunity for women in media during the earliest stages of Afghanistan's reconstruction and established a system in which men currently possess a near monopoly on "experience" and "professionalism."

However, the profit motive of Tolo TV, combined with the organization's interest in establishing itself as capable of relating to Western supporters, has advanced the place of female producers in remarkable ways. In part, this results from the financial strength of the station, which draws upon the resources of its partner organization Newscorp to provide expensive services such as child care and door-to-door shuttle services, which are particularly important to women working in the dangerous environment of contemporary Kabul. These benefits are, for many potential female employees, absolute necessities that are often unavailable at the smaller-scale media operations that exist throughout the city.

Tolo has also made a concerted effort to hire women as producers, particularly in the areas of family and lifestyle programming, which are associated with primarily female audiences. Tania Farzana, for example, was recruited back to Kabul, after years in the United States, to produce a local adaptation of *Sesame Street*. Numerous other women, many of whom grew up in Afghanistan during the Taliban period, have risen to similar roles as producers within the organization. However, in speaking to a dozen female producers in Kabul in the spring of 2014, I was unable to locate one who considered an Afghan, not Western, woman to be her ultimate boss.[23]

In my attempt to identify the most experienced female producers in Afghan commercial television, I was consistently steered toward women between the ages of twenty and twenty-three. Rokhsar Azamee ranks as one of the most experienced female producers in Afghanistan, despite having left the industry at twenty-two. Feverishly working from the age of seventeen after being introduced to Tolo management by a neighbor, Azamee produced several programs, primarily in the health and morning talk show genres. Having freelanced at a number of local stations in Kabul, Azamee enthusiastically attests to the freedom allowed women at Tolo TV as well as Ariana TV, another for-profit station. She suggests that these outlets, especially Tolo, encourage female freedom of expression by never introducing the concerns of "the government" or religious leaders into programs on sensitive topics such as health and education. This is not to say, however, that working at Tolo comes without risk. As Wazmah Osman notes in her history of postinvasion Afghan culture wars over television, women who work at Tolo, particularly on air, face precariousness in the most literal sense. A famous, tragic example is that of Shaima Rezayee, an on-air personality murdered after months of criticism from conservative cultural elements.[24]

Perhaps with such factors on her mind, Azamee, at an age at which her Western counterparts would have been fighting over volunteer internships at local stations, reached what she felt to be a natural conclusion to her television career. She moved into the more lucrative and stable telecommunications industry.[25] This remarkable trend toward youth currently cuts across gender lines at Tolo, although trends suggest that young men are more likely to remain with the organization for the long term. Although Kabul University offers a degree in journalism, Tolo TV recruits its creative staff by casting an enormously wide net, bringing in large numbers of young people with negligible skill sets and quickly assigning them surprising levels of responsibility. Most recruits wash out quickly, while the survivors take on relatively high-ranking producing roles within months.

This system succeeds in bringing in a fair number of women alongside a much higher proportion of men. However, Tolo's trial-by-fire approach is far better suited to the lifestyles of young Afghan men. The hours are long, sometimes bordering on abusive.[26] In a cultural space in which women working at night and women engaging in the public sphere are both points of great controversy, this system of long hours and high stakes at young ages is particularly precarious for women. Ultimately, it is untenable for most Afghan women to continue working such hours for the pedestrian pay that even the well-funded Tolo is able to offer.[27] There are many men willing to endure these conditions during their twenties, gaining professional experience and prestige while putting off family life and the economic exigencies that come with it. However, this is less of an option for women, many of whom wish to marry during this time period.

As a result, the Afghan for-profit mediasphere is remarkably successful in bringing women to positions of responsibility in production but is far less successful in keeping them there. In my interviews with producers at Tolo TV, the station was often described as a benevolent institution insofar as it granted expressive freedom to young women and opened doors, including opportunities at Western media organizations like the BBC. It is not, however, a stabilizing force for women wishing to gain an economic foothold in Afghanistan's uncertain economy.

THE NONCOMMERCIAL SECTOR

As the United States supported Tolo TV in the hopes that market forces would, among other things, encourage greater female media participation, numerous smaller, nonprofit projects were put forth with this explicit goal. To a significant extent, the United States outsourced this aspect of the Afghan media sphere, building gaps into a system of small local radio stations to be filled by allied nations with projects geared specifically toward female empowerment. Although American policy papers written throughout the 2000s emphasize the importance of nonprofit, women-produced media, they also cede many logistic elements to the French and Canadian governments.[28] This strategy makes a certain sense. America had overtly promised increased female access to the public sphere in the buildup to the war. However, once the invasion began, the realpolitik of post-Taliban Afghanistan provided ample incentive to create distance between the U.S. government and controversial media initiatives.

The most striking example of this danger is the story of Afghan Radio Peace, a single-room station broadcasting from Jabal Saraj in Parwan Province. Uniquely, the station's origins predate September 11. In a meeting in France in March 2001, a group of French women's rights leaders challenged Northern Alliance leader Ahmad Shah Masoud in exactly the way Abirafeh argues postinvasion NATO forces could not challenge Afghan leaders.[29] As the world focused on the evaporation of women's rights under the Taliban, French leaders pressed Masoud on his position on women in the Afghan public sphere. Putting the famed military leader on the spot, the group offered to fund a radio station in Northern Alliance territory, provided a woman be made manager. Masoud accepted and Zakia Zaki, a controversial local advocate for women's rights, took charge of Afghan Radio Peace. The French agreed to pay for a year of Zaki's salary, oil for an electric generator, and fifteen days of basic radio training with French broadcasting professionals.

By the time the station opened in October 2001, much had changed. Masoud was assassinated on September 10, one day before America's invasion of Afghanistan was made inevitable. However, operating in a semiautonomous space at the mouth of the Panjshir Valley, Zaki's small station was truly revolutionary. For six years, the station functioned on a combination of foreign money and local revenue strategies built primarily on classified-style hyperlocal advertising. As NATO and USAID took over rural radio broadcasting in Afghanistan, the French withdrew support, forcing the station to play American-funded public service programming to bring in the money necessary to remain on air. From 2005 to 2007, the station flourished under this model, airing foreign-produced material as well as a selection of local programs rarely focused specifically on women's issues but steeped in the values that brought Zaki to anti-Taliban activism.

In 2007, however, tremendous changes took place. NGO support in Afghanistan began to falter from fatigue, and the Taliban began to reassert itself nationally, largely through increasingly daring suicide attacks. With these disruptions came a campaign specifically targeting female journalists and other public figures. On June 6, 2007, Zaki was murdered. Her death had a massive effect on both Afghan Radio Peace and female media participation throughout the country. In the years following Zaki's assassination, little support has flowed to the station, with no foreign institution wishing to rebuild it to its previous place. Zaki's husband, Abdul Ahad Ranjbar, has taken over what has become a quiet outlet broadcasting twelve hours a day, half of which is American-funded national programming for which the station receives a few hundred dollars to keep the gas generator running.[30]

If there is a figure who has picked up Zaki's mantle, it is Farida Nekzad, whose career has run the gamut of Western-supported noncommercial media in Afghanistan. Nekzad began her media career as a refugee, working in Pakistan when the Taliban controlled Kabul. Inspired by a neighbor who worked for state media during the years of Soviet control, Nekzad received an education in journalism at Kabul University, before the Taliban banned female enrollment. In Pakistan, Nekzad found work with the BBC. When she returned to Kabul in 2002, Nekzad was a rare woman with the credentials necessary for managerial-level work with Western-funded media institutions. This experience allowed her to find employment with the Institute for Media, Policy and Society (IMPACS), a branch of the Canadian government encouraged by USAID to

THE COST OF BUSINESS   113

create three rural women-run stations in the relatively peaceful northern region of Afghanistan.

According to Sarah Kamal, a scholar who worked at the IMPACS station in Mazar I Sharif, the project fell into many of the unreflective patterns so often seen in Western approaches to women's development. In addition to early difficulties in recruiting women to work at the station due to local cultural resistance, the outlet was plagued by a disconnect between the needs of listeners and the expectations of international organizations. Foreign funders and local religious leaders required all programming be preapproved and "pressed the radio station towards adopting a scripted and more formal radio voice over spontaneous conversational dialogue in its programming."[31] Ultimately, the station failed to reach its intended female audience, as Western ideas of individualism and journalistic professionalism created a growing gap between the voices on the air and those listening.[32]

However, this professionalized, Westernized understanding of how to run a radio station has had one significant side effect: it has produced numerous female journalists prepared to succeed in Westernized organizations, often at better pay. The station's current director, Mobina Khairandish, describes the outlet's function as much in terms of training women producers as reaching the sort of audience envisioned by IMPACS when it made the original investment in 2005. Now financially stable, though reliant on occasional contracted projects for NGOs, the station has become a training ground for local women wishing to gain a foothold in the world of media. Despite ongoing difficulties with local groups who question the appropriateness of women on the radio, recruitment issues have more or less disappeared, with small but consistent numbers of young women arriving at the station to work each year.[33]

Although critics like Kamal question the station's ability to truly engage with large numbers of local listeners, it is undeniable that journalists trained at the station have moved on to jobs both within Afghanistan and abroad. In a creative maneuver, the outlet has taken young women whose families discouraged them from taking on public roles and positioned them as journalistic trainers. For example, local offices of Nai Supporting Open Media in Afghanistan, an Internews-funded institution for media education, now feature alumna from the Mazar I Sharif station. Other former employees work across the globe, primarily in media assistance organizations whose goals model the idealized, arguably disconnected, approach to journalism put forth by IMPACS. Although IMPACS perhaps failed in its attempt to train producers capable of connecting to a local audience, it succeeded in training Afghan women for a world of precarious labor in the overlapping fields of media production and media assistance. A project originally intended to suture community bonds may ultimately serve as a training ground for individuals entering an era of transitory and inconsistent labor conditions.

Farida Nekzad became the IMPACS project's greatest local success, leveraging her time with the Canadian organization to procure a position as the codirector of Pahjwok News. Set up as an independent NGO, Pahjwok—funded by Internews (and thus USAID) and based in Kabul—serves as the main domestic wire service in Afghanistan. While at Pahjwok, Nekzad oversaw tremendous changes in Kabul's journalistic landscape, particularly with regard to women. As universities began producing the first generation of post-Taliban journalism graduates, a number of women sought work at organizations like Pahjwok.

Nekzad, in a unique position of power, made a number of policy changes that have had a significant impact. Most obviously, she instituted a hiring quota for women, arguing that the increase in female journalism graduates required a change on the part of the organization. Remarkably, for a brief period in 2006, Pahjwok employed more female than male journalists. More subtly, Nekzad fundamentally changed local newsroom culture, temporarily suspending the traditional practice of separating men and women at company lunches. In Nekzad's view, lunchtime gender segregation, which remains prevalent throughout Afghan business, government, and NGO culture, represented a significant stumbling block to gender equality. "They make big decisions over lunch," she notes. "People think that men are funny and women are quiet because they are in the other room."[34]

The ugly events of 2007, however, forever changed Nekzad's career and undid a number of the changes she had instituted. After Zaki's death, Nekzad began to receive increasingly violent threats, followed by multiple attempts on her life. Women no longer applied for positions at Pahjwok at the same rate, for fear of reprisals. When Nekzad became pregnant, she quit the organization for America to safely raise her child. Upon returning in 2010, she found a very different landscape. Pahjwok was once again dominated by men, with lunches resegregated and only men in managerial positions.

In response, she took over a fledgling competitor, Wakht News. Housed in a three-room apartment off of a main street in Kabul, Wakht currently operates a frequently updated web site that is routinely cited by mainstream Afghan media. Nekzad has attempted to restaff the organization with women but has found the task nearly impossible. As Western NGOs have fled Kabul over the past five years, little grant money is available for anything but well-established, typically male-dominated institutions. As a result, Nekzad was forced to pare back her budget. Although women can sometimes be hired for lower salaries, their presence adds to a company's expenses. While traveling in the city is dangerous to anyone, men are able to ride public transportation and hire taxis when they are unable to walk. For women, this is too dangerous, adding significant private transportation costs to employer budgets. Nekzad's new organization thus faces a familiar conundrum in public service Afghan media. Those organizations that are big enough to maintain a large, diverse staff are deeply entrenched in traditional modes of office culture that work to the disadvantage of female workers. Those that might be willing to challenge these norms, however, are unlikely to receive enough funding to successfully hire women, given the significant additional expense.

CONCLUSION

Reflecting on the popularity of the Afghan women's cause in the period following September 11, Lila Abu-Lughod notes the deeply troubling parallels between the American rhetoric of the time and the colonial era discourse of "saving Muslim women."[35] The American government, media, and seemingly much of the population understood the plight of women under Taliban rule in terms that were both culturally reductive and historically myopic. Generalizations about Muslim and Afghan women abounded, while reflections on the role of the West in shaping Afghan history were all but absent.[36] The American-led war effort was praised for freeing Afghan women from the Taliban but rarely critiqued for assuming that all people ought to pursue Western, neoliberal visions of individual agency and free expression.

It is both easy and entirely appropriate to set American media assistance efforts in Afghanistan within this context. Although efforts were made to incorporate local voices in the new Afghan media system, this system was nonetheless built upon presumptions of the superiority and universality of Westernized media systems. Whenever possible, wealthy entrepreneurs were afforded benefits. When for-profit media was not suitable, America and its allies employed an NGO model that David Harvey found to be deeply intertwined with the neoliberal state system, often emphasizing individual rights over community needs.[37] Both of these approaches appealed to the notion of "saving" women critiqued by Abu-Lughod, in the former case through the magic of the profit motive, in the latter via the largesse of Western cosmopolitanism.

In this chapter I have strived to move beyond the simple neoliberal critique, attempting to consider more closely the specific, concrete impact of American policies on the work of female Afghan media workers. It would be foolish and dishonest to deny that the American-imposed system of media that currently dominates Afghanistan has brought hundreds of women into the public sphere in ways previously impossible. In the nonprofit realm, rare, privileged, and remarkably determined individuals like Farida Nekzad have succeeded in using small openings imposed by the West to create new opportunities for female voices. Furthermore, in considering the words and experiences of women working in the field, it is apparent that, given the circumstances, the profit-oriented media systems decried by Barker do, in fact, offer a greater range of expression to women. Although the Afghan government attempts to exert control over all media, the economic might and global cachet of Tolo TV have allowed the station to push boundaries, thus providing greater autonomy for producers like Rokhsar Azamee.

And yet it is necessary to note that, despite the rhetoric of security and nation building surrounding American media efforts in Afghanistan, increased female expression has by no means removed the precariousness of Afghan labor. In some cases, it has actively encouraged new elements of uncertainty, particularly for women. Most obviously, violence, death threats, and terror still plague the lives of female producers, although this situation predates the immediate post-2001 American involvement in the region.[38] More subtly, both NGO media initiatives and for-profit businesses place women in disproportionately precarious circumstances. Although NGOs train and hire women at admirably high rates, their funding is fickle, with donors often falling away over time. As seen in the case of Nekzad's Wakht News, women are often the first to lose their jobs.

In the realm of commercial outlets, such as Tolo TV, female producers are valued as a short-term means to attract women viewers and positive global press. Perhaps, over time, economics will encourage the outlet to offer long-term stability to the most successful female producers. However, given Afghan economy's remarkable instability and foreign dependence, this seems unlikely. Women will likely continue to leave for more lucrative, stable, and culturally acceptable positions, leaving most of the prestigious yet highly taxing production jobs to the men. Yes, Afghan women now have access to jobs that did not exist fifteen years ago and would never have been open to females even if they had. However, these new opportunities have combined the precariousness of war and reconstruction with the sorts of precariousness described throughout this volume in even the calmest mediaspheres.

NOTES

1. Vincent Brossel, Jean-François Julliard, and Reza Moini, *Afghanistan: What Gains for Press Freedom from Hamid Karzai's Seven Years as President?* (Paris: Reporters Without Borders, 2009), 3.

2. George W. Bush, "Remarks by President George W. Bush at the 20th Anniversary of the National Endowment for Democracy," National Endowment for Democracy, www.ned.org/remarks-by-president-george-w-bush-at-the-20th-anniversary/.

3. George W. Bush, "Transcript of President Bush's Address," *CNN*, September 21, 2001, http://edition.cnn.com/2001/US/09/20/gen.bush.transcript/.

4. Lynn Spigel, "Entertainment Wars: Television Culture after 9/11," *American Quarterly* 56.2 (2004): 249.

5. Carol A. Stabile and Deepa Kumar, "Unveiling Imperialism: Media, Gender and the War on Afghanistan," *Media, Culture & Society* 27.5 (2005): 766.

6. Ibid., 773.

7. Lina Abirafeh, *Gender and International Aid in Afghanistan: The Politics and Effects of Intervention* (Jefferson, NC: McFarland, 2009).

8. Zoya, John Follain, Rita Cristofari, and Rita Wolf, *Zoya's Story: An Afghan Woman's Struggle for Freedom* (New York: HarperCollins, 2002).

9. Latifa, *My Forbidden Face* (London: Virago, 2002).

10. Abirafeh, *Gender and International Aid in Afghanistan*, 28.

11. Islah Jad, "The NGOⒶisation of Arab Women's Movements," *IDS Bulletin* 35.4 (2004): 34–42.

12. Abirafeh, *Gender and International Aid in Afghanistan,* 30.

13. Ibid., 16.

14. Daniel Lerner, *The Passing of Traditional Society: Modernizing the Middle East* (New York: Free Press, 1958).

15. Miller. "NGOs and 'Modernization'and 'Democratization'of Media: Situating Media Assistance." *Global Media and Communication* 5.1 (2009): 16.

16. Herman Wasserman and Shakuntala Rao, "The Glocalization of Journalism Ethics." *Journalism* 9.2 (2008): 163–181.

17. Miller, "NGOs and Modernization," 16.

18. Michael Curtin, *Playing to the World's Biggest Audience: The Globalization of Chinese Film and TV* (Berkeley: University of California Press, 2007).

19. Michael J. Barker. "Democracy or Polyarchy? US-Funded Media Developments in Afghanistan and Iraq post 9/11," *Media, Culture, and Society* 30.1 (2008): 119.

20. Abirafeh, *Gender and International Aid in Afghanistan,* 19.

21. Habib Amiri, personal communication, June 2013.

22. Barker, "Democracy or Polyarchy?" 109–130.

23. This is not to say that such a person might not exist. However, the trend of young women serving as producers under slightly less young males was remarkable in its consistency during my Skype and Facebook interviews.

24. Wazhmah Osman, "Thinking outside the Box: Television and the Afghan Culture Wars" (PhD diss., New York University, 2012), 132.

25. Rokhsar Azamee, personal communication, June 2013

26. I realize this is a serious accusation, but I firmly believe it to be the case. In my discussions, multiple young male producers, whom I will not name in this context, attested to working shifts lasting over twenty-four hours. To them, these tasks seemed more or less akin to that of a college student pulling an all-nighter—stories recounted with nostalgia but nonetheless indicative of labor exploition.

27. A lead producer of multiple high-rating Tolo shows might make as little as $1,200/month in a city that suffers from considerable housing and food inflation.

28. Colin Soloway and Abubaker Saddigue, *USAID's Assistance to the Media Sector in Afghanistan* (Washington: USAID, 2005).

29. Abirafeh, *Gender and International Aid in Afghanistan,* .

30. Abdul Ahad Ranjbar, personal communication, June 2013.

31. Ibid., 408.

32. Ibid., 409.

33. Mobina Khairandish, personal communication, June 2013.

34. Farida Nekzad, personal communication, June 2013.

35. Lila Abu-Lughod, "Do Muslim Women Really Need Saving? Anthropological Reflections on Cultural Relativism and Its Others," *American Anthropologist* 104.3 (2002): 785.

36. Ibid., 784.

37. David Harvey, *A Brief History of Neoliberalism* (London: Oxford University Press, 2005), 78.

38. Which is not to say, however, that America did not play a role in bringing Afghanistan to the state it is currently in.

9

"No One Thinks in Hindi Here"

Language Hierarchies in Bollywood

Tejaswini Ganti

"Immy, can you tone it down a bit?" I was watching a film shoot at the Marriott Renaissance in Mumbai in July 2014, and the director, Vikram Bhatt, was instructing the lead actor, Emraan Hashmi, about his body language during a tracking shot where he had to stride resolutely across the hotel's ballroom. When Bhatt's assistant director began to block the shot for Hashmi, Bhatt bellowed in Hindi from his position in the back of the room, "Arre beta, thode dheere se jaao! [Hey son, go a little slower!]." He then spoke on the phone in Gujarati with a marketing representative from the music company that had released the soundtrack of his soon-to-be-released film. I noticed that the sheets of Hindi dialogue used by another assistant director to monitor actors' accuracy were written in Roman rather than Devanagari script.

A Hindi film set is a highly multilingual environment, and it is common to hear several languages spoken, but the linguistic bifurcation illustrated in this example, where Bhatt spoke in Hindi with his assistants and in English with his lead actor and screenwriter, is a manifestation of the increasing presence of English in the everyday life of the Hindi film industry. In 1996, when I started fieldwork on the production culture of the film industry, I was surprised by how prevalent English was as a lingua franca, especially among the actors, directors, writers, art directors, designers, and others responsible for the creative labor that goes into a film. For below-the-line workers, Hindi was merely one language in a complex linguistic universe that included Marathi, Bengali, Tamil, Telugu, Gujarati, and Punjabi. This is a testament to the tremendous linguistic diversity of India—18 official languages but 122 languages with at least 10,000 native speakers—and the cosmopolitan nature of the Hindi film industry, where people hail from every linguistic region of India as well as other parts of South Asia (or beyond) and are not necessarily native Hindi speakers. According to the 2001 census, while Hindi is spoken by 53.6 percent of the population, there are fifty different types of Hindi.[1]

India is perhaps unique among film-producing nations for having at least eight major film industries, all distinguished by language, and for producing films in about twenty languages every year. The polyglot nature of the contemporary Hindi film industry fits into the broader history of filmmaking in Mumbai. Mumbai, as a colonial center of commerce, has always been marked by tremendous linguistic, ethnic, and religious diversity, and this diversity has been apparent in the world of filmmaking from its origins: early Indian cinema featured Parsi and Gujarati capital, Marathi directors, and Anglo-Indian performers.

With the advent of sound in 1931, Mumbai filmmakers had to choose which language to make films in; Hindi offered the largest market, but which type of Hindi? Filmmakers finally settled on a version, referred to as Hindustani by the British, that had operated as a sort of lingua franca throughout northern India.[2] Thus Mumbai became the only city in India where the language of the film industry's output was not congruent with the dominant languages of the region, Gujarati and Marathi. This was in direct contrast to other major centers of film production in India, such as Kolkata, Hyderabad, Chennai, and Trivandrum. Thus the Hindi film industry, unlike other Indian language film industries, has not had recourse to a regional state apparatus to promote its interests. Other states in India promote filmmaking in their official languages by offering incentives and subsidies, whereas Hindi films are not identified with any one particular state.

Whether it is the earmarking of subsidies for filmmaking in specific languages, the promotion of a particular dialect as a normative standard in advertising, the daily translations undertaken by news agencies, or Hollywood studios' local language production strategies, language—as a category of socio-political identity, a form of labor, a set of commodified skills, and an object of market exchange— plays a critical role in the political economy of media industries.[3] Referring to the increasing opportunities and attractions afforded by the Hindi film industry and the growing international profile of Bollywood, this chapter discusses how changes in language or code choice within Hindi cinema and the increasing significance of English in the production culture of the film industry concretely animate the transformations that have taken place in the political economy and social world of the Hindi film industry since the advent of neoliberal reforms in India mandated by the International Monetary Fund in 1991.

The changes I have characterized elsewhere as gentrification have resulted in a situation in which two apparently contradictory phenomena are taking place within the contemporary industry:[4] the spoken language in many contemporary

Hindi films is much more diverse and regionally specific than in films from earlier decades, at the same time that fluency in Hindi appears to be waning among certain elite categories of creative workers (writers, directors, actors, producers), resulting in a situation where English has attained a certain primacy and status and putting those whose primary language is Hindi in a far more socially and economically precarious position within the industry. This chapter discusses the reasons for and consequences of this paradox and illustrates how language and linguistic competence become sites for the elaboration of distinction, the performance of cultural capital, and the enactment of new hierarchies within the Hindi film industry. I argue that the turn toward localized registers of Hindi in film dialogue is integrally connected to the increased prevalence of English within the film industry, as both phenomena emerge from structural transformations that have beset the industry since the mid-2000s.

These transformations have reduced the economic precarity that typified Hindi filmmaking for much of the industry's history. Flexibility, fragmentation, decentralization, and their associated occupational/employment insecurities, which are cited as characteristics of a global late-capitalist order, have actually been defining features of the Hindi film industry since the end of World War II. Dramatic changes in the structure of the Hindi film industry were initiated after the Indian state recognized filmmaking as a legitimate industrial activity in 2000. Official designation as an industry paved the way for a greater variety of financing for filmmaking, including loans from banks and other financial institutions, and initiated a number of structural changes commonly characterized as "corporatization," where high-profile Indian conglomerates established new production-distribution companies or existing production, distribution, or exhibition concerns became public limited companies listed and traded on the Indian stock market. These new regimes of finance and organization in the film industry transformed it from a very undercapitalized enterprise (with accompanying high rates of attrition and stalled films) to one where raising capital was no longer an obstacle. However, these very conditions have produced a scenario where Hindi has become marginalized within the *Hindi* film industry.

This chapter is divided into three main sections, based on fieldwork conducted with screenwriters, writer-directors, directors, and journalists in Mumbai in August 2013, January 2014, and August 2014. First, I provide historical background on the multilingual nature of the Hindi film industry, including the long-standing presence of English. Then, I discuss how contemporary members of the film industry assess the relationship between English and Hindi within the industry and outline the impact, especially on screenwriting labor, of the growing reliance on English within the creative process. Finally, I examine how certain filmmakers deploy their linguistic skill in Hindi as a form of cultural capital and a mode of elaborating distinction within the film industry.

ENGLISH AS A LINGUA FRANCA IN THE HINDI FILM INDUSTRY

If I'm making a Hindi film, I'm a Tamilian, but my DOP is a Malayali, and my editor is from Gujarat, so our common language is English.
—SRIRAM RAGHAVAN, WRITER-DIRECTOR

When reflecting upon the linguistic history of the Hindi film industry, two features stand out: the relative insignificance of fluency in Hindi/Urdu as a prerequisite for acting, directing, or even writing; and the consistent presence of English as a language of trade discourse, commentary, and professional nomenclature. As mentioned previously, the industry emerged in multilingual Mumbai rather than the regions of northern or central India referred to as the Hindi "heartland" and drew personnel from all over the subcontinent and beyond. While standard histories of Indian cinema point out the diverse ethnic and linguistic backgrounds of actors and directors during the silent era, making special mention of how actors and actresses who could not speak Hindustani were displaced by stage actors and courtesans with the arrival of sound, the scenario is actually more complex.[5]

Even with the advent of sound in 1931, directors and actors came from diverse linguistic and national backgrounds. For example, Bombay Talkies, which left an important legacy in the postindependence Hindi film industry in terms of stars and directors, had many Germans in its employ. One of its directors, Franz Osten, who did not know any Hindi, directed some iconic Hindi films from this era. Throughout its history and continuing till the present, there have always been a few directors working in the industry who knew very little or no Hindi at all. This holds true for actresses as well. One of the top stars of the 1930s was the Australian-born Mary Evans, renamed "Fearless Nadia," who gained fame in action/stunt films despite her heavily accented Hindi. Presently, women from non-Hindi-speaking parts of India as well as from as far afield as Australia, Brazil, Canada, Great Britain, Sweden, and the United States continue to try their luck in Bollywood.[6]

Even in the scripting process, English has played an important role starting from the early sound era. During the 1930s, in studios like Bombay Talkies, scripts and dialogues were initially conceived of in English by the writer (who was referred to as a "scenario" writer), after which the dialogue writer translated them into Hindustani.[7] Since scripts were often written by individuals who were not proficient in Hindustani, the autonomous dialogue writer emerged as a staple of Hindi cinema. The credits for a script were broken down into three components: story, screenplay, and dialogue, with each element attributed to a different individual—a practice continuing into the present. As a result of the varying ethno-linguistic backgrounds of Bombay film personnel, writers who were fluent or had a facility in Urdu were in great demand as dialogue and lyric writers, since Persianized Urdu was a valorized register for song lyrics and dialogues.[8] Many well-known

Hindi/Urdu poets, playwrights, and novelists supported their literary endeavors by working in the Hindi film industry, and scholars have pointed out that after the partition of British India into India and Pakistan, whereby Urdu became the official language of Pakistan, the only site in India where Urdu was kept alive, and even flourished, was the Hindi film industry.[9]

In this multilingual context—Urdu writers, German directors, Bengali actors, Marathi singers, Parsi producers, and so on—it is not surprising that English emerged as a lingua franca for cultural producers based in a British colonial port city. While Hindi was (and remains) important as the language within the diegesis and that of consumption, English served (and continues) as the primary language of professional nomenclature and discourse about Hindi cinema and filmmaking. The English terms *director, producer, writer, actor,* and *film* are part of daily parlance within and outside the industry, rather than the Hindi equivalents *nirdeshak, nirmata, lekhak, abhineta,* and *chalchitra.* In contrast to films made in other Indian languages, the opening and closing credits for mainstream Hindi films have been in English since the 1930s. The Devanagari (Hindi) and Nasta'liq (Urdu) scripts make an appearance in a film's title, but only after the prominent appearance of the title first in Roman script. One reason is perhaps because Hindi films are the only ones to have been consistently distributed nationally since the 1930s and internationally since the 1940s.

The most prominent forms of journalistic, critical, and trade commentary about the Hindi film industry have been in English since the 1930s. Film reviews, interviews with stars, industry news, celebrity gossip, and trade reports are carried out in English-language periodicals, whether *Filmland, Filmindia,* or *Blitz* in the 1930s–1960s; *Filmfare, Trade Guide,* or *Screen* since the 1950s; or *Film Information* or *Stardust* since the 1970s. While there are several Hindi fanzines and newspapers that cover Hindi cinema, they are quite marginal in terms of their impact or readership within the industry. The main trade journals, *Trade Guide, Film Information,* and *Box Office India,* which carry box-office figures and report about the business of the film industry, are in English.

If English has always played a prominent role in the Hindi film industry, how is the contemporary moment distinctive? The most drastic difference is English's changed status and value relative to Hindi. While English has served as a necessary lingua franca throughout the industry's history, it is increasingly operating as a language of production, creativity, and decision making since the mid-2000s. This change has to do with key demographic shifts in the film industry: namely, the intensification of kinship networks whereby a significant number of leading actors, directors, and producers represent the second, third, or even fourth generation within the industry; and a larger number of creative personnel drawn from urban social elites whose formal schooling has been wholly in English. Since the turn of the millennium, as Hindi filmmaking became more lucrative and rationalized, taking on an aura of professionalism and respectability that it had not traditionally enjoyed, social elites and film industry progeny gravitated toward the film industry as a viable career path.[10] In the next section I discuss how these shifts are implicated in industry members' assessments of the state of Hindi within the film industry.

THE PRECARIOUS STATUS OF HINDI IN THE HINDI FILM INDUSTRY

During my fieldwork in Mumbai in 2013 and 2014, several observers and members of the Hindi film industry lamented that the knowledge of Hindi had become so abysmal that the language appeared to be in a precarious position within the industry. Anupama Chopra, a noted film critic and television host, stated bluntly during our conversation, "Hindi is a secondary language now." She relayed the travails of producing a Hindi version of her popular English-language weekly television show, *Front Row with Anupama Chopra*—a talk show that mixes film reviews, interviews with actors and directors about their upcoming releases, and group discussions about important issues or key trends within the industry. The challenge of producing the Hindi version, according to her, was that "no one thinks in Hindi here," especially the younger generation of actors, who, though quite voluble and articulate in English, were unable to express themselves in Hindi. Chopra recounted how since it was so difficult for many actors to speak entirely in Hindi, they frequently devolved into English. She noted how in an episode on the relationship between Bollywood and fashion, eight minutes had to be cut from a thirty-minute segment because of the inability of the guests to converse about the topic in Hindi. Chopra quipped, "We would all breathe a huge sigh of relief after we finished the Hindi version, and then sit back and think [referring to the English version], 'Now we can relax and have fun!'"

Social class, generation, and geography are the central reasons offered by industry observers for waning fluency in Hindi. The two main social groups identified as having a poor knowledge of Hindi are actors and directors who grew up within the film industry, nicknamed "star kids," and upper-middle-class residents of Mumbai, dubbed "South Bombay types."[11] What these groups have in common is limited formal education in Hindi as a result of going to elite English-medium schools in India or boarding schools abroad, as well as the absence of a Hindi-speaking milieu by virtue of growing up in an elite social world in Mumbai where the primary language is English. Ajay Brahmatmaj, the film editor for the Hindi-language *Dainik Jagran,* the most widely circulated newspaper in India, discussed how in the current generation of actors, those who are from Mumbai and especially from film families speak Hindi only when they are compelled to with their domestic labor and household staff, and hence their knowledge of Hindi is limited to a very simple register. He said (in Hindi), "Many of them say they practice their Hindi, but with whom? With their cook, driver, and vegetable vendor. Now, the conversations with such individuals will be limited in terms of the vocabulary, not more than one hundred to two hundred words. At the most it will be '*gaadi lao*' [bring the car], now '*gaadi lao*' is hardly Hindi!"[12] Screenwriter Kalpana Chadda, a native of Delhi, who started working in the film industry in the early 2000s and who had learned and spoke English only in school, described how colleagues and friends regard her as an anomaly for being comfortable in Hindi, asking her frequently, "Why do you speak in Hindi so much?"[13] She reflected, "Delhi is very Hindi, friends speak to each other in Hindi, but in Bombay it seems not to be appropriate to speak in Hindi and to date that's the joke about me."[14]

Chadda spoke at length about the challenges faced by screenwriters like herself who "think in Hindi" in an industry run by people who primarily "think in English." One particularly ironic manifestation is when she is hired to write a screenplay but not dialogue. Since a screenplay has to have dialogue, the screenwriter will put in "dummy" or placeholder dialogue, after which the dialogue writer takes over and crafts the speech in the film. Although she is instructed to write the screenplay in English, Chadda ends up writing her dummy dialogue in Hindi because of her facility with the language, but then has to translate them into English for the director, producer, and actors, even though the film will ultimately be in Hindi. Chadda said she felt like telling filmmakers, "Why don't you just keep this dialogue and throw it away and let the writer write something else because it is double work for me to make the dialogue into English."[15] She also mentioned that she was much less precise in English, but according to her, most directors and producers from Mumbai are unable to comprehend an entire screenplay in Hindi. She asserted, "They won't be able to listen to a script written completely in Hindi. They won't get it. When it is in English, they'll get the craft and say, 'Oh this scene is tight' because English lends itself to crispness. Hindi is very difficult for you to go crisp on it. And we can't use difficult words because everybody is not familiar. If I use good Hindi words, I'll write a crisp Hindi script, but I can't do that—I have to use colloquial and general words."[16]

Notice that Chadda mentions "listening" to rather than "reading" a script. The dominant convention in the film industry is to orally recount a script, and it is commonplace to hear actors assert in interviews that they decided to work in a particular film after "hearing the script." Key members of the production team gather to hear the writer or director relay the film's screenplay. These sessions, referred to as "narrations" in the industry, are undertaken for the purpose of pitching or having a project green-lighted as well as recruiting the cast and crew. Since a script is often judged on how well it is narrated, Chadda explained that the practice of narrating a script disadvantaged writers who had limited proficiency in English.

While Chadda related the difficulties writers face with producers and directors, others spoke of the challenges of working with actors who had limited Hindi skills. Kamlesh Pandey, president of the Film Writers Association, who has written the dialogue or screenplay for a number of prominent films starting in the late 1980s, was vociferous in his criticism of the state of writing and Hindi in particular. Pandey blamed urban, English-educated writers and industry insiders for the poor state of Hindi, and criticized the prevalent practice of having to write Hindi dialogues in Roman rather than Devanagari script because of the inability of many younger actors to read Hindi. Pandey complained, "Hindi has come to such a state that it has to be read in Roman, and hence I'm afraid the *lipi,* the script will soon become extinct. In cinema, *Devanagari lipi* [script] has more or less disappeared."[17] For those writers who specialize in writing dialogue in Hindi, either from the outset or adapting someone else's English dialogue, an actor's facility with the language has significant consequences for the writer's creative labor. For an individual who is fluent in Hindi, which is a phonetically based language and alphabet, having to write dialogues in Roman script involves more effort, especially since the screenplay of a Hindi film on average comprises about seventy-five to eighty scenes and tends to be dialoguecentric.[18]

Another impetus to transliterate Hindi into Roman script is connected to broader efforts to refashion the film industry into a professional, corporatized site with greater emphasis on planning, preproduction, and rationalization of the production process.[19] An important artifact of such planning is the "bound script," which has achieved a near totemic status within the film industry. The desire for a complete typed script with dialogue available in advance, supported by a younger generation of computer-literate screenwriters and assistant directors who have had some formal film training, has led to an increase in the use of screenwriting software such as Final Draft, which is an English-only application. Hence, even if actors can read Hindi, screenwriters who utilize such software have to write their dialogues in Roman script, and then may have to transcribe the dialogue separately into Devanagari for veteran actors who find it alienating to have to read Romanized Hindi. Chadda, who uses Final Draft, remarked, "It's so strange that we have a multibillion-dollar Hindi film industry, but we are slaves to English. We even write the Hindi word in English."[20]

Writers also related that they had to think harder about vocabulary and syntax when actors were not fluent in Hindi. Pandey complained that he was unable to be subtle in his dialogue writing since actors did not understand nuance or idioms specific to Hindi. Writer-director Sriram Raghavan mentioned that he had to keep in mind an actor's facility with Hindi when composing dialogues because good lines could ring false depending on the actor's ability to deliver them. Sameer Sharma, a writer-director who has written dialogues for films helmed by directors who knew little to no Hindi, related his frustration: "I think the sad part is that most actors today have a diction problem, so they don't really try, and there are directors who don't correct them because they themselves have a problem. That's very visible, and it's very irritating for somebody who knows the language, but they get away with it so they don't work hard."[21]

Writers thus feel they have to work harder to make it easier for actors to read and speak Hindi, rather than actors expending the effort to improve their language skills. This appears as another manifestation of the starcentric nature of the Hindi film industry. Ever since the decline of the studio system in the aftermath of World War II, the Hindi film industry is star oriented, star driven—and many would complain, star controlled. In the next section I discuss how language becomes critical to some filmmakers' attempts to redefine or challenge mainstream paradigms of filmmaking.

HINDI "INDIE"

From 2006 on, a number of films produced by A-list production companies have utilized local registers of Hindi that set them apart from earlier films.[22] With a few exceptions, these films forgo the use of major stars and are set in small towns or subaltern spaces of large cities. Screenwriter Anjum Rajabali commented that the generic Hindustani of earlier eras of filmmaking was disappearing and that in contrast to the past, when characters spoke in the same dialect and register regardless of region or social class, in contemporary films, "characters' language is rooted in the cultural milieu in which they exist—not just region-specific, but also area-specific, city-specific, and locality-specific."[23] Rajabali explained this shift in terms of a greater concern with authenticity and realism. Devika Bhagat, a writer-director trained at New York University's Tisch School of the Arts, asserted that it was not possible to have a uniformity of speech across an entire film when its characters represented a wide array of socioeconomic backgrounds. Discussing her directorial debut, Bhagat described the characters and their various milieus: "I have a boy who's from the Dharavi slums, he speaks in Mumbaiya tapori language. And then there is a middle-class IT professional who speaks in Hinglish, so for each character, the language is specific to their background, their region, their attributes, so that's why there cannot be a pure form of Hindi anymore."[24]

This quasi-ethnographic attention to linguistic detail reflects the tremendous concern of a newer generation of filmmakers with gesturing toward a form of realism in mainstream cinema. One way to index the "real" is through spoken words and dialogue. Even if the rest of the production design is in the realm of fantasy and spectacle, dialogue can mark the rootedness of a film. In many recent films, the setting is actually not integral to the narrative. For example, certain films that showcase a Delhi Punjabi vernacular could have been set anywhere in India, as Delhi was not crucial to their plots; they could have easily been set in Mumbai.

These films are anchored to a particular place not by the story but by the language and the register of the dialogue.

Language has become an important way to distinguish among films; it is being foregrounded not just in songs but also in dialogue and speech. Thus language, in terms of dialect, accent, slang, and proverbs, has become an important part of the mise-en-scène, akin to songs, action, locales, and sets. Dialogue has always been important in Hindi cinema, but the turn to the colloquial helps to "dress the dialogue" in a different way. Writers are less reliant on clever turns of phrase or memorable dialogue because mere showcasing of the vernacular is enough. Writers can demonstrate skill not by cleverly crafting witty or memorable dialogue but by merely sounding nonstandard and "rustic."

Industry professionals offered two main explanations for this turn to the vernacular. One was framed in terms of a backlash of sorts by filmmakers, who were mostly from the Hindi-speaking north and outsiders to both Mumbai and the industry, against the dominant paradigm of filmmaking in the late 1990s and early 2000s. Referring to filmmakers like Anurag Kashyap, who is heavily identified with gritty, violent, dark dramas frequently set in nonmetropolitan sites, writer-director Sriram Raghavan stated, "There was that big phase of the Yashraj and Karan Johar films, which were shot largely abroad. Anurag and that group made it even more specific about certain areas [in India] because it was a reaction to some of these big films—that there were too many of them and they were seeming fake."[25]

Director Tigmanshu Dhulia asserted that the artifice of films from this period was a result of Mumbai-bred filmmakers catering only to diasporic audiences: "Because films were being catered to the sensibility of the NRIs [nonresident Indians], the language became fairly easy, poetry was lost, subjects and story lines became very frivolous. Suddenly we stopped making rooted films, and because we were getting revenues from abroad, we stopped making films for Indians." Dhulia went on to describe how filmmakers who grew up in the Hindi film industry—the second- and third-generation professionals who began their careers in the 1990s—"had not seen India; they'd only seen Bombay."[26] Due to their limited experience of India, according to Dhulia, such filmmakers only made "films about films; they were creating characters out of *filmi* characters, because they had no experience of India, of life; they thought Bombay is India."[27]

Dhulia claimed that people coming from outside Mumbai played a significant role in transforming Hindi cinema and the film industry. In Dhulia's words, outsiders enabled cinema to "find geography." Referring to himself and a number of other filmmakers, Dhulia remarked, "We came with our experiences, and so we started making films about the characters we knew, about the region we knew, so that is why the change of character and of language; we became very area specific. Now films have a geography, whereas earlier films didn't have a geography at all."[28] Sameer Sharma pointed out how even if the "bosses"—those who control finance and distribution—are from Mumbai, many of the directors, such as Anurag Kashyap, are outsiders who are becoming producers themselves and thus are able to green-light or foster films that are set in nonurban or nonmetropolitan settings. With reference to his own directorial debut, *Luv Shuv Tey Chicken Khurana*, a quirky comedy produced by Kashyap and set in Punjab, which employed Hindi heavily laced with Punjabi expressions, idioms, and humor, Sharma explained that although Kashyap is not from Punjab, he was able to understand a script that was rooted in a small town milieu by virtue of not being from Mumbai. Sharma stated, "It's important that people who are actually from outside can influence the making of certain films, which may not be understood by a producer who is only from Bombay."[29]

Sharma's remarks illustrate how even filmmakers who self-identify as "outsiders" or as "indie" work very much within mainstream structures of finance, distribution, and exhibition. In fact, their use of Hindi can be seen as another way to assert and perform their "independence" from "Bollywood," so that their linguistic ability becomes an important form of cultural capital that allows them to distinguish themselves within the industry.[30] The overwhelmingly positive critical reception of such directors—including Dibakar Banerjee, Vishal Bharadwaj, Abhishek Chaubey, Tigmanshu Dhulia, and Anurag Kashyap—by the English-language media in India, mostly for their "authentic" portrayals of the "Hindi heartland," illustrates the success some filmmakers have had with an outsider or renegade image.

However, rather than indexing the "real" or "geography," the Hindi in such films circulates as an exotic parlance or a simulacrum of the Indian hinterlands within English-speaking cultural spheres. The widely divergent responses between English-language and Hindi-language media regarding Anurag Kashyap's *Gangs of Wasseypur* provide a case in point. Screened at Cannes in the Directors Fortnight in 2012, this tale about a long-running blood feud between the families of an outlaw and a corrupt politician in Bihar was widely celebrated in the international and Indian press for "redefining" Indian cinema and identified as a potential crossover success. Interestingly, some media analysts noticed that the Hindi press was quite underwhelmed with the film and pointed out that reviewers for Hindi newspapers dismissed the film's claims to authenticity and argued that it simply pandered to metropolitan stereotypes under the guise of realism.[31] With respect to the dialogue, one analyst pointed out, "The English-language media were fawning about precisely the sort of things the Hindi reviewers noticed as false, including the language with its extravagant crudity."[32] I contend that it is only as a result of English becoming the unmarked, naturalized language of production and discourse within the film industry that filmmakers are able to deploy Hindi as a self-consciously marked commodity.

The second reason for the turn to the colloquial has to do with changes in the political economy of the film industry. The fact that some filmmakers are able to utilize language in a way that would have been regarded in an earlier era of film-making as limiting or alienating one's audience has to do with changing structures of finance, production, distribution, and exhibition that have reshaped the Hindi film industry's audience imaginaries—issues I have explored in detail elsewhere.[33] For example, Tigmanshu Dhulia, referring to his 2012 film *Paan Singh Tomar*, a biopic about a celebrated and medaled Indian steeplechase runner who is forced by circumstances to become a bandit, stated, "The language was Bundelhi; it was not even Hindi and I was scared that . . . I thought the audience would not even understand the language, but they did! So now cinema has changed, and I think it has changed for the better."[34]

One of the biggest changes in the political economy of the Hindi film industry since the advent of multiplexes and corporate production and distribution companies is the diminished significance of the "universal hit"—films that do well all over India and across all demographics. This is due to the structural transformations in filmmaking caused by the entry of corporate production companies and multiplexes, which have altered ideas of commercial success in the industry. Multiplexes, with their high ticket rates, revenue-sharing arrangements, and financial transparency, have managed to transform even low to moderate audience attendance or ticket sales into a sign of success. The entry of the Indian organized industrial sector into film production and the ability of established producers to raise money from the Indian stock market have diminished the role of traditional territorial distributors, who were always perceived by filmmakers as averse to cinematic experimentation. Many corporate producers have ventured into both all-India and overseas distribution and possess a much higher threshold for financial risk. These corporate distributors can either rely on profits from some territories to offset losses from others or profit from their investment by reselling distribution rights to individual territorial distributors. A universal hit is simply not as necessary within this new financing and distribution scenario. Thus there is less anxiety on the part of the financing side of the industry if a film appears limited in its appeal.

Sameer Sharma asserted that filmmakers now have a greater opportunity to express their individual style: "Previously you had to cut across to a whole section of the audience, and your way of making was dictated by the fact that a film should work both in New York and in Patna. But today, it's become more flexible. I think people have gotten more confident that you don't have reach out to everybody."[35] Sharma's statements illustrate how the reduced value of the universal hit within the industry has expanded the criteria of success to the benefit of filmmakers. While the previous structure of the industry rewarded   in terms of both economic and symbolic capital—only filmmakers who strived for universal hits, the contemporary structure enables those filmmakers who are unable to achieve or are unconcerned with broad appeal to also raise money and earn prestige and status within the industry.

CONCLUSION

Filmmakers' prestige and status is critically connected to the ability to circulate within elite social spheres, such as international film festivals, and to garner praise from the English-language press in India and abroad, as seen in the divergent responses to *Gangs of Wasseypur*. Not all "outsiders" or primary Hindi speakers from northern India are able to leverage their linguistic skills in the same manner as the filmmakers mentioned in this essay. Linguistic skill or fluency in Hindi serves as a form of capital only for those who are also fluent in English—that is, filmmakers like Anurag Kashyap, who are internationally celebrated in prestigious film festivals, such as Cannes and Toronto, and garner a great deal of media and critical attention within India. Those film professionals who know only Hindi, with limited proficiency in English, are condemned to remain assistants (to a variety of department heads), dialogue writers for hire, or language tutors, and are frequently marginalized in the social networks that provide a chance at upward mobility in the industry. Therefore, it appears that while not knowing Hindi is not much of a setback or obstacle to participating in the Hindi film industry, not knowing English can be a problem.[36]

The Hindi film industry has always been and had to be self-conscious and reflexive about language because of its commercial box-office orientation. In the early years of the film industry, language choice was thought about in terms of intelligibility and access to the largest market. Here I have argued that filmmakers consciously consider code choice as a way of marking a film as distinct within a crowded marketplace and of garnering symbolic capital within the film industry. Both are choices born of commercial considerations, but they speak to different moments and transformations in the political economy of the Hindi film industry. Thus, language/code choice helps make visible, or perhaps more appropriately, audible, the changing political economy of the film industry, as well as the changing social relations within it.

NOTES

1. Ananya Vajpeyi, "Hindi, Hinglish: Head to Head," *World Policy Journal* 29 (Summer 2012).

2. *Hindi, Urdu,* and *Hindustani* are not self-evident and neutral terms, but rather index a long, complex history starting from colonialism when British administrators along with language activists drew boundaries between Hindi and Urdu. At the level of colloquial speech, Hindi and Urdu are mutually intelligible and interchangeable.

3. Tejaswini Ganti, "Mumbai vs. Bollywood: The Hindi Film Industry and the Politics of Cultural Heritage in Contemporary India," in *Global Bollywood,* edited by Anandam P. Kavoori and Aswin Punathambekar (New York: New York University Press, 2008); Arlene Davila, *Latinos Inc.* (Berkeley: University of California Press, 2001); Lucile Davier, "The Paradoxical Invisibility of Translation in the Highly Multilingual Context of News Agencies," *Global Media and Communication* 10.1 (2014); Courtney Brannon Donoghue, "Sony and Local-Language Productions: Conglomerate Hollywood's Strategy of Flexible Localization for the Global Film Market," *Cinema Journal* 53.4 (2014); Judith Irvine, "When Talk Isn't Cheap: Language and Political Economy," *American Ethnologist* 16.2 (1988).

4. Tejaswini Ganti, *Producing Bollywood: Inside the Contemporary Hindi Film Industry* (Durham, NC: Duke University Press, 2012).

5. Eric Barnouw and S. Krishnaswamy, *Indian Film* (New York: Oxford University Press, 1980); B. D. Garga, *So Many Cinemas: The Motion Picture in India* (Mumbai: Eminence Designs, 1996).

6. Such actresses are usually dubbed over by voice artists fluent in Hindi.

7. Debashree Mukherjee, "Bombay Modern: A History of Film Production in Late Colonial Bombay 1930–1948," (PhD diss., New York University, 2015).

8. Ibid.

9. Sumita Chakravarty, *National Identity in Indian Popular Cinema 1947–1987* (Austin: University of Texas Press, 1993); Mukul Kesavan, "Urdu, Awadh and the Tawaif: The Islamicate Roots of Hindi Cinema," in *Forging Identities: Gender, Communities and the State,* ed. Zoya Hasan (New Delhi: Kali for Women, 1994).

10. For a more in-depth discussion of the social and structural transformations that have beset the industry since the late 1990s, see Ganti, *Producing Bollywood.*

11. "South Bombay" refers to the oldest and most expensive parts of the city, often synonymous with "old money" and an Anglicized elite, and also happens to be the farthest geographically from the northern and western suburbs that comprise the heart of the film industry.

12. Interview with Ajay Brahmatmaj, Mumbai, August 7, 2014.

13. I have assigned a pseudonym as she is still trying to establish herself within the industry and did not want her frank remarks attributed to her.

14. Interview with Kalpana Chadda, Mumbai, August 2, 2014.

15. Ibid.

16. Ibid.

17. Interview with Kamlesh Pandey, Mumbai, August 28, 2013.

18. The Hindi alphabet contains fourteen vowels, forty-one consonants, and fourteen conjunct consonants—a total of sixty-nine characters, conveying a much wider phonetic range than the twenty-six-character Roman alphabet.

19. See Ganti, *Producing Bollywood*; and Tejaswini Ganti, "Sentiments of Disdain and Practices of Distinction: Boundary-Work, Subjectivity, and Value in the Hindi Film Industry," *Anthropological Quarterly* 85.1 (2012).

20. Interview with Kalpana Chadda, Mumbai, August 2, 2014.

21. Interview with Sameer Sharma, Mumbai, September 2, 2013.

22. *Omkara* (2006), *Ishqiya* (2010), *Band Baaja Baraat* (2010), *Paan Singh Tomar* (2010), *Vicky Donor* (2012), *or Gangs of Wasseypur* (2012)

23. Anjum Rajabali, personal communication, March 27, 2014.

24. Interview with Devika Bhagat, Mumbai, August 29, 2013.

25. Interview with Sriram Raghavan, Mumbai, August 28, 2013.

26. Interview with Tigmanshu Dhulia, Mumbai, January 25, 2014.

27. Ibid.

28. Ibid.

29. Interview with Sameer Sharma, Mumbai, September 2, 2013.

30. Pierre Bourdieu, *Distinction* (Cambridge, MA: Harvard University Press, 1984).

31. Anand Vardhan, "A Landmark Departure," *The Hoot,* July 5, 2012, www.thehoot.org; Shougat Dasgupta, "Art or Artifice," *Tehelka,* January 21, 2012, www.tehelka.com.

32. Dasgupta, "Art or Artifice."

33. Ganti, *Producing Bollywood.*

34. Interview with Tigmanshu Dhulia, Mumbai, January 25, 2014.

35. Interview with Sameer Sharma, Mumbai, September 2, 2013.

36. Knowledge of English is more important for above-the-line workers than those below the line.

10

Complex Labor Relations in Latin American Television Industries

Juan Piñón

The transformation of the Latin American television industry clearly exposes the profound impact of neoliberal policies throughout the region, including the multiplication of distribution windows, trends toward media concentration, and changes in the modalities by which global media corporations are rooting in local and national television industries. Miller and Leger argue that runaway productions are the means by which Hollywood outsources production to developing countries to realize cost advantages via flexible labor, low wages, low prices, tax incentives, cheap accommodations, and access to material, cultural, and symbolic infrastructure, all the while maintaining tight central administrative and financial control.[1] This New International Division of Cultural Labor (NICL) allows global corporations to expand their transnational presence; however, capital accumulation and profit revenues stay close to the conglomerates' homes. Given this new media industrial order, Hesmondhalgh argues that media conglomerates acting as large bureaucracies increasingly rely on professionals from small production houses to provide creativity and innovation.[2]

Given this scenario, labor conventions in Latin American television are changing dramatically. The incursion of global media conglomerates in local markets across the region has caused unanticipated alliances with local independent production houses, or "indies," which have traditionally been subject to the disproportionate power of the major national television networks in their respective countries. This combination of circumstances has led to disparate outcomes. On the one hand, the presence of global conglomerates has problematically spurred the region's further incorporation into global capitalism, allowing penetration of Western media in countries where they were formerly confronted by institutional, linguistic, and cultural barriers tied to dynamics of local television consumption. On the other hand, these circumstances present an opportunity for indies to produce different kinds of television projects for national and regional markets, bypassing the long-standing monopoly of national television networks.

The fact that there are just a few indies in each domestic market with the capacity to produce for television networks with national distribution is symptomatic of their precarious status, and exposes their vulnerable position within an industry dominated by national or multinational media conglomerates.[3] Following Miller's reasoning, "Cultural labor incarnates this latter-day loss of life-long employment and relative income security among the Global North's industrial proletarian and professional-managerial classes";[4] accordingly, the very existence of indies relies on access to media professionals obeying the dynamics of flexible labor, nonunion status, and lack of long-term health or retirement benefits, which are crucial to the sustainability of their business models. These labor conditions are at the core of what Curtin and Sanson describe as "precarious livelihoods," which are "indicative of a new world order of social and economic instability."[5]

I argue that there is a fundamental difference among the production dynamics of film and television in transnational settings that are largely shaped by the relation with local/national audiences. So it comes as no surprise that some authors in this volume, such as Szczepanik in the case of transnational ventures with television conglomerates in the Czech Republic[6] or Keane in the case of television in China,[7] recognize the impact of the NICL and its insidious effects on creative labor and local economies and also complicate the landscape, avoiding a causal and unidirectional effect of these global processes. For instance, in Latin America, where Hollywood cinema overwhelmingly dominates the box office in every domestic market, a different scenario appears in television, where the programming of national/regional networks overwhelmingly dominates prime time and achieves high ratings because of the cultural proximity of their products.[8] As a result, while multinationals still rely on the advantageous agreements they receive in national markets and the flexible labor their productions require, these global television corporations also need indies and local professionals, who become valuable assets, albeit temporarily, helping to connect their content with local audiences.[9]

So indies of different sizes with diverse financial and technical infrastructures now participate in projects ranging from low-budget documentaries and journalism to midbudget games and reality shows to the most expensive fictional series, telenovelas, and movies. Indies' status across the region has grown because they can provide professional staff and talent to produce innovative narratives along with linguistic and cultural input that transnational corporations need to penetrate national and regional markets. In spite of these new opportunities for indie producers, it's not clear that these new opportunities have as yet had a positive effect on wages and working conditions.[10]

A BRIEF OVERVIEW OF THE LATIN AMERICAN
TELEVISION INDUSTRY

Throughout Latin America since the 1950s, television has been the primary audio-visual medium. During this decade, the growth of a national television institution was central to the process of modernization and nation building across the region.[11] Simultaneously, U.S.[12] technologies and the commercial model of broadcasting[13] were important engines for the growth of the medium across the region; Sinclair and Straubhaar have described this process as an interdependent relationship in which U.S. economic, commercial, and technological interests intertwined with the interests of national economic and political elites.[14] Within this pattern, national markets developed in relatively distinctive ways.[15] The development of Latin American television was shaped by specific conditions that include market size (population and purchasing power), market structure (monopoly, oligopoly, and competition), broadcasting regulations (private-commercial, state-owned, or hybrid), social and political instability (military coups, social movements, revolutions, and repression), and the visibility and impact of previously established cultural flows across the region, particularly radio and film.

As for content, U.S. programming became a television staple across Latin America during the early years, but national productions took the lead in countries where producers were able to achieve comparable production values.[16] Prime-time television in major markets, such as Mexico and Brazil, has been largely monopolized by national networks that produced most of their programming in-house. These not only dominated their national markets, they also became leading exporters, and their studios became the primary employers of the television labor force in their domestic markets. In smaller markets with lower production capacities, prime time has been populated with content coming from these major regional producers rather than U.S. studios, due largely to audience preferences for culturally proximate programming.[17]

In major markets in Latin America, the leading networks were free to produce and broadcast their own content with little regulatory oversight. They built impressive studio facilities and dominated distribution, thereby limiting the possibilities for independent producers. However, the development of the industry across the region did not follow the same patterns. In Mexico, Brazil, and Venezuela, hegemonic networks dominated domestic markets from the very beginning; in contrast, in Argentina, Chile, and Peru, TV production was disrupted or fragmented as a result of dramatic political changes brought about by military coups in the 1970s and authoritarian forms of government throughout the 1980s and the 1990s.[18] Colombia, which was similarly affected by political uncertainties, developed a hybrid television model wherein networks were state-owned but the content was largely produced by private production companies (*programadoras*).[19] In the long run, certain levels of media atomization, with an array of independent production entities and market competition, boosted creativity and stylistic diversity in these countries.[20]

During the 1990s, the implementation of media policies of privatization, deregulation, and liberalization coupled with new technological scenarios triggered the emergence of new windows of delivery through broadcasting, cable, satellite, and the Internet. Deregulation also encouraged a trend toward vertical and horizontal integration that enhanced the muscle of the already powerful national networks, allowing them to build alliances and expand into new sectors.[21] However, new national television networks have been launched in parallel, establishing new competitors that are scrambling to secure talent and content to ensure their economic survival. This scenario has been complicated by the slow but steady increase in the presence of transnational networks through cable and satellite television. An increasing localization effort made by global conglomerates (Comcast/NBC-U, 21st Century Fox, Disney/ABC, Sony, Viacom, and TimeWarner/HBO) has resulted in them tailoring programming that could be successful locally in a Latin American market, as well as luring audiences in the U.S. Hispanic market and other countries in the region. Independent producers have thus become a key resource within specific national markets to achieve a successful presence locally and to reach a larger, regional market. This has produced a struggle for talent in which dominant national television networks have tightened their grip, leading to lawsuits against actors and producers working with competing networks.[22] Therefore, global conglomerates, such as Sony, 21st Century Fox, and Comcast/NBC-U, have had to look elsewhere for professional teams and talent, increasingly establishing alliances, albeit temporary ones, with indies that house professional labor and talent, through joint ventures, coproduction, or takeovers.

INDEPENDENTS IN THE CONTEMPORARY
LANDSCAPE OF TELEVISION INDUSTRIES

The Ibero-American Observatory of Television Fiction (Obitel) reports that in 2013, there were forty-eight national television broadcasting networks in seven of the most important Latin American markets.[23] Despite this seeming diversity, the domination of these national markets still falls in the hands of a few corporations. Out of the forty-eight networks, only twelve play a prominent role in these seven major markets. In most cases, two networks hold more than 90 percent of the national audience share.[24] There is a correlation between these networks' prominent market position and their capability to produce their own prime-time content, in particular fictional programming. Big-budget projects such as telenovelas are mostly produced in-house by these networks, but in today's competitive environment these networks increasingly hire indies to produce series and miniseries that require innovative approaches.

The pressure to innovate derives from the fact that the multinationals are making use of cable and satellite services to gain a foothold in national markets. By 2013, 55 percent of Latin American households had access to these new services, and in some key markets, such as Argentina, more than 80 percent of households had access. These changes are reflected in ratings as well. Latin American Multichannel Advertising Council (LAMAC) reports that broadcast TV audience share fell from 86 percent in 2005 to 70 percent in 2014, while pay TV audience share rose from 14 to 30 percent in the same period.[25] Moreover, the pay TV audience is generally more affluent and therefore more desirable to ad-based and subscription television companies. Given this media landscape, transnational television networks are increasingly making investments to localize programming with the aid of local indie producers.

The new battle to effectively capture "desirable commercial audiences" in a newly populated industrial scenario brought about innovation but also the rehashing and remaking of "proven ideas and formulas" to successfully appeal to national and transnational audiences. In the case of indies working for the television industry, their size, budget, and production capacities are reflected in the kind of television programming they can offer their clients. In today's television landscape, there is great demand for documentaries, global formats (particularly reality TV), and fictional formats (particularly series), which range from small- to large-scale productions.

Despite the growing number of independent production houses, most have a short life span, and very few produce for the national television networks that can reach mass audiences. "Here, house productions last very few years," acknowledged an executive producer of Laberinto Producciones in Colombia.[26] While his production company is twenty years old, his assertion underscores the rarity of its position. In a similar statement, an executive producer from Argos Communication, Mexico, states that most transnational companies looking to produce a telenovela would have to select from only a few production houses: "Anybody who pretends to have strong presence in Mexico by producing more than a hundred episodes is going to face complications. In Mexico only we can do that."[27] Similarly, an artistic director from Del Barrio Producciones in Perú recognizes that "there are really few production houses that have the economic means to produce at that level."[28] These assertions reveal the challenges these production houses face in the context of their structural industrial relationship with the gatekeepers of distribution: the television networks. A handful of networks have the power to decide what gets produced and distributed nationally and, ultimately, internationally. National TV networks set the terms in contract negotiations, generally offering one of three options: they offer a flat producer's fee and retain the copyright; they forge a coproduction agreement based on the investments of the respective partners, with each retaining distribution rights for specific territories; or they agree to broadcast a program that is fully financed by the independent production house, which retains the copyright. In spite of these three options, most indies can't risk producing their own content because a single failure would likely bankrupt the company. Most commonly, an indie producer will pitch an idea to the networks. If the network is interested, it offers the first option and the producer accepts, reasoning that there will be a secure flow of income to keep the studio staff employed. When dealing with successful producers, networks commonly offer "exclusive" conditions through "volume content agreements," signing the producer for a number of projects. In other cases, a network will sign an agreement with a successful producer that gives it a "first look" at all new projects. Such agreements allow the network access to top material and give it the option to buy a project and shelve it for an indefinite period so that it doesn't fall into the hands of a competitor.

GENRE AND FORMATS DIVISION OF LABOR

The key role indies play at local, national, or transnational levels results from their flexible accommodation to television networks' needs. The networks' requirements matched with the capacity and infrastructure of local indies largely define the kind of genre and television formats that indies can afford to produce. Channels like Discovery or NatGeo have employed smaller indie houses to produce television formats that do not require large numbers of employees. Documentaries, docureality, and journalism have become an important source of content production for indies, as they permit cheaper formats and shorter time commitments. At the same time, these productions represent spaces for innovation and creativity by the producers and scheduling flexibility for the networks.

Fictional programming, in contrast, requires major commitments from both network and producer, so larger indies, some with international reputations, tend to prevail in this genre. Fictional programming is costly, requires larger infrastructure, and quite crucially, depends on access to top-line talent. This is especially true with telenovelas, which usually involve the production of around one hundred episodes. By contrast, series and miniseries provide a more secure space for indies for a couple of reasons: economically, they are shorter projects that involve less risk and demand for resources; creatively, they offer scope for innovation that telenovelas rarely offer. While series have fewer episodes than telenovelas, the fact that they continue through different seasons can ensure the economic well-being of the indie and its employees for several years. For networks, in contrast, telenovelas help them make optimal and daily use of their studio infrastructure and human resources. Keeping larger projects like telenovelas in-house allows the promotion of network talent and the full exploitation of commercial opportunities.

THE ASYMMETRICAL RELATIONSHIP BETWEEN INDIE
HOUSES AND TELEVISION NETWORKS

Even though independents provide creative possibilities free from the constraints of network in-house productions, most still lack the economic, technological, and labor capacity to produce their own content without the financial backing of a television network or a major sponsor. An executive producer from Blind Spot, Mexico, describes this model as one of "interdependency."[29] Even in cases where a production house has the means to produce its own content, the executive producer argues, "they still depend on having clients who want to buy this specific content." In some way, the producer from Blind Spot is subtly recognizing its condition of *dependency* on clients and television networks.

Argos is an interesting example of the challenges faced by indie producers, even though it is one of the most important indie houses in the large television market of Mexico. Its prestige as a leading producer of "quality fiction for TV" was achieved initially when Argos worked for TV Azteca (1995–2000) and produced some of the most innovative telenovelas from that decade. Ultimately a battle over distribution rights led TV Azteca to part ways with the indie in 2000.[30] That year Argos reached an agreement with Telemundo to produce 1,200 hours of fictional programming, but in this case Argos used its leverage to secure a share of distribution rights in international markets.[31] A screenwriter working with the Argos team recalls that Telemundo was willing to make concessions so long as Argos would shape its production to accommodate a specific U.S. Latino demographic as well as Mexican audiences.[32] Argos worked exclusively for Telemundo until 2007, then with TV Azteca again until 2010, when it struck a production agreement with Cadena Tres, a rising new network targeting upscale audiences.[33] Argos was encouraged to innovate as a way to enhance Cadena Tres's profile. As one Argos writer described it, "I was expressly asked to be polemical and controversial with a new project called *Las Aparicio*. It was delightful to have almost total freedom."[34] Seeking to distinguish itself from the dominant networks, Televisa and TV Azteca, Cadena Tres "had nothing to lose and too much to gain." However, the precarious positon of independents is interestingly exemplified by Argos's executive producer when he talks about its relation with Cadena Tres. He remembers that the indie, challenged by the economic crisis of the time, proposed a new business model: "First, Cadena Tres provides part of the cost while Argos provides an in-kind contribution *[pago por especie]* and some economic investment, and then both look for a third partner."[35] Argos invited Colombia's Caracol TV as a third partner, but the producer recalls that "when two television networks got together [Cadena Tres and Caracol TV], they asked themselves, what do we need Argos for?" So TV Caracol and Cadena Tres moved along on a new production agreement, leaving Argos behind.

Increasingly, there is a great deal of transnational deal-making between networks and independent production houses, much of it motivated by the desire to attract audiences in multiple markets. The key role of Argos is best exemplified by the indies' collaboration in Telemundo's *La reina del sur* in 2011, a coproduction that included RTI (Colombia) and Antena 3 (Spain). *La reina del sur* featured a transnational flow of characters with a drug trafficking narrative that was filmed in Bogota, Mexico City, Miami, and Melilla, Spain, with production teams in each location, a strategy I call "reglocalization," based on a "network cities system of production."[36] *La reina del sur* proved to be one of the most successful telenovelas in recent memory for Telemundo. Later, *El señor de los cielos* (2013), a new coproduction of Telemundo with Colombia's Caracol TV and the collaboration of Argos, became the second most popular production in Telemundo's history, only surpassed by *La reina*. That telenovela earned an Emmy in 2014[37] and propelled a new collaboration between Telemundo and Argos to produce new successful seasons of *El señor de los cielos 2* (2014), 3 (2015), and 4 (forthcoming), but this time without Caracol TV. This series of successes set the stage for a new programming/production strategy that Telemundo has called "super series."

The new set of corporate relationships that localized transnational ventures producing Spanish-language fictional programming is best exemplified by HBO's incursion into Mexico in partnership with Argos and by Sony's into Colombia in partnership with Laberinto Producciones. After prior experiences in Argentina and Brazil, HBO in 2007 announced its strategic partnership with Argos to produce *Capadocia* (2008) for Mexican and regional markets.[38] By 2014, HBO had experience producing with indies across the region, with eighteen television series produced in Argentina, Brazil, Chile, Mexico, and Uruguay. While working for HBO on *Capadocia,* one screenwriter remembers that she had a lot of creative freedom, which allowed the inclusion of "a lot of things that were vox populi, but nobody expected to see on television, not even on cable."[39] At the same time, "the expectation was to have an international product with high production values, with high-quality scripts." Because of these expectations, "the budget and investment of the company were considerably higher," and she added, "they paid us very well."[40] She recognizes that HBO supervised the project but never really interfered in creative decisions or practiced any kind of censorship.

Sony's presence in the Colombian television market can be exemplified by the production of *Los caballeros las prefieren brutas* with indie producer Laberinto Producciones.[41] Sony's partnership with the Colombian indie seems to be similar to HBO's and Argos's in Mexico, as described by an executive producer from Laberinto Producciones. Sony read the scripts and supervised the project but did not interfere too much with creative decisions. The producer explains, "For Sony it was an experiment that had its own risks, and they tried to understand how it works from a different creative point of view. They saw that some things function differently in Latin America, and they were open to that."[42]

In contrast, argues the Colombian producer, when a national network deals with an indie, it tries to interfere as much as possible in creative decisions to ensure that the product meets the network's goals. For instance, some of the most sensitive decisions in which networks intervene are in casting, to promote their own talent, followed by interfering in narrative strategies to please clients and their target audience. For example, an artistic director from Del Barrio Producciones in Peru argues that "sometimes we approach the network to pitch a story, and we want to make it with specific leading talent. Sometimes the channel buys the story but objects to the leading talent, and we need to change it."[43]

LABOR STRUGGLES, ACCOMMODATIONS, AND STRATEGIES OF SURVIVAL

Creative professionals face an array of challenges in their mostly unstable work settings across the region. These involve a lack of steady jobs and an absence of work benefits such as health insurance, retirement funds, paid vacations, and maternity leave. Most workers are nonunionized, and their employers are themselves subordinate to the power of national networks and multinational conglomerates. Both workers and management sense the precariousness of their situation. Their only leverage resides in the growing demand for content and the fierce competition for talent. Given that, the relationship between these rather small business entities and their creative labor is shaped by complex and intertwined conditions of professionalism, emotional attachment, creative styles, and in many cases "family"-style ties and relationships.

There are several sizes and modalities of production indies bring to the audiovisual realm. Many houses produce advertising and corporate and institutional content as a way to maintain a healthy income. They also keep their payrolls trim, commonly anchored by three to ten permanent office employees and a network of freelance creatives. Indies typically rely on the prestige and connections of particular professionals, mostly the producers themselves. So, while a company might be initially founded by a famous actor, director, writer, producer, or venture capitalist, most commonly its ongoing operations are led by a producer who is the owner, co-owner, or CEO of the company.

While varying in size, indies nevertheless tend to have similar staffing patterns. They routinely hire administrative personnel for the office, including accountants, administrators, secretaries, and office assistants. In larger companies, especially those producing fictional programming, there is also a second group of permanent employees, mostly technicians and manual laborers. In some cases, there is an editor on staff and a few other below-the-line professionals who enjoy permanent contracts and legal benefits such as health benefits, retirement funds, vacations, and compensation in case of a layoff. Yet they employ mostly a nonunionized workforce.

When launching a particular project, the company hires above-the-line creative professionals on temporary contracts at higher wages but with no legal benefits. These professionals are nonunionized, and although many are paid quite well, their work stints are unpredictable, punctuated by regular periods of unemployment without benefits. These professionals include writers, directors, actors, photographers, casting experts, art and costume designers, and many others. They constitute a floating labor force that offers its services either to independent producers or to fill the needs of network in-house production teams on particular projects. However, there are some working conditions that vary by country. In Mexico, freelance laborers take care of their individual health expenses and save for retirement. In Uruguay, individuals are hired through a personnel company that provides benefits, while in Colombia workers have benefits via payroll.

In terms of stability, freelancers are in the most vulnerable position, always pursuing the next gig by offering their services to multiple clients in different audiovisual sectors. At the same time, some workers embrace the flexibility and freedom of being able to change jobs and negotiate working conditions. An executive producer from the Uruguayan indie house Microtime argues, "There are professionals who prefer a freelance status because that allows them to manage their lives. They take vacations when they want. They do not want to ask permission from their boss, producer, and that kind of flexibility works very well for them."[44] At the same time, this kind of freedom comes with a downside: according to an Argos screenwriter, "I cannot plan my life more than two or three months in advance. If I have earned money from a project, I need to save and take care until I find the next one."[45] Interviewees explained that forging a good professional reputation is essential to keeping themselves in the labor force. Intelligence, talent, technical and artistic abilities, and work ethic are considered to be essential elements for survival. Work continuity and stability are linked to gaining the producers' trust.

Interestingly, the small number of highly visible indie productions and their small size tend to create tight relationships within professional circles. Work relations are permeated with emotional ties and a sense of common artistic purpose. Some executive producers from indie houses refer to their permanent staff members and regular freelancers as family, saying they want to take care of professionals who have worked with them for a long time by offering a sense of stability. An artistic director from Del Barrio says it's "because we know that these workers have families, and they have worked for us too many years. So, yes, there is an emotional element."[46] Thus, just as emotional and pecuniary relations are intertwined, so too is the artistic sensibility that permeates some of the indie shops. This is often described as a common outlook on how television should be made, a shared understanding in the realm of either aesthetics or ideology. As opposed to the conventions of in-house network productions, these creative teams believe that indie shops are the perfect space to make something different. The professional profiles of the leading indie producers seem to permeate the institutional culture of their production houses, creating personal bonds around common artistic goals, including innovation and brand distinctiveness that set them apart from the dominant network studios.

CONCLUSION

The new media landscape, with its myriad windows of video distribution and the changes brought about by digital conversion, appears to offer new opportunities to regional indie producers. It remains to be seen, however, if these opportunities can be translated into real improvements in labor conditions. There are already urgent questions about low pay and unstable labor conditions prevalent in the region.

Moreover, the transformation of the media landscape as a result of larger structural processes offers a complex industrial scenario in which the integration of the region into global capitalism leads to battles between national and transnational corporations. In this scenario, different entities are taking advantage of the structural conditions and flexible labor of indie producers. A visible element that underscores the differences among national television industries has been the nature and role of indie productions within these national markets. However, in spite of these differences, the indie production sphere first emerged in relation to powerful national television networks. Those relations have recently been challenged by the emergence of a new generation of "indies" wholly owned by large conglomerates or independently owned but closely related to them. The presence of transnational companies now competing with national networks or collaborating with them offers opportunities to professionals, but at the same time they are competing in an industrial space that would otherwise have been occupied by local companies. Fox-Telecolombia (21st Century Fox), Teleset (Sony), RTI (NBC), Cuatro Cabezas (Eye-Works), Endemol, Zodiak (Di Agostini), and FremantleMedia are striking "volume agreements" with television networks that allow them continuity in production but also show the large professional and financial capabilities of these "indies."

Beyond these new transnational indies, national and local entities are struggling to survive by deploying a variety of strategies. Their existence and roles go far beyond the realm of television industries, offering a diversity of services to different companies and producing a variety of programming, including films, documentaries, and corporate or educational videos. Consequently, they need to be flexible and scale their workforce to the shifting demands of their clients. As described by the executive producer from Blind Spot, producers need to have the capacity to bring the right people to a specific project, but they also need to have the economic resources to deliver. Prestige, capacity of delivery, and proven success are required elements in this equation. Success in delivery defines some level of continuity for these indies, while failure may lead to their demise.

Similarly, professionals working for indies offer their services to an array of potential clients, opening doors for possible future projects. To lessen the anxieties of job uncertainty, professionals actively work at networking and diversifying their skills. Some of the professionals revealed that they combine short-term and long-term strategies to survive. As the artistic director from Del Barrio Producciones explains, working for advertisers pays well, while producing television series is not as profitable; however, waiting for a paycheck from an advertising firm takes several months, while working for television offers a monthly paycheck.

The defining feature of independent production houses is that they are separate from the corporations that own the means of content distribution: the television networks. This definition is also at the center of their vulnerability, which has been reframed by professionals as a space of opportunity. While lacking the stability of permanent jobs, these professionals are motivated by notions of innovation and creativity as well as specific ideological convictions and aesthetic commitments. They believe that talent and skill can create success, while their emphasis upon gaining the trust of producers is a prevailing notion that fits into a market-oriented economic approach which requires the *illusion* of free competition. Within this ideological framework, this free-floating army of professionals seems to conceive of unionized labor and hiring quotas as constraints upon the very specific creative needs of particular projects. The lack of permanent job status is also reinterpreted as a lifestyle choice representing agency and freedom. Following Bourdieu's explanation of the dynamics of the field of cultural production, these professionals take innovation, socially–oriented narratives, and quality production as their reasons for working for indies as an assumed restricted space within the larger field of television production.[47] Paradoxically, the precarious conditions of this sector seem to be precisely the ideological engine that supports professionals' imagined conditions of freedom, creativity, and innovation.

NOTES

1. Toby Miller and Marie C. Leger, "Runaway Production, Runaway Consumption, Runaway Citizenship: The New International Division of Cultural Labor," *Emergences* 11.1 (2001): 89–115.

2. David Hesmondhalgh, *Cultural Industries,* 2d ed. (Los Angeles, CA: Sage, 2006).

3. In the last five years there has been a reformulation of telecommunication laws in the main domestic markets across the region with respect to quotas on the distribution of national and independently produced content with economic incentives for independent productions; however, the results of such legislation are uneven.

4. Toby Miller, chapter 2 in this volume.

5. Michael Curtin and Kevin Sanson, chapter 1 in this volume.

6. Petr Szczepanik, chapter 7 in this volume.

7. Michael Keane, chapter 16 in this volume.

8. Joseph Straubhaar, "Beyond Media Imperialism: Asymmetrical Interdependency and Cultural Proximity," *Critical Studies in Mass Communication* 8 (1991): 39–59.

9. Among the most visible indies are Argos, Adicta Films, El Mall, Lemon, and Canana Film, Blind Spot in Mexico; RTI, Teleset, Vista Producciones, FoxTelecolombia, Laberinto Producciones, BETV in Colombia; Cuatro Cabezas, Underground, Ideas del Sur, RGB, Chris Morena, Pol-ka, and Endemol in Argentina; Del Barrio Producciones, Imizu, Teatro Libre, and Sol Entertainment Producciones in Perú; and Bueno Puerto Producciones, Valcine Producciones, Wood Producciones, and My Friend Entertainment Producciones in Chile. Conspiração Filmes, HBO O2 Filmes, and Mixer Brazil represent the most visible examples of a much larger group of indies.

10. The recognition of the Latin American television context is the product of years of research as part of the Ibero-American Observatory of Television Fiction (Obitel); but this chapter is based on ethnographic work done at NATPE in summer 2012, and a handful of interviews done in Fall 2014 with high executives and above-the-line creative personnel from independent production houses: Blind Spot and Argos (Mexico), Laberinto Producciones (Colombia), Del Barrio Producciones (Peru), and MicroTime (Uruguay). The pool of interviewees from independent production houses is composed of six top executives. Their shared characteristics are active involvement in the production of television programming for television networks in their countries as well as involvement in coproduction or commissioned productions, particularly fiction, with a U.S. or global media conglomerate.

11. Jesús Martín-Barbero, "Memory and Form in the Latin American Soap Opera," in *The Television Studies Reader,* ed. Robert Allen & Annette Hill (London: Routledge, 2004).

12. James Schwoch, *The American Radio Industry and Its Latin American Activities, 1900–1939* (Urbana: University of Illinois Press, 1990).

13. Noreene Janus, "Advertising and the Mass Media in the Era of the Global Corporation," in *Communication and Social Structure: Critical Studies in Mass Media Research,* ed. Emile McAnany, Jorge Schnitman, and Noreene Janus (New York: Praeger, 1981).

14. John Sinclair and Joseph Straubhaar, *Latin American Television Industries* (London: British Film Institute, 2013).

15. Elizabeth Fox, *Latin American Broadcasting: From Tango to Telenovela* (Bedfordshire: University of Luton and John Libbey Media, 1997); Elizabeth Fox and Silvio Waisbord, eds., *Latin Politics, Global Media* (Austin: University of Texas Press, 2002).

16. Joseph Straubhaar, *World Television from Global to Local* (Los Angeles: Sage, 2007).

17. Joseph Straubhaar, "Beyond Media Imperialism: Asymmetrical Interdependency and Cultural Proximity," *Critical Studies in Mass Communication* 8 (1991): 39–59.

18. Guillermo Orozco, ed., *Historias de la televisión en América Latina* (Barcelona: Gedisa, 2003).

19. Ibid.

20. Nora Mazziotti, *La industria de la telenovela: La producción de ficción en América Latina* (Buenos Aires: Paidós, 1996).

21. Raúl Trejo, "Muchos medios en pocas manos: Concentración televisiva y democracia en América Latina," *Revista Brasileira de ciencias da comunicacao* 33.1 (2010): 17–51.

22. For instance in Mexico, TV Azteca sued Alan Tatcher for working with indie Nostromo in a new reality show for Telemundo in 2006; TV Azteca also sued talent working with indie Argos in a series for Cadena Tres in 2013.

23. There were five in Argentina, six in Brazil, seven in Chile, five in Colombia, seven in Ecuador, five in Mexico, six in Peru, four in Uruguay and fourteen in Venezuela. Guillermo Orozco and María I. Vasallo, eds., *Transmedia Production Strategies in Television Fiction* (Porto Alegre, Brazil: Globo Comunicação e Participações and Sulina Editora, 2014).

24. In Mexico, Televisa and TV Azteca hold 95 percent of the audience share; in Colombia, RCN and Caracol TV holds 97 percent; in Venezuela, Venevision and Televen 81 percent; in Brazil, TV Globo holds 40 percent; in Argentina, El Trece and Telefe hold 60 percent; in Peru, America TV, ATV and Frecuencia Latina hold 86 percent; and in Chile Canal 13, Chilevision, and TVN hold 70 percent of the audience share. Ibid.

25. LAMAC, "Penetracion de TV de paga," *Latin American Multichannel Advertising Council,* www.lamac.org/.

26. Interview with executive producer from Laberinto Producciones, Colombia, November 25, 2014.

27. Interview with executive producer from Argos, Mexico, January 29, 2013.

28. Interview with artistic director from Del Barrio Producciones, Peru, November 27, 2014.

29. Interview with executive producer from Blind Spot, Mexico, November 19, 2014.

30. Telemundo kept the distribution rights in the United States, Canada, and Puerto Rico. Mary Sutter, "Telemundo, Argos to Link," *Variety*, October 13, 2000, http://variety.com/2000/tv/news/telemundo-argos-to-link-1117787691/.

31. Joe Flint, "Productora Mexicana dará telenovelas a Telemundo," *Mural*, October 2000, 5.

32. Interview with screenwriter for Argos, Telemundo, TV Azteca, HBO, Cadena Tres, August 22, 2006.

33. Nikolas Maksymiv, "Imagen y Argos Anuncian una Alianza," *Noticias financieras* (Miami), January 21, 2010, ProQuest (466639295).

34. Interview with screenwriter for Argos, Telemundo, TV Azteca, HBO, and Cadena Tres, November 26, 2014.

35. Interview with executive producer from Argos, Mexico, January 29, 2013.

36. Juan Piñón, "Reglocalization and the Rise of the Network Cities System in Producing Telenovelas for Hemispheric Audiences," *Journal of International Cultural Studies* 17.6 (2014): 655–671.

37. Sara Bibel, "Telemundo's 'El Señor de los Cielos' Wins First-Ever International Emmy for Non-English Language U.S. Primetime Program," *TVbythenumbers*, November 25, 2014, http://tvbythenumbers.zap2it.com/2014/11/25/telemundos-el-senor-de-los-cielos-wins-first-ever-international-emmy-for-non-english-language-u-s-primetime-program/332190/.

38. Hernán Casciari, "HBO con acento latinos," *El país*, February 2009, http://blogs.elpais.com/espoiler/2009/02/hbo-pero-con-acento-latino.html.

39. Interview with screenwriter for Argos, Telemundo, TV Azteca, HBO, and Cadena Tres, November 26, 2014.

40. Ibid.

41. Marie A. De la Fuente, "Sony Will Sell Telenovelas at Mip," *Variety*, March 29, 2009, http://variety.com/2009/film/news/sony-will-sell-telenovelas-at-mip-1118001742/.

42. Interview with executive producer from Laberinto Producciones, Colombia, November 25, 2014.

43. Interview with artistic director from Del Barrio Producciones, Peru, November 27, 2014.

44. Interview with executive producer from Microtime, Uruguay, December 1, 2014.

45. Interview with screenwriter for Argos, Telemundo, TV Azteca, HBO, and Cadena Tres, November 26, 2014.

46. Interview with artistic director from Del Barrio Producciones, Peru, November 27, 2014.

47. Pierre Bourdieu, *The Field of Cultural Production: Essays on Art and Literature* (New York: Columbia University Press, 1993).

11

Labor in Lagos

Alternative Global Networks

Jade Miller

Just as Hollywood production frequently departs the greater Los Angeles area for less expensive shooting locations worldwide, Hollywood studios have also expanded their interests globally, investing in everything from Bollywood studios to telenovela-producing corporations.[1] In this sense, the Los Angeles-based film and television industry is indeed a multilevel "global Hollywood," as Miller and his colleagues convincingly illustrate in their so-titled book.[2] Accordingly, the individuals who make up global Hollywood's workforce are both geographically diverse (in "runaway production" locations from New Orleans to Prague) and industrially diverse, working on domestic film and television productions as well as major international projects, all of which increasingly rely on Hollywood capital. Global Hollywood's workforce, then, may include the labor on a Universal Studios movie shooting in Prague, labor on a Bollywood movie that is partly funded by a subsidiary of Sony Pictures, and labor on a telenovela produced by a company with ownership links to NBC. While the dynamics of employment differ among locations, as other chapters in this book illuminate, interest and investment from Hollywood require significant transparency in distribution and management at the very least. This generally means a corporate structure with a few behemoth companies dominating production and neoliberal governance: local and national policymakers and large private companies working in tandem to establish the sort of regulations, policies, and practices, including reliable copyright and contract enforcement, that are attractive to foreign direct investment (FDI) and formal domestic bank investment.

Entertainment production worldwide also exists outside Global Hollywood's networks. In this chapter, I critically examine the relationships among labor, distribution, informality, and power in one such industry: the massively popular southern Nigerian movie industry known as Nollywood.[3] Its productions dominate screens and mediascapes across sub-Saharan Africa and throughout the global African diaspora, though exact numbers about its production output and income are challenging to discern.[4] Counting and demonstrating sales are not just relevant to demonstrating an industry's importance for academic study or popular journalistic pieces. Rather, opacity (and the accompanying general inability to codify formal sales figures) is a defining part of Nollywood's structure and strength,[5] shaping nearly every part of the industry's day-to-day operations and practices. In particular, this opacity reinforces the power of the film distributors known as "marketers," who leverage their gray-market knowledge to control the Nollywood marketplace. While an industry predicated on personal relationships may appear to risk breeding disorder, Nollywood is in fact quite organized, a result of the marketers' self-governing practices and the industry's guild-based infrastructure. Consequently, Nollywood remains largely disconnected from formal global networks of labor organization, financing, and distribution,[6] but is nevertheless a nexus point for its own set of global flows and linkages.

Using a series of onsite observations and interviews with practitioners in the Lagos-based industry, my analysis reveals how global concerns about the precarious nature of local labor are shaped in this context by the particular brand of informality that characterizes Nollywood. If we take precarity and informality to be linked, we can see Nollywood as a particularly informal industry with a particularly precarious workforce, marked by limited recourse for labor grievances. I assess Nollywood's informality as a phenomenon forged out of a very specific place: Lagos, a rapidly growing, often overflowing megacity and an alternative media capital, a hub for global flows and connections that utilizes few of the formal dominant networks that mark Global Hollywood.[7] In this way, this chapter grounds the reality of local media labor in the specificities of the actual places where that labor works. In short, the structure of Nollywood reflects the specific architecture and shape of Lagos.

I would also like to be specific about what I mean when I discuss industrial informality in Nollywood. Film industries from Hollywood to Bollywood can be said to feature informal elements at many levels of production, especially in relation to labor practices like recruitment. And Nollywood features some formal elements in its production inputs and distribution outlets.[8] The distinction between formality and informality, then, is not a dichotomy. Rather, it is a continuum with no industry falling fully at either extreme. Additionally, the question of what exactly informality is and whether it should be celebrated has been subject to much scholarly debate, particularly in the context of media distribution studies, and Nollywood has been at the core of many of these arguments.[9] There has been concern over the potential to exoticize and "Orientalize" Nollywood via an overabundance of focus on the informality in the industry.[10]

Accordingly, to demystify the discussion of Nollywood's informality, I wish to be very clear about what exactly I mean by informality in Nollywood, and the ways in which it is a conscious choice in a global power play. This study understands the basic intersecting constituents of Nollywood's industrial informality to be 1) *not documenting sales* or most other distribution figures in any publicly accessible/ scrutinizable fashion, 2) *not utilizing legal contracts* for employment or other business relationships, 3) *not using agents* or other formal inputs such as accredited schools for talent recruitment, 4) *not pursuing copyright violations* via legal frameworks, and 5) *privileging undocumented financing and distribution networks* and spurning alternatives. It may be noted that four of these five elements begin with the word *not*. This is because our understanding of informality as an industrial feature worthy of mention exists only because of the existence of formality in these areas in other industries. While there may be some level of informality in other global movie or television industries, the dominance and intersection of these elements in Nollywood's day-to-day functioning render the industry *predominantly* informal as opposed to the fragmented informality that characterizes the global media industries that compete for Hollywood's production, coproductions, partnerships, or investments on the international stage. And point 5 underlines the conscious and active choice by Nollywood's marketers to utilize informality as a means to maintain power and thwart challengers.

THE CONTEXT: NOLLYWOOD THE PLACE

"Where is Nollywood?" asked a neophyte on a public Nollywood message board. The mirthful and mocking responses were plentiful. "Nowhere!" said many, while others were more specific, citing places where one can, indeed, see Nollywood at work. One answer is Surulere. This is the neighborhood in mainland Lagos where many producers, directors, and other creative professionals maintain offices and live. A more specific answer might be O'Jez's, a bar in Surulere's National Stadium that serves as a meeting point for socializing and making business deals. With the exception of O'Jez's, chance encounters with Nollywood elites are a rare occurrence in Surulere. Offices, workspaces, and production sites are unmarked; the streets are largely residential. Jonathan Haynes, writing on the geography of Nollywood, notes that the small amount of capital per entrepreneur means that large spaces marking flashy movie industries—studios, theaters, large office complexes—don't exist here, as Nollywood functions largely behind small unmarked doors.[11] It's a massive industry that remains hard to see and hard to quantify.

Another answer to the message board query could be Alaba Market, a vast sprawling electronics market on the outskirts of Lagos, which also serves as Nollywood's distribution nerve center. Journeying there in a taxi, one emerges from the city's densely populated urban maze into a dusty spread of low-lying disconnected buildings speckling the landscape before arriving at the market itself. Alaba is a city unto itself, with streets, churches, banks, and apartments, all low, dusty structures built from inexpensive materials. The market, according to a rough and unsourced estimate from over a decade ago, may be the epicenter of 75 percent of West Africa's electronics trade, may house 50,000 merchants, and may net $2 billion each year.[12] At Alaba, one can purchase anything from new flat-screen televisions to used generators to, of course, movies for home viewing.

Alaba's location is a logical one for the largest Nigerian (and West African) electronics market, directly between two sources of product importation: one formal (the Apapa port) and one informal (the Benin border at Seme).[13] The peripheral location isolates Alaba from government officials, allowing it to thrive on formal neglect. The market can spread as far as it would like without running into anything that the city would consider important enough to protect or regulate. The only efforts at delimitation are internal, and the market's infrastructure is mostly self-made. Merchants have private radio-wave towers to ensure mobile phone service, and operate private generators to ensure power. In their study of Alaba as urban form, architect Rem Koolhaas and his colleagues reference a statistic that, even though it may lack veracity, gives an idea of the scale and atmosphere of the market: that Alaba has the highest concentration of generators in the world. Alaba's self-governance has also included private development of a parking lot, local secretariat, fire station, and local library.[14]

Despite its fragmented connection to formal trade and governance, Alaba has forged its own global network and emerged as a central hub in the circulation of electronics in West Africa, as well as in Nollywood's own circulation networks. The market mirrors Lagos itself, a global megacity that is often said to be growing "off the grid." Possibly home to 21 million,[15] with less than a third connected to public water supply,[16] Lagos may be on its way to becoming the third largest city in the world, depending on how you count and who is counting. In understanding Lagos, the fungibility of its population estimates speaks to the culture of Lagos at large: mostly informal, undocumented, and difficult to officially count for those who make their living counting such things (and it is worth noting that counting such things has significant financial implications, as population and business figures directly affect applications for everything from loans to grants).

Both Alaba and Lagos are central locations in the production and distribution of Nollywood titles. The growth of their infrastructures serves as not just context but also metaphor for the logics that guide industrial operations in Nollywood. The next two sections of this chapter will detail those specific conventions, focusing on the informal networks that structure Nollywood's industrial organization and labor processes.

IMPLICATIONS OF OPAQUE DISTRIBUTION

While Nollywood produces movies, it is not technically a "film" industry. Movies are not shot on celluloid nor are they usually intended for big-screen projection in cinema houses. Instead, Nollywood movies are shot on video and largely viewed in private or in small public screenings. Though there are constant televised screenings of Nollywood movies, some informal public screenings in video parlors,[17] and a growing trend of some higher-end titles utilizing a splashy initial release and short run at expensive cinema houses,[18] the vast majority of profits in Nollywood come from physical direct-to-consumer sales. Most Nollywood movies are financed and distributed by one group of people, known as "marketers." Despite the name, they serve multiple roles for each movie: executive producers, marketers, *and* distributors. Essentially small-scale entrepreneurs with experience in the gray- and black-market electronics trade, marketers leverage their knowledge of Nigeria's informal, undocumented marketplaces and open-air bazaars to structure their business dealings in the movie business. While many creative workers in the industry bemoan the lack of everyday cinema houses, affordable to the poor and lower middle class and contributing to a local cinema-going culture,[19] the marketers flourish in an environment that leaves them in control of most authorized distribution.

Once finished movies have been pressed at the disc replication plant, the marketers package them with the appropriate graphics and release them to the markets on the next Monday. These movies flow through distribution hubs and subhubs, usually first focused on places like Alaba (the Lagos market) and Onitsha (the city in the Igbo-dominated southeast that is home base for a large number of production companies). Copies are then sent to nearby cities for sale at their markets, and they fan out to smaller hamlets from there, much the way electronics fan out from Alaba across the nation. These distribution networks are held together through trust, personal connections, and informal exchange as opposed to legally binding contracts, a prominent feature in any informal economy.

"Piracy" is part of both the heritage and the current functioning of the video distribution system,[20] although I will refer to it here as unauthorized distribution in order to remain value neutral. Despite the marketers' public proclamations that unauthorized distribution is decimating the industry, they themselves are not fully operating on the legal side of copyright law in all of their business dealings. Instead, one might say that they operate in a gray area, obtaining certain rights for movies and then overstepping them and hiding profits. The core professional experience of the marketers comes from a background in electronics trading, including unauthorized distribution of foreign movies. As Brian Larkin has illustrated,[21] their success in distributing the movies they produce comes in no small part from using the same distribution networks they forged years before to distribute unauthorized copies of Hollywood, Bollywood, and Asian action movies, and is augmented by their ability to operate behind closed doors and out of the sight of any potential regulators.

The current process of financing an average Nollywood movie is inextricable from the informality of its distribution. Again, while movie industries worldwide seek diverse funding sources (of varying degrees of legitimacy and reliability), the avoidance of transparent distribution in Nollywood delimits the potential to attract bank loans or other formal investors, as investors tend to require confirmed sales figures and reliable sales projections. The marketers' often antagonistic relationships with the government over taxes and other documentation issues mean that loans and grants upon which other film industries can rely are not part of the landscape for most moviemakers in Lagos. Instead, individual marketers tend to finance their own productions. Those in charge of distribution—the marketers— are the only ones who can make financial decisions and calculate risk, a confidence that comes from their exclusive control over (informal) distribution networks and associated knowledge of the (opaque) marketplace. This oversight establishes a level of collective power among the marketers that is intentionally difficult to usurp and that repels investment attempts by outsiders.[22]

Moreover, these marketers zealously guard their power by policing the informal relationships that enshrine their authority, which is particularly important as we analyze the structure of the industry. The strength of their informal networks trumps most attempts at formal takeover, and this strength is derived from informality: opacity in sales figures and distribution networks, and informality in industrial organization. Informality, however, is not the same as describing the industry as a disorganized, chaotic collective. In the absence of governance by legal institutions or the centralized formal power of major corporate studios, control is enforced by a mass of small enterprises whose internal organization helps preserve their collective interests, best represented in the marketers' guild (FVPMAN).

FVPMAN is just one of the many guilds constituting Nollywood's internal infrastructure.[23] Guilds, each boasting an elected national leadership, represent almost every aspect of the industry from marketers to makeup artists. Guilds provide, in essence, internal governance for the industry, standing in for legal contracts and labor regulations. While they appear centralized and visible, akin to unions, guilds are neither transparent nor formal, neither registered with nor regulated by the government, and subject to no external oversight. For instance, in the absence of legal contracts, guilds are meant to solve disputes. In theory, a grieved party takes his or her grievance to the guild's leadership, who work to solve the dispute with the offending party's guild. In practice, however, a dispute between an elite and an underling will rarely result in a disruption of the status quo, and there is no recourse to formal legal litigation as a corrective. Nollywood sets are full of empty complaints about labor practices, from unpaid labor to unsatisfactory working conditions.

While most guilds deal primarily with internal labor issues, the collective power of the marketers' guild, FVPMAN, is immense. In the past the guild has made attempts to space out movie releases to counteract periodic "gluts" in movie releases. FVPMAN also has cut down on production at times to address the same issue. Attempts to dethrone the marketers have consistently ended in failure, whether the attempts come from blocs of creative workers or government authorities, both wishing more control over the industry. For instance, Nollywood stars are a central mechanism through which movies are branded and sold to the public. Marketers rely on their images to help secure financial success. Nollywood stars are thus widely recognizable and glamorous, though fame secures most of them only a modest fortune. To make a consistent living, most stars must work frequently, and those demanding extravagant fees can fall out of favor with the marketers. FVPMAN acts quickly to shut down productions or blacklist actors if the organization feels the marketers' power is being chipped away by an overentitled celebrity. Heightened budgets and salaries in a bigger-budget nonmarketer branch of Nollywood, now known as "New Nollywood," have yet to evoke industrial change: workers must work so *frequently* that New Nollywood's limited slate won't sustain them, and the marketers still set the terms for the bulk of the industry.

For such a young industry, Nollywood is subject to constant speculation on the shape of its future. Various plans to shift that future in one direction or another come from both within and outside the industry. New plans to "formalize" in one way or another are near constant, including cinema construction schemes and various licensing initiatives put forth by the government and guilds. Some of these new ideas die before they are born, while others persist but only affect a small subset of the industry during their tenure. As with most cultural industries, the real power of the industry is centralized with those who control distribution. In Nollywood, this still means the marketers. Locating power in creative industries is key to understanding their functioning, and understanding the marketers as the nexus of power here is key to understanding Nollywood's persistent informal infrastructure. This informality can be a source of industrial strength to reinforce dominant power structures, and thus integration into formal global networks is unlikely to serve the best interests of those in authority (here, the marketers). This informality also marks the experience of labor and the nature of production and distribution in Nollywood in a manner that exceeds anything seen in industries that rely on theatrical release, official legal contract enforcement, and relative transparency in distribution statistics.

PRECARITY, REPEAT COLLABORATION, AND INDUSTRY ENTRY

Creative work and precarity in labor tend to go hand-in-hand, as the individual case studies in this volume collectively illustrate. In creative industries worldwide, creative workers tend to form new teams for each project.[24] This can range from the culturally temporary work structure in the technology sector, in which workers expect to work at companies for only a few years before shifting job title and project,[25] to the extremes of per-project team reformation in the creation of movies, television shows, and songs. On this end of the creative industries, workers are largely freelance and must constantly find new work as they coalesce for the completion of a single project.

In movie industries based on theatrical release logic, being hired on a film may mean several months of work on a single project—perhaps even a year or more—depending on one's role in the process. Nollywood instead operates on an industrial logic favoring rapid, inexpensive production. Instead of pouring money into a single title and laboring over an extended time frame, most Nollywood production moves at a brisk pace, as can be seen in other straight-to-video industries worldwide.[26] This is an extreme form of precarity, as a living is forged in Nollywood from working every week or every day, going from production to production. As informality in distribution entrenches power in the hands of the marketers, it also heightens precarity for Nollywood's nonmarketer labor force, as they lack recourse to legal protections and collective bargaining.

Nollywood production is marked by velocity. It is not unusual to shoot ten scenes in one day, with two to three weeks of shooting per movie a common scenario.[27] With one week of preproduction and one week of editing and packaging, a video film *can* go from inception to sale in four weeks, though three months is a much more common scenario, and New Nollywood titles take even longer. An in-demand worker can easily shoot two movies in one month. With modest pay from any individual movie, workers make a living mainly through quantity, and some can be found working nearly every day, ending one movie project to begin another.

Movie industries worldwide are mostly marked by freelance labor agreements, with crews coming together in new and different formations for project after project. Researchers from Caves[28] to Currid[29] have noted the weight this gives to informal relationships that may bridge friendship and business: if you must rely on your reputation to secure employment in a business marked by whom you know, social relationships are a core motor of your career and professional development. Despite the prominence of guilds in Nollywood, people usually hear about jobs from either someone they have worked with before or the recommendation of a friend. While this is not unusual in other movie industries, the lack of formal recourse to government labor regulation, talent agents, or managers marks Nollywood as particularly informal. Furthermore, the sheer number of projects that Nollywood workers must pick up to support themselves—many more than in movie industries marked by theatrical release of higher-budget projects—means that the informal is even more important to workers as a means through which to ensure their continued financial stability. Because of this quantity-based logic in production and labor, repeat collaborations are particularly common, and maintaining trust among individuals in those working groups is an essential survival tactic.

This trust is not easy to come by: breaking into the industry can be challenging. Entry into Nollywood is often based on family, ethnic, or other preexisting ties. There is little formal training in the industry, and many workers learn along the way. Some efforts to institute training programs via moviemaking schools have begun, but these have not become a reliable mechanism for feeding talent into the industry. Gathering places, like O'Jez's, the bar and restaurant in the National Stadium, can provide another opportunity to network one's way to the top. Industry events such as premieres, awards ceremonies, and elaborate birthday banquets are the type of invitation-only places where major business deals are negotiated. A bar like O'Jez's, which is open to the public, is less likely to yield dramatic results. It does, however, provide the chance to see and be seen, and people make an effort to hold personal meetings there, in order to be observed by others in the industry. In such instances, industry aspirants may find themselves only a few degrees removed from a critical phone number; personal introductions are common occurrences in these locations, helping novices connect with senior players in the industry.

Apprenticeships are often a low-cost entry point into the industry, especially for producers and technical crew. It is commonplace across Nigerian industries for a "big man" to train a number of "boys" to work under his mentorship,[30] and it is no different in Nollywood. This tradition is thought to ensure personal loyalty. One midlevel producer I spoke with, for instance, runs a production company whose in-house editor is the producer's former barber, someone the producer trained for the position. This way, the producer says, "I know he will always be loyal to me." Other industry workers teach themselves. One postproduction special effects artist I interviewed, for instance, learned his craft from free online tutorials on special effects software, such as Video Co-Pilot, Cinema 4D, and After-Effects. His training was a side pursuit based on personal interest while he was enrolled in another field of study at university. University education is common among the creative arms of the industry (producers, directors, editors, and so on) though not a requirement. Marketers are usually not university educated, as they often work in the marketplaces from a very young age and gain their knowledge from those experiences. Some of the rancor and distrust between marketers and directors is based on that point alone.

Guilds structure the industry. While crew and big-name stars are hired through personal connections, nonstar actors are usually enlisted through auditions. Auditions tend to be formal, well-attended affairs, with members of the leadership of each guild expected to attend and make sure everything is operating in a respectable fashion. For guilds with many members and limited work—for instance, the Actor's Guild—guild membership also forms the framework through which creative workers look for and find work. The power of the guild, regardless of who is in charge, stands in for a legal system in industry disputes, and it can also serve as a mechanism for resisting external interference in the industry status quo, be it from governmental or foreign interlopers. And it is the marketers' guild, FVP-MAN, where industry power is concentrated, in an opaque and cohesive collective of small- to medium-size distributors. The core of government efforts to control Nollywood has been aimed at interrupting this bloc and promoting the emergence of a few corporatesque national distributors that could be more easily controlled. This governmental strategy of control (actively promoting the emergence of a few corporate giants as opposed to a diversity of dispersed small distributors), implemented in many government bids for control over media industries worldwide (perhaps most notably in early U.S. radio development), has thus far failed in Nollywood, as the cohesiveness and collective opacity of the marketers, schooled by years of actively avoiding government notice, has made them challenging consolidation targets.

We can thus see informal, undocumented transactions as the building blocks of the industry, structuring its organization and labor processes. And we can see extreme precarity as characteristic of Nollywood labor. While informal connections and trust also form the basis of the working relationships of most other contract-based creative industries, including most of those highlighted in this volume, what is distinctive about Nollywood is that this is the *only* currency. There is no recourse to formal political or legal systems or institutions, like talent agencies, to help structure industry operations. At once a source of immense strength for those who control the distributive mechanisms, the southern Nigerian film industry's self-governed informality remains an ever-present challenge for workers who lack equal footing and for those looking to codify it with standards based on structured global networks, from which the industry remains disconnected. Such tensions have and will continue to shape Nollywood.

CONCLUSION

The functioning of Nollywood as an industry is inseparable from its location in Lagos, in Nigeria, and from a place of disjuncture with dominant formal global entertainment industry production and distribution networks. Alaba's rise to regional centrality in the outskirts of the urban core mirrors Nollywood's rise in a state of disjuncture with formal media industry networks and domestic government oversight. In both settings, a functioning industrial order emerged from an architecture that would be inhospitable to corporate formality. In Alaba, we can see individual fixes through the individual mobile phone towers and the sea of personal generators blanketing the previously barren landscape on the side of the highway from central Lagos to Benin. In Nollywood, we can trace this thread throughout the industry. Financing, for example, is usually done by the eventual distributor in the absence of reliable sales estimates or accountability. Production relationships are built on trust, not contracts, and entry to the industry is rarely through formal schools, as apprenticeships acquired through personal connections rule.

Another commonality is that both Alaba and Nollywood share deceptively organized governance. While both have been mostly ignored by Nigeria's and Lagos's actual government,[31] both are indeed governed: self-governed. In Alaba, we can see this through the libraries, firehouses, and schools built by the massive collective of small merchants housed in the market. These merchants are held together by the urge for self-preservation as well as the Nigerian tradition of group organization. In the same way, we see Nollywood's marketers (some of whom are the very same small-stall owners of Alaba) controlling the industry with the firm hand of confident self-organization. They maintain star salaries at a manageable level, control gluts, create stars, and maintain distribution networks that rapidly disseminate new cultural products to the most remote of Nigeria's hamlets. Unlike the precarity defining the work of most of Nollywood's labor, the opaque organization of Nollywood's marketers means they enjoy relative stability, as they themselves control the industry. Although they are threatened by "illegal" distribution practices, they are also strengthened by them, particularly those of their own genesis, and they have recourse to their non-movie side businesses, including electronics trading.

At the same time, it is important not to overromanticize the informal. While the marketers are happy with the current system, those on the industry's creative side as well as foreign and government forces have made and continue to make significant efforts to delimit the industry's informality in favor of an industrial structure with room for bigger budgets, theatrical screenings as a norm, and wider global recognition—in short, an industry in which they could achieve their artistic visions while still selling to their core domestic audiences. Yet we can see the current brand of informality that marks Nollywood as closely linked to the environment from which it was born: an environment that encourages small-scale enterprises with opaque business practices, meant to avoid notice by government officials. This informality thrives particularly well in areas characterized as both the urban and the global margins, even as they may be central in their own alternative networks. In this way, we can see the specificities of the local ingrained in the everyday realities of media labor in Nigeria's internationally popular movie industry.

NOTES

1. Amelia Arsenault and Manuel Castells, "The Structure and Dynamics of Global Multi-media Business Networks," *International Journal of Communication* 2 (2008): 707–748.

2. Toby Miller, Nitin Govil, John McMurria, Richard Maxwell, and Ting Wang, *Global Hollywood* 2 (London: British Film Institute, 2008).

3. This chapter does not directly compare Nollywood to Hollywood. To compare the two is to suggest that Nollywood is a less-funded imitator of Hollywood, when it is more accurate to view Nollywood as on its own trajectory, growing out of and flourishing in a different position in the global economy. However, in the context of this edited volume, I engage in a general comparison of Nollywood to more formal global media industries worldwide, as part of this book's charge to illuminate how *global* concerns about labor issues play out across a diversity of contexts.

4. It has become popular in recent years to cite a UNESCO statistic that Nollywood is second only to Bollywood in number of titles produced per year, but scholars have questioned the significance of such a statistic in comparing theatrical and home-viewing based industries. See Carmela Garritano, "Introduction: Nollywood—an Archive of African Worldliness," *Black Camera* 5.2 (2013): 44–52; and other articles in that Nollywood special issue of *Black Camera*.

5. See Brian Larkin, "Degraded Images, Distorted Sounds: Nigerian Video and the Infrastructure of Piracy," *Public Culture* 16.2 (2004): 289–314, for a full argument on informal distribution as a source of industrial strength.

6. Despite recent efforts in formalization in cinema, online, and satellite distribution, the core of industry profits are still in physical copies sold in networks of domestic open-air markets.

7. Jade Miller, "Global Nollywood: The Nigerian Movie Industry and Alternative Global Networks in Production and Distribution," *Global Media and Communication* 8 (2012): 117–133.

8. See ibid. for an analysis of Nollywood's formal inputs, such as cameras and sound equipment.

9. See Ramon Lobato, "Creative Industries and Informal Economies: Lessons from Nollywood," *International Journal of Cultural Studies* 13 (2010): 337–354.

10. Matthew Gandy, "Learning from Lagos," *New Left Review* 33 (2005): 36–52; Alessandro Jedlowski, "Nigerian Videos in the Global Arena: The Postcolonial Exotic Revisited," *Global South* 7.1 (2013): 157–178; Nyasha Mboti, "Nollywood's Aporias Part 1: Gatemen," *Journal of African Cinemas* 6 (2014): 49–70.

11. Jonathan Haynes, "Nollywood in Lagos, Lagos in Nollywood Films," *Africa Today* 54.2 (2007): 131–150.

12. Figures, to be taken with many grains of salt, are derived from Rem Koolhaas, Harvard Project on the City, Stefano Boeri, Sanford Kwinter, Nadia Tazi, and Hans Ulrich Obrist, *Mutations* (New York: ACTAR, 2000).

13. Ibid.

14. Koolhaas et al., *Mutations*. And counting comparative global generator density by neighborhood is perhaps the epitome of figures that could never be accurately counted.

15. See Elizabeth Rosenthal, "Nigeria Tested by Rapid Rise in Population," *New York Times*, April 14, 2012, www.nytimes.com/2012/04/15/world/africa/in-nigeria-a-preview-of-an-overcrowded-planet.html. This statistic is at the high end of estimates; the population may well be lower.

16. National Bureau of Statistics of Nigeria, *Annual Abstract of Statistics, 2012*, 115–117, www.nigerianstat.gov.ng/nbslibrary/nbs-annual-abstract-of-statistics/nbs-annual-abstract-of-statistics.

17. Those who made the movie see no direct profits from this.

18. Jonathan Haynes, "New Nollywood: Kunle Afolayan," *Black Camera* 5.2 (2013): 53–73; Moradewun Adejunmobi, "Evolving Nollywood Templates for Minor Transnational Film," *Black Camera* 5.2 (2014): 74–94.

19. Connor Ryan, "Nollywood and the Limits of Informality: A Conversation with Tunde Kelani, Bond Emeruwa, and Emem Isong," *Black Camera* 5.2 (2013): 168–185.

20. See Larkin, "Degraded Images, Distorted Sounds."

21. Ibid.

22. Those advocating loudest for more formality are those who would likely lead the industry were the marketers to lose control. This small group of big-name Nollywood producers and directors make movies that emerge from a largely separate self-financed system known sometimes as "New

Nollywood." This chapter, however, deals not with "New Nollywood" but with the bulk of the industry, which produces the majority of titles and employs the vast majority of workers.

23. It shouldn't be all that surprising that the institution of guilds has proven so popular in structuring primarily informal Nollywood. Nigerian society is full of organizations and leadership positions. It is not uncommon for people to spend their little spare time going from meeting to meeting: church governance groups, church committees, groups of those originally from the same village, and so on. It seems that anyone who is anyone (and many who are, in effect, nobodies) holds or has held a leadership position in some organization or another. Ascendency to leadership in any organization is afforded a high degree of respect and importance, and leaders of even the smallest of these organizations are usually hailed by their title in public.

24. Richard Caves, *Creative Industries: Contracts between Art and Commerce* (Cambridge, MA: Harvard University Press, 2002).

25. Annalee Saxenian, *Regional Advantage: Culture and Competition in Silicon Valley and Route 128* (Cambridge, MA: Harvard University Press, 1996).

26. Ramon Lobato, *Shadow Economies of Cinema: Mapping Informal Film Distribution* (London: British Film Institute, 2012).

27. A popular cinematographer suggests that ten to fifteen days is the bare minimum for a movie shoot, while a "good" movie will take twenty-one or more days. Shooting has been taking longer in recent years.

28. Caves, *Creative Industries*.

29. Elizabeth Currid, *The Warhol Economy: How Fashion, Art, and Music Drive New York City* (Princeton, NJ: Princeton University Press, 2007).

30. In Nigeria, a wealthy, successful man is usually referred to as "big," and underlings and servants are often referred to as "boys," no matter their age.

31. With the exception of sudden dramatic overtures, such as former president Goodluck Jonathan's disjointed multimillion-dollar funding scheme late in his tenure or the censorship board's ill-fated efforts to restructure distribution.

12

Creative Precarity in the Adult Film Industry

Heather Berg and Constance Penley

In this chapter, we examine the conditions of precarity in porn work, situating those conditions in the context of a changing industry and a political economic moment in which uncertainty is the most stable feature. Though we can link precarious conditions to their social contexts, we do not suggest that such conditions are inevitable or historically neutral. As Chuck Kleinhans insists, "Precarity is not a necessary result of [global political economic] changes. Rather, it is a deliberate policy and aspect of neoliberalism in its relation to the labor force."[1] Porn workers' precarity emerges out of an industry struggling in the wake of global recession, rampant piracy, and a hostile legal environment, but precaritizing policies are not a necessary response to these socio-political conditions. Instead, deliberate policies make porn workers precarious—policies ranging from independent contractor laws that excuse employers from labor regulations and proscribe union organizing, to formal and informal anti–sex worker codes that render sex workers especially vulnerable to both state and employer abuse, and of course, the mundane but not inevitable rules of the wage relation under capital.

We are equally interested in creative precarity—the resourceful ways porn workers resist, navigate, and exploit the precarity they confront. We suggest that taking seriously these forms of resistance can deepen our understanding of precarious labor in creative fields and in the world of work more broadly. Why? Because the conditions of precarity that appear to be recent historical developments in other industries have long shaped porn work. The "*new* gig economy [emphasis added]," brought on by "massive changes that have generated the expansion of precarious employment," is not, for instance, so new for porn workers, who have long pursued diversified income streams to get by.[2] The adult film industry is not exceptional, then, but it may be predictive. Workers' struggles there speak to the conditions that increasingly characterize labor in the current political economy, and we are well served to pay attention to the strategies they deploy in confronting them.

We must begin by mapping the adult film industry, because so little is known about it, and what is thought to be known—such as the oft-repeated claim that it is a $10–12 billion industry—turns out to be completely made up though almost never challenged. The establishment of porn studies as a scholarly discipline— with the inauguration of the journal *Porn Studies* in 2013, the growing number of university courses offered and dissertations undertaken, the availability of more archives and collections for historical research, and the efforts of academics and industry professionals to engage in productive conversations about the current and future shape of the industry—helps make this mapping possible. *The Feminist Porn Book: The Politics of Producing Pleasure* is the first collection, for example, to bring together writings by feminists in the adult industry and essays by feminist porn scholars.[3] But even as space opens up for academic discussions of pornography, the casualization of the professoriate and the erosion of the academic freedom ensured by tenure bring their own precarity to researching controversial areas such as the adult industry.

CONTOURS OF THE INDUSTRY

Though increasingly diffuse, the adult film industry occupies a central role in the spatial and political economy of California's San Fernando Valley. We focus our inquiry there in the interests of space and precision, while also attending to the growing production centers of Las Vegas, San Francisco, south Florida, and globally, Brazil and Eastern Europe. A small roster of production and distribution companies, including Manwin, Bang Brothers, Brazzers, West Coast Productions, Evil Angel, Wicked Pictures, Larry Flynt Productions, Playboy Enterprises, and Vivid Entertainment, dominates the adult film industry landscape. But as production costs rise and potential profits from large-scale productions decrease,[4] small, boutique production companies producing niche content increasingly populate the adult film industry. In using the term *industry*, we do not suggest a monolithic, static, or internally consistent body. Instead, we mean to indicate the dynamic networks of workers, management, and institutions that take part in the production process of adult film, all of which are affected by regulatory policies such as Measure B, the 2012 Los Angeles County mandatory condom law that saw more than a 90 percent drop in adult film production permits issued.

Studio executives, investors, producers, talent agents, directors, crew, performers, postproduction editors, and distribution and marketing staff are key players in adult film production. Common institutions connect these actors: trade publications distribute industry news and host annual trade and award shows; the industry's trade organization, the Free Speech Coalition, lobbies on its behalf and, since the 2010 collapse of what had been an industry-run health clinic, sets the terms for recommended sexually transmitted infection (STI) testing panels and exposure protocols; the Adult Performer Advocacy Committee (APAC), since the fall of 2013, provides worker education such as the *Porn 101* video and brings performers together to advocate on their own behalf in discussions of testing protocols and other informal policies; and private but industry-specific testing clinics clear performers for work. Other institutions and actors, while not of the porn industry, are intimately connected to it: multinational software development firms design web platforms and process credit card payments, real estate agents coordinate filming locations, beauty service providers specialize in readying performers for work, publicity firms cater to performers and adult businesses, and nonprofit organizations such as the Aids Healthcare Foundation build political identities and funding bases through their relationships with (or stark opposition to) the industry. In describing the contours of the "industry," we think it is important to include organizations and institutions that could not exist without the adult industry, such as for-profit "porn addiction" therapies, religious antiporn initiatives like the XXX-CHURCH, which sends its preachers on the college circuit to debate with porn stars ("Jesus loves porn stars!"), and the antiporn feminists who spend extraordinary amounts of time and energy fighting not only the adult industry but those who think it merits study rather than blanket condemnation (Stop Porn Culture).

We also understand the "industry" to encompass the satellite industries—including erotic dance, webcam, escort, and novelty—that enjoy a symbiotic relationship with the adult film industry. This relationship has three dimensions: first, income streams from satellite industries economically sustain adult film performers, securing a reserve army of performer labor for whom the film industry is not financially responsible. Were such income streams not available, it would be difficult if not impossible for performers to maintain themselves amid the vicissitudes of demand, filming schedules, industry, and other factors that mean a performer might work twenty days one month and two the next.[5] Second, many performers describe the increased earnings they can draw from satellite industries by marketing themselves as "porn stars" as a primary reason for taking on porn performance.[6] Dominic Ace, an adult industry publicist and photographer who has worked as a roadie for performers on feature dancing tours, explained it this way: "You've got web sites, you've got Skype shows, you've got privates [escorting], you've got fan clubs, you've got custom videos, appearances, feature dancing, Verified Call [a service that connects fans to performers via cell phone], a ton of different revenue streams. . . . You don't make money doing scenes, *a scene is a marketing tool* [emphasis added]."[7] Talent agents for film frequently recruit in erotic dance clubs and on webcam sites, and adult actresses report having begun careers in these fields, later moving into the film industry. Finally, production companies and agents who sign performers to exclusive contracts may be, depending on the specific terms of the contract, entitled to a percentage of workers' earnings in satellite industries.

Porn workers push the boundaries of the industry to meet their financial needs, as well as satisfy desires for autonomy, flexibility, and work-life balance. Porn performer and single parent Raylene explained that her average take from three to five hours of webcamming work was comparable to her film performance rate, but webcamming allowed her to have greater control over her schedule and working environment: "I was able to work alone, in my house, during school hours, and then, you know, have the rest of the evening with my child and make a better living at home than when I was in front of the camera."[8] Those performers who prefer satellite industries to adult filmmaking describe taking just enough film gigs to maintain their "brands." In line with Dominic Ace's description of scenes as "marketing tool[s]," performer Venus Lux noted, "When you're in porn, especially transsexual porn, it's not a money making thing. It's for the fame, that's it. The chain reaction of the fame means you can eventually get money."[9] Management too is keenly aware of the industry's reliance on satellite industries. Christian Mann, a longtime board member of the industry's trade organization and general manager of distribution giant Evil Angel, compared the porn industry's increasing reliance on alternative profit streams to similar trends in the mainstream music industry. "The reality is," he wrote, "albums don't make money anymore. Record stores are gone, right? So the saving grace for the music industry has been concert tickets."[10]

CONDITIONS OF AND RESPONSES TO PRECARITY

Performers' deft cobbling together of various income streams and tactical manipulation of their personal "brands" give the lie to the idea of porn workers as passive victims.[11] This is not to say that porn workers do not confront modes of work organization that constrain their autonomy and working conditions and threaten their well-being. It is, instead, to center on the creative ways in which they resist such conditions of precarity. Similarly, porn workers do not simply react to top-down management; just as often, changes in management style represent capital's desperate responses to workers' manipulating the system in ways management never anticipated. One performer explained, for example, that it is possible to identify clauses of an exclusive performer contract that correspond directly to work-arounds developed by previous contract stars. Listing individual clauses, she named each one after the performer who discovered a new way to assert power in the workplace. If this is a sobering reminder of management's tireless drive to constrain worker resistance, we might also remember that workers are often one step ahead.

We now take a step back to sketch the conditions of precarity confronted by porn workers. We will then return to an exploration of the ways they can be understood as creatively precarious. Like other industries in advanced capitalism,[12] the adult film industry more and more relies on a flexible, itinerant, and deskilled workforce. While the pool of porn performers was a small and close-knit one in the 1970s and early 1980s, today's seemingly endless supply of eager new performers limits current workers' ability to negotiate the terms of their labor with agents, producers, and directors. Internet piracy and employers' increased interest in casting amateurs further depress wages and job opportunities. The growing popularity of amateur aesthetics also decreases the demand for professional camera operators, directors, editors, and scriptwriters.

The porn industry operates free of most external labor regulations governing pay, employment discrimination, occupational health, and benefits. This is in part due to the industry's liminal legal status. Industry-specific regulations typically focus on age record-keeping requirements[13] and obscenity prosecutions,[14] rather than working conditions. Regulations governing occupational health, wages, and employment discrimination are clumsily borrowed from noncomparable industries, such as nursing in the case of blood-borne pathogens. Recent attempts at passing industry-specific workplace health legislation have proven unsuccessful. The Safer Sex in the Adult Film Industry Act passed in Los Angeles County in November 2012 has remained largely unenforced. In the face of overwhelming dissent from performers, anemic legislative support, and concerns about funding and enforcement, AB 1576, the proposed statewide legislation mandating a whole range of rigorous health and safety requirements, including condom use and employer-provided STI testing, failed in August 2014. Workers and management oppose external policy on the grounds that it would undermine what they maintain is the industry's robust and effective self-regulation, which includes twice-monthly STI testing for performers and industry-wide filming moratoriums in the event of a positive HIV result. Indeed, workers suggest that that the industry's testing system has suffered in the wake of the 2011 downfall of the Adult Industry Medical Foundation (AIM), which served as an autonomous and centralized testing and treatment clinic. Significantly, outside organizations campaigning for greater state involvement in the porn industry's health protocols were instrumental in AIM's closure.

Adult industry workers' precarious legal status is solidified by their designation as independent contractors. To a large extent, independent contractor law is organized explicitly to excuse employers from their responsibilities to workers. Employers can, fully within the bounds of the law, pass on to workers a broad range of production costs, including STI testing, wardrobe, makeup, and transportation. Workers have little legal protection from discrimination in hiring or pay disparity. Rates for black women performers are a fraction of those of their white counterparts, for instance,[15] plus-sized performers too are underpaid, and male performers can be blacklisted based on rumors of their having had same-sex sexual encounters. Independent contractor status means that workers cannot legally unionize and that they have fewer legal protections in the event of retaliation against even informal organizing efforts.

Independent contractor status also affects porn workers in ways that extend beyond the letter of the law. Employers and workers alike make a host of often inaccurate assumptions about legal entitlements based on what they assume being an independent contractor entails. Though producers are legally required to secure production insurance, few do, and this gives workers little recourse in the event of on-set injury or infection. Even in uninsured workplaces, workers are entitled to make workers' compensation claims against their employers but rarely do. Standard industry rhetoric maintains that the nature of porn work makes identifying the precise cause of (and hence the party responsible for) a work injury difficult, but employers escape financial responsibility even for those injuries that are plainly traceable to a particular set. In one extreme instance, veteran performer Prince Yahshua sustained significant injury to his penis during a scene. The injury required $120,000 in surgery and follow-up care that left Yahshua out of work during his months-long rehabilitation. He covered these costs out of pocket save for a $20,000 check the production company sent of its own accord. When asked why he chose not to file a workman's compensation claim, Yahshua pointed to his independent contractor status. He added, "It worked itself out," noting that he has since continued to work consistently in the industry.[16] Other workers who reported having been injured on set suggested that paying medical costs out of pocket was a small expense in comparison to the wages they would surely lose had they filed a claim.

In spite of the various ways independent contractor status can increase profit for employers and vulnerability for workers, most workers do not identify establishing employee status as a priority, and many have found ways to make the independent contractor status work for them. Performers find tax and legal benefits associated with incorporating their own names and brands—a number of performers are their own LLCs—which is not possible for employees.

On a more abstract level, performers report that they prefer the idea of working for themselves, perceiving that this affords them greater autonomy as they negotiate schedules, wages, and work tasks. Independent contractor status may give workers more freedom to seek out alternative income streams, another way performers can be understood to be creatively precarious.

Adult film performers are skilled at diversifying income streams, a strategy that has become increasingly important as both performance rates and casting opportunities in film diminish. In addition to the satellite industries we previously outlined, performers maximize their incomes by creatively monetizing quotidian moments of their lives: they sell their used underwear, make money while sitting in Los Angeles traffic by charging fans for a cell phone chat, and command fees for opening their birthday parties to the public. Performers also make marketing opportunities out of the mundane, sharing Twitter photos of their morning showers, fitting DVD signings into family vacations, and engaging fans as they watch favorite sports teams. Though these opportunities could be read as discomfiting evidence of the market's encroachment into even the most intimate spaces of workers' lives, they could also be said to represent workers' creative strategies for negotiating precarity. Part of what we find so instructive about porn work is that both things are undoubtedly true.

The Amazon "wish list" is a nearly ubiquitous feature on performer web sites and social media. Performers invite fans to buy them lingerie, sex toys, and cosplay gear, but also novels, records, and daily essentials such as vitamins and shampoo. Performers self-consciously use wish lists as a means to supplement unpredictable earnings and, sometimes, to compensate for payment they feel production companies wrongly withhold. Gay porn performer Conner Habib offered this explanation to his Twitter followers: "Why is it okay for porn stars to have wish lists? [Because] we don't get royalties even though studios get our images forever."[17] Other performers have suggested that they find it hard to be too concerned with piracy when sales only enrich production companies. Were residuals and royalties standard practice, performers might make more of an effort to encourage fans to "pay for [their] porn," as the industry slogan goes. As it stands, it may be more efficient for performers to leave antipiracy advocacy to employers and focus their marketing efforts on the alternative income streams for which their porn performances serve as advertisement. Performers are acutely aware of the areas in which they have power, and they manipulate them brilliantly.

Facing the threat of retaliation and legal barriers to formal organizing, porn workers devise creative methods of not only individual but also collective resistance. We caution against a view of labor organizing that recognizes only those forms of action legible in law and mainstream union movements. Apart from various unsuccessful attempts to join the Screen Actors Guild, porn-worker organizations have not, for the most part, sought to replicate a labor union model.[18] Instead, they focus on mutual assistance, information sharing, and education. Club 90 in the early 1980s served as an education and support group and inspired an off-Broadway play in which Club 90 members performed.[19] Led by Nina Ha®tley[20] in the late 1980s, the Pink Ladies' Social Club served as a support group but also a space in which performers shared material information about rates, working conditions, and which bosses were best to work for. Under Har®tley, a trained nurse and veteran performer, the organization provided health information, educating performers about which sex acts posed the greatest risk of sexually transmitted disease transmission, safer sex methods, and the signs of sexually transmitted infection. Ha®tley has continued to play a key role in industry organizing, and held a leadership role in the Adult Performer Advocacy Committee.

With a series of on-set HIV transmissions in 1997 and 1998, performers again came together to emphasize health in their organizing efforts. Founded by former performer Sharon Mitchell, the Adult Industry Medical Foundation (AIM) served as a centralized testing and treatment clinic and provided a space for performer education, offering the video primers *Porn 101* and *102* to new performers curious about how to negotiate rates, STI risks, consent, and financial matters such as the importance of paying your taxes in a state where it is legal to have sex on camera. The Erotic Entertainers Guild (1997) and Adult Performers Union (2003) focused on establishing a wage floor and continued to push for performer-centered health-care protocols. These organizations have been short-lived, due in part to industry management's consistent harassment of the workers involved. Ha®tley explained, for example, that even Pink Ladies' Social Club, hardly a militant organization, drew management retaliation: "We were instantly branded as lesbian unionizers and barely worked for six months."[21]

Fear of management retaliation may partially explain more recent groups' special efforts to distance themselves from labor unions and any suggestion of labor-management conflict. The Adult Performers Association (2011) made explicit that "*everyone* in the industry will benefit from our research and efforts [emphasis added],"[22] but its leaders, Nica Noelle and January Seraph, were nonetheless subject to harassment and threats.[23] The Adult Performer Advocacy Committee (APAC, established in 2013 and still operating) has similarly positioned itself as a voice for performers, but one not in conflict with industry management. Reviving AIM's educational tradition, APAC produced an updated version of *Porn 101,* introducing new performers or those just thinking about going into porn to topics ranging from sexual health to contract negotiation. APAC has met with greater institutional support, with the porn industry's trade organization (the Free Speech Coalition) initially offering meeting space and legal counsel and its trade magazines disseminating APAC's press releases. This level of support may owe to APAC's leadership, which includes top performers in the industry, many of whom also hold management roles.

Citing parallel features, including competition among workers, the transience of the workforce, the reality that workers hold multiple positions simultaneously, and management's concentrated power, industrial relations scholar Gregor Gall suggests that craft organizing of the sort Dorothy Sue Cobble describes in waitresses' unions might allow for organizing in the porn industry.[24] An additional challenge of organizing porn work is the frequency with which those involved shift between management and worker roles. In addition to pursuing various satellite industries (and making new subindustries of their own), porn workers resist precarity by shifting between the roles of manager and worker. After a short time in the industry, most performers will have at least dabbled in management, producing content for their own web sites or clips stores, working as directors for established production companies, or starting production companies of their own. This fluidity challenges the strict class divisions that have been central to state, activist, and academic approaches to labor organizing. That performer groups can consist of worker-managers does not nullify their organizing work, but it no doubt affects the organization's perspective and priorities. Seeking a purer organization untainted by management interests misses the point, though, because the potential to shift between worker and manager roles is indispensable to workers seeking control over labor processes.

DO-IT-YOURSELF ETHICS, CLASS, AND BOUNDARY WORK

In addition to resisting the vulnerabilities precarity brings, some porn workers describe precarity as both a potential job benefit and what allows them to be creative. Shifting between worker and manager roles is one way porn workers respond to precarity not by seeking greater stability but by exploiting flexibility to their advantage. Though some performer-cum-managers, like the iconic small business owner, simply prefer to be their own bosses, autonomous production is also a space in which workers refuse status quo labor practices, casting opportunities, rates, and representational politics. Worker-produced porn also makes managers of workers, generating conflicting interests and riven class positions. The medium trades in tensions that orthodox analyses of creative labor cannot account for.

At the most basic level, self-producing gives worker-managers control over the products in which they are featured. In an industry in which the most successful performers carefully craft their personal brands, what benefits a performer's brand may be less advantageous to agents, directors, and studio heads. Authorial control can be a powerful tool. Performers may choose to wait to perform anal sex, for example, until they can command the highest rate possible, and many also perceive that slowly doling out new types of scenes to fans helps to ensure career longevity or, in industry speak, to avoid getting "shot out." Agents, however, prefer performers who "do everything" right away, as this ensures more bookings (and thus commissions) in the short term. With a self-replenishing reserve army of labor, agents have little interest in counseling performers for longevity. Directors and producers too have ready access to new talent and are most invested in the current production's profits. In this context, performers can choose to self-produce the sort of content, such as a first anal scene, that promises higher sales. Leading up to these productions, workers can use performances for other production companies both to gather start-up capital and to advertise the self-produced content from which they profit most. Worker-producers may also use self-production as a long-term planning strategy to the extent that continued sales can generate earnings for years, money that contract performers (who do not receive royalties) will never see.

Though mainstream porn is home to a proliferation of small production companies led by current and former performers, do-it-yourself (DIY) ethics are most strikingly embodied in amateur, independent, and queer and feminist porn. We now focus on these forms to consider the ways such small-batch production simultaneously responds to, perpetuates, and refuses precarity. Web technology has radically changed the landscape of the porn industry, making not only content but also production hyperaccessible. *C'lick Me: A Netporn Studies Reader* explores these shifts, foregrounding the role of DIY ethics in contemporary Internet pornography. Rejecting any static social meaning of pornography, the anthology's editors recognize the ways porn producers and users (and where the two meet) modify pornography's meaning through their interactions with it. Netporn "can contain a critique of commercial work ethics and gender roles," they suggest.[25]

Performers take on self-production to create alternatives to available work. Those who do not fit the metrics of physical attractiveness currently in vogue may find better luck producing their own content and creating a niche around their personal brand. Sites such as Suicide Girls and Burning Angel initiated the alt porn genre in the early 2000s to feature tattooed and pierced bodies that, while overwhelmingly white, cisgendered, and thin, did not fit into available porn genres at the time. Queer porn production emerged from the desire to include bodies invisible in mainstream porn, but also had more expressly political aims. Frustrated by the homogeneity of alt porn, Courtney Trouble developed No Faux, now Indie Porn Revolution, the first site to market itself as "queer." Unable to find work in alt porn as a plus-sized performer, Trouble took to self-production in part to make space to explore her own desires on film. Imagining that others might desire such a space as well, they[26] wanted to create "something that's truly representative of underground communities and give people a place where they can explore their desires on film."[27] Those who may find a home in queer porn include transgendered and gender queer performers unwilling or unable (read: without surgically altered gender-conforming bodies) to work in mainstream "tranny" porn, plus-size performers who do not conform to the BBW (Big Beautiful Woman) genre's own strict rules, those with visible disabilities, and some people of color. In her essay on the practice of directing and producing feminist pornography, director and author Tristan Taormino insists that pornographic representations are entirely bound up with production practices. As a feminist pornographer, she works to "capture some level of authenticity, a connection between partners, and sense that everyone's having a good time. Think of it as organic, fair-trade porn."[28]

Amateur porn presents another space that privileges "authentic" self-expression. Trading on the idea of porn as a mode of self-expression, amateur sites and film distributors seek amateur producers who, as Farrell Timlake, the owner of the largest amateur porn distributor, put it, "want to be doing it for the exhibitionist thrill." Timlake describes Homegrown Video's scenes as an "authentic" alternative to "paint by numbers porn."[29] We read this too as political. As with other forms of DIY porn, amateur emphasizes the experience of the performer as much as that of the consumer. Again, they may be the same people.

For others, mainstream work is available but requires performing in scenes they feel are degrading or otherwise politically problematic. Roles for black performers are extremely limited, for example, and those available often require workers to perform exaggerated tropes of racialized sexuality. These roles are also poorly compensated, black performers earning a fraction of the rates their white counterparts do.[30] Historian Mireille Miller-Young describes self-produced porn as a way for black women performers to assert control over the images they portray. At the same time, self-produced ventures need buyers to survive, so black women performers weave together mimetic performance of expected tropes with portrayals that refuse these roles. For black women porn site producers, she writes, "netporn proffers an intensely politicized space where the line between exploitation and empowerment, pleasure and peril, community and alienation is totally blurred."[31]

We find that blurriness compelling. That DIY porn is as much about process as profit contributes to ongoing discussions in media industries scholarship about the dialectics of precarity and creativity. Workers sometimes seek out precarious conditions to enable greater creative expression. With the exception of those self-producers, such as some black women performers who choose DIY in part because it can offer better pay, DIY porn overwhelmingly pays less than mainstream. Those amateur distribution companies that pay at all offer $500–$1,000 for a film, to be distributed among all those who participated. Queer production companies pay $200–$400 flat rates for a scene, regardless of performers' gender presentation, race, body type, or the type of sex they perform. Mainstream rates vary widely along these lines, but a standard rate for female performers is $800–$1,200.[32] Mainstream productions typically employ a host of crew and support staff, whereas DIY productions are drastically pared down. There is no need for scriptwriters, after all, in "unscripted" sex. Films designed to appear more authentic require less postproduction labor.

From a sex-work organizing perspective, DIY porn might be understood to reinforce the idea that sex work is unskilled. More broadly, we are well aware of the widespread management strategy of replacing professional with amateur labor. But DIY, a medium workers initiated precisely in reaction to "professional" pornography, pushes against this critique too. To the extent that focusing on "authentic" sexualities stabilizes them as natural[33] as it frames them as unproduced (that is, unlabored), DIY may serve to stabilize identities as it destabilizes economies. Though DIY production entails greater economic precarity, is that such a bad thing among those for whom stability is personally and creatively toxic? This is, of course, a familiar coupling in the political economy of late capitalism. It puts in relief a set of tensions we cannot and do not wish to smooth over.

NOTES

1. Chuck Kleinhans, "'Creative Industries,' Neoliberal Fantasies, and the Cold, Hard Facts of Global Recession: Some Basic Lessons," *Jump Cut: A Review of Contemporary Media* 53 (2011), www.ejumpcut.org/currentissue/kleinhans-creatIndus/text.html.

2. Martha King, "Protecting and Representing Workers in the New Gig Economy: The Case of the Freelancers Union," in *New Labor in New York: Precarious Workers and the Future of the Labor Movement*, ed. Ruth Milkman and Ed Ott (Ithaca, NY: Cornell University Press, 2014), 150–170.

3. Tristan Taormino, Constance Penley, Celine Parreñas Shimizu, and Mireille Miller-Young, eds., *The Feminist Porn Book* (New York: Feminist Press, 2013).

4. Interviewees estimate that, whereas a producer could expect to quadruple his or her investment in the late 1990s, one might double an investment today. Transcripts for all interviews cited in this piece are in Heather Berg's possession. For more on the broader project of which they are a part, see Heather Berg, "Labouring Porn Studies," *Porn Studies* 1.1–2 (2014): 75–79. For a recent update on the economics of porn production, see Alexander Poe, "Seven Directors Focus on the Current Condition of Porn," *XBIZ: The Industry Source* (August 20, 2014), www.xbiz.com/news/183848.

5. None of the thirty-three female performers interviewed made a living off film work alone.

6. Gay porn performer Christopher Daniels, for example, explained that the "sole reason" he took on porn performing is because he learned that escorts who are also porn performers get more bookings and can charge on average $100 more per hour than their nonperformer counterparts. Christopher Daniels, interview by Heather Berg, Los Angeles, April 9, 2014. Female performers in "straight" porn who pursue escorting or erotic dance can command at least double the earnings of their nonperformer counterparts. Tara Holiday, phone interview by Heather Berg, February 22, 2014.

7. Dominic Ace, interview by Heather Berg, Reseda, CA, November 8, 2013.

8. Raylene, interview by Heather Berg, Reseda, CA, October 29, 2013.

9. Venus Lux, phone interview by Heather Berg, June 30, 2014.

10. Christian Mann, "Christian Mann, General Manager, Evil Angel Productions," in *Distribution Revolution: Conversations about the Digital Future of Film and Television*, ed. Michael Curtin, Jennifer Holt, and Kevin Sanson (Berkeley: University of California Press, 2014), 121–131.

11. Antiporn feminist writing is rife with constructions of porn workers as passive and un-self-aware. In Catherine MacKinnon's telling, for example, Linda Lovelace "was pornographed," Playboy's consumers masturbate "over the positions *taken by* the women's bodies [emphasis mine]," and pornography is "sex forced on real women . . . women's bodies trussed and maimed and raped and made into things to be hurt and obtained and accessed." Catharine MacKinnon, *Feminism Unmodified: Discourses on Life and Law* (Cambridge, MA: Harvard University Press, 1988), 128.

12. See, e.g., Cristina Morini, "The Feminization of Labour in Cognitive Capitalism," *Feminist Review* 87.1 (2007): 40–59, doi: http://dx.doi.org/10.1057/palgrave.fr.9400367. Andrew Ross, *Nice Work If You Can Get It: Life and Labor in Precarious Times* (New York: New York University Press, 2009).

13. *Sexual Exploitation and Other Abuse of Children: Record Keeping Requirements*, 18 U.S.C.A., 2000.

14. See Constance Penley, "Collision in a Courtroom," in *Images, Ethics, and Technology*, ed. Sharrona Pearl (New York: Routledge, 2015).

15. See Mireille Miller-Young, "Putting Hypersexuality to Work: Black Women and Illicit Eroticism in Pornography," *Sexualities* 13.2 (April 2010): 219–235, doi:10.1177/1363460709359229.

16. Prince Yashua, interview by Heather Berg, Canoga Park, CA, February 28, 2014.

17. Conner Habib, Twitter post, October 23, 2013.

18. Though performers have repeatedly sought inclusion in mainstream Hollywood's Screen Actor's Guild, their presence has remained unwelcome due to both mainstream's sex negativity and SAG's policy of only organizing workers on sets where collective bargaining contracts exist. See Gregor Gall, *An Agency of Their Own: Sex Worker Union Organizing* (Washington: Zero Books, 2012), 28.

19. Legs McNeil, Jennifer Osborne, and Peter Pavia, *The Other Hollywood: The Uncensored Oral History of the Porn Film Industry,* 2nd ed. (New York: HarperCollins, 2009), 373.

20. Nina Ha⊛tley's name is trademarked; this is her preferred spelling.

21. Nina Ha⊛tley, interview by Heather Berg, Los Angeles, CA, February 17, 2012.

22. Gall, *An Agency of Their Own,* 31.

23. Nica Noelle, e-mail interview by Heather Berg, October 14, 2013.

24. Gall, *An Agency of Their Own,* 31.

25. Katrien Jacobs, Marjie Janssen, and Metteo Pasquinelli, "Introduction," in *C'lickme: A Netporn Studies Reader,* ed. Katrien Jacobs, Marjie Janssen, and Metteo Pasquinelli (Amsterdam: Institute of Network Cultures, 2007), 1.

26. *They* is Trouble's preferred gender-neutral pronoun, as it is for other gender queer and trans people, including Jiz Lee and Papi Coxxx..

27. Courtney Trouble, interview by Heather Berg, Emeryville, CA, March 18, 2014.

28. Tristan Taormino, "Calling the Shots: Feminist Porn in Theory and Practice," in *The Feminist Porn Book: The Politics of Producing Pleasure,* ed. Tristan Taormino et al. (New York: Feminist Press, 2013), 261. For a critique of discourses of authenticity in queer and feminist porn, see Heather Berg, "Sex, Work, Queerly: Identity, Authenticity, and Laboured Performance," in *Queer Sex Work,* ed. Mary Laing, Katy Pilcher, and Nicola Smith (London: Routledge, 2015).

29. Farrell Timlake, phone interview by Heather Berg, January 23, 2014.

30. Mireille Miller-Young, *A Taste for Brown Sugar: Black Women in Porn* (Durham, NC: Duke University Press, 2014).

31. Mireille Miller-Young, "Sexy and Smart: Black Women and the Politics of Self-Authorship in Netporn," in *C'lickme,* ed. Jacobs, Janssen, and Pasquinelli, 207.

32. Average rates drawn from performer interviews.

33. See Julie Levin Russo, "'The Real Thing': Reframing Queer Pornography for Virtual Spaces," in *C'lickme,* ed. Jacobs, Janssen, and Pasquinelli.

13

Strategies for Success?

Navigating Hollywood's "Postracial" Labor Practices

Kristen J. Warner

This chapter makes a case for precarity as a historical state of being for marginalized men and women of color in the entertainment industries. As a preface to underscore what follows, I want to recount two recent experiences that make explicit the larger stakes I'm concerned with here. First, at the originating conference for this collection, a key debate focused on the gendered division of labor and how debates about "progress" often obscure the ongoing marginalization of women from the screen media workforce. Scholars made resoundingly astute points about the ways women continue to suffer under the tyranny of patriarchy in the culture industries and articulated many powerful ways in which we—scholars and practitioners— might engage in the struggle for change and equality. Yet what was missing in this conversation was what is often missing from conversations about identity politics: explicitly marking out the white racial identity of the women we were discussing. I spoke up, named the exonmination, and filled in the gap. Women do not all experience precariousness and contingent labor in the same way. Some women have more access to opportunities than other women simply by virtue of their racial identity, and while all women certainly suffer under patriarchal labor regimes, some suffer less and some suffer more. My intervention in the conversation, then, was to insist on the importance of intersectional cultural analysis when discussing women and labor in the entertainment industries, and insist that any intervention we discuss must be attuned to those differences. Because in a conversation where, to crudely paraphrase Gloria T. Hull, Patricia Bell Scott, and Barbara Smith,[1] all women laborers are assumed white and all racial or ethnic minority laborers are assumed male, we can't begin to address the precarious creativity of women of color without first making them visible in our conceptions of screen media work.

While attending panels about working in the industry at the third annual Austin Television Festival (ATXFest), I encountered another instance when the conversation erased the specific experiences of women of color in the entertainment industries. At the festival, I listened as successful casting directors, staff writers, and showrunners shared their workaday experiences in the field. In a panel on working as an assistant, four women—three white women and one ethnically ambiguous woman—described how they each got their start in the business. Each woman had an internship that then led to permanent employment. They further explained that they garnered the necessary skills for their profession not through college but through their work as assistants or in online extension courses. Lastly, and most relevant to this essay, when asked about accessing entry-level assistant positions, each panelist agreed that leveraging existing relationships and networks was absolutely crucial to employment in the entertainment industries. Indeed, even the panelists' own hiring practices reinforced this "truism." They discovered new talent through alumni networks, family members, and friends. Reflecting on this panel conversation, I found precariousness to be an inevitable function of their career choice. Yet I also found that the panelists enjoyed the privilege of stabilizing some of that uncertainty for others by hiring those who reproduce their identities and social relations, and thus offsetting precarity for those who are most like them. I mention this example not only because professional networks are largely racially myopic, but also because the reproduction of identities and social relations vis-à-vis networking and mentorship directly serves a racially unjust status quo. In short, its superficial innocence masks a much more troubling reality: to assume that access to creative work simply depends first on "whom you know" and then on being "the best person for the job" ultimately obscures the power structures that systematically exclude men and women of color from availing themselves of similar opportunities for networking *and* jobs in the first place.

Both anecdotes reinforce a major crux of the discussion that follows. First, discursive maneuvers that reframe racially myopic professional networks and practices as an ideologically benign function of the creative industries raise the precarious stakes for laborers of color—they effectively neutralize arguments about systemic discrimination and inequality by displacing structural concerns in favor of questions about skills and talent. You're simply good enough to get the job or you're not. Likewise, much like my opening anecdote suggests, this discourse risks framing genuine concerns about parity and progress as the product of a contemporary moment marked by extreme precariousness for everybody rather than a function of the socio-historical circumstances of a group of workers whose precariousness has been an ever-present condition of their existence. When meaningful conversations about diversity are outside the confines of common industrial logic (that is, it's not a problem that exists), the strategies and tactics people of color deploy to gain visibility, secure employment, and maintain careers as creative laborers deserve sustained consideration.

In this chapter, then, I first establish the stark realities of minority employment in the creative industries before outlining how industry professionals abdicate responsibility for structural problems by reframing the issue as one about skills and talent. Such discourse, I argue, is predicated upon the exnomination of its normative ideological basis. In the second section of the chapter, I draw focused attention to how this discourse affects casting for film and television roles. Here I briefly consider how casting directors reproduce normative identities (and thus limited opportunities for actors of color) in their workaday practices. I then conclude by outlining three strategies racial and ethnic minority performers have adopted to contend with their precarious circumstances, and at what cost. Ultimately, I argue that necessary and meaningful political intervention on behalf of a diverse labor force is displaced by persistent notions of "talent" and obfuscated by the simple need to find work in whatever ways possible.

My analysis draws from interviews with media professionals in industry trade journals, conference panels, social media platforms, and my own fieldwork. I borrow John Caldwell's notion of industrial reflexivity to reframe the workaday experiences and explanations of these "insiders" as a process of self-fashioning and self-theorizing their own identities and interests within existing structures and categories.[2]

MINORITY EMPLOYMENT: DISMAL DATA AND INDUSTRIAL PUSHBACK

The lack of a diverse labor force in both above- and below-the-line talent is not simply anecdotal. In April 2014, the Writers Guild of America (WGA) released their latest "Hollywood Writers Report," the organization's study on the state of diversity in the film and television industries.[3] The report's findings prompted much debate, and rightfully so, as the data indicated a dismal state of affairs for film and television writers: for instance, minority television writers had increased their share of employment by only 1 percent, and women remained underrepresented by a factor of two to one among television writers.[4] Hollywood's lack of diversity also extended to directing. In 2014, the Directors Guild of America (DGA) diversity report indicated that of the 3,500 episodes analyzed from more than 200 scripted television programs produced in the 2013–2014 season, 69 percent were directed by white males,[5] 12 percent by white females, 17 percent by minority males, and 2 percent by minority females—a statistic unchanged from the previous year's study.[6] The numbers are no better in acting, where the Screen Actors Guild (SAG) reported that in 2008, white actors dominated television and film roles (70.7 percent). Rounding out the casting data, African Americans represented 14.8 percent of television and film roles, Latinos 6.7 percent, Native Americans 0.30 percent, and unknown/other 4.1 percent.[7] Lastly, official statistics for casting directors are more difficult to secure because they are not represented by organized labor to the same degree as other creative professions. They do have a professional society—the Casting Society of America—whose leadership profile follows a pattern similar to employment data collected and distributed by the guilds. Its twenty-six-member leadership team is all white with the exception of one Latino; its gender split is roughly equal.

Such are the data that characterize the premier occupations within Hollywood's labor force, capturing the degree to which the great majority of feature films and television productions resist multiculturalism. Indeed, despite some small signs of progress (often disproportionately celebrated with self-congratulatory discourses), the film and television industries have yet to initiate any meaningful measures that might correct the staggering lack of diversity in their labor force. In fact, the last time the industry's exclusionary hiring practices received serious and sustained public criticism was the fall 1999 television season—more than fifteen years ago—when none of the season's twenty-three new prime-time series featured a single person of color in a leading role. Civil rights organizations and media advocacy groups threatened boycotts and litigation, publicly demanding immediate action from the networks to rectify the troubling lack of minority characters.[8] The public shaming and negative news coverage generated some momentum in favor of minority employment both in front of and behind the camera. Networks immediately began casting people of color in supporting roles across a number of series—a liberal "sprinkling" of multiculturalism to quell the controversy. In a structural attempt at change, many networks created in-house diversity positions—executives charged with the futile task of encouraging television showrunners to increase the number of people of color employed on their productions.

Despite such responses, the momentum produced limited success and short-lived interest. Diversity executives are considered all bark and no bite; without the authority to hire or fire, they lack the power to intervene effectively. They furthermore claim that efforts to diversify personnel require fundamental change at every employment rank within a network, and that change remains a far-off reality.[9] Furthermore, in the NAACP Hollywood Bureau's 2008 report, the organization stresses that, despite some gains, the primary objectives it negotiated during the 1999 talks have been largely abandoned by the networks.[10] As Vicangelo Bulluck, former executive director of the NAACP's Hollywood bureau, posited, "The trend definitely seems to be going in the wrong direction."[11] Indeed, nine years after one of the most public industrial shakedowns, employment data retells the same story each year, which further suggests that even if advocacy groups are still pursuing their diversity agendas, the networks have generated strategies to allow them to opt out.

With less than substantial improvement to its exclusionary hiring practices, the television and film industries have nevertheless become emboldened in their apathy about the lack of diversity both in front of and behind the camera. Report after report citing the dearth of employment for creative labor of color has had little effect on how the major Hollywood players choose to conduct their business. Certainly, it is not in their best interest to admit that racial and ethnic diversity is simply a low priority or an unnecessary distraction. In short, no matter how dismal the employment data, diversity just isn't a problem for many of those individuals in positions with enough power to do something about it. Instead of direct acknowledgment, they employ discursive stopgaps that redirect conversations about employment into discussions of competence and skill—ironically, as I will outline below, concepts that perpetuate familiar ideological beliefs about racial identity.

For example, in response to coverage of the 2013 WGA "Writers Report," the anonymous commenter "Heartsick" at *Deadline Hollywood* expressed frustration at the pressure coming from diversity executives as well as talent agents to racially integrate his writing staff. Describing literary agents calling him to suggest writers of color for his staff, Heartsick recalls asking: "What piece of writing have you read that indicates this person would be right for my show, and the answer INVARIABLY is: they haven't read the person, they're just calling to con me into hiring someone based on irrelevant, invidious categories that should have no place in the employment of writers."[12] Heartsick is frustrated with agents who allegedly send him ill-prepared writers of color—a phenomenon he doesn't attribute to white writers also seeking employment—because they interfere with his ability to identify talent based on how well they "fit" with the creative sensibility among his writing staff, a criterion that in his mind transcends racial difference. One can only imagine how many Heartsicks exist in the Hollywood hierarchy. But here's the critical point: if diversity was an organic industrial practice implemented in staffing hires based simply on postracial notions of fit, talent, and worth, then by extension Hollywood would be a much more hospitable place for ethnic and racial minorities.

Commentators on *Deadline* are not the only industry-minded folks maintaining that anonymity is the only way to honestly respond to these shameful data-filled reports. One of the more recent trends on Twitter is the emergence of Mystery Hollywood. The "Mysterys," as they label themselves, are anonymous industry workers/insiders who claim they hold enough clout in the industry that revealing their personal identities would wreak havoc on their professional lives. Mysterys' racial, ethnic, and gender identities remain unclear unless their Twitter handles or avatars make explicit such differences. The juxtaposition between how Mysterys occupy the socially mediated space as exnominated white and/or male identities and the manner by which they self-fashion personas as successful entertainment industry laborers using the Twitter platform to "tell the truth" anonymously creates some complicated spaces of navigation for a person of color follower. Consider a small section of a Twitter screed by a Mystery account called "DevelopmentHell Exec (DHE)": "Am I the only one sick of hearing about the plight of women in the film and TV industry? It's 2014. Just do something awesome, you're in. Or how bout just making GOOD FILMS? Women-centric, men-centric, alien-centric, muppet-centric, Wall-E-centric. Whatever. Quality > politics."[13] Similar to Heartsick, DHE's Mystery account allows him to speak his truth about the manner by which diverse employment is discussed in Hollywood. It also allows him[14] to free himself from the focus on employing different kinds of gendered and racial bodies to instead focus on the abstract and apolitical notion of "good work" that cares not about the body from which that work is produced. For DHE, the data suggesting how far white women and men and women of color lag behind white men in all facets of the industry is representative not of a racist structure but of natural selection, sifting out those who create "quality" work from those who are unqualified for the business.

Regardless of how many popular press articles, pie charts, and data graphs consistently demonstrate that marginalized bodies are not allowed opportunities to prove they can produce quality work, the ideological frames perpetuated by the likes of Heartsick and DHE dissociate the structural racism from common industry practices. Creative talents are rewarded with access and opportunity, regardless of the racial or ethnic identity of the worker. The few minority workers who do enjoy some success function as evidence that the best talent does indeed rise to the top. Yet such discursive logic obscures that Hollywood is an industry built around relationships, networking, internships, and apprenticeships—a classed set of practices from which people of color are systemically excluded.

CASTING DIRECTORS: PRECARIOUS LIMBO GATEKEEPERS

By the very nature of the career, casting is an overlooked and underresearched component of the filmmaking process. To claim success, the casting director must identify such high-quality talent that his or her part in locating the actors is effaced in favor of an assumption about the process as organic and natural: the actor "just fits" the role. Put simply, good casting happens when no one notices the casting director's work. Even casting directors themselves elide the skills and expertise required to do their jobs well—in my conversations, they repeatedly claim they "just know it" when they meet the right person for the part. It's much more likely that casting practices parallel the sort of creativity described by Keith Negus: "Creative practice is not approached as inspirational and radically new, nor as something that everybody does in a kind of everyday creative way. Instead, ongoing cultural production involves working with recognizable codes, conventions and expectations."[15] In other words, casting is not an exclusively intuitive, inspirational, or mystical act. Rather, it is a learned and socialized professional skill. Instead of knowing the right actor when you see her, casting directors understand that the "right" person must adhere to the standardized codes, conventions, and expectations of the industry they service. Casting directors know how to practice their trade because they were trained by other casting directors; identifying the right person is a learned and learnable skill and constitutes the knowledge capital shared among professional networks. A number of current casting directors who spoke with me were trained by the greats—the Marion Doughertys, the Ellen Lewises—and frequently compare this relationship to graduate education.

Casting is a freelance occupation. Casting directors establish careers—and financial sustainability—from job to job. This precariousness further enshrines and reproduces the standard codes and conventions that define the "right" person for the role. Radical or nontraditional casting techniques jeopardize the trust casting directors must maintain with producers and other professionals in their network, especially for casting directors who are young or new to the profession. Indeed, at an ATX Fest panel on casting, Jen Euston, casting director for *Orange Is the New Black,* said that it was only after she became an established casting director with ongoing and recurring work that she could walk away from a job because she disagreed with the creative vision of the producers or the network bosses. She described this privilege as an outcome of a long and arduous career—a freedom she earned that isn't available to everyone in her profession. This anecdote underscores how the precarious nature of casting (indeed, much creative work) keeps most professionals tethered to the same ideological frames as those from whom they must gain employment. Learning casting conventions and reinforcing the status quo increase a casting director's chances for success, but these requirements limit access and opportunity for those individuals who fall outside established codes.

My ongoing research project has been to track mechanisms the film and television industries have promoted as strategies that occasionally allow individuals—like casting directors—to circumvent the racial myopia of professional networks and practices. After spending time observing and interviewing casting directors about the ways they can or cannot incorporate diversity into their workaday practices, I identified colorblind casting as the most prominent contemporary strategy to improve diversity in the postracial era.[16] Colorblind casting is the process of excluding racial identities from character descriptions, a tool to increase the number of racial or ethnic actors in front of the camera by ensuring the role is open to (literally) any body (type). While my earlier research investigated how colorblind casting informed the decisions of casting directors and how the practice affected onscreen representations, in what remains of this chapter I turn to the place of agency for actors as they navigate an industry and its gatekeepers, all operating under race- and gender-blind assumptions disconnected from the systemic obstacles designed to exclude specific individuals and representations from common business practices. Racial and ethnic minority actors are forced to play along with this game to secure employment in an industry that is always already characterized by chance, instability, and insecurity. Accordingly, actors of color are doubling down on their precariousness. As they turn to strategies to circumvent these obstacles, we find not minority groups engaged in *collective* resistance against systematic exclusion but *individual* minority actors availing themselves of whatever strategies will increase the odds in their favor, ultimately (and unsurprisingly) establishing a set of practices that not only reinforce normative white ideals by exnominating the racialization conventions of the "right fit" for whatever jobs are available but also reproduce subtle tactics of antiblackness through disavowing racial discrimination as an industrial reality. I explicate this dual process in the discussion below by identifying three strategies that help actors of color circumvent their precarious careers. These strategies are blindcasting, ambiguously raced performance, and universal discourse.

STRATEGY 1: BLIND CASTING

The physical embodiment of visual difference rather than a qualitatively meaningful representation of difference, blind casting is an illusion of equality and parity in casting. In other words, it functions as a form of diversity you can count rather than a notion of diversity that accounts for the nature of the roles or content. Blind casting thus operates as a way to increase diversity in physical difference without investing in any associated cultural differences. Colorblind casting logic is useful to guilds like the Screen Actors Guild (SAG-AFTRA). Because the guild has no authority over or investment in the form or quality of the employment (that is, the guild does not regulate content), it cares less about the nature of the role than about counting that role as an employment gain for their members. Colorblind casting logic thus offers an easy method to assuage dual concerns: it makes available more job opportunities for the least employed sectors of the guild's membership and imbues those job opportunities with an air of "respectability" because of the way colorblind logic evacuates any cultural specificity in its operating logic in favor of normative whiteness.

Yet, underpinned by neoliberal race logic, colorblind casting deploys a universal, "we are all the same" rhetoric that only superficially addresses the issues of diversity, employment, and racial representation in television and film. Its resolution relies solely on visible difference. Blind casting thus forces minority actors who desire employment to input cultural differences and output a standardized form of whiteness. Moreover, that this input/output practice has become so commonsensical makes acknowledging its existence a bit of a conundrum. Colorblind logic holds that race is no longer a meaningful barrier to accomplishments, so pointing out continuing injustice as a consequence of racist structures is now, in fact, a racist act. When I make visible the dissonance that occurs when blind casting places an actor of color in a narrative context that, say, isolates him or her from a larger community of color, *I* am the racist for making a fuss over what Stuart Hall calls "matter out of place."[17] Rather than identifying how this process erases a community's socio-historical specificity, the logic requires that we celebrate its evacuation of race as an issue at all. Diversity matters now only inasmuch as the networks (and guilds) can count the representation of visible difference.

Yet identifying "matter out of place" is one way to observe the failure of the blind casting strategy. If blind-casting roles for actors of color ultimately normalizes them to the degree that they become culturally illegible, the same effects can reveal the dangers of such an enterprise. When writers do not consider racial difference and history as part of their character's backstory, they too often succumb to a set of unintended racially troped pitfalls. Consider the blind-cast role of the Black character Bonnie Bennett—a witch—in CW's *The Vampire Diaries* (*TVD*). Bennett, whose original surname in the book series, McCullough, was changed to Bennett as a consequence of the casting decision, is a central character in the televised series. According to the original material, Bonnie McCullough is a fair-skinned redhead. Yet Bonnie Bennett signifies as an African American teenager. While it is a laudable effort on the part of the network and its executives to diversify *TVD*'s ensemble cast, the failure to adjust the character's backstory to account for the long history of racialized imagery of Black women and witchcraft opens the series to a number of accidental pitfalls. In the series, Bonnie belongs to a family of witches who historically served as slaves to the lead actors. Continuing in the tradition, Bonnie's servitude to her white friends results in her sacrificing her life for theirs. Finally, unlike Bonnie's female counterparts, who are immersed in teen sexuality and coupling—a vital convention of the teen drama—Bonnie is rarely paired with a love interest. Instead, her sole devotion is to those she serves. Collectively, these tropes raise troubling historical associations with Black representation and further perpetuate the sort of symbolic violence against Black female bodies that blind casting's postracial ethos is intended to counter.

Despite the pitfalls, blind casting remains a viable option for employment when few other promising opportunities exist for actors of color. Moreover, because the parts are written normatively, many actors themselves celebrate the opportunities as "respectable" alternatives to race-specific casting calls, which often perpetuate troubling stereotypes.

STRATEGY 2: RACIALLY AMBIGUOUS PERFORMANCE

A second strategy deployed by underrepresented groups to circumvent the industrial barriers to employment is self-fashioning as a racially ambiguous actor.

Recalling the earlier statistic from SAG-AFTRA, racially unknown/other actors accounted for 4.1 percent of all roles in 2008. The category "racially unknown/other" designates actors who did not select a racial or ethnic identity on the surveys SAG-AFTRA sends to identify the racial and ethnic makeup of its membership. According to interviews with guild representatives, members opt not to self-identify because they fear it will relegate them to the limited roles intended for a particular racialized group. Implicit in this trend is the practice of "passing" among those actors who believe they can be cast in roles with a racial identity other than their own.

For instance, the biracial identities of Jessica Szohr from CW's *Gossip Girl* and Rashida Jones from NBC's *Parks and Recreation* remain "unmarked" in these texts and others in which they appear. Similarly, Troian Bellisario's racial ethnicity is ambiguous enough to allow her to pass as just one of the (white) girls in ABC Family's *Pretty Little Liars*—even though reading her body suggests there is something "not quite white" about her character. Beyond indeterminate racial identities, racially or ethnically ambiguous performers find themselves cast as *multiple* races and ethnicities. Blair Redford's ambiguous look allowed him to be Latino for ABC Family's *Switched at Birth* and American Indian for ABC Family's *The Lying Game*. While the logic behind this strategy might increase an actor's employment opportunities by expanding the number of types through which his or her look is interpreted, it also privileges (oftentimes racist) assumptions about the look of a given racial group.

Racially ambiguous performers also amplify colorblindness's insidious power. As a strategy, it not only makes race something that is "unseen" but detaches racialized bodies from their socio-historical contexts. In other words, the actors function as empty signifiers in that their bodies can be read by audiences in multiple ways, and they can be placed in infinite settings without being tethered to a reality rooted in the socio-historical specifics of their racial and cultural experiences. Furthermore, racial ambiguity allows the network to claim diversity without engaging with the concept beyond superficial (physical) differences.

STRATEGY 3: UNIVERSAL DISCOURSE

The final strategy I want to discuss is one that, unlike the first two, is applicable to a variety of laborers in the film and television industry. It concerns distributing and marketing film with predominately Black casts that are also written, directed, and/or produced by Black creative talent. From films like *The Best Man Holiday* (2013) to *Think Like a Man* (2012), and *Think Like a Man Too* (2014) to the *About Last Night* (2014) remake, publicity and advertising largely frame these films within a universalist discourse—one designed to assure (white) mainstream audiences that the experiences onscreen are both "human" and "relatable" even though the characters may not look like them and elements remain that are, in fact, quite culturally specific.[18] Consider the promotional strategy for *Think Like a Man*. According to a 2012 *Vulture* article, while Black producer Will Packer devoted a large portion of his marketing and advertising budget to flying the cast to events with large numbers of African Americans in the audience, he deployed an alternative strategy to draw white audiences. Here he relied heavily on "crossover" comedian Steve Harvey—who hosts the daytime game show *Family Feud* and wrote the film's source material—as the movie's messenger. "Packer has deployed Steve Harvey . . . to sell the 'everybody's welcome!' message to the general public, sending him out to tub-thump . . . on CBS's *This Morning* and ABC's *The View,* shows that Packer explains, 'don't necessarily over-index with African Americans.'"[19] Moreover, to target white women, Packer and his team stressed the romantic comedy conventions of the film via a television campaign that, according to one former studio marketing head, looked "like classic Romantic Comedy 101. In fact, it looks like a Nancy Meyers movie, with black people. Which is fine. . . . All it has to be is funny, and make it clear that the concept has no race."[20] Yet at what cost comes this universal rhetoric? Extra labor taken on by the actors and producers during these press junkets and promotional events to sell the film as fitting for "all" is expected from marginalized bodies if they desire to reach a mainstream audience. Films with predominately white casts are not expected to sell their films (domestically at least) as universal and relatable because they always already operate within the normative and authentic standards by which we judge the human experience. Similar to blind casting, the burden falls on the person of color to perform his or her "sameness" as a mechanism to ensure that the preferred demographic is not alienated from the production. As Packer asserts, "There is a process to get those audiences. It starts with making a film like this, which is broad, smart, and one where there's no cultural or ethnic specificity that would not be relatable to mainstream Americans."[21] Black cast films, then, are not a niche production; they are the benign reflection of a large, multicultured world that poses no threat to liberal sensibilities and consumption practices.

Universal discourse underscores the historical precariousness of minorities in the creative industries whose labor always existed under this double bind structure that equates success with being both similar to and different from the normative order. Such a double bind recalls how Clyde Taylor defines the mode of Black film production in early cinema as one of "unequal development," that is, a phenomenon that exists where there is "an exploitative/dependent relationship that ultimately results in a more powerful society drawing from the less powerful selected goods and resources without regard for what the loss of those resources will mean to the exploited."[22] According to similar logic, universal discourse insists that for creative laborers of color to participate in the film and television industries, they must embrace a rhetoric of sameness that not only elides their unequal professional footing but also encourages them to lose any sense of socio-historical specificity. Yet what must it mean to be a minority worker who, to find employment, must not only cross over to mainstream filmmaking but also disavow elements of his or her own racial identity to remain gainfully employed? Unequal development epitomizes precarity. It considers the minority worker—whose skills are utilized and borrowed, or more specifically, appropriated, for a variety of purposes—always operating on a conditional and probationary basis. Once the current diversity zeitgeist ends, so does the work.

I would extend the universal discourse to branding and would draw attention to how showrunner Shonda Rhimes, most recently described as a "revolutionary,"[23] tells the story of how when she looked at an invitation for an award ceremony at which she was to be honored and saw that she was described as the most powerful Black female showrunner, she scratched out the modifiers *Black* and *female*.[24] While I understand her desire to not be limited or constrained by those modifiers if she, in fact, *is* the most powerful showrunner of any description, her rationale that white men do not have to name themselves is based in structural power and an inherent specialness that allows them to be ex-nominated. They don't have to be named because it's common sense. Thus though Rhimes's refusal to take the modifier may for her be an insistence to transcend, the rhetoric ultimately reinforces the very whiteness implicit in industry. Further, while her strategy attempts to upend the "unequal development" of being considered successful only in relation to other Black female television producers—of which there is one: Rhimes—as opposed to being placed in contention with the predominately white male showrunners, by shrugging off those identity modifiers Rhimes reinscribes herself in a universalist posture. A posture that ironically makes racial difference a type of pathology one needs to be cured of, thus reinvigorating the very tenets of unequal development she hopes to quash.

CONCLUSION

Throughout this essay I tried to illustrate different ways that various creative laborers at various levels of access navigate precarity—from the anonymous (white) gatekeepers who stress that precarity is not a diversity issue but only an issue for those who lack the necessary skills; to the casting directors who find themselves stuck in a precarious limbo with insufficient power to break the status quo despite unparalleled access to diverse pools of talent; to actors of color whose precarious existence means they must strategically plan to circumvent the system even if those strategies benefit individuals at the expense of collective forms of resistance. Ultimately, the uncertainty of employment forces all these groups into their own strategies and tactics of negotiation. And while employment and maintaining one's livelihood is the point, the danger of such precarious livelihoods is that oftentimes survival takes precedence over all other factors—including the need for cultural resonance and specificity. That precarity results in the maintenance of a white heteronormative status quo is not shocking, but demands that future research consider the historical and discursive ways creative men and women laborers of color have survived in spite of the uncertainty as a guidepost for understanding issues of labor at all levels.

NOTES

1. Gloria T. Hull, Patricia Bell Scott, and Barbara Smith, eds., *But Some of Us Are Brave: All the Women Are White, All the Blacks Are Men: Black Women's Studies* (New York: Feminist Press, 1993).

2. John Thornton Caldwell, *Production Culture: Industrial Reflexivity and Critical Practice in Film and Television* (Durham, NC: Duke University Press, 2008).

3. Darnell Hunt, "The 2014 Hollywood Writers Report: Turning Missed Opportunities into Realized Ones" (July 2014), www.wga.org/uploadedFiles/who_we_are/HWR14.pdf.

4. Ibid.

5. It should be noted that white males directing decreased by 3 percent in contrast to the year before, while minority males increased by 3 percent, although the study cites that the increase can be attributed to a higher number of episodes directed by Tyler Perry, who solely directed episodes for his three television series.

6. Directors Guild of America, "Employers Make No Improvement in Diversity Hiring in Episodic Television: DGA Report," September 17, 2014, www.dga.org/News/PressReleases/2014/140917-Episodic-Director-Diversity-Report.aspx.

7. Screen Actors Guild, "2007 and 2008 Casting Data Reports," www.sagaftra.org/files/sag/documents/2007–2008_CastingDataReports.pdf.

8. Katie M. Kleinman, "Minorities in Prime-Time Television," November 15, 1999, www.katiekleinman.com/portfolio/minoritiesmedia.php.

9. Jennifer Armstrong and Margeaux Watson, "Diversity: Why Is TV So White," *Entertainment Weekly*, June 13, 2008, www.ew.com/ew/article/0,,20206185,00.html.

10. NAACP, "Out of Focus—Out of Sync Take 4: A Report on the Television Industry," December 2008, http://action.naacp.org/page/-/NAACP%20OFOS%20Take4.pdf.

11. Armstrong and Watson, "Diversity."

12. Heartsick, comment on the Deadline Team, April 14, 2014, 10:53 A.M., "WGA Diversity Report: Women Writers See Gains in TV, Slide on Film Side," *Deadline Hollywood*, April 14, 2014, http://deadline.com/2014/04/writers-guild-minority-report-2014-women-writers-714478/.

13. DevelopmentHell Exec, Twitter post, May 30, 2014, 3:46 P.M., https://twitter.com/DevHellExec.

14. Based on the pattern of Mystery account titles, the assumption is that unless modifiers are in place that suggest otherwise, the owners of said accounts are white males.

15. Keith Negus, "The Production of Culture," in *Production of Culture/Cultures of Production* (Thousand Oaks, CA: Sage, 1997), 362–363.

16. Kristen Warner, *The Cultural Politics of Colorblind TV Casting* (New York: Routledge, 2015).

17. Stuart Hall, "The Spectacle of the Other," in *Representation: Cultural Representations and Signifiying Practices,* ed. Stuart Hall (Thousand Oaks, CA: Sage, 2003), 236.

18. For evidence of this trend, look at the press junkets for the films and note how often the actors stress that these are movies "for everybody."

19. Claude Brodesser-Akner, "*Think Like a Man* Is the Best-Testing Film in Hollywood—but Can It Win Over Black Men and White Audiences," *Vulture*, April 10, 2012, www.vulture.com/2012/04/think-like-a-man-kevin-hart-will-packer.html.

20. Ibid.

21. Ibid.

22. Clyde R. Taylor, "Black Silence and the Politics of Representation," in African-American *Filmmaking and Race Cinema of the Silent Era: Oscar Micheaux and His Circle,* ed. Pearl Bowser, Jane Gaines, and Charles Musser (Bloomington: Indiana University Press, 2001), 3.

23. Mark Harris, "The Shonda Rhimes Revolution: Finishing What *The Sopranos* Started," *Grantland,* October 16, 2014, http://grantland.com/hollywood-prospectus/shonda-rhimes-scandal-abc/.

24. Lacey Rose, "Shonda Rhimes Opens Up about 'Angry Black Woman' Flap, Messy *Grey's Anatomy* Chapter and the *Scandal* Impact," *Hollywood Reporter,* October 8, 2014, www.hollywoodreporter.com/news/shonda-rhimes-opens-up-angry-738715?utm_source=twitter.

14

Games Production in Australia

Adapting to Precariousness

John Banks and Stuart Cunningham

In this chapter, we pay full attention to the structural conditions and human cost of precarious labor in a particular local instance of the games industry. But at the same time, we attempt to shift the debate on precarity from the existential (the creative individual attracted to industries promising autonomy and meaningful work and finding only casualization, no work/life balance, and poor management) and the totalizing (all work under regimes of neoliberal hypercapitalism is increasingly characterized by precarity; indeed a whole new class—the precariat[1]—is posited as emerging) to a focus on analysis for actionable reform.

Significant "creative destruction"[2] through the global financial crisis (GFC) led to games industry restructuring and consolidation, including withdrawal of major publisher investment in many dispersed regional hubs of games production. More fundamentally, major platform shifts and new business models started before the global downturn and continue through this contemporary period of slowdown in the world economy. There has been major consolidation at the console production end of the games industry, with more expensive blockbuster or AAA titles, a hollowing out of the midrange games market, and rapid growth and proliferation of casual gaming and mobile applications with unprecedentedly lower production costs and barriers to entry.

What has happened to one such regional hub, the Australian games industry, spatially remote from the centers of publisher power and hubs of creative ferment?

A recent "perfect storm" of factors has arisen to change the face of the Australian games industry. The industry had grown on the model of work for hire producing "catalog fillers" for the major publishers; very little original IP was produced. And while very few AAA titles were made in Australia, games companies had a reputation for quality. However, the business proposition was buttressed by more than a decade of favorable exchange rates, which (literally) underwrote international investment. The industry by 2007 was structured around approximately forty-five midsize small businesses.[3] Notable companies included Krome, Pandemic, THQ StudioOz, Creative Assembly, Torus, and 2K.

The global financial crisis saw higher-end production scaled back, a withdrawal by the major publishers from spatially distended supply chains, and a new preference for formally affiliated production companies. At the beginning of 2007, the Australian dollar was 75 cents on the U.S. dollar. During the GFC, the Australian dollar became a "currency haven," such that by the start of 2012 it was worth US$1.02, gutting the industry of its price advantage. Of even greater structural consequence for the industry was the simultaneous explosion of apps-based mobile casual games play based on the smartphone platform and later the tablet.

Official statistics tell a stark story of destruction of value. Of the 1,431 reported employees in 2007, only 581 remained by mid-2012, and reported game development income had dropped from A$116.9 million to just A$44.4 million.[4] The industry's spatial pattern in 2007 evidenced a significant presence in Queensland and Victoria, with additional studios in New South Wales, the Australian Capital Territory, and South Australia. By 2012, the majority of the bigger studios had closed, and the industry had retreated to be concentrated in Victoria. Those whose doors had closed or who had radically downsized included Krome, Pandemic, THQ StudioOz, BlueTongue, Team Bondi, SEGA Creative Assembly, and Tantalus Media Brisbane. The major studios remaining included Halfbrick (Brisbane), 2K Australia (Canberra), and in Melbourne, Big Ant, Torus Games, Tantalus, and Wicked Witch. According to the Games Developers Association of Australia (GDAA), the main advocacy and professional association for the industry, somewhere between 60 and 70 percent of industry workers had either moved to another industry (many skills, preeminently programming skills, are very transferable) or had left Australia for more resilient industry locations or those better supported by government policy and programs.[5]

In 2014, the GDAA characterized the industry as composed of two hundred formally registered businesses, of which 92 percent are considered to be independents.[6] It defines *independent* as a typically small-scale enterprise that concentrates exclusively on original IP and self-publishes on the new digital platforms (Apple App Store, Android, Steam). It estimates about eight hundred workers now in the industry. This is a recent history of an industry much reduced in turnover and traditional employment, but which has transformed its revenue base from 80 percent work for hire to 75 percent original IP—an almost complete reversal in the balance between business models.[7]

But, invoking Joseph Schumpeter, how "creative" has this destruction been? A rigorous critical organizational-studies analysis of the Australian industry advances the argument that severe power differentials between publisher and producer/developer have persisted across this momentous industry restructure and continue to compromise local agency in global supply chains.[8] An equally rigorous media-studies argument anatomizing poor labor conditions in the industry globally is nevertheless clear that "the most plentiful and well-paying jobs in the video game industry continue to be those provided by major video game publishers either directly or indirectly."[9] Neither view offers much comfort for the idea that this destruction could be in any way "creative."

These perspectives, however, contrast with the self-understanding of many of those games workers (whom we have interviewed for the research that supports this chapter) who survived the shakeout or are sufficiently new to the industry to know no other conditions. Culturally and industrially, original IP—and the conditions under which it can be prioritized—tends to be championed by these developers against fee-for-service and as a normative aspiration. Industrially, a dominant narrative in the industry has been the desire to move from fee-for-service (where the company is a price taker and doesn't control its own destiny) to original IP. Culturally, this aspiration also speaks to many developers' creative impulse and is actually enshrined in the advocacy and the definition of indie established by the representative body, the GDAA. It is reinforced by normative criteria built into state policy and program funding support.

Given the degree to which higher-end fee-for-service business has dried up, while essentially self-publication on major digital distribution platforms (Apple's App Store, the Google Play Store, Steam, and so on) has grown exponentially, necessity has become a virtue. Conditions have crafted an industry that is much reduced in terms of turnover and traditional employment but now operates within a disintermediated value chain that radically forces the pace of innovation. Despite much commentary that treats Apple, for example, as basically yet another global corporation "taking their (un)fair share of financial profits,"[10] near-global dissemination via the digital platforms on a 30/70 split of income derived represents an ostensibly better deal than the power asymmetries enshrined in dealing with the major publishers.[11]

Australian companies, in particular Halfbrick after its huge success with *Fruit Ninja* (2010), made hay while the sun shone in the early days of apps-driven games and became a sort of template for national ruminations on how to succeed in the new environment.[12] It is distinctly harder now to capture attention: massively lower barriers to entry create conditions in which it is estimated that more than 1.3 million apps are now available on the App Store with duplication across the platforms, of which around 20 percent are games.[13] Mobile games production is markedly less driven by the crunch associated with games development under the dominant business model of fee-for-service work, in which development schedules were driven by milestones at the behest of large international publishers. This has led,

Antony Reed suggests, to a situation where the industry has seen much less attrition in last few years. Furthermore, there is arguably a great deal more innovation activity in original IP. Indeed, there is runaway innovation,[14] with the rapid shift from games as a product to games as a service driving the mobile apps purchase price points to zero, accompanied by the proliferation of in-app purchasing. And these rapid shifts have in turn been challenged by a return by some to premium mobile app pricing as well as premium pricing for games released through Steam.

THEY *STILL* MAKE GAMES

It is to these identities and motivations—the scripts games developers have written for themselves to adapt to the new conditions—and their relation to business models and production cultures that we now turn.[15]

Predominantly, we encountered a sense of pride in the fact that these developers were *still* making games. They had found a way to survive the changes upending the Australian industry. Many emphasized that they were now doing this more on their terms and that the shift from fee-for-service to original IP meant they enjoyed greater creative control and autonomy. In describing this sense of creative control, none of the developers were remotely Panglossian about the precariousness they and the workers around them routinely face. Many recounted the pain of downsizing and seeing fellow workers lose their jobs, with many needing to leave the country for work in the United States, Britain, and Canada. Others told us about their companies coming repeatedly to the brink of closure and yet finding a way to keep the doors open. Nevertheless, this assertion of creative control came through in a comment by Dean Ferguson at 5Lives (a Brisbane-based group of five developers making the Kickstarter-funded game *Satellite Reign,* 2015): "It's probably the first time in a number of years where I've felt like I'm crafting a game and not simply part of a cog. Before 'the crash,' I worked with and formed great relationships with many very creative people, with really well-meaning people, including publishers, but it often came down to pure economics much of the time. It could be a real struggle to just craft something, and while it sounds tacky, a lot of us do this largely for the love of crafting."[16]

Morgan Jaffit, director of Brisbane's Defiant Development, put the case even more strongly: "Australia has a history of terrible work-for-hire projects and shitty lowest-bidder poor-quality games. It not only erodes your studio but I think it kills your soul too."[17] Trent Kusters, founder and director of Melbourne-based League of Geeks, also noted the importance of "having an impact on the medium, and the progression of the medium, and where that is happening. That you as a creator, you're not just pumping out some crappy title that's, you know, just going to turn a quick buck. If you want to make things that matter, you need to have a cultural understanding. You need to be involved in that, the discussion of the cultural zeitgeist of game development and games as a medium, and you can see a clear pattern between the people that are right now developing great games and the networks that they move within."[18] The values that these leaders of what has emerged as a profoundly different Australian games sector associate with "indie" game development need to be carefully interrogated; they are in no way opposed to commercial interests or business sustainability. Creative adaptation, experimentation, and opportunity have arisen under conditions of profound uncertainty and precariousness.

Many developers clearly feel there is a great deal more innovation potential—and identity reinforcement—in original IP. On the other hand, viewed from an industry-wide perspective, some companies continue to pursue fee-for-service work to offset the risk associated with free-to-play—and indeed with making original IP games generally. For some developers, work-for-hire remains important to the sustainability of their studios. Therefore, we now posit a typology of approaches to funding and releasing games in the overall ecology of the sector and then briefly profile companies that exemplify this range of approaches.

Along with licensed IP, there are five distinct variations on the exploitation of original IP: subscription, premium payment, free-to-play with in-game monetization, advertising supported, and pay-to-play. The subscription model is consistent with the games-as-service approach, where at the beginning of each period, usually monthly, the player pays to stay engaged with the game. This is typical of games like *World of Warcraft*, which continues to have a significant player base ten years after launch. The premium model is very much traditional in the games industry and is consistent with the games-as-product approach. The consumer pays for a complete experience with a one-off payment. Such a model is typified in AAA titles, such as the *Call of Duty* series (2003–) or titles like *Minecraft* (2011), but a quite different level of premium pricing also applies to variations on free-to-play.

Free-to-play can be adopted in a variety of forms, placing this category in both games-as-product, where you pay to unlock additional content but expenditure is capped—for example, *Puzzle Retreat* (2013)—or in a games as service form, where there is no cap on monetary expense (for example, *Clash of Clans* [2012] or Kixeye's *VEGA Conflict* [2013]). The advertising-supported revenue model leverages advertising as the primary source of income by inserting advertising at regular or semiregular intervals; it is most typical of browser-based flash games. The final model is the pay-to-play monetization model. Typified by the original arcade machines, each play of the game requires an input of credit for the player to progress. The developers that we discuss in this chapter have tended to focus on emerging opportunities of free-to-play and premium payment approaches, especially in the context of the shift toward games-as-service models.

The funding for games development takes a variety of forms, depending on the availability and the scale of the project. Briefly, these sources include government funding, in the form of loans or grants with funds available not just for development costs but also for travel or to engage marketing expertise; crowdfunding through platforms like Kickstarter; the traditional publisher model, where the developer is engaged to produce content at a set fee and with set milestones for delivery, essentially work-for-hire; variations on the work-for-hire approach that may involve undertaking projects such as game installations, serious games, or nongaming apps; and securing donations, where donations are received against the development costs.

As an index of the stakes involved in this challenging innovation space, consider the case of Halfbrick, the company that bet the farm on original IP on mobile game platforms. Halfbrick has continued this approach with recent releases like *Fish out of Water* (2013), *Collosatron* (2013), and *Bears versus Art* (2014). While the company's recent releases experiment with various approaches to free-to-play and in-app monetization by drawing on analytics and metrics to inform their design, development process, and decisions, they have not as yet managed to repeat the stellar commercial success enjoyed by *Fruit Ninja* (2010) or the lesser but still substantial success of *Jet Pack Joyride* (2011). Halfbrick had led the industry in adapting to the shift from work-for-hire to original IP titles for mobile devices.[19] In front of the pack when mobile games were all paid for upfront, success has so far eluded the company after the market shift to free-to-play and games-as-service.

Wicked Witch, which was started, like Halfbrick, in the late 1990s, is different. It mixes work-for-hire with original IP development. During the industry decline, Wicked Witch radically downsized, almost closing. However, by continuing fee-for-service work for domestic sports titles that were not subject to the exchange rate crisis, together with developing original IP games for mobile devices, Wicked Witch has managed to rebuild a fifty-person studio. This makes them one of the largest companies in the new ecology. Successful titles include *Catapult King* (2012), released for both Android and iOS devices. Wicked Witch has also released *Whac-a-Mole* (2014) for Mattel, a conversion of the classic arcade game for Apple devices, and *Jet Run: City Defender* (2014), a free-to-play game with in-app monetization, for iOS and Google Play. Wicked Witch CEO Daniel Visser observed that in his opinion the free-to-play model was becoming "a race to the bottom that is so intense that we're going to end up paying people to play our games."[20] Free-to-play is becoming such a crowded market, with such great potential for destruction of value, that developers need to explore other models, including premium payment titles for mobile platforms.

Melbourne-based League of Geeks exemplifies such an approach. League of Geeks is not banking on chasing the mobile free-to-play market. Since 2011, this group of developers, including designers, programmers, and artists, have come together to make *Armello* (2015), a game they describe as "a swashbuckling adventure that combines RPG elements with the strategic play of card and board games, creating a personal, story fuelled experience."²¹ Structured as a core creative team of four directors and a loose coalition of programmers and artists who contribute collaboratively to the project, they are located in the Arcade in inner-city Melbourne, a game development space shared with other companies that has the look and feel of a creative start-up and is supported by the Victorian government. League of Geeks garnered attention in 2014, when they raised $305,000 from Kickstarter to keep the *Armello* project progressing. Director Trent Kusters describes League of Geeks as a game development collective rather than a formal studio.²² Kusters left the Australian industry in 2011–2012 to seek work overseas. He said that through this period he felt "disenfranchised" by the big studio developer culture. He worried that in such an environment he could end up being "a little cog in a big wheel, tweaking combat timings on some NPC for, you know, some multimillion dollar game." In contrast to Wicked Witch, Kusters emphasized the importance of developing original IP, saying that fee-for-service work was "like quicksand."²³ Unlike Australian developers who retain some fee-for-service work to balance the risks associated with an original-IP-only approach, Kusters believes relying too much on fee-for-service can compromise a studio's ability and commitment to create original IP.

The game development engine Unity was becoming widely available by the late 2000s, offering low-cost but high-quality technology for making games. Combined with digital distribution opportunities through the App Store and Steam, this radically changed the possibilities for making and releasing games. Kusters noted the emergence of online indie developer communities using productivity tools to manage distributed collaborations among teams around the world. *Armello* relied on a distributed network of developers that Kusters sees as exemplifying his vision of a game developer collective. Some developers were engaged through a points-based system in which they would receive a cut of the profit from *Armello* based on their contribution to the project. Others worked on the project through an arrangement that combined points with contracted and paid employment. *Armello* also raised funds to continue development through Kickstarter, but both national and state government funding was critical to *Armello*'s viability. League of Geeks plans to release *Armello* as a premium title rather than pursuing a free-to-play approach with in-game monetization. This model of indie development, Kusters says, is about "adapting to the current climate. . . . The market completely shifts underneath us all the time. We just have to be agile. We just have to do what we need to do, and that's basically how we came up with the model . . . that doesn't require us to have cash."²⁴ This is a business model that marshals government backing, deferred points-based payment systems, and crowdfunding to underwrite passionately conceived games that depend on innovation, reputation, and point-of-difference from most standard mobile games product.

Sharing office space in the Arcade complex with League of Geeks, Voxel Agents (a small studio of five or six employees) pursues the opportunities of original IP and free-to-play game releases for mobile devices with successful titles like the *Train Conductor* (2009) series and *Puzzle Retreat* (2013). Voxel Agents is tackling the shift toward games-as-service, which requires regular content updates and the use of metrics and data analytics to respond to player behavior. Voxel's Simon Joslin noted the value of working in a collaborative space such as the Arcade, which permits both formal and informal sharing of knowledge and experience about the rapidly changing video games market.²⁵ This includes access to small specialist firms, such as Surprise Attack, which offers consulting services to developers as they seek to develop effective business models that embrace the demands of games-as-service, particularly expertise in game monetization and effective use of data analytics. Both state and national government support for business development was critical as they experimented with various approaches to the games-as-service model. Joslin noted that while the shift to original IP provided greater creative control, changing business models to games-as-service, especially free-to-play games like *Candy Crush Saga* (2012), may compromise the craft of making quality game experiences. He worried—as did other developers—that many of the monetization strategies associated with in-app game purchases relied on mechanics that may be addictive. He discussed the ethical and craft implications of free-to-play: "It's a complex question, a gray area. . . . There are points where I've played games and I feel that's the wrong way to do it. . . . I wouldn't feel comfortable doing that to my players."²⁶ He talked about the steep challenge of adapting existing game design knowledge and skills to create engaging and compelling free-to-play titles while making effective use of metrics and analytics.

So far, with the exception of Wicked Witch, we have emphasized GDAA-defined indies in this survey of the precarious but widening range of business models and company and developer identities. But some U.S. company presence remains in the country. Kixeye, situated in Brisbane with a staff of some fifty to sixty, manages the distance from centers of developer culture by being a wholly owned subsidiary of San Francisco–based Kixeye, a developer of online browser-based strategy and combat games, such as *Battle Pirates* (2011), *War Commander* (2011), and *VEGA Conflict* (2013). The studio director, George Fidler, a veteran of the industry, emphasized the fundamental challenge of shifting from a work-for-hire and games-as-product model to a games-as-service market environment.²⁷ He suggested that while the fundamental skills of programming, art, and good design were still crucial, new skill sets and expertise in digital retail now needed to be integrated into the production process and studio culture. Australian development studios still lacked the skills crucial to successfully making the shift to games-as-service. Fidler commented that the work-for-hire origins of many Australian studios and developers meant that they perhaps had not gained the market discipline of focusing on a core competency or a core market. Speaking of the games-as-service shift, Fidler concluded that for Australian developers, "it'd been tough to create those kinds of games early in the cycle, because the expertise simply wasn't there." By expertise, he clarified the product manager and producer skills required to combine and balance retention, monetization, and engagement: "We've got thousands of game designers in Australia. No problem at all, but we have very, very few experienced product managers, and that's meant most of the attempts have fizzled out, because if you think of the build-measure-learn cycle, we built, we didn't quite know what we were measuring, and we learned nothing."[28]

PRECARIOUSNESS AS A FUNCTION OF POLICY AND INDUSTRY CULTURES

In the overwhelmingly nonunionized games industry, advocacy for the sector is largely conducted by professional associations, and support is offered through state policies and programs.[29] This section considers the extent to which precariousness is a product of policy, advocacy, and industry self-governance.

A key feature of the games industry is that it is poorly understood by the political class. This is despite its size and growth rates globally dwarfing anything remotely comparable, and is an outstanding example of creative content and use driving technological innovation and take up, not the other way round, as is usually constructed in innovation policy and business strategy. It tends to fall between the three "stools" of cultural policy, industry and innovation policy, while its main interface with the political class and the wider populace is around social and educational policy concerns (violence, game-playing addiction, claims and counterclaims about educational benefits). Inconsistent or nonexistent policy support, particularly compared to other cultural industries, such as film and television, contributes to precariousness. Such policy inconsistency across different countries, as well as policy entrepreneurship or arbitrage between countries in bidding for the services of this high-skill component of the "creative class," contributes to the hypermobility of games creatives.

In Australia, federal policy and programs supporting the industry had been piecemeal,[30] seeking to fit games into the established cultural template developed over decades for the arts, film, and television. They required developers to articulate game proposals as forms of storytelling to measure the cultural significance of the game. The long march toward a realistic balance between cultural and industry policy for the creative sector was accelerated by the industry transformations of the last five to seven years. Government accepted that very little original IP was being created; that Australian developers were locked into a fee-for-service system; that the country was no longer attractive to licensed IP; and that oversees competitive incentives were "luring" talent away from the country. A significant A$20 million package was developed, the Australian Interactive Games Fund, whose objectives were to promote industry growth and sustainability, support the development of new intellectual property, encourage skills retention and renewal, and maximize the creative opportunities of fast broadband.[31] With a change of government, however, the initiative was cancelled with only half the money spent.

At a state or provincial level, the policy rationale for support has been equally uneven, with an equal or perhaps even greater impact on precariousness for the labor force. The state of Victoria has been most consistent in its approach to games, which are recognized as a core component of the state's industrial and employment base in its information and communication technology sector. Effective advocacy for the sector forestalled a cost-cutting attempt to close down support in 2012. Funding and programs in support of the sector are administered through a mainstream screen agency. The approach in Queensland was exclusively industrial and remained positive while the industry was generating jobs as midsize small businesses proliferated in the pre-GFC period. The collapse of several of the larger companies effectively eliminated games from a standard industry development policy logic as pursued within a department of state development and saw the policy focus narrow to a minor part of the screen agency's remit. Government did little to arrest the collapse of the industry in the state, and has done little since. New South Wales, the most populous state and the one with the largest slice of GDP, had rarely focused policy and program attention on games, leading to the irregular doughnut shape of the industry's geography.[32] The effect of such policy variability is clear—Victoria has seen strong 15–20 percent growth in each of the last few years, while Queensland has not grown strongly out of the downturn. The mobility and associated uncertainties faced by game workers are often forced on them by the volatility of an industry whose profile with government is equally volatile.

Policy fluctuation and failure contributes to precariousness; so does the industry's reputation for poor management. Some of its notoriously poor working conditions can be attributed to the immaturity of the industry and the need for self-governance reform. The industry's still overwhelmingly male-dominated production base needs to change if it is to attract the best talent, improve balance and sustainability, and capture value in a rapidly evolving consumption environment. Women and girls now account for 48 percent of all gamers. The high skew toward men and boys—more than 78 percent in the console core demographic—underlines that women are in the majority in the more casual gaming areas of the market.[33] GDAA survey data for 2014 suggests that, of the approximately eight hundred people now working in the industry, some 26 percent are women, and most of these are programmers and artists. This is beginning to align with the IGDA's most recent survey results, which report 22 percent women employees globally in September 2014.[34]

Management deficit is by no means confined to gender. Casey O'Donnell's loving but forensic description of the "secret world of videogame creators" does not spare the industry.[35] Tacit knowledge has been poorly converted into transferable knowledge. This is a critical shortcoming because the daunting complexity of bringing together engineers, artists, designers, marketers, and managers in intense iteration can lead to crunches, "intense and extended periods of socially mandatory overtime, and a seemingly perpetual start-up environment for game development companies."[36] There is little industry formalization and representation. Invoking the analytical work of Gina Neff and David Stark, O'Donnell asserts that the industry is in a state of "permanent beta." Cross-disciplinary collaboration—which causes unremitting creative tension at the level of the firm and poses some of the most challenging project management tasks in contemporary industry practice—is absolutely necessary for the industry's future. The tendency is for the industry, because of its closed opacity (and, as we have seen, because of its extreme volatility), to continually reinvent the wheel. O'Donnell stresses the great breakthrough by Unity when it made transparent authoring knowledge of great value, for example, for developing country industries.[37] All of these factors contribute to working cultures and conditions that see 50 percent leave with up to ten years exposure.[38] On the other hand, Australian industry, GDAA claims, is rare in the way it shares knowledge and resources among industry players now that the industry is composed overwhelmingly of indies. This is not typical of companies based in the United States, and was also not common when Australian developers were producing licensed IP, as a result of nondisclosure agreements.

A better articulation of the broader value of the industry to the society and economy can address precariousness. Antony Reed, an industry advocate, asserts that "this industry could make such a huge contribution if only it was understood better."[39] Advocacy, he argues, should seek to raise awareness of, for example, the value of game design input into health and education; the transferability of games skills into mainstream IT or the burgeoning apps industry; and the highly skilled entrepreneurial games workforce, which any country should seek to retain as part of its creative class. This draws on evidence that uncertainty of work in games is mitigated to some extent by the capacity to work outside the sector (due to the high transferability of skills, particularly of programmers). There is also some evidence that companies and individuals manage precarious original IP development with sourcing licensed IP opportunities within the growing domestic apps industry, so-called serious (edutainment) games, and a small range of domestic purchasers of games products and services (sourcing licensed IP domestically can be more sustainable because it is not subject to currency fluctuation).

CONCLUSION

Deuze, Martin, and Allen stress the importance of mapping what they call "gamework": "the key issues informing and influencing the working lives and professional identities" of developers in the global computer and video game industry.[40] Deuze and his colleagues were writing at a time when the dominant model involved developers working for large studios making games for publishing conglomerates like Electronic Arts. However, as we have seen in the case of the Australian industry, several options for making games and different workplace models confront developers. Some developers celebrate the creative freedom they experienced following the shift toward producing original IP games for mobile platforms, while others caution about the compromises associated with in-app monetization mechanics. The turmoil transforming the Australian games industry exemplifies precariousness. But it also includes adaptive experimentation in studio culture and associated changes in professional developer identity so as to continue the craft of making games in the midst of uncertainty. Analysts who have been very close to the industry and its developer culture, such as Casey O'Donnell, suggest that the current situation presents an opportunity to recapture the industry's craft basis, the sustaining heart of the developer culture, stressing that gaming is not just a software industry.[41] Creative destruction in the Australian games industry has been extraordinarily two-edged. As Gina Neff comments in the broader context of creative labor, "The trick for future media and business revolutions will be to find ways to support venture labor, so that innovative and creative jobs can also be stable and good jobs."[42]

To achieve this, programs designed to support the industry need stability and predictability. Turning the public support spigot on and off according to political whim and policy fashion escalates precariousness. Furthermore, the industry needs better management practices. In addition to providing a more welcoming workplace for women and managing the crunch, it needs to learn how and when to cooperate as well as compete, and how to identify and incorporate new skill sets to deal with "runaway" innovation. Advocacy needs to articulate the wider value of the industry to society and economy, and to emphasize viable career structures within it. Precariousness, we have suggested, is an addressable matter—one that governments, the industry as an associative entity, and those who *still* make games can work on together.

NOTES

1. Guy Standing, *The Precariat: The New Dangerous Class* (London: Bloomsbury, 2011).
2. Joseph A. Schumpeter, *Capitalism, Socialism and Democracy* (New York: Routledge, 2006 [1942]).
3. ABS, "8515.0—Digital Game Development Services, Australia, 2006–2007," last issue April 8, 2008.
4. Ibid.; ABS, "8679.0—Film, Television, and Digital Games, Australia, 2011–2012," last issue June 18, 2013.
5. Antony Reed, CEO, GDAA, interview with the authors, Melbourne, August 28, 2014.
6. Ibid.

7. Antony Reed, e-mail message to authors, September 30, 2014.

8. Rachel Parker, Stephen Cox, and Paul Thompson, "How Technological Change Affects Power Relations in Global Markets: Remote Developers in the Console and Mobile Games Industry," *Environment and Planning A* 46.1 (2014): 168–185.

9. John Vanderhoef and Michael Curtin, "The Crunch Heard Round the World: The Global Era of Digital Game Labor," in *Production Studies: The Sequel!* ed. Bridget Conor, Miranda Banks, and Vicki Mayer (New York: Routledge, 2015).

10. Larissa Hjorth, "Games: Mobile, Locative and Social," in *The Media and Communications in Australia,* ed. Stuart Cunningham and Sue Turnbull (Crows Nest, NSW: Allen & Unwin, 2014), 281.

11. See John Banks, "The iPhone as Innovation Platform: Reimagining the Videogames Developer," in *Studying Mobile Media: Cultural Technologies, Mobile Communication, and the iPhone,* ed. Larissa Hjorth, Jean Burgess, and Ingrid Richardson (New York: Routledge, 2012), 155–172.

12. John Banks and Stuart Cunningham, "Games and Entertainment Software," in *Handbook of the Digital Creative Economy,* ed. Ruth Towse and Christian Handke (Cheltenham: Edward Elgar, 2013), 416–427.

13. "Number of Available Apps in the Apple App Store from July 2008 to September 2014," October 12, 2014, www.statista.com/statistics/268251/number-of-apps-in-the-itunes-app-store-since-2008/; "Most Popular Apple App Store Categories in September 2014, by Share of Available Apps," October 12, 2014, www.statista.com/topics/1729/app-stores/.

14. Innovation, captured in Schumpeter's powerful phrase *creative destruction,* can have extraordinarily two-edged social, economic, and cultural effects. Runaway innovation occurs when change outstrips even its progenitors' comfort and control. See, e.g., David Lane, "Towards an Agenda for Social Innovation," European Centre for Living Technology, www.insiteproject.org/wp-content/uploads/2014/02/Social-Innovation-Manifesto_INSITE.pdf, 2–3.

15. The research on which this chapter draws includes semistructured interviews conducted in Q3 2014 by the authors with sixteen developers from eight development studios, as well as with leaders in the games association and in government program support.

16. Dean Ferguson, interview with John Banks, August 21, 2014.

17. Morgan Jaffit, interview with John Banks, November 27, 2014.

18. Trent Kusters, interview with John Banks, September 24, 2014.

19. For a short history, see Banks, "The iPhone as Innovation Platform."

20. Wicked Witch CEO Daniel Visser, interview with John Banks, September 23, 2014.

21. "Armello Press Kit," http://press.armello.com/.

22. Trent Kusters interview.

23. Ibid.

24. Ibid.

25. Simon Joslin, interview with the authors, August 29, 2014.

26. Ibid.

27. George Fidler, interview with the authors, September 10, 2014.

28. Ibid.

29. The Media, Entertainment & Arts Alliance (MEAA), the largest and most established union and industry advocate for Australia's creative professionals, has no section for games.

30. Christian McCrea, "Australian Video Games: The Collapse and Reconstruction of an Industry," in *Gaming Globally,* ed. Nina Huntemann and Ben Aslinger (Basingstoke: Palgrave Macmillan, 2012), 203–207.

31. Screen Australia, "Australian Interactive Games Fund Industry Consultation: Objectives and Context," www.screenaustralia.gov.au/gamesoptions/category/Objectives-context.

32. Queensland, the major northern state, and Victoria, the major southern state, have been the twin centers of the Australian industry; the largest state located between them (New South Wales) has had a smaller proportion of the industry.

33. Entertainment and Software Association, "2014 Sales Demographic and Usage Data: Essential Facts about the Computer and Video Game Industry," ESA (2014), www.theesa.com/wp-content/uploads/2014/10/ESA_EF_2014.pdf; DataGenetics, "Casual Games Demographics," www.datagenetics.com/blog/december12010/.

34. IGDA, "Press Release: IGDA Developer Satisfaction Survey Results Are Released," www.igda.org/news/179158/Press-Release-IGDA-Developer-Satisfaction-Survey-results-are-released.htm.

35. Casey O'Donnell, *Developer's Dilemma: The Secret World of Videogame Creators* (Cambridge MA: MIT Press, 2014).

36. Ibid., 28.

37. Ibid., 74.

38. Ibid., 161.

39. Antony Reed, interview with the authors, August 28, 2014.

40. Mark Deuze, Chase Bowen Martin, and Christian Allen, "The Professional Identity of Game-workers," *Convergence* 31 (2007): 336.

41. Casey O'Donnell, "This Is Not a Software Industry," in *The Video Game Industry: Formation, Present State and Future,* ed. P. Zackariasson & T. L. Wilson (New York: Routledge, 2012), 17–33.

42. Gina Neff, *Venture Labor: Work and the Burden of Risk in Innovative Industries* (Cambridge MA: MIT Press, 2012).

15

Redefining Creative Labor

East Asian Comparisons

Anthony Fung

People often fantasize about Hollywood's workforce being composed of innovative people imbued with refined tastes and aesthetics. They are further imagined as being well paid and therefore able to enjoy a rosy bohemian or bourgeois lifestyle, as opposed to other industrial workers. This romantic vision of the hip Hollywood creative may be apocryphal, but few would deny that the industry has long prospered because it has been able to foster and harness the creative energies of its employees. Moreover, Hollywood has served as a model for other creative industries in the United States, including gaming, animation, software, and information technology (IT).

This paper offers an alternative perspective on creative labor by investigating the values and attitudes of workers in Asia. The data of this study is based on my face-to-face interviews with workers in different kinds of game-related companies in China, South Korea, Malaysia, Singapore, and Vietnam, as well as observation in their working sites from 2011 to 2013.[1] These locales vary from large-scale factory-like game enterprises with over one thousand workers to small companies operated by a few personnel; they include online or video game companies, game distributors, and production houses that focus on animation, character design, or programming for online, mobile, and web games. The interviewees include workers of all levels: owners, artists, programmers, distributors, and promoters. These interviews cover various modes of creative labor in East and Southeast Asia. By comparing the lifestyles of these Asian workers with their U.S. counterparts, this chapter suggests that "creative labor" in East and Southeast Asia does not conform to the model described above, due largely to different industrial practices and cultural contexts as well as different experiences with processes of globalization.

Given these divergences, the term *cultural labor* is more apt and comprehensive, indicating the ways video game production varies around the world. Moreover, this essay highlights distinctions *within* this Asian region, noting different attitudes, practices, and working conditions.

Three modes of cultural labor are theorized: in Korea, *progressive artists,* who are innovative in developing their entrepreneurship; in Southeast Asia, *skilled conformers,* who are "the arms" of the Western giants; in China, the *contented bourgeoisie,* who are skillful but less creative under state censorship. The presence of these emerging forms of cultural labor in Asia challenges the ethnocentric view of creative labor that has largely been shaped by North Atlantic tradition.

Previous studies of creativity suggested that research on creativity has been limited by ethnocentric boundaries in a world of cultural pluralism, implying that the traditional Western model of creativity is not appropriate in Southeast Asian countries. Maharaj Krishna Raina investigated the labor and lifestyles of Southeast Asian creative workers, concluding that they varied greatly from their Western counterparts.[2] Beth Hennessey proposed that the concept of creativity is not applicable across nations, suggesting that creativity is constituted by both apparent and embedded values of different nations and is dependent on social agreements about what precisely constitutes creativity.[3]

PROBLEMATIZING CREATIVITY

The study of creative labor or the creative class attracted substantial academic interest in the 1990s. Richard Florida might be one of the first researchers to describe the emerging occupational, demographic, psychological, and economic profile of the American creative class.[4] In his view, it is a privileged group that not only excels in creativity but leads a modern bohemian lifestyle. Moreover, this unconventional artistic existence is often associated with material comforts, cultural capital, and above-average working conditions. Problematizing the assumption that workers in creative industries are by default creative opens up a new imaginative space for conceptualizing this kind of labor.

David Hesmondhalgh and Sarah Baker's book on creative labor is perhaps the most recent and comprehensive work to synthesize and problematize the concept of creative labor in the United Kingdom.[5] They challenge the assumptions of autonomy, well-paid work, and the high quality of life of the cultural laborer. Moreover, recent debates about the concept of creativity have suggested that it is highly variable and contextually embedded.[6] Hence the assumption that being creative is natural when technology and capital are in place is problematic. Similarly, in a study of artists and administrators for digital game companies in a small city in Canada, Laura Murray and others showed that they were often involved in contractual relationships with the audience and hence were swayed by the latter's feedback, a relationship that challenged notions of autonomous creative genius.[7]

Creative industries in the United States, which usually involve exporting cultural commodities, are a crucial driver of economic revenue and account for a large portion of the country's GDP. Other nation-states share these priorities, whereas for some countries, factors such as political interest and the vested interests of autocrats are more important. Yet even in countries like China, where political priorities prevail, cultural exports are seen as a way of exercising soft power and developing the economic power of their media and film industries.[8] Under such circumstances, creative labor might benefit from top-down support for their industries, even though key elements of creativity, such as free expression, cultural tolerance, and the marketplace of ideas, may be stringently limited. The intriguing question is whether we redefine or requalify this type of creativity. If so, what specific characteristics might define alternative notions of creative labor?

In an effort to more accurately profile those working in the creative industries, I use the term *cultural labor* instead of *creative labor*. Whether it is creative or noncreative depends on the specific sociopolitical context. In China's political environment, cultural labor is not "creative" enough to construct a virtual game world that would enable universal suffrage and voting. Yet an employee of Netease, a major online gaming platform, explains that Chinese game planners are often smart enough to bypass and outmaneuver constraints imposed by political leaders in order to launch and operate popular games.

In other words, the socio-political contexts in which creative industries are developed and sustained, and in which creative laborers work, produce, and are reproduced, result in different conceptions of creativity. When explained in terms of maneuvering around boundaries, creativity might be very limited; however, when understood in terms of entrepreneurial strategies aimed at navigating both market and political structures, they comprise a broader scope of cultural labor.

SUBCONTRACTING AND SUBCONTRACTED CREATIVITY

A comparative perspective on creativity labor should also take into account the new international division of cultural labor in relation to creative industries, which is a result of cultural globalization.[9] Florida, in the new edition of his book, also mentioned the global effects of the creative class,[10] acknowledging that cultural globalization would inevitably create differences between people working in the center and those working on the periphery. The difference is a reflection of the dependence of new creative satellite cities or nations on the global media hub or transnational creative industries. As a value chain of cultural industries, it is a strategy for big transnational companies to search for the cheapest locations to "manufacture" cultural products using low-cost, labor-intensive processes in developing countries. However, for creative industries, the relocation of production is not simply a direct transference of manual labor from the established economy to developing countries. Game industries, for example, involve highly skilled labor in programming, computer graphics, and artwork. Thus contracting companies from the United States have to ensure that the skills and techniques in programming games are adopted by the contracted companies, and the aesthetics of the artwork have to be consistent throughout development. It is quite common that multiple subcontractors are used, but this doesn't mean that all those working on the project share a collective vision. The contracted labor will most likely feel complacent about the arrangement; they often feel diffident about adopting the aesthetics of the giant lead companies. For example, Disney often subcontracts for artwork and Nintendo for animation, using many small- to medium size teams for numerous aspects of a production. Moreover, the exploding popularity of online gaming among Asian consumers has further stimulated an expansion in the number and variety of companies operating in the gaming industries.

Despite the energetic growth of the gaming sector, Asian cultural labor is largely subordinated to global creative industries. The latter set the overall agenda for developing popular titles and prescribe aesthetics for the subcontractor to follow. In other words, global companies subcontract their version of creativity to game developers who must uncritically accept guidance from above. This involves standardization of both the professional knowledge needed to produce the work and the values and aesthetics needed to appreciate and legitimize the production. To understand the complex workings of market-submarket and prescribing and prescribed creativity requires a theoretical model that takes into account both the value-free cultural work and the potential commodification and fetishization of mass cultural production.

Reconciling critical theory, neo-Foucauldian, and liberal-democratic approaches, Banks's critical framework on cultural work is useful here for examining the de facto nature of creativity and cultural labor across the neoliberal and capitalist markets dominated by multinational enterprises. In the context of Western cultural economies, he argues that there are always tensions between autonomous production on one side and corporate functionality of production and governmental prescription on the other, and this creates a spectrum of arguments from the discourse of moral, empowering cultural labor to the subordinated, alienated workers, with some alternative and moderate discourses in the middle.[11]

Putting the global context of cultural production of game industries in Banks's framework, we can assume that while there are relatively free autonomous cultural workers in the major market of Western Hollywood production, there are also subcontracted cultural workers struggling in many other parts of the world, where the conditions for subcontractors vary by firm, location, and job. To understand the uneven and diverse terrains of game labor, it is important to critically survey differences in the condition of cultural labor among geographic locales without assuming that their lives, wages, working conditions, and (dis)empowering possibilities are equal. What follows is an overview of three important production locales: Southeast Asia, South Korea, and the People's Republic of China. As we will see, government policies, market dynamics, and cultural specificity all have a significant impact on working conditions and on the attitudes and values among game company employees.

THE DEPENDENCY OF SOUTHEAST ASIA

Many local game developers in Southeast Asia, mostly small- and medium-size companies, were start-ups in the 1990s or 2000s. They sustained themselves through contracted, skilled work that they accepted from international game companies seeking to outsource projects. Although some companies produce small-budget games, such as mobile and flash games, they also produce quality art assets for global titles. They are perfect subcontractors for cross-platform games that operate on consoles and PCs, as well as mobile devices.

Several global game companies have chosen to set up studios in Southeast Asia because skilled talent there can be hired at lower pay rates. Such companies include Electronic Arts, Lucasfilm, Koei, Gevo, and Ubisoft in Singapore; Codemasters Studios in Malaysia; Square Enix and Gameloft in Indonesia; Activision, Bioware, Bungie, and Eidos in the Philippines; and Gameloft in Vietnam. In addition to serving as satellite production hubs, these operational outposts are sometimes used to distribute products in Southeast Asia as well.

KOREA AS A RISING GLOBAL EXPORTER

In East Asia, countries like Korea and Japan have a long history of colonial dependence, but they are not satisfied with being culturally colonized nations. In recent years, the concept of exporting culture has taken hold, particularly in Korea because of strong government support. Nowadays, Korea is the major hub for creative industries both in Asia and globally, particularly the games industry. One major breakthrough in addition to financial support is that state policies encourage a sufficient supply of cultural labor to support the industry.

The year 1997 was a watershed year, when the Korean government announced a scheme to boost the local games industry, including a plan to set up a Korean Game Promotion Centre (KGPC). This not only meant that governmental policy was focused on developing the Korean games industry, but it also set in motion a series of related state initiatives that attempted to reverse one-sided importation of culture from the U.S. and European markets. Early efforts involved the reorganization of governing bodies. For example, in 1998, the games industry had officially been grouped with cultural industries, implying that games were not only entertainment but also part of the national cultural arena. The launching of KGPC in July 1999 and its Japan branch two months later marked major steps in the government's plan to nurture its national games industry. The mission of KGDI (Korean Game Development and Promotion Institute, later renamed the Korean Game Industry Agency [KGIA]) was to establish a strategic platform between the government and the games industry. The strategy included providing the industry with overseas market information, infrastructural support, and subsidies for research and development. In this way the government provided industry practitioners with timely technological and marketing advice.

The formation of the Ministry of Culture and Tourism (MCT) in 1998 and the transfer of the cultural assets policy portfolio, including the games industry, to MCT's jurisdiction served to enhance industry expansion. The launch of Cyber Korea 21 one year later accelerated the development of the online games industry, particularly by speeding up broadband technology development, rapidly increasing the number of Internet users in Korea, and enhancing national Internet education. Moreover, the subsequent launch of the Korean Creative Content Agency (KOCCA) provided these industries with additional support, including equipment rental, investment, technological training, international marketing advice, and research support for medium- and long-term development, as well as developing strategic partnerships with overseas buyers and suppliers. To nurture talent for the booming games industry, the Korean government started the Games Academy in November 2000. A games investment association and a games investment valuation association were established in December 2000 and June 2001, respectively, to nurture talent and obtain venture funding and investments to meet the needs of the rising games industry. Such outcomes were indicative of the visible success of a state-led industry policy.

The critical mass of cultural labor formed under the state-driven model unquestionably adhered to the philosophy of the state, although in fact it is neither a free-market nor a neoliberal model, but is instead similar to the Hollywood model for cultural export. Consequently, the mind-set of workers in the Korean gaming sector is very close to the values and lifestyles of their American counterparts, largely because the United States is regarded as Korea's benchmark of cultural exportation.

CHINA'S GLOBAL EXPANSION

Like Korea, China changed from an importer of online games (initially from Korea) to a major international player and exporter. According to the official statistics released by Ministry of Culture, in 2010 the total annual revenue of mainland China's online games industry reached $5.7 billion. It also became a substantial exporter of online games. In 2011, Chinese game companies generated $360 million in overseas sales revenue from thirty-four games that performed especially well in Southeast Asia, North America, Korea, and Japan. Such success has encouraged China's game giants to extend their overseas reach by acquiring major game titles and companies. In 2011, Tecent's acquisition of Riot Games, the developer of *League of Legends*, for about $230 million is typical of the global expansion of China's game companies. *League of Legends* is the most popular PC game in North America and Europe, with an average of 27 million gamers daily.

However, the industry developed much faster than the regulations did. Before 2004, there were no regulations or cultural policy to drive or control the industries.[12] In subsequent years, Chinese authorities introduced a series of regulations: the Regulation on Digital Publication in 2007, the Regulation on Publishing of Digital Publication in 2008, and the Administration of Software Production in 2009. A censorship system was promulgated in August 2010, when the state delegated such censorship to the provincial level (People's Congress Decision on the 5th Batch Cancellation of and Delegation of Approval to Level of Management and Controlling Unit). In the name of protecting minors, most of the regulatory guidelines focus on controlling violence and indecency. However, my interviews with the committee responsible for censorship revealed that ideological controls are fairly common, thus hindering the import and publishing of foreign games in China.

Despite these stringent controls, the authorities have not hindered private investment and game support. Instead, as incentives, tax reductions are given to game companies that export, and the provincial and local authorities set up technology areas or cultural clusters to cater to the needs of game companies. The challenge for game companies, as I will describe, is the general lack of talent and the high cost of recruiting teams to develop games.

MODES OF CREATIVE LABOR

The conditions in which creative goods are produced affect labor. In the U.S. context, Richard Caves explained that the production of creative goods is largely susceptible to basic economic properties, including commitment and devotion of labor, skills needed, product differentiation, time and demand, and costs incurred.[13] However, in nonfree markets and nondemocratic states, many other factors shape, foster, or dictate the conditions of how cultural labor is produced, trained, and socialized. As explained earlier, on the social level, in Asia the state plays a prominent role in driving creative industries that require appropriate types of workers. Even more directly, the state plays an active role in training and nurturing cultural labor for emerging industries. To a certain extent, cultural workers adhere to the values and worldview prescribed or controlled by the state. Even if they are not totally synchronized, in areas like Asia, workers' innovation under the current neoliberal market is always driven by, intertwined with, and managed by the state and multinational enterprises.[14]

On the institutional level, the specific features of creative industries structure the know-how, attitudes, and type of creativity needed. This is not just a matter of employing talent. When cultural workers invest their time in creative industries, they internalize the norms and roles imposed by these corporations. The entire range of cultural production, from unpaid digital laborers who participate in the production of blogs and free content to paid, highly skilled cultural labor, is "channeled" and "structured" within capitalist processes of consumption and production perpetuated in multinational corporations.[15]

In summary, both macro and medium organizations have set boundaries for cultural labor, and hence shaped their values, lifestyles, and even political ideologies. I am not arguing that cultural labor is deprived of free will. Nor do I posit that such labor lacks "creativity," understood in the Western context. However, rarely can the cultural labor in a particular locale go beyond the ideological boundaries of the workplace and the political or regulatory system of the regime. This chapter formulates a framework that takes into account two major dimensions: creative dependence and creativity tolerance.

In the tumultuous drive toward cultural globalization, subcontracting activities have become a key issue in creativity dependence. The less jobs are subcontracted by the creative industries, the more autonomy companies have to develop their own creativity. On the contrary, the more creative industries depend on subcontracting work, the more labor must have the professional skills and standards that the company requires. In other words, the creativity of the subcontracted labor can only be a replication or derivation of the subcontracting global companies.

The cultural, economic, and political context plays an important role in determining the motivations of cultural labor.[16] In addition to financial incentives, the so-called atmosphere, or "people climate," plays an important role in attracting talented workers to creative enterprises.[17] This is further affected by the ideology of the state, which shapes the overall tenor of public attitudes toward innovation and diversity.[18] From the perspective of political economy, stronger politico-economic control diminishes the creative expression in the cultural products.

THREE MODES OF CULTURAL LABOR

The two dimensions of creativity dependence and creativity tolerance yield four possible quadrants or formations of cultural labor. The fieldwork in Asia yielded at least three modes of cultural labor.

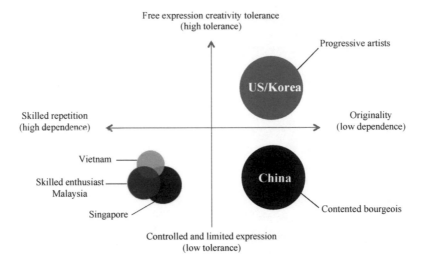

FIGURE 1. Modes of Cultural Labor (in Game Industries)

Progressive Artists

Cultural labor in Korea works in a democratic, free-market environment where the business model of games depends on both internal consumption and export. The conditions of the market, the democratic system, and the business models of the games companies are similar to those in the United States. Koreans used to be the leading players in the games market in Asia and still contribute to many leading games on the market. One of the most important games is *Aion: The Tower of Eternity,* a MMORPG released by NCsoft, a major Korean game developer. It was first released in Asia in 2009, and by May 2009 had acquired 3.5 million subscribers in the region, where China is the largest market under its operator Shanda Interactive Entertainment. *Aion* was later localized for Western markets, including North America, Europe, and Australia.

My interview with a former NCsoft programmer who was involved in developing *Aion* revealed the conditions of Korean cultural labor. The venue of the interview was picked by the interviewee: the backyard of a stylish coffee shop in the Bochun area, a district featuring well-preserved traditional Korean houses where artists reside. During the interview, I saw visitors going back and forth taking photos. The interviewee was well aware of the overly romanticized lifestyle of cultural labor in the area. Because of their strong programming skills and sophisticated tastes, which are in high demand, they are able to pursue a relatively uninhibited lifestyle. The interviewee is now a graduate student at Seoul National University writing a thesis on the Korean creative industry. He has confirmed that he will return to work at NCsoft after completing his graduate degree. Coincidentally, another programmer I met was also a graduate student, at Yonsei University. As he explained, he became interested in games when he was in high school. His mother promised to pay his tuition at a private game college where students studied game programming, if he passed his college entrance exams with flying colors. He did, which allowed him to study game design and work for a game company while also studying as an undergraduate student at Yonsei. The money he earns as a game developer is considerable and allows him to pay the tuition at Yonsei, which is one of the most expensive private universities in Korea.

The information revealed in the interviews suggests that these cultural workers are part of an educated elite in Korea. They can be regarded as middle-class workers with a flexible schedule and relative creative autonomy. They readily switch between studies and work, and living expenses are not a financial burden. Hence, they resemble artists enjoying a high standard of living. Moreover, they are able to live in downtown Seoul, which is unaffordable for many university graduates. The interview with another Seoul National University student who wanted to enter the industry revealed that the expected average annual salary was around two to three million Korean Won (US$20,000–30,000), which is not a particularly high salary, but the increments could be very high, depending on performance.

I deliberately discussed politics in Korea with them, particularly asking them about President Park Geun-hye, the first woman president in East Asia and the daughter of Park Chung-hee, president of South Korea from 1963 to 1979, when South Korea was a military dictatorship. Interestingly, the interviewees did not seem concerned with politics and soon changed the topic to the history of gaming in Korea, game development, and the support provided by KOCCA. This does not mean that they were not reflective or critical, but it is a significant shift from their parents' generation, when educated young Koreans were passionate about politics. Unlike the old days under authoritarian rule, they have a strong belief in the current electoral and democratic system, which allows individualism and generally supports creativity. Subscribing to civic nationalism, they highly value the authorities' rapport with the games industry.

Skilled Conformers

Cultural laborers working in the Southeast Asian region, including Singapore, Malaysia, and Vietnam, can be considered skilled conformers. In the major cities in these countries, cultural workers take pride in subcontracted jobs from Hollywood and elsewhere. In response to our question of why Singapore was chosen to inaugurate a Disney game in Asia, the CEO of Infocomm said that for Disney, "it is difficult to have control in other countries. [Singapore] is the only place that they will feel that everything will be accomplished according to their plan."

Asian cultural labor perceives China as the most profitable market in Asia aside from the United States and Europe (the CEO of the distributor of *World of Warcraft* in Singapore concurred). If these small- and medium-size Asian companies could break into the Chinese market, American game giants would entrust them to be the distributors to the Chinese market. The dependence on the American market, in their view, is not imbalanced; instead their view aligns with the government's point of view, and they feel privileged to be the "Asian arm of Hollywood." They believe that their creative industries have greatly contributed to making Singapore an international cosmopolitan city on par with the professional standards of Hollywood. In 2014, the Singaporean government aimed to attract Disney and Lucasfilm to locate their Asian headquarters in a futuristic horseshoe-shaped building, the Sandcrawler, in Fusionopolis, the new cyber area of Singapore. In a joint effort, the National University of Singapore and the Media Development Authority launched the Singapore Hollywood Attachment Programme, which networks with top IDM (Interactive Digital Media) institutions in the United States to place Singaporean students. These are conscious efforts by Singapore to keep up with the West. In short, they want to follow, conform to, and defend the Western standard of creativity.

On the other hand, the philosophy of cultural labor is synchronized with the official ideology of the state. Executives and employees of major game companies in the region express a strong sense of social contribution and harmony, values they share with the authorities. Infocomm, the Singapore game distributor mentioned earlier, launched many offline activities to attract online game players to socially beneficial causes, including their blood donation event. Virtual gifts were given to players who participated in the event.

According to the CEO of a major Malaysian game company, Codemasters Studio, both the company and its employees embrace global standards while also maintaining local values. Codemasters, which has been in operation for seven years, is like many other companies in Southeast Asia. It started by producing CGI for Pachinko and now focuses on subcontracted game art for overseas clients in North America, the United States, the United Kingdom, Europe, and Japan. The CEO of the company explained that he is proud of the fact that most employees were trained in Malaysia but they are all familiar with creative products from around the world. Given that awareness, he notes, "When you talk about style we are quite flexible. I will say that it is our strength actually. So we don't really favor any type of style, but we are quite flexible. When we actually talk to people like those from the UK, or from the U.S., we communicate quite well. Moreover, I think the main strength is our communication."

The strength of these Malaysian laborers, as they see it, is that they embrace Western aesthetics. In fact, most feel "superior" in that they share among themselves values that are not local but cosmopolitan. In other words, they regard

Western values as more modern, trendy, and worldly than indigenous Malaysian values. As we found in our fieldwork, most of these workers display Western pop culture decorations—including posters, toys, and games—in their offices, work spaces, and production sites to demonstrate their artistic, avant-garde, modern values. Their work spaces provide a stark contrast to other offices in Kuala Lumpur.

Contented Bourgeois

Cultural labor in China is characterized by contented bourgeoisie. China's domestic cultural market is as large as the American market, and in Asia, China competes with Korea for exports. There is always a perceived shortage of talent in the market. The entire cultural labor market in China can be explained by the literal Chinese translation of Yu Xin's (513–581) ancient Chinese expression "Crouching tiger, hidden dragon." The essence is that China is full of talent that remains unseen and undiscovered. The fact is that in major Chinese cities and universities, this hidden talent has to be actively sought by major game companies. They prefer to appear as "curling roots"—crouching tigers that are content with politics and society as long as their lives are settled. Thus if game companies want to expand, they must provide incentives to attract workers from leading universities and other game companies.

The head of a game engine programming team at Perfect World Company—one of the largest online game companies specializing in MMOPRG in China and an IPO company on the NASDAQ—described the trajectory of his work experience. He started with a Taiwanese company and produced the strategy game *Three Kingdoms*. He then was brought in by Perfect World to lead a game production team. When asked about his views on developing games, he offered a very pessimistic response, saying that it is very difficult to break out of the corporate culture to launch a small start-up. Although his team is exceptionally talented, with the capacity and know-know to develop a full-fledged game engine on its own, the path is full of obstacles.

The biggest problem is financing. He mentioned that at least two phases of capital investment are required to develop a game. On average, RMB 12 million is required in the first year, mainly for salary, and in the second year, a special bonus or commission has to be distributed to the team. The high investment makes it impossible for him to start his own business. Hence most people seek refuge in big companies, where the corporate culture is pragmatic rather than imaginative or spiritual. The guiding principle is the contractual relationship, which specifies incentives based on commissions or stock options. When asked how long he would continue to work for this game company, he responded, "Right now I am quite distressed. The day drags—it's okay to stay in a big company. People resigned because [the job] is too demanding and life is too stressful. I am now twenty-six. I am too old; I can't move."

However, in terms of salary relative to living standard, these workers in fact lead affluent lives. Based on our estimation of his monthly salary, which is at least RMB 30,000, the interviewee could live luxuriously. However, he rented a small, old apartment and worked long hours, and he said that he did not have much of a personal life in the city, since he devotes most of his time to his job.

We heard similar concerns from the vice president of Perfect World. The interview was conducted in a canteen on the ground floor of a complex located in the Shangdi district of Beijing, an area designated for high-tech industries. Despite the building's postmodern appearance, office decorations hardly reflected the bohemian values of the so-called cultural laborers. Against the plain gray walls and floor, the tables were packed close to each other, and people sat back-to-back on low-budget chairs in a closed, noisy, stuffy environment. In contrast to this dull, monochromatic interior, the food was extraordinary! The entire interview was conducted in a quiet corner of the canteen. I was on my way out after finishing the interview when I came cross a senior programmer sitting at a crowded table outside the canteen. He seemed socially detached and relatively subdued. I would say that he and his team, who sat around him, were quite content with the bland office environment.

This visit to Perfect World immediately deflated my fantasy about these cultural workers. It seems that on both organizational and individual levels, the lifestyles of these workers were among their lowest priorities. My visits to the game production sites of the giants, Perfect World and Qilin, as well as to smaller-scale game companies, reconfirmed my presumption that these workers were concerned with sales figures, not lifestyle. In contrast to high-tech companies like Yahoo! and Gamania, which equip their offices with coffee bars and play corners against walls of highly contrasting orange and gray, these companies have large-scale offices with endless partitions and small cubicles where a programmer or artist sits.

It could be said of cultural labor in China that despite the "creative" nature of the industries, the programmers, artists, and marketers in these game companies resemble industrial workers in their tastes, aesthetics, and lifestyles. Their offices and hubs, sometimes called creative clusters, resemble factories where games are produced on computers and servers instead of machines on an assembly line.

The blind pursuit of wealth amid a chaotic market is typical of China. From the perspective of cultural laborers, because they are constantly exploited by the system, what matters to them is the immediate financial reward, not a fancy lifestyle that might not be sustained for long. While the individualistic pursuit of desire is on par with those in the creative industries in the United States and Europe, other factors differ. On the individual level, the assumption of a democracy of economic agents is not valid because China is not a state that allows free choice.[19] In the market, if competition or entrepreneurial actions drive knowledge, then that knowledge, hence creativity, does not exist because the market, particularly the cultural market (for example, media, books, and films), is dominated by a very few wholly or partly state-owned companies.²⁰ Even when creativity exists, it is distorted. In this unregulated "market," both investors and entrepreneurial consumers seek to navigate an array of choices to maximize their benefits without the baggage of intellectual property and copyright as in the West.²¹ As many interviewees expressed, once a game of considerable popularity is published by a small company, major players simply clone it and improve its quality.

CONCLUSION: CREATIVE INDUSTRIES WITH OR WITHOUT CREATIVITY

The three modes of cultural labor discussed in this study reveal key differences in the working conditions and lifestyles of game company employees in Asia. Of course, the reality is more complicated than the theoretical constructs. The positions of cultural labor, the changing nature of the creative industries, the political atmosphere, and the degree of urbanism in which the creative industries operate could change the nature and relative positions of the three modes of cultural labor.

The findings showed that the concept of creativity is relative. As long as the political economy of transnational corporations is robust and stable, the global division of labor remains. However, there must be locales in which creativity is highly valued and protected for global cultural production; at the same time, there must be dependent satellite locales in which creativity is less valued, as they are serving the center of production. If creativity industries are ideally meant to foster cultural diversity, social inclusion, and a wider development pathway—as clearly indicated in UNESCO's 2013 report on the creative economy—the Asian cases indicate that conditions on the ground are more complicated.²² Given the existing economic structures, the creative economy in some Asian countries is deemed dependent and secondary, and their creativity, if any, is derivative of the transnational corporations.

Besides the impact of global hierarchies, we have also seen that the internal dynamics within a nation greatly affect the conditions of cultural labor. Where governance is top-down and state-driven, cultural workers subscribe to ideologies of development ranging from capitalist democracy and neoliberalism to socialist economy, cultural nationalism, religious economy, and state corporatism. For example, for China and Korea, national cultural policy basically dictates the development of creative industries, the content produced, and the products exported, whereas in Malaysia, Vietnam, and Singapore, cultural workers are still immersed in the illusive gaiety of prescribed creativity. The different philosophies of cultural policy nourish two very different modes of cultural labor. Cultural policy also varies according to the regime, the regional economy, and the relative competitiveness of creative industries in the region. Taken as a whole, these forces and influences encourage us to consider the cultural valences and the theoretical implications of concepts such as precarity, creativity, and creative labor.

214   ANTHONY FUNG

NOTES

This work was fully supported by a grant from the Research Grant Council of Hong Kong Special Administrative Region (Project no. 4001-SPPR-09).

1. Data collection was conducted from 2011 to 2013. The research team interviewed seventy informants in China, South Korea, Malaysia, Singapore, and Vietnam. All are practitioners in the game industry, including online games, mobile games, handheld games, console games, computer games, and arcade games.

2. Maharaj Krishna Raina, *The Creative Passion: E. Paul Torrance's Voyages of Discovering Creativity* (Stamford, CT: Ablex, 2000).

3. Beth Hennessey, "The Social Psychology of Creativity," *Scandinavian Journal of Educational Research* 47.2 (2003): 253–271.

4. Richard Florida, *The Rise of the Creative Class and How It's Transforming Work, Leisure, Community and Everyday Life.* (New York: Basic Books, 2002).

5. David Hesmondhalgh and Sarah Baker, *Creative Labour: Media Work in Three Cultural Industries* (New York: Routledge, 2011).

6. Todd Lubart, "Cross-Cultural Perspectives on Creativity," in *The Cambridge Handbook of Creativity,* ed. James C. Kaufman and Robert J. Sternberg (New York: Cambridge University Press, 2010), 265–278.

7. Laura Murray, S. Tina Piper, and Kirsty Robertson, *Putting Intellectual Property in Its Place: Rights Discourses, Creative Labor and the Everyday* (New York: Oxford University Press, 2014).

8. Michael Keane, *Creative Industries in China: Art, Design and Media.* (Cambridge: Polity, 2013).

9. Toby Miller, Nitin Govil, John McMurria, Richard Maxwell, and Ting Wang, *Global Hollywood 2* (London: British Film Institute, 2008).

10. Richard Florida, *The Rise of Creative Class, Revisited* (New York: Basic Books, 2012).

11. Mark Banks, *The Politics of Cultural Work* (New York: Palgrave Macmillan, 2007).

12. Anthony Fung and Vicky Ho, "Cultural Policy, Chinese National Identity and Globalization," in *Global Media and National Policies: The Return of the State,* ed. T. Flew, P. Iosifidis, and J. Steemers (New York: Palgrave Macmillan, 2016).

13. Richard Caves, *Creative Industries: Contracts between Art and Commerce* (Cambridge, MA: Harvard University Press, 2002).

14. Maureen McKelvey and Sharmistha Bachi-Sen, eds., *Innovation Spaces in Asia: Entrepreneurs, Multinational Enterprises and Policy* (Cheltenham: Edward Elgar, 2015).

15. Tiziana Terranova, "Free Labor," in *Digital Labor: The Internet as Playground and Factory,* ed. T. Schola (New York: Routledge, 2013), 33–57.

16. Murray, Piper, and Robertson, *Putting Intellectual Property in Its Place.*

17. Florida, *The Rise of Creative Class, Revisited.*

18. Florida, *The Rise of the Creative Class.*

19. Pitman Pott, "Belief in Control: Regulation of Religion in China," in *China Quarterly* 174 (2003): 317–337.

20. Ibid.

21. Lucy Montgomery, *China's Creative Industries: Copyright, Social Network Markets and the Business of Culture in a Digital Age* (Cheltenham: Edward Elgar, 2010).

22. UNESCO, *Creative Economy Report 2013 Special Edition: Widening Local Development Pathways* (2013), www.unesco.org/culture/pdf/creative-economy-report-2013.pdf.

16

Unbundling Precarious Creativity in China

"Knowing-How" and "Knowing-To"

Michael Keane

In the industrially developed countries they run their enterprises with fewer people and with greater efficiency and they know how to do business. All this should be learned well in accordance with our own principles in order to improve our work.

—MAO ZEDONG, ON CONTRADICTIONS, 1956

They say low wages are a reality
If we want to compete abroad.

—BOB DYLAN, "WORKINGMAN'S BLUES #2"

Job security is under unprecedented threat in many developed nations as a consequence of the mechanization of work.[1] In addition, rising production costs are seeing the relocation of production to low-cost locations. This is a well-known story. Emerging economies are achieving substantial growth by providing cheap labor and preferential investment policies. For China, already an economic powerhouse, a foreign country's insecurity is their security: the "made in China" phenomenon manifests in products that are designed elsewhere and fabricated in China. Much of this outsourced production involves components. Economists call this "trade-in-tasks," "unbundling,"[2] or OEM (original equipment manufacturing).

In this chapter, I attempt to unbundle precarious creativity, a concept that is somewhat ambiguous and misconstrued.[3] I look at the relationship between creativity and knowledge capital. Knowledge capital is a currency that is much sought after in the PRC and in some respects overseas players are temporary custodians: the relationship of knowledge capital to "precarious creativity" is therefore worth exploring.

I begin by contextualizing precarity in China's workforce. Following this, I explore the idea of knowledge. I discuss the distinction between "knowing-that" (propositional knowledge) and "knowing-how" (the acquisition of abilities and skills). I then turn to the question of how knowledge capital and precarious creativity apply to China's media and cultural industries, specifically animation and television. In the final section, I explain variants of precarious creativity by drawing on a heuristic called the "cultural innovation timeline," which shows how many policy makers and commentators see the gap between China and its competitors closing. I argue that it is closing because employment is mobile and because knowledge (know-how) is being transferred. But it is also closing because the world is coming to China, not because China is going to the world. In the conclusion, I examine censorship, the "elephant in the room." The precariousness of expression in China affects all cultural and media workers, Chinese and foreign. Finally, I argue that the value of know-how is augmented by "knowing-to," a disposition that emanates from cultural and political contexts and constitutes a crucial modality of knowledge capital for persons looking to operate successfully in the Chinese market.

CONTEXTUALIZING PRECARIOUS CREATIVITY

The notion of precarity and the neologism *precariat* have emerged in academia over the past decade to account for the way the labor market is reorganizing in many developed economies in response to flexible forms of capitalism; for instance, an increasing number of jobs are listed as casual without fixed incomes or benefits. Skills learned in schools and universities, such as reading and theorizing, are losing value in occupations that rely on on-the job learning.[4] When this argument is extended to art, design, and media sectors, we are informed of the condition of "precarious creativity." On the surface, this coinage conjures up a dark side to creativity. In contrast to a wide-ranging consensus among educators, psychologists, and business leaders that creativity is positive and aspirational, there are now negative externalities to consider, among which is the apparently transient nature of employment in many creative sectors. Many scholars opt to use *precarity* as a corrective to euphoric claims associated with the creative economy, particularly that it is expanding globally and generating more meaningful jobs.[5]

When used to refer to cultural and creative labor, *precarity* normally picks up on the employment insecurity of workers in industry sectors affected by technological convergence—for instance, music, film and TV production, online games, and design—rather than those providing lower-level service jobs in the same industries.[6] Of course, creative work itself is difficult to define, and it is beyond the scope of this essay to investigate gradations of creative labor intensity. What can be argued, however, is that creative products and services sold to consumer markets are generally produced by people with specifically acquired skill sets.

My own research into media parks and creative clusters in China identified that 95 percent of creative workers had tertiary degrees, mostly undergraduate (54 percent).[7] Moreover, such technical and managerial skills can be easily learned or transferred when businesses move offshore, particularly when R&D sharing is part of the market entry equation.[8] For instance, AnnaLee Saxenian has characterized the migration of the Taiwanese integrated circuit (IC) supply chain to Shanghai in the early 1990s as "perhaps the greatest transfer of managerial and technical skills in human history."[9]

In China, where the nation's capital stock has accumulated largely by virtue of "sweat industries," the discourse of creativity juxtaposes productivity gains and labor market transformation. It promises a way to lift masses of people out of polluting, repetition-based industries and move them into value-adding service sectors while at the same time revitalizing domestic cultural and content industries by making them internationally successful; it offers what might be termed "cultural soft power" dividends.[10] Indeed, gains in expertise and innovation in new media sectors, which are less burdened by regulation, are assisting the Chinese government in its mission to extend the nation's soft power internationally. The key factor is knowledge—or more specifically, know-how. The concept of know-how is by now fairly well entrenched in management literature. In speaking of China, moreover, it is worthwhile noting the epistemological distinction between *knowledge-that* and *knowledge-how*, as elaborated by Gilbert Ryle in the 1940s.[11] Knowledge-that constitutes propositional knowledge, things that we know about the world. Ryle believed that knowing-how is a "higher-grade disposition," associated with "abilities and propensities" as well as "capacities, habits, liabilities and bents."[12]

Many view the challenge in terms of "catching up" with and learning from advanced soft-power nations in terms of acquiring more know-how. While the Chinese government is reluctant to openly identify such "know-how-rich" nations, there is no doubt that most practitioners in the creative industries target Western developed economies as well as Japan and South Korea. These have become China's "soft power competitors."[13] The acquisition of foreign know-how, in addition to codified intellectual knowledge (knowledge-that), readily obtainable from reports and scholarship, offers a key that can unlock secrets of innovation.

For a Chinese person, the chance to work in a foreign company may be the means of acquiring both crucial know-how and know-that. But how long the worker stays with a company depends on salary, job satisfaction, and career expectations. The inclination to change occupations can be explained in terms of "compensating differentials," that is, the coexistence of monetary and nonmonetary elements of employment.[14] People undertake jobs for a variety of reasons: in many creative industries, some work for less or work long hours because they enjoy the work they are doing and the people they associate with. Moreover, in a market like China, where there are plenty of job openings in new media sectors, workers can experience significant mobility. Taking knowledge gained, including IP, elsewhere is therefore another variant of precarious creativity. In short, the Chinese government hopes that the transfer of international knowledge together with an understanding of markets and consumer preferences might contribute to the rise of Chinese media influence. Whether this rise signals the receding influence of international media in China is a moot point.

A CHINESE POLITICAL ECONOMY FRAMEWORK

There are several ways of understanding precarious creativity in China. The first is to recognize that China, like many other countries, faces new opportunities from information abundance. Technology is having an impact on traditional patterns of life, as distant friends and potential customers are connected instantaneously through apps like WeChat and Taobao. Second, rapid urbanization has significantly altered the demographic pattern of Chinese society. One study estimates that China will have more than two hundred cities of over one million inhabitants by 2025.[15] Urbanization changes the mobility of the workforce as more people are drawn to opportunities in big cities. Third, the One Child Policy, instituted in 1978 to curb population growth, has skewed population demographics, giving rise to a generation without siblings.[16] Fourth, recent liberalizations in the household registration system *(hukou)*,[17] have increased people's ability to change employment. In tandem with unprecedented mobility and technological change, skill shortages are appearing in the workforce, a problem that is bound to continue over time as a result of the One Child Policy, with fewer young people transiting into the labor market.

Industries need labor. In China the term *industry* has an ever-present relationship with economic modernization. Policy documents emanating from Beijing, particularly the five-year economic and social plans that underpin the allocation of key government resources, emphasize the industrialization of welfare, manufacturing, education, and even culture.[18] Whereas the English word *industry* comes from the Latin *industria* and refers to "diligence, activity and zeal," the dominant term in China until recently was *gongye,* literally the "activity of physical labor."[19] The use of the body, more than the mind, reminds us of the agrarian base of Chinese society until the mid-twentieth century. The sustainability of the Chinese economy from a so-called feudal agrarian system prior to the Chinese Revolution in 1949 to the socialist commune system of the late 1950s was founded on manual labor. The ensuing rise of export-led manufacturing in the 1980s and 1990s entailed further separation of mind and body, resulting in an intensification of production lines throughout the country.

By the turn of the century, this "new factory system" was well entrenched, drawing migrant laborers into working conditions that were often unsafe and exploitative. Migration to cities led to increasing social fragmentation and exacerbated informal employment.[20] Laborers, predominantly male, toiled in urban construction projects from high-rise buildings to ostentatiously named "cultural and creative clusters,"[21] while female workers offered housekeeping *(baomu)* duties for urban residents or serviced the bodies of the middle class in thousands of massage parlors. Sweatshops proliferated on the fringes of cities, taking in work from overseas clients. As Loretta Napoleoni comments, "In the second half of the first decade of the twenty-first century China becomes the center of the global assembly line, the pieces produced at lower costs in neighboring countries and put together in Chinese factories."[22]

However, it is difficult to equate precarity in such labor-intensive sectors with media and cultural industries. In the latter, we see widespread transfers of knowledge capital that can translate into social mobility. Indeed, the zones of attraction and influence for China's creative classes are distinct from the labor-intensive Special Economic Zones (SOEs), which have led to a proliferation of sweatshops and global assembly lines. Beijing and Shanghai in particular draw creative migrants into their cosmopolitan orbits.[23]

While the precariousness of creative work is the subject of a number of important studies,[24] precarity in China's cultural and creative industries requires us to be cognizant of social and political context. I will return to this point in the conclusion. In most usages, precarious creativity refers to unstable employment in occupations that generate symbolic goods and services—for example, design, VFX and film, and software. Most international depictions relate to market economies where the hand of government is at a distance.[25] In a country where freedom of expression is constrained by politics, the term *precarious creativity* implies something quite different. The hand of government is very visible. Even when it is less evident, for instance in design, fashion, and music, there is usually a need to appease a government official somewhere. This situation reflects the organization of cultural production under socialism, still the prescribed ideology in Chinese schools today.

KNOWLEDGE CAPITAL

The importance of knowledge to creative industries is on the surface uncontroversial. Most people accept the proposition that the creative industries are knowledge based. Knowledge is a cognitive capacity, conventionally understood as expertise. In conventional media and cultural sector value chains, expertise is valued as an input into content generation, delivery, and sales (that is, marketing). Knowledge capital, sometimes referred to as intellectual capital, includes the workforce (human capital), demands and preferences of audiences and consumers (customer capital), and systems, products, processes, and capabilities (structural capital).[26] While this is invariably knowing-that, it embodies know-how.

Knowledge capital can be sticky: it is often difficult to transmit or export. The term *absorptive capacity* describes the capacity to absorb knowledge that presents as "spillovers," the latter term implying unintended consequences of actions. Both spillovers and absorptive capacities exist because an organization or an individual cannot capture all the benefits resulting from inventive activity. A good example is business precincts where there are convivial spaces in which people meet and share ideas informally. Localized spillovers and cultures of interaction frequently occur when participants are close to the knowledge source. Such clustering allows the exchange of tacit knowledge: that is, people may become smarter by interacting with each other. Creativity, learning, knowledge networks, and innovation occur because of skilled labor markets and movement of people. Media capitals like Hollywood and Mumbai, and technology hubs such as Silicon Valley, provide evidence of how knowledge capital is shared.[27]

In the past few years, a rise in collaborative production opportunities in China together with the construction of cultural parks and media bases has led to significant transfers of knowledge capital: this includes human capital, customers, and structural capital as well as technological know-how.

MEDIA: THE GAME CHANGES

One senses a strong belief among China's creative workforce in the rising power of Chinese media and cultural production. At the moment workers are in demand in China; pay, conditions, and job satisfaction exceed many other service occupations. While data from the National Bureau of Statistics is not fine grained in term of occupational categories, it does indicate that salaries in "culture, sports, and entertainment" occupations are higher than other service industries, not a surprising finding considering the amount of investment, both domestic and foreign, that has taken place over the past several years. In addition, the largest increase in salaries is in the category "information transmission, computer service, and software." In 2009, the average wage for workers in this area was RMB 58,154 (approx. US$9,500); in 2013 had become RMB 90, 926 (US$14,800).[28] Discussions of bonuses paid by domestic technology and games companies like Tencent can be found online.[29] Successful projects can deliver dividends to creators that often exceed monthly salaries.

Job opportunities are increasing, allowing workers to move from place to place, from job to job. The animation and gaming industry, despite its reliance on outsourcing contracts, is a case in point. Cities such as Beijing, Shanghai, Suzhou, Hangzhou, Wuxi, Guangzhou, Shenzhen, and Dalian are competing to be the "animation capital" of China, and there is a relative shortage of "talent." Video gaming is indicative of demand. Data shows that salaries in the games industry are highest in Beijing, where the category "technology R&D" (*jishu yuanfa*) dominates; in

Shanghai and the Guangzhou-Shenzhen region, salaries are less than Beijing and more focused on "product design" *(chanpin cehua)*.[30] As I discuss below, while talent is frequently nurtured in foreign companies, workers are hard to retain because there is somewhere else to go and companies willing to pay more.[31] Shaun Rein, author of *The End of Copycat China,* says:

> A lot of Chinese feel like they can't make it to the top of their organizations in multinationals. They're moving to the Chinese private sector where companies have a lot of money for research and development. And there's no bamboo ceiling. So why be the country head of R&D for 3M when you can be the global head of R&D for a private Chinese company? It's happening that a lot of multinational companies now have to realize that their biggest competitors are often people that they trained directly over the past decade.[32]

This scenario now plays out in creative sectors. Many international companies have established offshoring operations, mostly in animation, software, design, and film production. In these environments, workers acquire knowledge capital through learning, sometimes in a "master-apprentice" system. Skills are molded by watching, listening and imitating, "learning-by-doing," illustrating Polanyi's tacit knowledge, essentially the acquisition of know-how. The foreign business introduces new ways of thinking about design while the locals provide cheaper labor. But cheap labor is not without transaction costs. Skills (and knowledge) are transferable, and many workers see no need to be loyal to the foreign master. When workers walk out the door, actual codified knowledge in the form of patterns (IP) might be lost. In the games industry, we observe a similar phenomenon.

In addition to a strong demand for graduates from China's communication universities in the new media sectors, there is another side of development that allows us to further unbundle the nuances of the term *precarious creativity* in China: this is the commercialization of broadcasting industries. As mentioned above, prior to the 1990s, media production was regarded as a public service. The term generally used in this regard is *public institution (shiye).* The largest *shiye* is China Central Television (CCTV), a cultural mothership that for most observers of China symbolizes the hegemony of the state. Ying Zhu has eloquently described CCTV's turn toward the market in *Two Billion Eyes.* The introduction of contract labor with higher pay, as opposed to ongoing employment, signaled a move toward the kinds of outsourcing practices common in most international media industries. When the broadcaster launched its flagship current affairs program, *Oriental Horizon (Dongfang shikong),* in the early 1990s, production work was contracted out, with less than 10 percent of workers remaining on CCTV's payroll.[33] The contracted workers became central to CCTV's talent identification. As Ying Zhu notes, CCTV poached talent from independent production companies, thereby refreshing its workforce. On the other hand, as her study points out, many of the best people at CCTV have left and moved into independent and digital media sectors.

Similarly, at Beijing Television (BTV) competition is coming thick and fast from digital media. In a focus group interview I conducted with several senior personnel, one person commented, "Jobs were relatively high paid a decade ago, but staff members have received no pay increases for eight years."[34] The same person said that his department recently recruited about a dozen workers. The quality was high, many being overseas returnees with postgraduate qualifications and media experience. He noted, "The expansion of digital sectors is providing 'talents' with better working conditions and pay, and as a result there is a lot of mobile human capital. Mobility is accelerated and as a result the turnover rate is very high. This [competition] might force us to raise salaries in the future."

At the time CCTV was renovating its operations in the 1990s, a number of leading production units emerged in television and film. Some of these, including Enlight Media,[35] were formerly within the system; in time they would become leading players in the provision of entertainment content, particularly television formats and live events. A new "variant" of precarity soon came into being. Regulations allowing licensing of private companies came into force in 2004.[36] With the exception of "foreigners," any person or enterprise can form a media production company in China as long the State Administration of Press Publicity Radio, Film and TV (SAPPRFT) ratifies the license. The performance of non-state-owned production units, although precarious under conditions of censorship, has helped fulfill quotas of domestic content required to fill schedules, thus thwarting the incursion of foreign media content from the United States, Europe, Hong Kong, and Taiwan, which had spiked in the early 1990s.[37] By the time China joined the World Trade Organization in 2001, the number of companies registered as private *(mingying)* had climbed to over three hundred, most of them plying their trade in TV serial drama production. By 2009, the number of independent production units in the broadcasting sector had exceeded four thousand, with 90 percent of drama production commissioned from such enterprises.[38]

While private companies have changed the game, it is necessary to add a caveat to the meaning of the term *independent*: that is, their existence is dependent on the dominance of the state in determining what content is suitable for audiences. Compared with the independent sector internationally, state-owned television stations maintain dominance in contract alliances; for instance, private production units might produce a show that is successful, but the rights are generally owned by the broadcaster. There are other uncertainties built in that make production precarious. Censorship is something that private entities need to be mindful of because production licenses are renewable. Moreover, when a program is successful, it might be replaced if the TV station decides to make its own version. This demonstrates the fragility of the concept of copyright in Chinese media industries. To maximize revenue and remain solvent, many production companies seek out and produce advertising content.

THE CULTURAL INNOVATION TIMELINE
RECONSIDERED

The question of how knowledge capital is circulated and deployed in generating successful cultural and media products leads me to reconsider the utility of the term *precarious creativity*. Rather than simply being a negative indicator, precarious creativity is adding to the knowledge capital of China's creative industries. In other words, many workers are moving from low-cost production to higher-end production and from low wages to higher salaries. People are moving from traditional broadcasting to new media, where the salaries are better. In the process some are identifying ways to innovate and internationalize rather than relying on the domestic market. To see how this plays out, I explore the cultural innovation timeline, a concept I have used elsewhere to explain the uneven development of China's creative industries. Essentially the cultural innovation timeline depicts how production moves from low to higher value offerings. In describing these processes, it underscores the centrality of knowledge capital and the role of cultural intermediaries.

The base level of the cultural innovation timeline is standardized production; for instance, deterritorialized production and outsourcing of call centers gives low-cost locations an opportunity to be included in global trade networks. Factories are established because land is made available for cultural and creative industry projects, often with the help of local governments.[39] Human capital in most of these instances is unskilled. Workers are paid low wages, and they work long hours. While there may be some status working in a design sweatshop or an animation outsourcing company, there is no desire to innovate; this is just a job. That is not to say, however, that there will be no learning on the job.

The second level of the timeline is imitation. Without the capacity to experiment or expend resources in content development, many producers of content follow the path of copycatting. China has a global reputation as a copy-nation, but again this needs to be put into the context of precarity. In the main, copying is a safe way of proceeding; if something has made money, it is reasonable to try it again, or tweak it a little bit. Shaun Rein says copying exists because you don't have to pay high upfront costs. While an offender might get fined by the government, this is usually cheaper than paying for the rights.[40] In addition to the economic dividends, there are cultural reasons for copy culture that would require a lengthy exposition.

In fashion we see clear evidence of this process. The fashion industry is populated by copyists; in responding to the question "How do you keep reinventing?" Ralph Lauren once said, "You copy. Forty-five years of copying. That's why I'm here."[41] In China today, fashion and textile manufacture coexist in a symbiotic relationship. Workers toil to produce textiles while the country's leaders exhort people to build an "innovative nation." The worker on the Chinese-owned production line in Shaoxing, the capital of the textile industry in Zhejiang Province, is unlikely to be concerned with the idea of an innovative nation; work is a means to put food on the table, hopefully providing a stable income. This is the ultimate sweat industry: long hours, cramped conditions, and low wages. Workers produce capital through duplication; in this context creativity is redundant.

In many foreign-owned design workshops, creative capital is configured differently. According to Tim Lindgren, an independent designer who took his production to Shanghai several years ago because costs in Australia had escalated to the point where he could not employ staff, "It's hard to keep high quality staff: they learn on the job and then leave to start their own business or find higher pay."[42] The mobility of workers in this situation is understandable. For the foreign design enterprise, it entails a search for staff replacements, not always so easy in a cross-cultural work environment. According to Lindgren, the other side of this dilemma is that patterns and designs (copyright) are lost, often appearing as high-priced garments in local markets.

Collaboration follows imitation, as content producers seek out alternative ways to capture value. Two examples of collaboration are pertinent to knowledge capital: film coproduction and TV formats. Coproductions in film are an interesting vehicle of knowledge capital transfer. They are categorized in three ways: the first is joint production (*lianhe shezhi,* or *hepai*), in which domestic and foreign parties make a joint investment of capital, services, or materials, and jointly share the benefits and risks of such "codevelopment." The second is known as assisted production (*xiezuo shezhi,* or *xiepai*). This is where a foreign party makes an investment to produce in China: equipment, apparatus, sites, services, and so on are provided by the Chinese party, which receives a fee for services. The third model is entrusted production or commissioned production (*weituo shezhi,* or *daipai*). Here the Chinese party is "entrusted" by the foreign party to produce content in China.

Joint productions are considered domestic productions. In discussion with producers in Australia, I have observed a preference for codevelopment over assisted production—that is, producers are endeavoring to make stories that will sell in the Chinese market, taking advice on how to proceed from locals. There is a sense of optimism, some believing that Chinese audiences will learn to appreciate stories that have new ingredients. *Codevelopment* suggests that the Chinese side is interested in cocreating with foreign entities rather than just supplying low-cost production services. To date this road is littered with failure. It is precarious from a market sense as well as reputation. If producers edit their stories to appease the Chinese government, the danger is that critical acclaim in international filmmaking communities will diminish. Yet the road most traveled is likely to be documentaries about the wonders of China, not the treatment of its dissidents.

In effect, different risks exist depending on whether a project is a joint production or a commissioned one. East Asian businesses in many cases have a better appreciation of the precariousness of working with Chinese scripts; for instance, Chinese screenwriters and producers invariably have a well-developed sense of how to self-censor. Chinese content is imbued with allegory, parody, and oblique references, one of the reasons it encounters audience resistance when exported.

While coproductions have helped Chinese television improve its markets and have injected new ideas, China's TV industry has struggled to export its brand. In television China's comparative advantage in overseas sales comes from adaptations of the four classics of Chinese popular literature *(sida mingzhu)*,[43] as well as historical serials about emperors, eunuchs, and court intrigues. This advantage has conspired to produce a glut of second-rate productions; even home audiences have turned away in large numbers, precipitating edicts from the SAPPRFT to rebalance production slates toward contemporary stories. In short, economic success in the home market does not equate to success abroad, and critical success abroad (as in the case of art house cinema) does not necessarily translate into economic success at home.

In the case of TV formats, a transaction is made between the domestic licensee and the format holder or distributor. According to the managing director of a leading international TV format distributer, Chinese television stations generally want more knowledge than other international partners. The TV format distributor in question not only sells the copyright of the TV format to the local TV station or production company but also provides direction on program localization, consulting on production, and even direct participation during the production and postproduction periods. This represents a difference from the format licensing business elsewhere; in China the foreign party is regarded like a consulting firm.[44] The Chinese want the know-how.

Following collaboration, the fourth level in the cultural innovation timeline is cultural trade. By the first decade of the millennium, the impetus to move programs out of China into international regional markets had increased. Coincident with the cultural trade impetus was the consolidation of production and management, first in media conglomerates and later in media bases or clusters (the late 1990s, early 2000s).

This consolidation constitutes level five of the timeline. I have earlier mentioned the virtues of clustering and the spillover effects that can accrue. Of course, this is the ideal. Clustering has a checkered history in China's reform period. In many instances, clusters function to attract business investment *(zhao shang)* more than attracting creative talent *(zhao chuang)*.[45] Moreover, the fact that China has hundreds of clusters in which outsourcing is the bread and butter indicates that there is still a market for semiskilled labor.[46] The massive injection of government funding in clusters is driving competition for talent and investment. Places are competing for creative talent and investment on a scale unprecedented in China, with local governments providing preferential policies, tax breaks, and free rent. In effect, precarity has a broader context in China. While employment is volatile and profits are uneven across the broad spectrum of commercial creative industries, the high level of government subsidy in constructing zones and parks has created a bubble.

In previous work on cultural and creative industries, I have described level six as constituting "peer communities" and "creative communities."[47] This is the online world, with more than 650 million participants. The activities of online producers are indeed precarious, so much so that much content is predominantly parody. It is posted, reposted, and then taken down, often by persons employed by the government to monitor unhealthy commentary. It is this meaning of precarious creativity, I feel, that characterizes China more than debates about job losses in the "creative industries," which are invariably construed as symptomatic of neoliberalism, a move that arguably succumbs to its own kind of reductionism.[48]

CONCLUDING REMARKS: THE (PRECARIOUS) ELEPHANT IN THE ROOM

A great deal of government investment has targeted the cultural sector in China over the past decade. As a result of market openings, many foreign players are lining up to take advantage of the "world's biggest audience."[49] The technological gap between China and the developed economies is closing fast because of the transfer of knowledge and the movement of human capital.

I have argued that the concept of precarious creativity requires rethinking if it is to apply to China. Of course, the conventional usage of *precarity* as depicted in much of the literature does apply, especially in manufacturing sectors, where sweatshops operate with impunity. Much work in the creative industries in China is project based, and we observe a marketplace for talent. In this latter sense, the key point is the mobility of workers in and across media sectors, and from foreign companies back to Chinese digital companies. While many foreign companies are struggling to retain talented workers, the new media challenge is significant, extending to state-owned media enterprises. As suggested by CCTV's poaching of talent from the independent production sector, even though the work may not be long-lasting, skills are in demand. Conversely, the example of BTV shows that digital media, from games to mobile media, is bent on securing the best "talent" and paying more money.

Despite the massive market for culture in China, government regulation undermines attempts to be taken seriously internationally as a soft power competitor. When competing for the hearts and minds of international audiences, two main challenges confront creators of film, television, and animation content. There are other elements of precarity that stymie China's outward-bound ambitions. The first is the challenge of credibility. An emphasis on historical revisionism and a propensity toward melodrama, while acceptable in the PRC market, fail to transfer into commercial success abroad. This in turn points to a second problem. There is a lack of understanding within China of how to make content that might be successful overseas and actually assist in reinvigorating "brand China."[50] Hence the demand for foreign know-how.

Another ubiquitous aspect of precarious creativity is really the "elephant in the room." What is the point of talking meaningfully about creativity in China if its existence is made perilous by censorship? In this context I want to add another dimension to our understanding of knowledge capital, namely "knowing-to." Whereas knowing-that and knowing-how provide ways to ascend the cultural innovation timeline, knowing-to comes into play at important times; for instance, a person might wish to push the boundaries of creative work, or a foreign producer might seek to promote a film coproduction in China. Knowing-to becomes an important modality of knowledge capital. Knowing-to manifests in four circumstances: first, anticipating outcomes (understanding the effects of an action or a policy); second, timeliness (making one's move at the right time); third, context (working in a way that takes account of others' political obligations and *guanxi*);[51] and fourth, "understanding weightiness" (knowing the relative weight of policies and regulations).[52] Knowing-to combined with knowing-that makes for good business in China. However, this does not guarantee good content, just survival.

Finally, it is worth considering how knowing-to applies to the Chinese leadership's attempt to rebrand China as a "strong cultural power" *(wenhua qiangguo)*, the latest rhetoric emanating from cultural industry think tanks. In China, precarity extends beyond employment; if someone expresses a view in writing that directly challenges the government or infers that a member of the Chinese political elite is corrupt, this person's employment may be terminated—and this may have consequences for personal liberty and the welfare of the person's family. The European Enlightenment view that creativity is about asking difficult questions, challenging authority, and destabilizing norms does not sit well with the government. The discourse of creativity is based on a harmonious vision of progress, captured in the soporific idea of a Chinese Dream, one in which all Chinese citizens are presumed to participate. That means 1.3 billion Chinese dreams. The problem in this rhetoric is that dreaming by definition is difficult to control.

NOTES

I acknowledge the support of the Australian Research Council in enabling this research to be undertaken. The author(s) declared no potential conflicts of interest with respect to the research, authorship, and/or publication of this article. The author disclosed receipt of the following financial support for the research, authorship, and/or publication of this article: Research for this paper was funded through the Australian Research Council Discovery-Projects DP140101643 Willing Collaborators: Negotiating Change in East Asian Media Production.

1. I use the term *developed nation* or *economy* rather than *West* or *Western*. A developed economy in this sense is where tertiary and quaternary sectors dominate the economy.

2. Robert Baldwin, "Globalisation: The Great Unbundling(s)," Economic Council of Finland, 2006, available at www.tinyurl.com/2ol2n8.

3. For instance, see G. Hearn, R. Bridgstock, B. Goldsmith, and J. Rodgers, eds., *Creative Work beyond the Creative Industries* (Cheltenham: Edward Elgar, 2014).

4. See Nestor Gabriel Canclini, "Precarious Creativity: Youth in a Post-Industrial Culture," *Journal of Latin American Cultural Studies: Travesia* 22.4 (2013): 341–352.

5. Boosterist claims of the creative economy proliferate in most countries. Much of this relates to errors in accounting, namely the propensity to count as creative things that are evidently not creative. The first book to advance the cause was John Howkins's *The Creative Economy: How People Make Money from Ideas.*

6. For instance, facilities maintenance, hospitality, domestic work. See Terry Flew, *The Creative Industries: Culture and Policy* (London: Sage 2012), 107.

7. From 251 valid surveys (from a total of 400) in Beijing (Fangjia 46, Shijingshan Cyber Recreation Park), Suzhou Industrial Park and Creative 100 (Qingdao), conducted May 2009 to July 2010. Michael Keane, *China's New Creative Clusters: Governance, Human Capital and Investment* (London: Routledge 2011).

8. See Seamus Grimes, "Foreign R&D in China: An Evolving Innovation Landscape," in *Innovation and Intellectual Property in China: Strategies, Contexts and Challenges,* ed. K. Shao and X. Fend (Cheltenham: Edward Elgar, 2014), 186–205.

9. AnnaLee Saxenian, *The New Argonauts: Regional Advantage in a Global Economy* (Cambridge, MA: Harvard University Press, 2006), 201.

10. The term *cultural soft power* in China is used to refer to China's attempts to move its cultural and media products into international markets. See Michael Keane, *Creative Industries in China: Art, Design, Media* (London: Polity 2013); and Michael Keane, *China's Television Industry* (London: BFI Palgrave, 2015).

11. Gilbert Ryle, *The Concept of Mind* (Chicago: University of Chicago Press, 1949).

12. Ibid., 45.

13. For a discussion of soft power competition regionally, see Beng-Huat Chua, *Structure, Audience and Soft Power in East Asian Culture* (Hong Kong: Hong Kong University Press, 2012).

14. For a discussion, see Jason Potts and Tarecq Shehadeh, "Compensating Differentials in the Creative Industries: Some Evidence from HILDA," in *Creative Work beyond the Creative Industries,* ed. G. Hearn, R. Bridgstock, B. Goldsmith, and J. Rodgers (Cheltenham: Edward Elgar, 2014).

15. McKinsey Global Institute, "Preparing for China's Urban Billion" (McKinsey and Company, 2009).

16. The One Child Policy refers to the policy adopted in 1978 that mandated that each family is allowed one child with the exception of minorities. The policy has undergone revision in the past few years, allowing people who were single children to marry and have two children.

17. The *hukou* refers to the household registration scheme initiated in the 1950s to maintain population control. It is essentially a work permit.

18. For a discussion, see Keane, *Creative Industries in China.*

19. The word *industrialization* is translated as *gongyehua*

20. Martin King Whyte, "The Paradox of Rural-Urban Inequality in Contemporary China," in *One Country, Two Societies: Rural-Urban Inequality in Contemporary China,* ed. M. K. Whyte (Cambridge, MA: Harvard University Press, 2010), 1–28.

21. Michael Keane, *China's New Creative Clusters: Governance, Human Capital and Investment* (London: Routledge, 2011).

22. Loretta Napoleoni, *Maonomics: Why Chinese Communists Make Better Capitalists Than We Do*, trans. Stephen Twilley (New York: Seven Stories Press, 2011), 41.

23. See Juncheng Dai, Shengyi Zhou, Michael Keane, and Qian Huang, "Mobility of the Creative Class: A Case Study of Chinese Animation Workers," *Eurasian Geography and Economics* 53.5 (2012): 649–670.

24. Mark Banks and David Hesmondhalgh, "Looking for Work in Creative Industries Policy," *International Journal of Cultural Policy* 15.4 (2009): 515–430; David Hesmondhalgh, David, *The Cultural Industries*, 2nd ed. (London: Sage, 2007); Andrew Ross, *Fast Boat to China: Corporate Flight and the Consequences of Free Trade: Lessons from Shanghai* (New York: Pantheon Books, 2006); Kate Oakley, "In Its Own Image: New Labour and the Cultural Workforce," *Cultural Trends* 20.3–4 (2012): 281–289.

25. For instance, see the other essays in this volume.

26. Alan Burton-Jones, *Knowledge Capitalism: Business, Work, and Learning in the New Economy* (Oxford: Oxford University Press, 1999).

27. For a discussion of media capital, see Michael Curtin, *Playing to the World's Biggest Audience: The Globalization of Chinese Film and TV* (Berkeley: University of California Press, 2007). For Silicon Valley, see Martin Kenney, ed., *Understanding Silicon Valley: The Anatomy of an Entrepreneurial Region* (Stanford, CA: Stanford University Press, 2000).

28. From National Bureau of Statistics and China Statistical Yearbook, Beijing.

29. See www.zhihu.com/question/19588383.

30. See www.zhuayoukong.com/122808.html

31. Dai Juncheng, Zhou Shangyi, Michael Keane, and Qian Huang, 'Mobility of the Creative Class and City Attractiveness: A Case Study of Chinese Animation Workers," *Eurasian Geography and Economics* 53.4 (2012): 649–670.

32. Interview with Shaun Rein, September 15, 2014, available at http://www.creativetransformations.asia/2014/09/innovation-creativity-and-the-chinese-dream/.

33. Ying Zhu, *Two Billion Eyes: The Story of China Central Television* (New York: Free Press, 2012).

34. Focus group discussion with representatives of Beijing Media Group, including production managers, marketing, and programmers, QUT, Brisbane, September 25, 2014.

35. Enlight media was formed in 1998 by Wang Changtian, a former producer at Beijing Television. For a discussion, see Yuezhi Zhao, *Communication in China: Political Economy, Power and Conflict* (Lanham, MD: Rowman & Littlefield, 2008).

36. Michael Keane and Bonnie Rui Liu, "China's New Creative Strategy: Cultural Soft Power and New Markets," in *Asian Popular Culture: The Global Cultural (Dis)connection*, ed. Anthony Fung (London: Routledge, 2013), 233–249.

37. Keane, *China's Television Industry*.

38. X. Yingdan, "90% from the Private Production in China's TV Drama Market," *Xinhua Daily*, May 28, 2007, www.ccmedu.com.bbs33_45123.html.

39. See Keane, *China's New Creative Clusters*.

40. Interview with Shaun Rein, September 16, 2014.

41. Eric Wilson, "O and RL: Monograms Meet," *New York Times*, October 25, 2011, www.nytimes.com/2011/10/27/fashion/oprah-winfrey-interviews-ralph-lauren.html?_r=1&.

42. Interview with Tim Lindgren, September 12, 2014.

43. *The Dream of the Red Chamber* (*hong lou meng*), *The Journey to the West* (*xiyouji*), *Outlaws of the Marsh* (*shuihu zhuan*), and *Romance of the Three Kingdoms* (*sanguo yanyi*)

44. Interview, Beijing, August 25, 2014.

45. Keane, *China's New Creative Clusters*.

46. See ibid.

47. Keane, *Creative Industries in China*.

48. I have elsewhere argued that the concept of neoliberalism is problematic and is not applicable to China. See, for example, Keane, *The Chinese Television Industry*.

49. Curtin, *Playing to the World's Biggest Audience.*

50. See the discussion by Yingchi Chu regarding horizons of expectation. Yingchi Chu, "The Politics of Reception: 'Made in China' and Western Critique," *International Journal of Cultural Studies* 17.2 (2014): 159–173.

51. *Guanxi* is usually translated as "personal relationships"; these may have political implications.

52. For a discussion of knowing-to in traditional Chinese philosophy, see Stephen Hetherington and Karyn L. Lai, "Knowing-How and Knowing-To," in *The Philosophical Challenge from China,* ed. Bryan Bruya (Cambridge, MA: MIT Press, 2015), 279–301.

17

Revolutionary Creative Labor

Marwan M. Kraidy

This chapter elaborates the concept of revolutionary creative labor. The Arab uprisings, particularly the conflict in Syria, have given rise to a notion of creative resistance. Various activists, journalists, academics, and curators have used that phrase to celebrate a gamut of expressive practices and forms encompassing graffiti, digital memes and mash-ups, handheld banners, political rap, and others.[1] The wording combines two terms with overwhelmingly positive connotations that evoke human ingenuity and agency. But if *creative resistance* is to convey anything beyond a nebulous concept of ingenious rebellion, it needs to be systematically explored and situated vis-à-vis notions of activism, creativity, and labor in cultural production. One way to achieve that goal is to theorize processes of artful dissent as revolutionary creative labor.[2]

In order to develop a working definition of revolutionary creative labor, this chapter draws on a study of the body and activism in the Arab uprisings based on primary materials, most collected in 2011 and 2012.[3] In this chapter I pursue the following questions: To what extent does the extreme duress of revolution shift our understanding of creative labor? Is revolutionary creative labor different from other kinds of creative labor? What does revolution add to our understanding of creativity and precarity in cultural production? To answer these questions, I engage with a few key texts. The chapter first zeroes in on the use of creativity in social movement theory, mainly in James Jasper's *The Art of Moral Protest*.[4] Then it reviews some work in media industries research that addresses precarity and creativity, namely Vicki Mayer's *Below the Line*.[5] A comparative analysis of "industrial" and "revolutionary" forms of creative labor follows. Finally, via brief references to the magisterial compendium provided by Hans Joas in *The Creativity of*

Action[6] and to Lazzarato's theory of immaterial labor,[7] the chapter concludes with a theoretical elaboration of revolutionary creative labor.

CREATIVITY AND LABOR IN SOCIAL MOVEMENT AND PRODUCTION STUDIES: A SNAPSHOT

Social movement theorists have rarely discussed activism in terms of creativity or labor. Though creativity is sometimes mentioned in its prosaic meaning and the word occasionally appears in titles of books on social movements, rarely is it systematically theorized or critiqued as a conceptual category.[8] Jasper's *The Art of Moral Protest* comes closest to a sustained conceptual treatment of creativity: the notion of artfulness is a cornerstone of the book's "cultural" approach to protest, which intends "to increase [the focus on] explanatory factors . . . to concentrate on mechanisms, not grand theories . . . to give the voice back to the protestors we study."[9] Jasper writes: "Protest movements work at the edge of a society's understanding of itself and its surroundings. Like artists, they take inchoate intuitions and put flesh on them, formulating and elaborating them so that they can be debated. Without them, we would have only the inventions of corporations and state agencies, products and technologies created to enhance efficiency or profitability." Jasper then concludes: "In order to understand these innovations, we need 'moral innovators' too: the artists, religious figures, and protestors who help us understand what we feel about new technologies."[10] By comparing activists to artists, Jasper anchors artfulness in the socio-political realm of activism, valorizing innovation not in its potential for commodification but for its ability to generate political-rhetorical value.[11]

For Jasper, *artfulness* refers to "experimental efforts to transmute existing traditions into new creations by problematizing elements that have been taken for granted."[12] Artfulness articulates biography and culture: beginning as individual creativity, it becomes strategic once shaped by a group, and subsequently it is enacted in protest. Examples include deploying widely familiar and emotionally evocative symbols and grafting new meanings onto existing symbols. Language is a primary vehicle through which activists project, manipulate, and redefine symbols. Having elsewhere in the book compared activists to artists, Jasper writes that "at the most extreme, ideologists operate as poets; they define emerging structures of feeling with new terms and images."[13] Invoking the "immense value we place on individual creativity,"[14] Jasper employs the notion of "tactical innovation," a mainstay in the social movements literature, which emerges at "the interplay of protest groups and their opponents."[15]

Unlike studies of activism, research on cultural production does not focus on Political aspects of labor.[16] But the two are alike in rarely grappling directly with creativity as a central conceptual category.[17] One exception is Vicki Mayer's study of workers in a television set factory in Manaus, Brazil, where the author endeavors to "deconstruct our received notions of creativity and to reconstruct a notion of creative action that is both social and individual in the practices of assembling."[18] Following an argument made by Joas and others that social context is key to understanding creativity, Mayer develops notions of creativity that "conjoin the interiority of mental labor with the exteriority of a world that enables its articulation."[19] In addition to emphasizing creativity's social dimension, Mayer shows that as a discourse creativity is deployed with discrimination for purposes of social distinction and control. But it is Mayer's discussion of creativity as a process of making do under structural constraints that is most relevant for my purposes, because it leads to two questions that are central to this chapter. What differences can we discern between deployments of "creativity" in media industries research and the trope of "creative resistance" used to describe some forms of dissent in the Arab uprisings? And how do these differences enable my elaboration of revolutionary creative labor?

"Creativity" is a strategic and discriminatory trope. It is strategic because its selective deployment reflects and perpetuates relations of politico-economic power. It is discriminatory because it is applied according to rules of exclusion and inclusion that serve criteria of social distinction. Considerations of power and distinction in creative labor differ between scholarship on media industries and research on Political forms of labor, such as activism and propaganda. In the television set factory Mayer studied, the discourse of creativity is reserved to operators in higher ranks of the industry, who exclude workers on the assembly line from creativity's definitional scope. As Miller has shown, proponents of "creativity" have stretched the term to encompass most ways in which any activity that could remotely be described as cultural is monetized.[20] In contrast, the creative resistance trope operates primarily according to political and ideological imperatives. *Creative resistance* refers to propaganda by people we like—in this sense *creative resistance* is a more glamorous, bottom-up cousin of the great euphemism *public diplomacy.* During the war between Israel and Lebanon in 2006, Hezbollah launched a range of stylistically bold, visually compelling propaganda videos, some aimed at mobilizing supporters, others psyops clips, many in Hebrew, aimed at demoralizing Israeli soldiers. Though the notion of resistance is central to Hezbollah's raison d'être, and though many of the videos were rhetorically sophisticated and aesthetically slick, to my knowledge no one called these "creative resistance." Most mainstream media coverage in the West referred to them as "propaganda," though in some aspects they resemble revolutionary videos of the Arab uprisings, and some of them even resemble U.S. Army recruitment commercials.

INDUSTRIAL AND REVOLUTIONARY: TWO TYPES OF CREATIVE LABOR?

As a mercurial term that is applied at once broadly (connoting a vast and varied semantic field) and selectively (according to considerations of political power and social distinction), *creativity* requires definitional work to be analytically useful. In this chapter I am not interested in developing a full-scale analytical parsing of *creativity*'s various possible definitions and applications. I am, however, keen on discerning differences between the kind of creativity that one sees in, say, a television studio or factory floor—industrial creative labor—and the kind of creativity manifest in revolutionary creative labor. What might some of these differences be?

One must begin with the rather obvious observation that the creative labor of Egyptian, Syrian, and Tunisian revolutionaries is more confrontational than the invisible, sanctioned, unsanctioned, and even subversive types of creativity that Mayer identifies on the Manaus factory floor. Manifestations of creative labor in the Arab uprisings are not flexible, reformist, or merely subversive: spawned under life-threatening conditions, they are *radical* rejectionist expressions of human affects and aspirations. Rather than trying to find ways to survive or thrive in the factory, revolutionaries seek to burn the factory down, clean the debris, and build a new and utterly different edifice. This is the first and most crucial difference between industrial and revolutionary creative labor.

The centrality of the human body is a second difference between industrial and revolutionary creative labor. Though concern with the body is not vital to most research on media industries, Mayer does grapple with corporeality as an important aspect of workers' experience, what she calls "the corporeal achievement of assembly," and she argues that "conditioning the body to do the physical work signified an important rite of passage in the social world of the factory."[21] Assembly workers regiment their bodies in new and uncomfortable ways with the purpose of increasing productivity. Nonetheless, "the corporeality of the act of assembling the television set could not communicate a creative act in itself simply because of its exclusion from the discourse of creativity."[22] In contrast, revolutionary creative labor, I would argue, is more deeply and more intimately entangled with the human body. This is primarily a matter of resources: factory workers are provided with the tools needed to satisfy the demands of capitalist production. Revolutionaries, in contrast, are often bereft of tools and resort to very basic media. The Syrian Masasit Mati collective, which created the famous *Top Goon* video series lampooning Bashar al-Assad, used paper, wood, and fabric to create finger puppets and human energy to operate the puppets. Using basic materials, they miniaturized the dictator by reducing him to a finger puppet and infantilized him through satire.[23] Of course, they also had a basic video camera and eventually set up a YouTube channel, but rather than being provided by "the system," these resources (most from the seventeenth century, some from the twentieth and twenty-first) were snatched "behind the back" of the dictator to express derision of his person and rejection of his rule.

This brings us to the third divergence. In the television set factory in Manaus, assembly-line workers are subjected to a range of *managerial* constraints that

Mayer groups under Taylorism, "parsing complex jobs into tasks,"[24] and Japanization, which consists of a gamut of "social surveillance techniques."[25] Working in tandem and sometimes in contradiction, these two top-down forces constrain workers as they create opportunities to overcome constraints. In Mayer's words, "Assemblers looked creatively for solutions to stressful limits because *they had no other choice. . . .* Yet workers' creativity could also overstep expectations, leading to disciplinary actions, dismissal, or even blacklisting."[26] In contrast, revolutionary creative labor is situated farther down the sanctioned–unsanctioned creativity that Mayer evokes in her analysis. Assembly workers' creativity is what I would call "making-do" creativity, whereas creative insurgency involves "breaking-bad" creativity.[27] The first is conjured up to cope with the system; the second is deployed to topple the system. The first is framed by top-down industrial-managerial models; the second is a bottom-up expression of pent up repressed subjectivity. The former involves bodily discipline—"The adaptation of her fingers to the fine manipulations of wires was an acquired skill"[28]—on the factory floor, while the second entails bodily insurrection on a literal and symbolic battlefield. In the first, Mayer points out, "unsanctioned creative actions generally stimulated more rules."[29] Whereas factory workers bent their fingers to the demands of capital, members of Masasit Mati moved puppets' fingers to utterly reject the Syrian dictatorship. The first is adaptation; the second, rebellion.

Whereas assembly workers face managerial (and social) constraints, Arab creative activists confront often brutal and sometimes murderous repression, which grows increasingly violent as uprisings endure. If Brazilian assembly workers focus their creativity on "eking out a living,"[30] Arab revolutionaries deploy creativity for the purpose of eking out a dignity, a political agency. Prerevolutionary creative dissent in countries like Egypt, Syria, and Tunisia—double-entendre parodies, strategically ambivalent artwork, and allegorical theater—can be described as subversive. In contrast, revolutionary creativity is a confrontational, no-holds-barred, high-stakes, high-risk, and potentially high-rewards gambit.

Industrial creative labor and revolutionary creative labor differ in a fourth way. Whereas the former occurs openly, the latter operates surreptitiously. In both cases, the visibility of creative labor is determined by the structural constraints already discussed. Though factory floor workers may engage in micropractices of subversion to improve their lives in the factory, they are subjected to a strong surveillance regime, and the lion's share of their labor is exceedingly visible to their managers. But if in the factory "absences were treated as the worst infractions,"[31] absence from the revolutionary public sphere constitutes an ideal situation for incumbent dictators—presence and visibility invite immediate repression. As a result, though security apparatuses attempt to spy on and capture activists, revolutionary creative labor must occur underground and be physically peripatetic to avoid arrest. In addition to resources, then, revolutionary creative labor's "trajectories of creative migration," as Michael Curtin called creative labor's movement across national boundaries,[32] are motivated primarily by the desire to physically stay alive, rather than by economic survival. Many Syrian revolutionary artists now live in Beirut or Berlin, and several prominent Arab uprising activists are political refugees in Europe.

A fifth and final difference between industrial and revolutionary creative labor is that the former is remunerated, however unfairly, while the latter is unwaged labor.[33] I list this difference in fifth place rather than earlier in the list because this contrast is not as extreme as it may appear. Though the creative labor of most activists in the Arab uprisings remained unrecognized and unwaged, there have been several exceptions reflecting the commercial and political co-optation of revolutionary creative labor. The Egyptian surgeon turned late-night comedian, Bassem Youssef, the so-called Egyptian Jon Stewart, started his show on YouTube during the Egyptian revolution. In time, one television channel picked up the show, then a bigger channel acquired it, to considerable commercial success and global critical praise. Subsequently, the show was streamed by the Arabic-language channel of the German broadcaster Deutsche Welle, before being shut down after the military coup of Abdelfattah El-Sisi in June 2013.[34] Youssef, already an affluent medical doctor, was one of a few revolutionary creative laborers who moved from unpaid to highly waged labor. The finger puppeteers of Masasit Mati, in contrast, tried crowdfunding their second season via Kickstarter, and when that effort failed, they received a grant from the Prince Claus Fund in the Netherlands. In effect, they leveraged their fame into financial support and official recognition from prestigious Western institutions, even if technically that does not constitute waged labor. But disagreements within the group led to its dissolution. Despite momentary success, then, revolutionary creative labor's mainstream prospects are as precarious as revolutionaries' ambitions for political rule.[35]

SUBJECTIVITY AND REVOLUTIONARY CREATIVE LABOR

This chapter has been grappling with the extent to which different contextual environments and constraints generate different types of creative labor with different levels of precarity. From the preceding critical comparison of what I called *industrial* and *revolutionary* creative labor, we can conclude that the extreme strictures of revolutionary contexts lead to a specific relation between the individual and the social. In *The Creativity of Action,* Joas singles out three metaphors, which emerged between 1750 and 1850, that are central to creative action: *expression,* from the work of Johann Gottfried Herder; and *production* and *revolution,* both elaborated by Karl Marx. Each of these metaphors, Joas argues, "represents an attempt to anchor human creativity in at least one of the three ways of relating to the world. The idea of *expression* circumscribes creativity primarily in relation to the subjective world of the actor." In contrast, "the idea of *production* relates creativity to the objective world, the world of material objects that are the conditions and means of actions." "And finally," Joas concludes, "the idea of *revolution* assumes that there is a potential of human creativity relative to the social world, namely that we can fundamentally reorganize the social institutions that govern human coexistence."[36]

Revolutionary creative labor, I conclude, entails the convergence of expression, production, and revolution. Revolutionary contexts are characterized by total upheaval—social and political but also economic and cultural—in which everything is up for grabs. These contexts of tremendous flux and peril require a total expenditure of resources, calling on people to mobilize to enact subjective and objective changes to the world they live in.

The definitional field delineated by expression, production, and revolution encompasses familiar axes of tension: the individual versus the social, the ideational against the material, the reformist in contrast to the radical. Such a field is a particularly apt space to grapple with the revolutionary creative labor emerging in the Arab uprisings. If, as Joas and Mayer argue, creativity entails coordinating a variety of means, responding to incentives, and working within constraints, and if, as I have already argued, revolutionaries respond to specific motivations and work within strictures distinct from the constraints of the factory floor (or, for that matter, the production studio), then revolutionary creative labor is indeed a distinct kind of creative labor.[37]

Revolutionary creative labor contributes to the creation of a subjectivity that is radically different from that of industrial labor. Jasper noted that artists can "generate and regenerate the very subjectivity they pretend only to display."[38] This echoes Lazzarato's argument about immaterial labor, which "presupposes and results in an enlargement of productive cooperation that even includes the production and reproduction of communication and hence its most important content: subjectivity."[39] Whereas Lazzarato argues that immaterial labor changes the relationship *between producer and consumer,* it is productive to think of revolutionary creative labor as changing the relationship *between ruler and ruled.* One important aspect of Lazzarato's thesis is that the shift from manual to immaterial labor transforms the three elements of what he calls the aesthetic model of labor—author, reproduction, and reception—by emphasizing their social rather than individual aspects. Creativity, Lazzarato concludes by way of brief mentions of Simmel's work on intellectual labor and Bakhtin's focus on social creativity, is social rather than individual, a point also made by Joas and Mayer.

Ordinary people from among the hitherto ruled, having become revolutionary activists, enact revolutionary creative labor to get rid of the ruler. Revolutionary creative labor, then, occasions a shift in subjectivity from the atomized docility of subjects under dictatorship to the collective rebellion of politicized agents in revolution. In Foucauldian terms, we can describe revolutionary creative labor as *a technology of revolutionary selfhood*. It mobilizes expressive and affective resources alongside the material resources of "noncreative" revolutionary labor—demonstrating in the street, staffing barricades, confronting security personnel, wielding sticks, shooting guns, tending to the wounded—to effect fundamental and political change.

The body is crucial to the project of revolutionary selfhood. As I have argued elsewhere[40] (though without grappling with the conceptual minutiae of creativity and labor), the body—as instrument, metaphor, symbol, medium—is central to revolutionary creative labor. Mayer explains how creativity pertains to Joas's concept of a "situation," by which he means "the ability of the body to move and communicate in an innovative way. . . . [C]reativity must be enacted through both the body and the social system of meanings that recognizes the action as different from the norm. . . . Creative action unifies the mind and body in doing something perceived as different. . . . This means that thought must be materialized, but also that the material is cause for later reflection."[41]

But in revolutionary contexts of the twenty-first century, the body must be understood as a central and agentive node among a panoply of other media—from cardboard to digital video—that are harnessed by revolutionaries in an all-out campaign to change their lives. The body, then, must be understood as the animator of what I elsewhere called "hypermedia space," a space of signification with multiple points of access created by interconnections among various media platforms.[42] In the case of the Arab uprisings, these include media that can be characterized as mainstream (television, newspapers), new (mobile devices, social media), and old (puppetry, graffiti), alongside the oldest of them all, the human body, which operates all other media.

Revolutionary creative labor, then, is an embodied, extremely precarious practice unfolding in a life-or-death situation, one among several kinds of labor (from physical struggle to mainstream media production) that challenge authoritarian leaders. Whereas, as Mayer argues, assembly-line work is a kind of creative labor that should to be situated within the broader context of media creativity, a different kind of creativity is at work in what I defined and explicated in this chapter as revolutionary creative labor. Indeed, a final distinction can be made between forms of creative labor that are embedded in localized contexts (the factory) which are otherwise not creative (the assembly line), what in this chapter I called industrial creative labor, and revolutionary creative labor, which consists of explicit and self-conscious forms of revolutionary creativity that are intended to be launched into broader trajectories of circulation. By enacting contextually new forms of political subjectivity and directing them at radical change, revolutionary creative labor seeks to find, congeal, and mobilize publics.

NOTES

Vicki Mayer—who alerted me to the work of Hans Joas—Michael Curtin, and Toby Miller have been key interlocutors on issues related to this chapter. I also thank Katerina Girginova for research assistance on creativity, Michael Curtin and Kevin Sanson for their useful feedback on the first draft of this chapter, and Marina Krikorian for editorial help.

1. Media stories and academic publications celebrating Arab revolutionary rap and graffiti have become so commonplace that we could talk of an a Revolutionary Graffiti Index or and Arab Rap Index, following what Miller, referring to Richard Florida's work, calls the Technological and Gay Indexes (Toby Miller, "A View from a Fossil: The New Economy, Creativity and Consumption—Two or Three Things I Don't Believe In," *International Journal of Cultural Studies* 7.1 [2004]: 60).

2. Clearly, this is only a small part of revolutionary labor at large, which includes demonstrating, confronting policy and security personnel, building barricades, feeding revolutionaries, tending to the wounded, and so on.

3. Marwan M. Kraidy, *The Naked Blogger of Cairo: Creative Insurgency in the Arab World* (Cambridge, MA: Harvard University Press, 2016).

4. James M. Jasper, *The Art of Moral Protest: Culture, Biography and Creativity in Social Movements* (Chicago: University of Chicago Press, 1997).

5. Vicki Mayer, *Below the Line: Producers and Production Studies in the New Television Economy* (Durham, NC: Duke University Press, 2011).

6. Hans Joas, *The Creativity of* Action (Chicago: University of Chicago Press, 1996).

7. Maurizio Lazzarato, "Immaterial Labour," in *Radical Thought in Italy: A Potential Politics,* ed. Paolo Virno and Michael Hardt (Minneapolis: University of Minnesota Press, 1996), 133–147.

8. For example, Benjamin Shephard, *Play, Creativity and Social Movement* (New York: Routledge, 2011), pivots around the notion of play; while Glenda Ballantyne, *Creativity and Critique: Subjectivity and Agency in Touraine and Ricoeur* (Leiden: Brill, 2007), focuses on subjectivity and agency. The "culture-jamming" literature does not apply in this context because it concerns relatively low-risk subversion of consumer culture in relatively stable, relatively democratic, industrialized countries.

9. Jasper, *Art of Moral Protest,* 378–379. Jasper identifies four basic dimensions that artful protesters use: *resources* like technology and money; *strategies,* individual and group tactics; *culture,* shared aspects of mental worlds and their physical representations; and *biography,* individuals' mental worlds, conscious and subconscious.

10. Ibid., 375.

11. Jasper uses *creativity* and *innovation* somewhat interchangeably, though definitional differences emerge in his discussion. The sociologist Doug McAdam has done extensive work on tactical innovation. For a summary introduction, see Doug McAdam, "Tactical Interaction and Innovation," *The Wiley-Blackwell Encyclopedia of Social and Political Movements,* ed. David A. Snow et al. (Hoboken: Wiley-Blackwell, 2013).

12. Jasper, *Art of Moral Protest,* 65.

13. Ibid., 159.

14. Ibid., 219.

15. Ibid., 99. For an argument about upbringing and social support as key biographical enablers of creativity in famously "creative" people, see Howard Gardner, *Creating Minds: An Anatomy of Creativity Seen through the Lives of Freud, Einstein, Picasso, Stravinsky, Eliot, Graham, and Gandhi* (New York: Basic Books, 2011).

16. *Political* with a capital *P* connotes issues of state power and resistance to it, as opposed to cultural politics.

17. Media, cultural, and music production scholars have addressed labor issues, though mostly focusing on the exploitation of labor by those industries. See Toby Miller et al., *Global Hollywood:Issue* 2 (London: British Film Institute, 2004); Mark Andrejevic, *Reality TV: The Work of Being Watched*

(Lanham, MD: Rowman and Littlefield, 2004); Matt Stahl, *Unfree Masters: Recording Artists and the Politics of Work* (Durham, NC: Duke University Press, 2013). The emerging literature on digital labor also focuses on the increasingly exploitative nature of capitalism; see Christian Fuchs, *Digital Labour and Karl Marx* (London: Routledge, 2014). This literature's socio-economic focus is helpful, but only indirectly, for studying a revolutionary setting.

18. Mayer, *Below the Line,* 33.

19. Ibid., 32.

20. Miller, "A View from a Fossil."

21. Mayer, *Below the Line,* 43.

22. Ibid.

23. See their YouTube channel at www.youtube.com/user/MasasitMati.

24. Mayer, *Below the Line,* 44.

25. Ibid.

26. Ibid., 47–51.

27. Jasper's definition of creativity as an "extreme form of flexibility" (*The Art of Moral Protest,* 94) has a matter-of-fact resonance in a revolutionary setting.

28. Mayer, *Below the Line,* 58.

29. Ibid., 56–57.

30. Ibid., 58.

31. Ibid., 59.

32. Michael Curtin, *Playing to the World's Biggest Audience: The Globalization of Chinese Film and TV* (Berkeley: University of California Press, 2007).

33. One aspect of the compatibility of revolutionary work with digital labor is that they are both unpaid. Though Lazzarato's elaboration of "immaterial labor" focused on the remunerated kind, there has been an active discussion of unwaged labor in the digital era at least since Terranova's 2000 article: Tiziana Terranova, "Free Labor: Producing Culture for the Digital Economy," *Social Text* 18.2 (2000): 33–58. Andrejevic's critique of reality television highlighted the unpaid "work of being watched" (*Reality TV,* 2004). Most recently, see the special issue of *TripleC,* "Philosophers of the World Unite! Theorising Digital Labour and Virtual Work—Definitions, Dimensions and Form," ed. Christian Fuchs et al.; especially Brian A. Brown, "Will Work for Free: The Biopolitics of Unwaged Digital Labour," *TripleC: Communication, Capitalism and Critique* 12.2 (2014): 694–712, www.triple-c.at/index.php/tripleC/article/view/538.

34. Marwan M. Kraidy, "No Country for Funny Men," *Al-Jazeera America,* February 26, 2014, http://america.aljazeera.com/opinions/2014/2/no-country-for-funnymen.html.

35. For more details, see Kraidy, *The Naked Blogger of Cairo.*

36. Joas, *The Creativity of Action,* 71 (emphasis in original).

37. I suspect that a systematic, theoretical, and comparative examination of "action" and "labor" would unearth fascinating overlaps and differences, but this falls outside the purview of this chapter.

38. Jasper, *Art of Moral Protest,* 154.

39. Lazzarato, "Immaterial Labour," 139.

40. Marwan M. Kraidy, "The Revolutionary Body Politic: Preliminary Thoughts on a Neglected Medium in the Arab Uprisings," *Middle East Journal of Culture and Communication* 5.1 (2012): 68–76; "The Body as Medium in the Digital Age: Challenges and Opportunities," *Communication and Critical-Cultural Studies* 10.2–3 (2013): 285–290; "The Politics of Revolutionary Celebrity in the Contemporary Arab World," *Public Culture* 27.1 (2014).

41. Mayer, *Below the Line,* 41–42.

42. I initially elaborated it in Marwan M. Kraidy, "Governance and Hypermedia in Saudi Arabia," *First Monday* 11.9 (2006), http://firstmonday.org/issues/special11_9/kraidy/index.html. For an application of the concept in the context of political activism before the Arab uprisings, see Marwan M. Kraidy, *Reality Television and Arab Politics: Contention in Public Life* (Cambridge: Cambridge University Press, 2010).

18

Precarious Diversity

Representation and Demography

Herman Gray

Conceiving of social inequality as a salient object of research for media industry studies is a tricky business. As a research matter, approaching inequality is mired in if not now displaced by a cluster of terms like *diversity, multiculturalism, difference, lifestyle,* and *niche.* Media's role in the production of inequalities based on class, race, gender, and sexual identification is displaced onto questions of access and representation, multiculturalism and diversity, branding and audience appeal. As the subject of media industry studies research, approaches to the study of diversity often direct researchers to see diversity as a discrete outcome and empirically track rates of diversity in the production and expression of media content.

Thinking with the possibilities opened up by renewed energies and critical foci in media industry studies, I ask what assumptions underwrite how diversity is thought in media studies of race and difference. What evidence locates, measures, and assesses its effectiveness as a social accomplishment? Is the study of diversity a salient means of getting at the role of media in the production of inequalities? As the editors of this collection suggest, following such a research agenda means starting with the methodological assumption that diversity, like studies of creative labor, operates at *multiple levels* and in *multiple registers,* including textual representation, reception, and production, as well as in the micro transactions that circulate among different sites.[1] Such transactions include critical discourses and industrial practices that organize and nominate media objects as significant and worth studying, as well as the legal and aesthetic disputes that make social differences based on race, gender, and sexual identification objects of legal oversight, political dispute, financial (dis)investment, and administrative management by studios, the FCC, global entertainment corporations, and guilds. As with studies of work objects, deep texts, and implicit ritualized relations, at each of these levels media researchers might aim to identify the quotidian practices of diversity and ask how is it framed, how it works, and to what ends.

Research on questions of diversity (as a gloss for inequality) seems especially suited to neoliberal approaches to studies of media industries as a robust site to generate new evidence about the actual practice of diversity in media organizations and institutions, its expression and production as a practical outcome of the *doings* that happen in particular and specific production and creative sites.[2] This includes researchers asking with respect to diversity, what do creative personnel understand themselves to be doing and what notions of diversity matter, how, and where do such understandings express themselves in their actual quotidian practice?

Diversity is also the object of contentious political, legal, and academic disputes. In the United States, diversity is a practical outcome, the momentary stabilization of a discursive logic and signifying system that produces material effects in the social world. As a proxy for addressing race and a disavowal of racism and inequalities based on gender, racial, and class difference, diversity operates in a shifting nexus of legal rulings, social claims, cultural practices, and media narratives about its practical life and effects. As a key location where diversity is practiced materially and symbolically, the media too is constantly undergoing economic, institutional, and technological change, marked by the appearance and disappearance of new platforms, synergies, financial entities, and international networks of finance and production. The cultural idea of diversity circulates in a media environment where, at least on the issue of race and ethnicity, social difference is a cultural signifier of a (purportedly) postracial America. Cultural signs of diversity, such as language, sexual identifications, school textbooks, and university admissions policies, are not only contested but extremely "hot" discursive objects. As the subject of news stories, reality television, and salacious entertainment, these signs of social difference veer between "postracial" racial insignificance and disputes about the primacy of racial and ethnic difference in access to economic resources and differential exposure to personal vulnerability and social insecurity, such as environmental toxins, police abuse, youth violence, and substandard housing. In this sense, diversity is also a technology of power, a means of managing the very difference it expresses, which prompts me to focus in this chapter on the social life of diversity as a working practice, social commitment, and policy goal in the media as well as media studies scholarship.

Industry, scholarly, and market inventories of the distribution of race and gender difference in media content look to representational parity as the most salient benchmark of diversity in the entertainment business. Of course, representational parity is essentially meaningless without demography as a reference point. Hence the path to diversity in entertainment media must always pass through the "assumed link between representation and demography," a link that has defined media studies of race and diversity in the United States over several generations now.

What are the conditions of possibility that produced the discursive alliance between representation and demography? Moreover, why (and how) did the discursive alliance between representation and demography come to settle on production as the site of correction and regulation that still organizes scholarly research, industry responses, and state intervention as means of addressing racial and ethnic disparities in U.S. media? In the remainder of the chapter, I detail the technological, discursive, social, and cultural conditions of possibility that gave rise to this initial alliance, then identify the subsequent shifts in media discourses of race and racism that give rise to a different problem space and set of research questions. Drawing on examples from recent media studies scholarship, I then consider some possible ways that researchers and scholars might approach media studies of difference, diversity, and representation that conceive of a different problem space for thinking about media and diversity.

PROBLEM SPACE 1: EMPLOYMENT, CONTENT, AND DEMOGRAPHY

Why diversity, not (in)equality? Or perhaps the assumption is that diversity is the expression of equality? Articulated most explicitly in the 1968 *Report of the National Advisory Commission on Civil Disorders,* or Kerner Commission Report, the discursive alliance between representation and demography turned on the conception of racial difference and the role that this conception played in contributing to the conception of blacks and the disadvantages and frustrations blacks experienced. Media was a crucial site for addressing grievances of disenfranchised blacks over lack of access to significant positions of employment and the exclusion of black images.[3] Addressing racial, class, and gender inequality was never the explicit aim of this alliance; access and inclusion was. Prodded by the Civil Rights Commission and left to their own devices, television networks, newsrooms, showrunners, and advertisers entered a generation-long cycle of lurching in fits and starts toward granting access and including people of color and women in mainstream media content and employment.

Media scholars and historians[4] suggest that there was at least shared agreement among members of the civil rights establishment, black cultural nationalists, and the policy establishment about the importance of aligning television news and entertainment content, media industry employment, and the demography of minority populations. Nowhere is this consensus on the alignment of content, demography, and employment more evident than in the Kerner Commission Report. As media scholar Vicki Mayer reads it, "The Kerner Commission Report of 1968, which concluded that media representation helped fuel national racial unrest, linked problematic discourse (stereotypes) not to mass communication per se but to employment within its related industries." She continues, "An explosion of publicly and privately financed quantitative studies of television content, employment practices, ownership patterns and cultivated audience effects buttressed social movement claims that distortions on the screen should be mediated through production practices and broadcast regulations."[5] For Mayer, issues of identity in studies of television production seemed tied to the labor that could be held responsible for the representations of race and gender on television. This historic conjuncture of the golden age of broadcast networks, the moral and political pressure of the civil rights movement, and news and entertainment content as the site of cultural affirmation, social recognition, and redress still remains the dominant framework for academic research on race and gender representation in media industries research, especially for cable and broadcast media and television. This reasoning and framework also continues to organize policy approaches to achieving media diversity.

Since 1965, for example, media and communication scholars, activists and pressure groups, journalists and critics, craft guilds and industry observers have provided periodic reports on the state of diversity in North American media and entertainment industries. These reports inventory the number of women, black, gay and lesbian, Asian American and Latino/Latina personnel employed in different production sectors of the U.S. entertainment media from showrunners and writers in television to directors and producers in cinema. These reports also monitor the state of diversity in front of the screen (according types of characters by genre, role, setting, action, and so on).

Consider a few recent examples that illustrate the continuing influence of the discursive alignment of representation and demography as a measure of racial and gender equality. In March 2014 a respected television critic and columnist, Mo Ryan of the *Huffington Post,* reported on the dismal state of affairs for diversity in entertainment television: "At the outlets responsible for many top programs, women and people of color are enormously under-represented as *creators.* If one focuses only on the last dozen years at AMC, FX, Showtime, Netflix and HBO, around 12 percent of the creators and narrative architects in the dramatic realm were women. . . . According to the most recent stats from the Writers Guild of America, about 30.5 percent of TV *staff writers* are women, and about 15.6 percent of TV writers are people of color; both numbers represent modest gains from the past. San Diego State University's Center for the Study of Women in Television and Film, which uses a different calculation method, puts the percentage of female TV writers for the 2012–13 season at 34 percent. . . . Yet according to SDSU's most recent study, 27 percent of women bear the title executive producer, and 24 percent are a 'creator'—numbers that have remained stagnant for a long time."[6]

Sociologist and media scholar Darnell Hunt authored one of the reports cited by journalists, industry observers, and pressure groups concerned about the state of racial and gender diversity in Hollywood. Hunt's *2014 Hollywood Diversity Report* tracks longitudinal data on the distribution of actors, writers, directors, agencies, and audience in film, cable, and broadcast outlets. According to Hunt, minorities fare better as leads in cable comedies and drama compared to broadcast at 14.7 percent, while women fare worse as leads in cable comedies and dramas than in broadcast at 37.2 percent. Minorities, in contrast, are more likely to be leads on reality and other shows than on comedies and dramas in broadcast.[7] Citing a Writers Guild of America West 2013 report, Hunt emphasizes that, according to the report, "diverse writers were underrepresented by a factor of about 4 to 1 among writer-producers with the most decision-making authority, both in the development of original network show concepts and in the day-to-day management of the storytelling process . . . despite the fact the minorities collectively accounted for 36.3 percent of the nation's population in 2010."[8]

In another highly respected state-of-the-industry report, Stacy Smith and her colleagues at USC's Annenberg School of Communication provide a highly detailed annual report on the dismal state of gender and racial diversity in the Hollywood film industry.[9] As with Hunt's *2014 Hollywood Diversity Report,* the San Diego State University study, and the Writers Guild of America West and Director's Guild of America findings, Smith's study is based on longitudinal data. Smith found a similar absence of gender, racial, and ethnic diversity in Hollywood, drawing conclusions similar to those of Hunt and other researchers. On the index of gender, participation seems somewhat more hopeful than on race and ethnicity, though the general trends suggest that despite industrial transformations in production, financing, and service delivery in television and film production overall, movement in racial and gender inclusion and participation has not kept up with these transformations.

What accounts for the persistent patterns of racial and gender exclusion reported in these empirical studies? Surely after years of reporting on such practices of exclusion, media executives, advertisers, content producers, and program purchasers are aware of the dismal state of affairs with respect to diversity in media industries. In the face of so much documented evidence about the lack of racial and gender diversity in television and cinema, what else might be going on? What else might account for the failure of these reports and the evidence they present to gain any lasting traction? What would it take at the level of policy prescriptions, industry practice, and guiding assumptions for this evidence to matter in ways that would change the practices of exclusion they report? Periodically, advocacy groups like the National Association for the Advancement of Colored People, the Mexican American Legal Defense and Education Fund, and GLAAD use these reports to leverage studio and network executives to hire more women and people of color, develop more content aimed at diverse audiences, and earmark job training programs to develop talent in different sectors of the industry.[10]

What if we shifted the angle of vision, treating inequality and the absence of diversity as a process? What if we see the absence of diversity, or more properly inequality, in media as a crucial component of the production of creative objects, labor relations, financing, distribution, and marketing, and not just discrete outcomes within the associated fields of production aimed at representational and demographic parity.[11] Why not expand the analysis to include the very way we *frame and interrogate* issues of diversity? As the handful of reports cited already show, research scholars, craft guilds, industry leaders, regulators, and advocacy groups understand diversity in media industries as a matter of whether or not television, cinema, and now different sectors of new media like gaming employ a diverse workforce, which by extension is presumed to result in more diverse content.

This continues to be an important goal to be sure, but it conceives of diversity as a fixed outcome, measurable in the number and distribution of discrete indicators like the number of minority showrunners or the number of women in lead roles. While this approach addresses questions of representational parity, it raises other questions, especially the relation between media industries and inequality, including whether correctives to inequality can be addressed by the exchange of bodies and experiences responsible for making content, rather than by exposing the assumptions, micropractices, social relations, and power dynamics that define our collective cultural common sense about the nature of social difference and the practices of inequality.

As a research agenda and public policy goal, by far the dominant approach to media diversity is framed from the vantage point of a problem whose specific roots go back over fifty years to black urban unrest, the golden age of network television, and a liberal consensus on the Great Society. In this discursive alliance, legal, cultural, social, and political assumptions located in the Great Society and the civil rights movement consensus set the terms of a framework that aligns demographic representation, the politics of representation, the conception of media and television as cultural sites of redress for racial injury, and the assumption that a corrective of the image will equal social justice and political parity. That is, the legal terms of state recognition engendered by the civil rights movement, the idea that demographic parity and media parity should be equivalent, that merely having diverse content would achieve demographic parity, and that minority access to the dominant image culture would equal social redress. So by dwelling on the conditions of possibility and the assumptions that frame media studies approaches to diversity and the empirical evidence by which media scholars measure its distribution and assess its efficacy, perhaps we can begin to account for why the discursive alignment that defines much of the research on diversity and the media has proved to matter so little in reordering the racial order of things in the media.

By conceiving of diversity as a social accomplishment and emphasizing the shifting, contested, and precarious nature of the social context and power relations that diversity elicits, organizes, and charges relative to its changing conditions of possibility, we might begin to ask different questions about media practices of diversity as a proxy for inequality. Diversity's precarity invites probing the shift in academic and popular discourses of diversity, especially legal disputes over the very meaning and conception of difference generated by a host of new legal and cultural claims and grievances. A good place to begin might be with the disarticulation between the problems to which studies of racial and ethnic distribution in content and production were generated to provide answers and our own conjuncture, on which these studies are called upon to comment.

THE CURRENT CONJUNCTURE

Among the most significant elements that define the current conjuncture with respect to media and diversity, we would certainly have to account for the impact of the new international division of labor and the new international division of cultural labor, including especially the rise of new media capitals and production centers, such as Bangalore, Lagos, and Hong Kong, along with highly skilled and unskilled labor forces.[12] These production centers generate specific content organized around nation, ethnicity, language, and history, all of which provides a sharp contrast to—while adding to and complicating—U.S. conceptions of diversity. So too the changing functions of culture within the global circulation of information, entertainment, and cultural products that scholars like George Yudice and Arlene Davila explain as the expediency of cultures. These expediencies add cultural diversity and celebrations of diversity and cultural differences to the working of culture and media, especially in terms of the circulation of content ranging from gaming culture to cinema.[13]

The post-network-television environment and the realignments of platforms for the delivery and distribution of content, as well as reception experiences and consumption practices, require a different research approach with diversity as a complex object of research.[14] In this context, multicultural programming content is very much an element of branding and marketing deployed by content producers to reach precise sectors of their desired markets (for instance, reality television shows about rural white working-class families, or programs about black church women or the ordeals of Silicon Valley high-tech employees). Seen from this perspective, it would seem that in the current media ecology, diverse characters, story lines, and content producers are no longer in short supply and that the alignment between representation and demography, now understood as identifiers for market segments and lifestyle choices, has, in the gloss of the postracial society, been fully realized. This is no longer a condition of content scarcity but one of saturation and hypervisibility.

Added to corporate transformations of the U.S. media ecology is the impact of juridical and legislative state institutions and practices in legally inscribing and authorizing color-blindness in voting rights laws and college admissions. Underwritten by the principle of color-blind legal and social practices, diversity, supplemented by its proxy multiculturalism, is the expressive form for the institutionalization of what Rod Ferguson calls minoritarian discourse. For Ferguson, the discursive life of minoritarian discourse is expressed explicitly as a value commitment to diversity in the culture of university classrooms as well as in scholarly research. Ferguson cautions that this value commitment has an increasingly normative function, and thus in his view is an operation of power/knowledge that works to exclude the social actors and political struggles that made race, ethnicity, and gender discursive sites of struggle around inequality and emergent sites of non-normative imaginaries.[15] This reordering provides the scholarly rationale and authority for the circulation of knowledge about lifestyle differences that find their way into production suites, executive offices, and media content.

The point is simply that unlike the conditions that produced the alignment of networks, studios, and the state as objects of political protest by groups and the alliance between demography and representation as the accepted means of redress, the conditions that define the present conjuncture are predicated on the cultural *recognition* of difference, the deployment of diversity as a social practice, and their normative operation as a discourse of management and regulation.[16] In short, the current conjuncture destabilizes the alliance between demography and representation as a response to exclusion, invisibility, and stereotypes and reorders it around diversity and multiculturalism as markers of consumer brands, lifestyle choices, and postracial cultural appreciation.

PROBLEM SPACE 2: DIFFERENCE AND POWER

In their critical assessment of studies of race and ethnicity in media and communication studies, David Hesmondhalgh and Anamik Saha observe that production studies has given woefully little attention to questions of race and ethnicity.[17] The lacuna they signal is as much the result of the analytic confinement and discursive linkages of race to people of color (and not the operation of whiteness) as it is to not appreciating the logic of creative practices, especially media, as a site of making race and practices of inequality. It follows too that inattention to race-making rather than racial representation in media studies assumes that the source of inequality and racism rests with individual preferences and dispositions of showrunners and directors, network executives, and advertising executives. Concerns with diversity and race as a practice of knowledge/power (what John Caldwell calls the deep texts of production cultures) are not endemic to the organization of media industries or research approaches to their study.[18] Designing studies of media and race in the current conjuncture at the least suggests foregrounding an analytic of governmentality, televisuality, neoliberalism, and the role of diversity in making race.[19]

To these I would add the need for systematic attention to media production and the operation of racial knowledge as a repetition of inequality (and knowledge about differences in race, gender, and sexuality) embedded in the routine habits, assumptions, practices, rituals, and organization of cultural work. Media industry and television studies might productively address some of the concerns identified by Hesmondhalgh and Saha by engaging with creative industry and production studies research agendas to identify sites, discourses, and practices of producing difference and to study race-making practices as power/knowledge that operates as a logic of production.

DIVERSITY AS QUOTIDIAN PRODUCTION PRACTICES

In her study of the shift in the nature of the work object, its impact on social relations among television writers in Los Angeles, and the precarity of their work as writers, television scholar and director Felicia Henderson examines the transformation of the traditional work product, the television season, as a key unit of analysis.[20] Specifically, she focuses on the shortening of the television season from twenty-two programs to thirteen, which is made possible by changes in delivery systems, viewing platforms, viewing practices, and contract negotiations.

The virtue of Henderson's insight is that her analysis of the writer's room as a site of creative production (like others in this genre) dwells on the structure of creative relationships, industrial settings, and the organizing logic that defines the production and creative processes rather than on individual personalities and attitudes of creative personnel. In terms of the applicability of her approach to a concern with race and diversity, Henderson's research commends attention to the organizational sites, creative processes, and social relations where the practices of diversity (or impediments to diversity) operate. Such an approach appreciates the fluidity and flexibility of evidence and analysis across time and space so that foundational categories, policy mandates, political stakes, and analytic conceptions can shift with the historical, technological, and political conditions in which they embedded and which they help organize and narrate. In other words, analytically it is useful to look at the conditions that structure and organize some of the foundational assumptions and questions about diversity and television (aims, means of realizing, forms of monitoring and assessing their effectiveness).

Henderson's approach suggests that the specific conceptions, conditions, and assumptions that produce diversity (or the twenty-two-episode season as a staple unit of network television) as a desirable goal in television are not static, nor is the nexus of institutions, interests, and stakes that support or oppose its actualization. Her approach encourages an analysis of diversity (or impediments to diversity) as a dynamic and flexible set of industrial, legal, cultural, and economic practices that the study of the precarity of creativity and diversity can bring to bear on the question. In other words, the specific conceptions, conditions, and assumptions that produce diversity as a goal and practice within creative media industries like television are not fixed, and neither is the nexus of institutions and logics that organize and express them.

The challenge is moving the research focus from the founding scene of the problem of racial access and image exclusion within television to the shifting conditions that shaped television and discourses of race, including the rise of diversity, since the Kerner Commission Report. What, in other words, are the implications for quotidian practices of inequality and making race that the shorter seasons, new delivery systems, new interactive platforms, new divisions of labor, and new relations of production crystalize? What might the impact of these developments be on the very terms within which we pose the question of inequality in television that diversity glosses? Such reframing moves the issue of diversity some way from the analytic social and political scene in which it initially appeared. It shifts the industry and analytic assumption of equating diversity and social equality with access and representational parity to one where the calculus of cultural, economic, and political difference as a basis of the production of inequality is central to media industry practices.

This approach to research on television and race scrambles foundational binaries that continue to inform industrial practice, academic approaches, and media activism: inside/outside, accuracy/stereotype, author/imitation. With respect to race and difference, the terrain is considerably more complex and urges different questions that creative industry studies might help clarify: 1) How is diversity and difference framed as a labor issue and as a matter of work process and contractual management? 2) In what respect does the international division of creative labor pressure local and national formulations of diversity as matters of representation, reparation, and labor? 3) In what respects do the new international division of cultural labor, the rise of new platforms and delivery systems, and the creative arrangements that drive new projects, genres, talent bear on the question of diversity in new and unforeseen ways, especially within different national formations defined by distinct racial projects and ethnic formations? 4) These conditions could just as well open the way for the media production of diversity as cultural normativity or a technology of power/knowledge deployed to reach lifestyle niches. A critical media industry approach to inequality (rather than merely diversity) would urge that media and ethnic/racial arrangements be located and analyzed within the context of racism, racial projects, and race making nationally and globally.

On this count, John Caldwell's insights about reflexivity, industrial knowledge, and practices and rituals among cultural producers are exemplary;[21] so too are Vicki Mayer's considerations of the inscription of knowledge in practices at all levels of the production process, as is Sarah Banet Weiser's work on the role of brands and branding as a mode of crafting and caring for the self in the construction of diversity.[22] Finally, Timothy Havens's explorations of the circulation of television content about blackness in the United States and the role of industry lore about race and diversity in the creative process are especially rich. So too are Darnell Hunt's studies of African Americans who use new media technologies to write, produce, and perform alternate and nonhegemonic conceptions of complex and intersecting minoritarian identities.[23]

CONCLUSION: FROM INVENTORY TO ATTACHMENT

Jennifer Petersen's *Murder, the Media, and the Politics of Public Feeling* might be taken as the kind of study that moves away from the dominance of concerns with parity and representation as routes to social and racial justice toward concern with the affective work of media in galvanizing feelings, organizing publics, and materializing grievance.[24] In her concern with emotional conflicts, legal adjudications, and social negotiations over the depiction, circulation, investment, and use of the coverage of the murders (and their aftermath) of Matthew Shepard and James Byrd, Petersen traces the circulation, disputes, and impact of the emotional economy of these events. She shows how they came to matter on questions of sexuality, race, gender, and nation. Petersen's study prompts media studies of race and diversity to consider not just what things mean but also how they matter, where, for whom, and with what effects.

To Peterson's emphasis on the relationship of media to public feeling and how things matter, I urge attention to the concerns mobilized by media content and the resonances it generates for *users as well as producers* of content. Engaging research this way may at the very least complement if not reimagine insights that the nexus between representation and demography now yields. Practically, this means moving away from the assumption that a bid on image accuracy and authenticity anchored by demography will provide some assurance of social parity. It suggests moving toward the possibility that a focus on resonance and attachment might critically address the complexities of race making and the production of diversity as a technology of power in the current conjuncture. Signaling matters of concern registers a different assumption, one that considers the inscription of racial meaning as endemic media work.

Complementing media studies of production, industrial organization, and routine media practices with critical research on the intensity, duration, and locus of emotional concerns engendered by media could direct critical analytic attention to forms of attachment and identification that do a bit more than document annual diversity effects in media. The alliance of discursive and social conditions of possibility that has defined much of media studies research on race and media for several generations now suggests that we have reached a critical limit of the capacity of the alliance of demography and representation to tell us enough about the practice, production, and normalization of diversity to matter. The annual research reports on representational parity have themselves become normative, organizing and fueling policy prescriptions, research agendas, guild training programs, marketing research, and branding campaigns. Perhaps it is time to ask that our research tell us a different story about the operations of power/knowledge and the role of media in the making of racial inequality (and its potential for the making of racial justice).

NOTES

1. Miranda Banks, "How to Study Media and Makers," in *The Sage Handbook of Television Studies*, ed. Manuel Alvarado, Milly Buonanno, Herman Gray, and Toby Miller (London: Sage, 2014).

2. John Caldwell, *Production Culture: Industrial Reflexivity and Critical Practice in Film and Television* (Durham, NC: Duke University Press, 2008).

3. "The News Media and the Disorders," in *Channeling Blackness: Studies on Television and Race in America,* ed. Darnell Hunt (London: Oxford, 2005); Kerner Commission, *Report of the National Advisory Commission on Civil Disorders* (Washington, DC: U.S. Government Printing Office, 1968); Arthur S. Fleming, Stephen Horn, Frankie M. Freeman, Manuel Ruiz Jr., Murray Saltzman, and John A. Biggs, *Window Dressing on the Set: Women and Minorities in Television* (Washington, DC: U.S. Commission on Civil Rights, 1977).

4. See, for instance, Aniko Bodroghkozy, *Equal Time: Television and the Civil Rights Movement* (Urbana: University of Illinois Press, 2012); Lynn Spigel, *Welcome to the Dreamhouse: Popular Media and Postwar Suburbs* (Durham, NC: Duke University Press, 2001); Laurie Ouellette, *Viewers Like You? How Public TV Failed the People* (New York: Columbia University Press, 2002); Sasha Torres, *Black, White, and in Color: Television and Black Civil Rights* (Princeton, NJ: Princeton University Press, 2003); Chon Noriega, *Shot in America: Television, the State, and the Rise of Chicano Cinema* (Minneapolis: University of Minnesota Press, 2000); Devorah Heitner, *Black Power TV* (Durham, NC: Duke University Press, 2013); Steven Classen, *Watching Jim Crow: The Struggle over Mississippi TV, 1955–1969* (Durham, NC: Duke University Press, 2004); Anna McCarthy, *The Citizen Machine* (New York: New Press, 2010); and Vicki Mayer, *Below the Line: Producers and Production Studies in the New Television Economy* (Durham, NC: Duke University Press, 2011).

5. Mayer, *Below the Line,* 13 (my emphasis); see also Kerner Commission, *Report of the National Advisory Commission on Civil Disorders.*

6. Mo Ryan, "Who Creates Drama at HBO? Very Few Women or People of Color," *Huffington Post,* March 7, 2014.

7. Darnell Hunt, "Hollywood Story: Diversity, Writing and the End of Television as We Know It," in *The Sage Handbook of Television Studies,* ed. Alvarado et al; Ralph Bunche Center, *2014 Hollywood Diversity Report: Making Sense of the Disconnect* (Los Angeles: UCLA, 2014).

8. Hunt, "Hollywood Story," 166.

9. Stacy Smith et al., "Gender Inequalities in 500 Popular Films: Examining On Screen Portrayals and Behind-the-Scenes Employment Patters in Motion Pictures Released between 2007–2012,"

Annenberg Report (Los Angeles: University of Southern California, 2013); Stacy Smith et al., "Race/ Ethnicity in 500 Popular Films: Is the Key to Diversifying Cinematic Content held in the Hand of the Black Director?" Media Diversity and Social Change Initiative (Los Angeles: University of Southern California, 2013).

10. Directors Guild of America, "'A Fair Shot': Women Directors on Television," www.dga/Craft/ DGAQ/All-Articles/1301-Winter (accessed September 19, 2014); Directors Guild of America, "DGA Report: Employers Make No Improvement in Diversity Hiring in Episodic Television," www.dga.org/ News/PressReleases/2014/140917.

11. Pierre Bourdieu, *The Field of Cultural Production: Essays on Art and Literature* (New York: Columbia University Press, 1993).

12. Michael Curtin, "Media Capitals: Toward the Study of Spatial Flows," *International Journal of Cultural Studies* 6.2 (2003): 202–228; Toby Miller, Nitin Govil, John McMurria, and Richard Maxwell, *Global Hollywood* (London: British Film Institute, 2001); David Hesmondhalgh, *The Cultural Industries* (Los Angeles: Sage, 2006).

13. George Yudice, *The Expediency of Culture: The Uses of Culture in the Global Era* (Durham, NC: Duke University Press, 2003); Arlene Davila, *Culture Works: Space, Value, and Mobility across the Neoliberal Americas* (New York: New York University Press, 2012).

14. Amanda Lotz, *The Television Will be Revolutionized* (New York: New York University Press, 2007).

15. Roderick Ferguson, *The Reorder of Things: The University and Its Pedagogies of Minority Difference* (Minneapolis: University of Minnesota Press, 2012).

16. Herman Gray, "Subject(ed) to Recognition," *American Quarterly* 65.4 (2013): 771–799.

17. David Hesmondhalgh and Anamik Saha, "Race, Ethnicity and Cultural Production," *Popular Communication* 11.3 (2013): 179–195.

18. Caldwell, *Production Culture.*

19. Laurie Ouellette and James Hay, *Better Living through Reality TV* (London: Wiley, 2008).

20. Felicia Henderson, "Options and Exclusivity: Economic Pressures on TV Writers' Compensation and the Effects on TV Writer's Room Culture," in *The Sage Handbook of Television Studies,* ed. Alvarado et al.

21. Caldwell, *Production Culture.*

22. Mayer, *Below the Line*; Sarah Banet-Weiser, *Authentic* (New York: New York University Press, 2012).

23. Timothy Havens, *Black Television Travels: African American Media around the Globe* (New York: New York University Press, 2013); Hunt, "Hollywood Story."

24. Jennifer Peterson, *Murder, the Media, and the Politics of Public Feelings* (Bloomington: Indiana University Press, 2011).

19

The Precarity and Politics of Media Advocacy Work

Allison Perlman

When Alex Nogales, president and CEO of the National Hispanic Media Coalition (NHMC), narrates the history of his organization, he tells a story of continuity and change. The core mission of the group—to integrate Latinas/os into more jobs behind and in front of the camera, ameliorate derogatory images of Latinas/os in the media, and advocate for telecommunications policies that serve the needs of Latina/o publics—has remained consistent since the NHMC was founded in 1986. What has changed, according to Nogales, is the organization's strategies, which have evolved with the group's experiences in media activism and advocacy. In his telling, the NHMC went from being a comparatively naïve organization, committed to addressing the exigent concerns of local communities, to a sophisticated group capable of exerting meaningful pressure on a national scale, especially via participation in the policymaking sphere.[1]

The NHMC's emphasis on media labor has been in keeping with the priorities of other identity-based media advocacy groups who have worked to bring people of color into media industry workforces at all levels. For the NHMC, to ensure that Latinas/os have access to these jobs is, like other equal employment advocacy, to enable them to participate in a sector that had historically discriminated against them; in addition, it is to transform the kinds of stories told and perspectives voiced in media texts, from news reports to entertainment programming. While securing Latina/o jobs has been a consistent goal of the NHMC, it has had to navigate a legal environment increasingly hostile to race-conscious policies to promote diversity and a regulatory system increasingly committed to media deregulation. In response, the NHMC, like other advocacy groups, has had to rethink how to promote diversity in the absence of what had been essential regulatory tools and in a climate unreceptive to such interventions.

Media advocacy, the kind of actions undertaken by groups like the NHMC, thus not only has been centrally concerned with media labor, but has constituted its own form of work. The work of media advocacy often is a labor-intensive enterprise, one that relies on myriad forms of capital—financial, cultural, institutional—to function. While media advocacy has often depended on uncompensated labor, from the work of volunteers whose contributions create the scaffolding upon which media advocacy efforts are built to the citizens who respond to calls to action by filing letters with or calling the Federal Communications Commission (FCC) or members of Congress, it also has been guided by media advocacy professionals. These are professionals in two senses of the term: they have expertise and they are compensated for their labor.

To examine media advocacy as work is to alter the kinds of questions we ask and the kind of narratives we construct. While there are meaningful differences in how scholars have understood the political stakes, moments of opportunity, and mobilizing structures and strategies of media advocacy efforts, what they share is an understanding of media advocacy as a *social movement* or as a form of *civic participation* that has sought to transform the media to meet the communication needs of citizens in a democracy. Media advocacy campaigns are often narrated as David-and-Goliath stories, in which public interest groups try to reform the media only to be defeated by better-resourced media corporations that more successfully manipulate public opinion and gain sway over public officials.

The emphasis of media advocacy scholarship, furthermore, often is the media advocacy campaign, a temporally bounded effort undertaken at a particularly propitious moment when political changes or new technologies introduce fissures that make reform seem possible.[2] Media advocacy has also often been analyzed along a success/failure binary, an assessment of how and why media advocacy has or has not attained its desired goals. As the first section of this article discusses, to see media advocacy as work is to shift our focus off outcomes and onto process and to rethink the success/failure binary that has structured much of media advocacy scholarship. Media advocacy for groups like the NHMC is a long-term, multifaceted commitment that shifts with technological, political, and regulatory changes, as well as with the increasing savvy of the media advocates themselves. Their work is continuing, not contingent on singular campaigns or issues. Viewed through this lens, media advocacy can be seen less as a rhythmic exercise in hope and failure and more as a continuous hum of activity that sometimes yields actionable policy changes, in which communities outside the official regulatory sphere make themselves legible as stakeholders in the policymaking process. To consider media advocacy as work is to see it as ongoing, cumulative, and flexible.

In addition, as the second section demonstrates, many contemporary media advocacy groups in the United States are engaged in *media work,* labor that contributes to, rather than interferes with, media production and the interests of media companies. Media advocacy, however, has been invisible to scholars of media labor, who mostly have been interested in how the production process under which media are made, as well as the occupational cultures and power relations structuring the mode of production, affects the narratives, values, and images that media audiences consume. Deploying ethnographic and historical methods, and focusing on a range of media, this subfield traditionally has focused on above-the-line workers (directors, writers, producers, and executives); labor within these texts is imagined as both the creative labor of artists and the managerial labor of executives, the friction between them understood as alternately stifling and generative for the production of media texts.[3]

More recent scholarship, however, has expanded the methods and subjects of media labor scholarship. John Caldwell, for example, has blended ethnographic research with sophisticated discourse analysis to investigate not only the diverse range of labor practices—both above and below the line—that constitute film and television production, but the discursive labor involved in shaping and sustaining the occupational cultures within the entertainment industry.[4] In a similar vein, Vicki Mayer, in her *Below the Line,* has broadened the definition of *production* to include the "invisible labor" that is constitutive of television production but frequently absented in both industry and academic discourse.[5] Conceptions of media labor thus have been extended to the myriad forms of work that contribute to media production and to the discursive formations that sustain its division of labor.

While media advocacy has often existed outside media production, it has also intersected with, and contributed to, both the workflow of media production and the underlying assumptions about audience and narrative that structure it. For decades, media advocacy groups' work with media producers has been a constitutive part of their reform efforts. Increasingly, however, this collaboration has extended to advocacy groups using their position as representatives of the public to promote the policy agenda of media corporations. As the second section discusses, for some organizations, media advocacy work thus has given way to media work, their adversarial role transformed into a collaborative—or, to some critics, collusive—one with media and telecommunications corporations.

MEDIA ADVOCACY AS WORK

In the United States, public participation in media policymaking is technically part of the process. The FCC is required to solicit public input on new policies or changes to existing regulations. By design, members of public are to have their say in the shaping of regulations; in actuality, the role of the public has been far more constrained. Not only have industry lobbyists and attorneys had far more purchase with policymakers than members of the public, but administrative law requires federal agencies to consult the public but does not require them to pay heed to what the public says.[6] As a result, a range of social movement and civil society organizations have included media advocacy in their broader fights for social justice and political reform, and a number of dedicated media advocacy groups have emerged with the mission to reform the media. Many of these groups have been engaged in media advocacy for decades and have adapted to changes in media technologies, regulatory decisions, and broader political and social conditions.

As Becky Lentz and I have argued elsewhere, media advocacy hinges on the acquisition of media policy literacy, a set of competencies to understand not only the processes by which media policies and laws are formed, debated, and enacted, but also how to participate in a milieu of action to effect meaningful change. This literacy forms out of experience; that is, it is through sustained participation in advocacy that individuals and organizations gain the capacity to critique the sociopolitical impact of media structures, media practices, and media representations, and to strategize how best to tackle them.[7] Part of this literacy involves recognizing the myriad functions of a media advocacy campaign. While campaigns have identifiable goals, they also make an advocacy group legible as a stakeholder in the policymaking process and can establish the group's credibility with fellow advocacy practitioners. The work of the NHMC, which has been committed to media reform for nearly thirty years, exemplifies the long-term, multifaceted, and flexible nature of media advocacy work.

The history of the NHMC shows the organization expanding its understanding of how media and communications matter to the Latina/o community and accordingly increasing the scale of its activities. When the NHMC first began its media advocacy work, it focused primarily on the practices of local broadcast stations. The NHMC utilized the petition to deny license renewal to broadcast stations as its primary means of redressing discriminatory employment practices and derogatory programming. The threat of a petition often would incline local stations to negotiate with the group rather than face the legal fees and irritations of a license challenge. In its early years, the NHMC reached agreements with local Los Angeles stations and soon extended its reach to television and radio stations in heavily Latina/o areas across the United States. The NHMC, in the process, also built ties with Latina/o groups in communities across the nation and began to establish its visibility as a Latina/o rights organization centrally committed to reforming media practices.[8]

Throughout the 1990s, the NHMC enlarged its focus to include not only local stations but also broadcast and cable networks, along with the media conglomerates that owned them. In addition to an extensive economic boycott of the entertainment holdings of Disney-ABC in 1997, the NHMC targeted media consolidation, specifically the merger of ABC and Disney and the sale of the Spanish-language network Univision to non-Latina/o interests, in its advocacy campaigns. The NHMC was especially concerned over the potential transformation of Univision, the largest Spanish-language television network in the United States at the time, into an adjunct to Mexican and Venezuelan media empires.[9] For the NHMC, media consolidation in the English-language sphere and foreign control of the Spanish-language sector would portend fewer jobs for Latinas/os, diminished opportunities for Latinas/os to gain control of their own stations, and the continued invisibility of Latina/o concerns and perspectives in the national media.

Throughout, the NHMC confronted a regulatory apparatus that was seemingly disinterested in enforcing existing policies, especially around media ownership restrictions. These experiences signaled to the NHMC a divide between policy and enforcement and exposed a persistent willingness on the part of the FCC and the federal courts to facilitate media consolidation even in the face of the commission's own rules against it. In addition, though the NHMC was not able to prevent the sale of Univision in the 1990s, its tenacity in fighting it established the organization as a formidable Latina/o advocacy group. Univision sent representatives to meet with the NHMC in the mid-1990s, and in exchange for ceasing their legal actions, the NHMC gained programming commitments in areas like children's educational television, which it viewed as critical to the needs of the Latina/o community.[10]

These experiences in the 1990s were highly instructive for the NHMC in its approach to media advocacy. It more fully committed to affecting policy at the national level—as Nogales states, the NHMC realized that the "big game" was being played in DC—and in the early 2000s hired two attorneys specifically to do policy advocacy work. In addition, its scope continued to increase as telecommunications issues of particular concern to the Latina/o community arose—for example, the expansion of broadband connectivity, the preservation of network neutrality, the maintenance of the Universal Service Fund. And as nativism accelerated in the United States in the mid-2000s over undocumented immigrants, the NHMC has made hate speech one of its top priorities, combatting what NHMC executive vice president and general counsel Jessica Gonzalez refers to as "low-hanging fruit," the programs that circulate what strikes the NHMC as particularly dangerous invective against the Latina/o community.[11]

Media consolidation has continued to be a top policy issue for the NHMC. Since 2003, it has worked continually to prevent the FCC from diminishing its ownership restrictions. And while it has fought some media mergers—most notably the 2011 proposed merger between T-Mobile and AT&T—it also has sanctioned mergers in exchange for concessions for communities of color. Perhaps most controversially, the NHMC encouraged the FCC to approve the merger of

Comcast and NBC-Universal in 2010. When asked to serve on a Hispanic advisory board, the NHMC and other Latina/o groups negotiated a memorandum of understanding (MOU) with Comcast and NBC-U for diversity measures such as the creation of a Hispanic Advisory Council, increased Latina/o representation in the companies' workforce, enhanced procurement diversity, and the expansion of Spanish-language broadcasting. Members of the NHMC subsequently held ex parte meetings with FCC commissioners in which they described the conditions of the MOU and asked, should the merger be approved, that enforcement of the MOU be written into its conditions.[12]

A galvanizing moment for the NHMC took place in 1999 and 2000, when it banded together with other identity-based advocacy groups to secure memoranda of understanding with each of the Big Four (ABC, CBS, NBC, and Fox) broadcast networks. Greg Braxton in the *Los Angeles Times* had reported that of the twenty-six new prime-time shows premiering across the major networks, not one had a person of color in a recurring role.[13] Working in a "grand coalition" with the NAACP, the Asian Pacific America Media Coalition, and Indians in Film and Television, among others, the NHMC secured MOUs that included hiring commitments, mentorship and training programs, commitments to work with minority-controlled vendors and production companies, and designations of in-house executives to promote diversity.[14] These MOUs were struck at a low point for minority advocacy work, as the federal courts and Congress by 1999 had eliminated or ruled unconstitutional all the rules adopted in the 1960s and 1970s to promote minority employment and ownership in broadcasting. Direct negotiations with the networks were, at this moment, the most immediate and advantageous way to bring more people of color into the television industry. It was this experience with the networks, according to Nogales, that shaped how the NHMC approached the NBC-Comcast merger.[15]

The NHMC was certainly not the only civil rights or advocacy group to support the merger. The NAACP, National Urban League, and National Action Network similarly secured an MOU with the two companies for programming and hiring commitments, as did a consortium of Asian American civil rights groups.[16] The stance of these organizations put them at odds with public interest and consumer advocacy groups who had been allies, especially over media consolidation issues, including Free Press, whose then president and CEO Josh Silver labeled the merger a "comcastrophe," fearing that with it would come an onslaught of greater levels of consolidation that would diminish diversity, raise prices, and gut network neutrality.[17]

While the NHMC feels ambivalent about its role—Nogales referred to the NHMC's action as something of a "cop-out"—its actions speak to a tension within its advocacy agenda. While philosophically the NHMC sees public interest harms in media concentration, it also, as part of its mission, has prioritized the inclusion of Latina/o perspectives and narratives in the media and Latina/o access to jobs within media industries. Its decision to support the merger thus speaks to the experience of the NHMC in unsuccessfully fighting mergers of the past, its assessment of the FCC's inclination to approve, and its estimation that this was the best way to secure some services to its community. And to be sure, identity-based media advocacy groups historically have butted heads with public interest advocacy groups over the issue of media consolidation. While the latter have imagined substantial public interest harms in enabling fewer companies to own more media properties, the former at moments have been willing to sanction media mergers in exchange for concessions, especially hiring and programming commitments.[18] When the NHMC supported the NBC-Comcast merger, it followed in a longer history of civil rights organizations choosing to secure benefits for their communities at a moment when it seemed like the regulatory sphere was inhospitable to considerations of minority media rights.

As the shifting strategies of the NHMC illustrate, examining media policy advocacy as work illustrates that it is an ongoing process in which advocates continually learn and revise the optimal way to intervene in the policymaking process. Their campaigns hinge on and are informed by previous experiences with advocacy. Accordingly, media policy advocacy is a cumulative process in which advocacy groups both acquire the skill sets and resources necessary to intervene in policymaking while at the same time adjusting their expectations of what can be accomplished at particular historical junctures. Sometimes, as in the case of the NBC-Comcast merger, this experience leads advocacy groups to work with media companies and to use their standing as public interest representatives to sanction their interests. In other words, as the next section addresses, media advocacy work can constitute *media work*.

MEDIA ADVOCACY AS MEDIA WORK

Media advocacy has long been concerned with shaping the parameters of what media production can be and how it can be profitable. Battles over, for example, media ownership limits, equal employment rules, children's television requirements, and indecency regulations are efforts to influence the labor conditions of media companies, the composition of their workforce, and the cultural products they make. While not engaged directly in the creative labor of media production, media advocacy groups frequently have intervened in the economic and cultural logics of production. In addition, media advocacy groups have contributed their labor to media producers. Frequently this work has been advisory—the reading of scripts, for example, to ensure that the politics of representation within them are not demeaning or harmful—and accordingly, it has been part of the mission especially of identity-based advocacy groups.[19] Work on behalf of media companies has more recently extended for some advocacy groups to their policy work, as they have supported positions that, to their critics, do the bidding of media companies at the expense of the communities they ostensibly represent. Critics of the NHMC's support for the NBC-Comcast merger have read its actions in this light.

This recent synergy of interests in the policy sphere between advocacy groups and media companies is inseparable from the increased financial support advocacy groups receive from media corporations. Fund-raising, as Gonzalez has put it, is the "dirty skeleton in the closet" of advocacy work.[20] While many media advocacy groups at first rely on volunteer labor, over time they require a sustained staff who can pursue both long-term and short-term objectives. Thus sustained media advocacy requires sustained access to financial support. Early media advocacy groups were funded by a combination of donations and grants from philanthropic foundations. Action for Children's Television (ACT), for example, founded in 1969 to combat commercialism in and raise the quality of children's programming, was supported by individual membership fees, higher donations from "benefactors," and grants from the Ford Foundation and the Markle Foundation.[21] Ford additionally was the primary funder of educational telecasters in the fifteen years leading up to the passage of the 1967 Public Broadcasting Act, and as Jefferson Pooley has demonstrated, Ford from 1998 onward has been one of the biggest benefactors of the media reform movement.[22]

While grants from philanthropic organizations and individual donations continue to provide substantial support for media advocacy work, they are either inaccessible or inadequate for many organizations. The NHMC, when it formed, relied on the volunteer labor of its members. In the 1990s, it formalized as an organization, secured its 501(c)(3) status as a nonprofit organization, and expanded the scope of its activities. While it initially had been difficult to attract foundation support, the NHMC in the 2000s secured a Ford Foundation grant to support its policy advocacy. Both Ford and the Media and Democracy Fund continue to support the NHMC, the latter also operating as an important advocate for the NHMC's work with other potential funders.[23] Professional and personal networks can be pivotal for media advocacy groups, often making the difference between being visible or invisible to potential funders, regardless of the significance of the organization's advocacy commitments or its credibility with the community it represents.

While foundation support has been crucial, it also can be insufficient. Thus a number of advocacy groups rely on corporate donations and sponsorship. The NHMC itself receives financial support from media companies like Univision, Entravision, Disney/ABC, and Comcast/NBC-Universal. This funding enables the NHMC's writers' program, a screenwriting workshop that prepares Latina/o writers for writing careers in the television industry, and its pitch program, which trains writers to package their ideas as "pitches" and connects them to executives at broadcast and cable networks. The NHMC's goals with these programs—to bring more Latinas/os into above-the-line creative positions in television—lines up well with the interests of media companies seeking not only potential new series but strategic hires that can underline their dedication to diversity.[24]

The NHMC also raises money through annual events that fuse the organization's fund-raising with its mission to promote Latina/o talent and to honor allies and advocates for Latina/o rights. These include an annual gala held in Beverly Hills to honor Latina/o performers; an annual conference that brings together industry personnel, artists, and activists in substantive conversation about contemporary media practices and Latina/o creators and publics; a local impact awards luncheon that honors local talent in the Los Angeles area; and an impact awards reception in Washington, DC, to recognize individuals in the policymaking and legislative sphere who have championed issues central to the NHMC mission. To organize these events, the NHMC has two staff members who spend half their time on fund-raising, along with one dedicated intern to support fund-raising, out of a total staff of six full-time and two part-time employees.[25]

With these activities, the NHMC operates a sort of para-industry, which trains creative talent and honors the accomplishments of media workers. In return, they strengthen the NHMC's identity as a Latina/o media advocacy organization and its personal ties with media professionals. Yet they also link the NHMC to companies whose policy objectives often contrast with its own. As both Gonzalez and Nogales insist, NHMC's record should quell concerns that it is a shill to the companies that help fund its work, as the NHMC has routinely taken positions contrary to their interests. The organization has been a consistent advocate of network neutrality, has filed comments or signed onto comments filed by other public interest groups in support of retaining current media ownership restrictions, and has aggressively opposed some proposed media mergers that it has seen as harmful to its community.

In addition, the NHMC has sought to distance itself from other civil rights organizations that have similarly accepted corporate monies but whose integrity allegedly has been compromised for it. As Juan González and Joseph Torres have argued, civil rights stalwarts like the National Association for the Advancement of Colored People (NAACP) and the League of Latin American Citizens (LULAC), which "used to rail against the injustices of the white media," now often advocate for policies that support media and telecommunications companies at the expense of the communities they represent.[26] For González and Torres, this turn constitutes a "startling and tragic" setback for minority media rights and is directly tied to the financial support provided to these organizations by media corporations.[27]

Most notably, in June 2013, David Honig and his advocacy group, the Minority Media Telecommunications Council (MMTC), came under attack as being under the sway of their corporate donors.[28] Honig is a long-standing media advocacy professional, who, prior to forming the MMTC, had worked for the NAACP on a range of minority media rights campaigns. Honig's longtime experience as an advocate for minority media rights put him in strong standing to advise civil rights groups on media policy issues. And so when the MMTC—along with the NAACP, LULAC, and others—supported diminished media ownership restrictions, opposed network neutrality, and backed media mergers, other media advocates cast suspicion on the integrity of the MMTC's position and the influence of corporate donations in its decision making.

The MMTC's about-face on media ownership issues is of especial concern. When the FCC voted in 2003 and 2004 to diminish its existing ownership restrictions, it faced an enormous public backlash and had its rules remanded by the Third Circuit Court of Appeals for procedural violations and failure to consider how the changes would affect female and minority ownership of broadcast stations.[29] When, in 2010, the FCC voted to repeal its newspaper-broadcast cross-ownership rule, the Third Circuit once again remanded the rule to the FCC and admonished it for not considering the change's impact on female and minority ownership of broadcast stations.[30] In each review, as the FCC has asked for comments on its ownership rules, the NHMC, often in collaboration with other advocacy groups, has drawn on the concern over levels of minority ownership to persuade the commission not to diminish or repeal existing regulations. Thus for one of the leading civil rights–based media advocacy groups to argue that media consolidation poses no harm to communities of color, and that the loosening of ownership restrictions could benefit them, is a tremendous opportunity for advocates of deregulation and the media companies who would benefit from it, and a substantial obstacle to public interest advocates who fear the impact of consolidation on the diversity and quality of the media.

The MMTC's opposition to network neutrality has similarly raised the ire of advocacy groups and elicited accusations that the MMTC and the civil rights organizations with which it works have forsaken a public interest agenda for a corporate agenda. Opposition by the MMTC, NAACP, LULAC, and National Urban League to network neutrality rules indeed echoes the claims of media companies that open Internet provisions would *harm* communities of color by reducing jobs and inhibiting the expansion of broadband into underserved communities. James Rucker, cofounder of ColorofChange.org, has characterized this advocacy as "the deployment of our civil rights organizations in support of a corporate agenda," one facilitated by the heavy financial support provided by telecommunications companies to these groups.[31] Honig has responded to these charges by reasserting that his organization and other civil rights groups are centrally committed to protecting communities of color, accusing his "netroots" critics of paternalism toward communities of color that in fact misunderstands their interests.[32]

In 2013, Nogales publicly admonished Honig and the actions of the MMTC, accusing Honig of having become "too chummy with the industry." Nogales also resigned his position on the MMTC's board because of concerns over the organization's ties to media corporations.[33] In this, Nogales joined a chorus of media advocacy group leaders who sought to delegitimize the MMTC as an advocate of the public interest broadly, and of the civil rights community specifically, on media regulation issues. In the process, Nogales was able to distance the NHMC from damning accusations that advocacy groups who accept corporate monies become corporate mouthpieces rather than watchdogs or opponents. Such a move was necessary for the NHMC to retain its credibility with its own community and with fellow advocacy practitioners.

Thus part of the current practice of media advocacy groups is to police what counts as an acceptable relationship with a media company and what constitutes advocacy capture, the process by which public interest groups adopt the priorities of their funders over those of their communities; it is to distinguish the kinds of media work that are acceptable forms of media advocacy work. Significantly, it is the ongoing, cumulative nature of media advocacy work that has rendered the recent actions of the MMTC, NAACP, and LULAC so threatening to other advocacy groups and their allies. The power of these groups' positions on media ownership and network neutrality hails from their clout as long-standing media advocates for communities of color and their past record of reform campaigns to ensure that the media meet the needs of a multiracial public. This work is what makes them credible advocates to policymakers, desirable allies for media and telecommunications companies, and heartbreaking adversaries to other media advocacy groups.

CONCLUSION: THE PRECARITY AND POLITICS OF
MEDIA ADVOCACY WORK

Precarity—the central theme of this collection—defines media advocacy work in many ways. The NHMC has been motivated by what it has seen as the precarious status of its community. Its work has been premised on the belief that Latinas/os' security—as well as their political, economic, and social rights—would be affected by their visibility within the media and their ability to access communication technologies. The capacity to enact reform is also precarious, as the outcome of advocacy campaigns rarely hinges only on the solidity of the arguments presented or the extent of popular support for an issue, but also depends on the ideological commitments of the regulatory community, the sway of industry interests, and the political culture at a historical juncture. The ability to do advocacy work is precarious, as groups not only have to continually raise money to support their organization, but consistently have to shore up their informational and reputational capital in order to be legible and credible stakeholders to regulators, other advocacy groups, and their own community. Indeed, the very precarity of media advocacy only underlines how critical it is to honor the ongoing labors of media advocacy groups who continually work amid uncertainty as to outcome as well as to their own survival.

When civil rights organizations become, in the words of Nogales, "too chummy" with the media corporations, when they use their standing as representatives of communities of color to promote the agenda of media companies, they only intensify the precarity of media advocacy work. Not only do they lend support to policies that most likely will diminish the diversity of voices in the public sphere, but they discredit the notion that communities of color have not been, and will not be, served well by deregulation. In this, they mask their media work as media advocacy work and upend the very purpose of media advocacy on behalf of the public interest.

NOTES

1. Alex Nogales, interviewed by Allison Perlman, July 10, 2013, offices of National Hispanic Media Coalition, Pasadena, CA.

2. Philip Napoli makes this very point in his wide-ranging overview of media advocacy scholarship. See Philip Napoli, "Public Interest Media Advocacy and Activism as a Social Movement," *Communication Yearbook* 33 (2009): 394–401

3. Hortense Powdermaker, *Hollywood: The Dream Factory* (New York: Grosset & Dunlap, 1950); Leo Rosten, *Hollywood: The Movie Colony, the Movie Makers* (New York: Harcourt Brace, 1941); Thomas Schatz, *The Genius of the System: Hollywood Filmmaking in the Studio Era* (New York: Pantheon Books, 1988); Todd Gitlin, *Inside Prime Time* (New York: Pantheon Books, 1983); Horace Newcomb and Robert S. Alley, *The Producer's Medium: Conversations with Creators of American TV* (New York: Oxford University Press, 1983).

4. John Caldwell, *Production Culture: Industrial Reflexivity and Critical Practice in Film and Television* (Durham, NC: Duke University Press, 2008).

5. Vicki Mayer, *Below the Line: Producers and Production Studies in the New Television Economy* (Durham, NC: Duke University Press, 2011).

6. Seeta Peña Gangadharan, "Public Participation and Agency Discretion in Rulemaking at the Federal Communications Commission," *Journal of Communication Inquiry* 33 (2009): 337–353.

7. Becky Lentz and Allison Perlman, "Media Advocacy Practice Produces Media Policy Literacy," presentation at the International Communication Association Annual Meeting, Seattle, Washington, May 25, 2014.

8. The NHMC, for example, in 1988 filed four petitions against stations in Los Angeles, and in 1989 went after WNET in New York for low levels of Latino employment. See Victor Valle, "Latino Group Challenges TV Licenses," *Los Angeles Times,* November 2, 1988, 1; Victor Valle, "Latino Coalition's Bid For KTTV: Full Assault, Long Odds," *Los Angeles Times,* November 10, 1988, H1, H13; Victor Valle, "Latinas/os Claim Job Bias at KCBS," *Los Angeles Times,* December 31, 1986, J1, J2; "NHMC Signs Landmark Agreement with KABC-TV," press release, November 11, 1993, Box 7, Folder 1, Papers of the National Hispanic Media Coalition, University of California, Los Angeles (hereafter NHMC Papers).

9. For documents relating to the Disney boycott, see Box 33, Folders 1–2, NHMC; for a discussion of the struggles of Spanish language broadcasting, see Allison Perlman, *Public Interests: Media Advocacy and the Struggles over U.S. Television* (New Brunswick, NJ: Rutgers University Press, forthcoming), chapter 6.

10. Notice of Appeal, *NHMC v. FCC,* filed October 20, 1992; Notion of Intention to Intervene, *NHMC v. FCC,* filed November 5, 1992, Box 32, Folder 2; Settlement Agreement, Entered into Between National Hispanic Media Coalition and the Univision Television Group, Inc., May 20, 1994; Letter from Enrique Baray to Armando Durón, October 18, 1995, Box 31, Folder 3, NHMC Papers.

11. Jessica Gonzalez, interviewed by Allison Perlman, April 17, 2014, offices of National Hispanic Media Coalition, Pasadena, CA.

12. Interview with Nogales; Electronic Filing, Correction to *Ex Parte* Presentation Letters, filed by Jessica Gonzalez, September 21, 2010, http://apps.fcc.gov/ecfs/comment/view?id=6016055968. See the letter to Genachowski outlining the terms of the MOU, http://apps.fcc.gov/ecfs/comment/view?id=6015694189.

13. Greg Braxton, "A White, White World on TV's Fall Schedule," *Los Angeles Times,* May 28, 1999, 1.

14. Interview with Nogales; Greg Braxton, "Groups Join to Protest Exclusion, Television: Coalition Forms in Response to the Absence of Minorities on New Shows in Prime Time This Fall," *Los Angeles Times,* June 25, 1999, 1; Paul Bernstein and Michael Schneider, "NAACP, NBC Reach Pact," *Daily Variety,* January 6, 2000,1; Lisa de Moraes, "TV Networks Adding Some Color For Fall: New Minority Roles Receive Little Applause," *Washington Post,* May 21, 2000, A01.

15. Interview with Nogales.

16. Letter to Chairman Genachowski from Benjamin Todd Jealous, Marc H. Morial, and Rev. Al Sharpton, December 16, 2010, http://apps.fcc.gov/ecfs/comment/view?id=6016064629; Letter to Chairman Genachowski from Karen K. Narasaki, December 15, 2010, http://apps.fcc.gov/ecfs/comment/view?id=6016064415.

17. Josh Silver, "Comcastrophe: Comcast/NBC Merger Approved," *Huffington Post,* January 18, 2011, www.huffingtonpost.com/josh-silver/comcastrophy-comcastnbc-m_b_810380.html.

18. Erwin G. Krasnow, Lawrence D. Longley, and Herbert A. Terry, *The Politics of Broadcast Regulation* (New York: St. Martin's Press, 1982), 57–58.

19. See Kathryn C. Montgomery, "Special Interest Citizen Groups and the Networks: A Case Study of Pressure and Access," in *Telecommunications Policy Handbook,* ed. Jorge Reina Schement, Felix Gutierrez, and Marvin A. Sirbu, Jr. (New York: Praeger, 1982), 241–254.

20. Interview with Gonzalez.

21. Donald Guimary, *Citizens' Groups and Broadcasting* (New York: Praeger, 1975), 125–126.

22. Jefferson Pooley, "From Psychological Warfare to Social Justice: Shifts in Foundation Support for Communication Research," in *Media and Social Justice,* ed. Sue Curry Jansen, Jefferson Pooley, and Lora Taub-Pervizpour (New York: Palgrave-MacMillan, 2011), 211–240.

23. Interview with Gonzalez.

24. Ibid.

25. Ibid.

26. Juan González and Joseph Torres, *News for All the People: The Epic Story of Race and the American Media* (London: Verso, 2012), 371.

27. Ibid., 372–376.

28. Jason McLure, "Civil Rights Group's FCC Positions Reflect Industry Funding, Critics Say," *Center for Public Integrity,* June 6, 2013, www.publicintegrity.org/2013/06/06/12769/civil-rights-groups-fcc-positions-reflect-industry-funding-critics-say.

29. *Prometheus Radio Project v. FCC,* 373 F.3d 372 (2004).

30. *Prometheus Radio Project v. FCC,* 652 F.3d 431 (2011).

31. James Rucker, "Net Neutrality, Civil Rights, and Big Telecom Dollars," *Huffington Post,* September 10, 2014, www.huffingtonpost.com/james-rucker/net-neutrality-civil-rights-orgs_b_5796944.html.

32. "David Honig Pushes Back against the 'Digital Activists," *Field Negro,* July 30, 2014, http://field-negro.blogspot.com/2014/07/david-honig-pushes-back-against-digital.html#.VBD1i1ZnylK.

33. McLure, "Civil Rights Group's FCC Positions Reflect Industry Funding."

20

Internationalizing Labor Activism

Building Solidarity among
Writers' Guilds

Miranda Banks and David Hesmondhalgh

Across the world, trade unions have played a major role in efforts by workers to improve their conditions, defend their rights, and promote social justice in people's working lives. Yet in the recent "turn to labor" in media and cultural studies, there has been little sustained consideration of unions.[1] The collective action and bargaining offered by unions are crucial in providing a means of limiting the problematic working conditions that, as a number of researchers have shown, are apparent in much media work, in spite of easy and flawed assumptions that the media industries provide high-quality or "easy" jobs.[2] The labor precariousness that is the subject of this collection would be much less likely to prevail in a situation where strong unions were able to negotiate collectively on behalf of workers. In addition, the best trade unions strive to counter inequalities and exclusions based on gender, class, ethnicity, and other dimensions of social power, and these too are real problems in the media industries. Yet many media workers feel uncertain about the value of trade unions, or anxious that affiliation or identification with them will lead to the loss of work. This chapter concerns efforts by professional and trade organizations to defend and improve the rights and conditions of writers as a community of workers in the media industries, both within particular nations and internationally. It explores these issues via a case study of the Writers Guild of America (WGA).

However, our concerns are not confined to the borders of the United States. We begin by discussing various obstacles and tensions facing organized labor in the media industries. Although here we focus on the United States and the United Kingdom, many of these issues can be found internationally. We then discuss some of the ways these issues have played out historically in the specific example of the WGA, before turning to a recent significant development that raises crucial questions about media labor in an era of internationalization or, as some would have it, "globalization": increasing efforts by the WGA to work with other writers' labor organizations abroad, not only to prevent outsourcing of work to cheaper locations (of course a problem in many industries, media and otherwise, in the global era), but also to build solidarity. Yet some of the same problems regarding tensions between solidarity and exclusion, fairness and privilege, can be found in the context of international media labor organization, though with intriguing new dynamics that we explore below. Those new dynamics can be properly understood only when explained in the context of problems facing organized labor in the media industries, and we begin this chapter with a historical perspective on these issues.

PROBLEMS FACING ORGANIZED LABOR IN THE MEDIA INDUSTRIES

In many countries, media industries have been fairly highly unionized for many years. In *The Cultural Front,* Michael Denning tells the story of how culture came to be a major ground for leftist activism in the United States during the 1930s and 1940s,[3] and he shows how this led to the American working class making its mark on dominant cultural institutions for the first time, but also how it led to the formation of organized labor institutions in the sphere of culture. For Andrew Ross,[4] Denning's perspective is a useful reminder that the industrialization of culture in the twentieth century was an opportunity for creative labor more than a threat. Industrialization made culture an object of mass production, and unlike workers in other industries, media workers could exert an influence on the shape and nature of the product. By contrast, Ross points out, "the non-commercial arts have long been a domain of insecurity, underpayment, and disposability."[5] In other countries too, the rise of media industries was accompanied by significant levels of unionization. For example, the networks that traditionally dominated British broadcasting (the BBC and ITV) were unionized from their formation in the 1920s and 1950s, respectively,[6] and so was U.K. journalism (the National Union of Journalists [NUJ] was founded in 1907). The U.K. Musicians Union was formed in 1921 and by the end of the 1990s had over 31,000 members.[7]

Across the world in the early twenty-first century, however, media trade unions of all kinds are facing significant challenges. Attacks on trade unions in general, launched with renewed vigor starting in the 1970s and 1980s, have continued to the present day across the globe, and in many countries union membership is in steep decline.[8] This, combined with the marketization of media industries enabled by government deregulation programs, has led to a real reduction in the influence of media labor unions. The power of trade unions in the media industries has almost uniformly diminished, professionally, economically, culturally, and politically. Examples can be seen in television, journalism, and music.[9] Rates of unionization are extremely low in the independent television production companies that have come to occupy a key place in the European television market. Journalists' unions have been significantly reduced in number and power, not only because of the technological "advances" of digitalization, but also because of changing employment laws and journalists' embrace of notions of "professionalism," which has drawn entrants to the occupation away from unions.[10]

Musicians' unions illustrate some of the problems facing collective worker organization in the new media landscape in a way that suggests the dangers of precariousness for screen workers. Few workers are employed permanently as musicians, and musical labor more often than not is carried out on a freelance basis, and therefore difficult to unionize. Musicians' unions play an important role in campaigning around various issues—for example, the regulation of live performance. But the collective bargaining over pay and conditions that is at the heart of modern trade unionism is elusive in the case of musicians outside live entertainment and orchestral work. What's more, some of the issues that musicians' unions take up on behalf of their members can have detrimental effects on musicians outside the union. For example, those who have already attained the status of authorship, and who are therefore more likely to gain fuller compensation through rights, are more likely to be members of a union (among other reasons, because they are more likely to feel that it is worthwhile to pay their dues). Income from "rights" of various kinds provides an important supplement to other income for many musicians and other precarious creative workers—though few workers can actually make a living from rights alone. It is perfectly understandable that unions and other associations of workers work to increase such income for their members by campaigning for stricter enforcement of intellectual property. Yet this can have the effect of stifling public culture and making content creation more expensive for workers who do not have the protection of a big company. This illustrates the potential tensions between goals that unions pursue on behalf of their members (payment via rights) and other potentially legitimate goals that might favor non-member media workers (more open access to culture). Such tensions between solidarity and exclusion recur constantly and internationally.

The fight for improved conditions for media workers faces other challenges even within the organized labor movement. The coexistence of the terms *union* and *guild* indicates some of the tricky issues regarding different kinds of workers, and different approaches to how they might best be protected by worker organizations. There are tensions in the media and communication industries between "craft unions," on the one hand, and those oriented toward general worker solidarity, on the other. There are also tensions between those organizations that represent above-the-line or "creative talent" workers, such as writers, actors, and directors, and those representing below-the-line "craftspeople," technical or support workers.

Worker organization in the media industries is divided between, on the one hand, craft unions and guilds, who often aim primarily to protect the pay and conditions of existing members who have gained entry to a limited field; and on the other, general unions that adhere to inclusive goals of solidarity and equality, and see themselves much more as defending workers as a whole. This in turn relates to a fundamental problem underlying all modern trade unionism: the tension between the pressure to act as a "businesslike service organization" or as an "expression and vehicle of the historical movement of the submerged laboring masses."[11] As Alan Paul and Archie Kleingarter have shown in the most important study of the topic, the unions or guilds representing "creative" above-the-line talent in the U.S. film and television sectors managed to expand membership and bargain powerfully for their members in the late twentieth century, in spite of regulatory and technological changes that might have harmed their effectiveness.[12] Some analysts have responded to the unfortunate connotations of *above-the-line* and *below-the-line,* terms derived from Hollywood accounting practices and seeming to suggest a hierarchy of labor, by treating above-the-line workers as somehow inherently privileged or more "creative" compared with technical and other workers. But in the media industries some technical workers enjoy very good pay and conditions, and many above-the-line workers suffer hardship.

Craft unions have some ambivalent features, as Vincent Mosco and Catherine McKercher have shown in a valuable account of labor organization in media and communication industries. Craft solidarity, they write, has "at times worked against the push toward mass unions, and at other times has encouraged it."[13] The International Typographical Union (ITU), which represented printers in the U.S. newspaper industry until 1986, for example, encouraged workers to identify with their union and to see it "as the institution that would provide them with a good living."[14] But Mosco and McKercher also recognize that craft solidarity can be destructive, and that the ITU, for example, tried the patience of workers as it grew into a more bureaucratic and professional bargaining institution concerned with "jurisdiction over the tools of the trade" to the exclusion of protection and promotion of the craft itself.

What is needed is strong union representation ensuring good working conditions and rights across all types of media work, nationally and internationally. Yet social and cultural changes have negatively affected trade unions in general, including media unions. One way of understanding this is via the concept of *individualization,* whereby workers tend to see organizations, and jobs, as opportunities for self-development rather than sources of commitment. For the most widely cited advocate of this concept, Ulrich Beck, individualization offers some new freedoms in that people become independent of restrictive traditional ties, but it also leads to competitiveness and isolation.[15] In the eyes of some commentators, this leads to "an individualistic and self-centered culture of contentment that sees no virtue in forms of collective association and solidarity."[16] Such developments perhaps help to explain how, in the contemporary media industries, in Susan Christopherson's words, "personal networks are recognized as the central mechanism both for individual career advancement and risk reduction."[17]

Organizations representing creative workers face all these challenges. They also face a challenge concerning how they are perceived more widely. In a fine analysis of changes in the U.S. film and television industries, Christopherson shows how middling budget productions are being eroded both by the huge demand for cheap programming in the era of multichannel television and by the blockbuster syndrome in movies, and how this has led to a strengthening of "defensive exclusionary networks"[18] that dominate access to the best jobs. Are guilds of creative workers examples of such exclusionary networks, reinforcing the privilege of the well educated and successful? This question of *privilege* cannot be separated from dynamics of inequality related to class, race, ethnicity, and gender. In the remainder of this chapter, we explore these issues by examining efforts by writers of film, television, and streaming media to defend—or better procure—their rights as employees within the major media industries, first by looking at some of the obstacles faced by U.S. writers in their own national context and then turning to their efforts to establish strong global connections among writers' organizations.

THE WRITERS GUILD OF AMERICA IN THE NATIONAL CONTEXT

In early November 2007, certain quarters of Los Angeles transformed overnight into walking districts. For the next five months, five days a week, dozens of writers, often spectacled, wearing jeans and T-shirts and always with picket signs, walked for hours in front of various gates of the major Hollywood studios. Across the country, dozens more in New York bundled up and braved the cold to protest their rights of labor and rates of compensation. These professional film and television writers walked en masse to protest stalled negotiations with the American trade organization the Alliance of Motion Picture and Television Producers (AMPTP). For the first time in nineteen years, the Writers Guild of America (WGA) was on strike. Nationally, a poll conducted two weeks after negotiations broke off showed that 63 percent of Americans sided with the striking workers (with 4 percent favoring the studios, 33 percent unsure).[19]

It is rare in the United States to see striking workers marching in a number of areas across the two largest cities in the country. Even more notable was the fact that these employees were neither blue-collar laborers nor white-collar workers. They were no-collar workers.[20] Unlike earlier strikes, this time writer-producers and showrunners also walked the picket lines, arguing that they could not separate their work as producers from their role as writers. The guild leadership specifically targeted showrunners early in the negotiations to get their support, not just for labor action but to read the letter of the law in such a way that their role as producers could not be separated from their role as writers. While as producers they were part of management, as writers they were employees of the studio. While some faces were familiar—Tina Fey, Rob Reiner—others had names that were familiar to audiences: Norman Lear and James L. Brooks. Still others were attached to beloved products that suddenly disappeared from homes across the globe. Writers were now positioned—in their role marching around the outside of studio buildings—as industry workers fighting for their rights.

The Writers Guild of America was first established as the Screen Writers Guild in 1933, though it was not granted a contract until 1942. The WGA, which comprises East and West branches, is the bargaining agent for professional writers who craft film, television, news, animation, streaming media, and video game scripts for American signatory companies. The Writers Guild has gone on strike six times, in 1959–1960, 1973, 1981, 1985, 1988, and 2007–2008. Three of these industrywide walkouts were protracted, lasting many months. As they had in every previous strike, in 2007–2008, these American writers marched in circles and demanded their rights, not as artisans but as workers in a media industry. This time, though, because of the globalization of film and television distribution, as well as the rise of YouTube—where many striking writers went to speak directly to audiences—more people than ever before were aware of a strike among working writers. Not just in the United States, but globally. And not just audiences, but other writers as well.

For the writers under its protection, the WGA as a guild provides union-oriented services: it convenes and mobilizes members, addresses their concerns, negotiates and enforces contracts, lobbies on behalf of its members, and represents the face of screenwriters to the outside world. But it is its final directive—preserving the art and craft of writing—that most clearly illuminates the subtle difference between a union and a guild. The WGA sees its protection, teaching, and preservation of the work of writing as the additive dimension that distinguishes it from a traditional trade union.

Yet during moments of economic crisis or labor negotiations, writers often feel compelled to define themselves as a union first and foremost. Bob Barbash, a writer on *Zane Grey Theater,* explained how this perception played out during a strike in 1960: "A tremendous amount of people in the Guild . . . resent the word 'union.' . . . [Every] morning I had to be carrying a picket sign in front of MGM. Now that is not a Guild. That's a union, man. When you are walking there and you are trying to stop people from crossing the line. We are an unusual group because we like to think of ourselves as [part of a] super, upper [tier of] intelligence. That we don't work on a loading dock . . . but if you are going to have a union, you are a union."[21] In contrast, the term *guild* implies a focus less on working conditions and more on championing the artistry of the profession. The difference is not merely one of terminology: it has resulted in a recurring tug-of-war across the entertainment industries between different groups of writers and sometimes even within an individual writer's conception of what they do and how their interests ought to be represented.[22] The internal friction is captured in shifting definitional terms such as *artist, worker, creative, laborer.*

Writers must join the guild if they have surpassed a certain quantity of work with a company that has signed as a contractual partner on the guild's collective bargaining agreement. A signatory company can be as vast as a multinational corporation or as limited as a small pro-union production company. An associate writer amasses units to gain full membership, and today writers must belong to either the WGA East (which uses the acronym WGAE) or the Writers Guild West (which prefers WGAw), depending on geography. The guild's stated objectives are voluminous. It contracts minimum rates for specific types of work, determines writers' screen credits, ensures payment of residuals, provides pensions and health benefits for members, engages in national policy debates concerning writers' interests, and provides continuing education for members and the community. Some writers have seen their induction into the guild as a sign of having "made it" in the industry. Others have felt membership to be a weighty burden foisted upon them. And still others have paid little attention to what membership meant. Then there are those who view membership as a life raft. Barbara Corday, creator of *Cagney & Lacey,* expressed deep gratitude for the benefits afforded to veteran writers: "First of all, having residuals. Lifetime medical insurance as a backup to Medicare, as a secondary insurance. How many people outside of Congress have things like that? It's just *phenomenal.*"[23]

Corralling this disparate group of workers, however, is an arduous task. The guild brings together thousands of individuals who predominantly perform solitary work. As Hal Kanter, creator of the series *Julia,* noted in the 1970s, "We writers are, collectively, a strange group of creatures and it's a frequent source of amazement to me that the Guild is such a well-run zoo!"[24] John Furia Jr., writer for *The Singing Nun* and president of the WGAw from 1973 to 1975, laughed as he pointed out, "We are the most individualistic group to band together."[25] Phyllis White, who worked on writing teams for various television series from the 1950s through the 1980s, noted the paradox of singular writers with unique voices aligning for a collective cause: "It's a Guild of individuals as no other union is. You've got the Teamsters and there are a certain number of Teamsters who do the same job. . . . They do the same hours. They do the same thing. We don't. . . . Trying to amalgamate this group . . . [of] nearly 5,000 into one union now is horrendous. It's amazing that it works at all."[26] White's sweeping claims around the specialness of writers' work are problematic: many trade unions cover diverse members with distinct job descriptions, and the work of writers is not as rarefied as she proclaims.[27] And yet the notion of collecting a community of workers who usually work alone does pose distinct difficulties.

Another major challenge for the Writers Guild is that it coexists with a number of other guilds and unions in the media industries. The other groups that negotiate with signatory companies include the Directors Guild of America (DGA), which represents directors, assistant directors, unit production managers, and production associates; the Screen Actors Guild–American Federation of Television and Radio Artists (SAG-AFTRA), which represents actors, extras, broadcast journalists, and puppeteers, among others; and the International Alliance of Theatrical Stage Employees (IATSE), which represents a diverse set of industry workers, from electricians to set carpenters, makeup artists, prop masters, cinematographers, editors, and art directors. The other three organizations service vastly larger constituencies than the WGA, and have needs so diverse that a united front proves tricky—especially when it comes time to negotiate with the monolithic Alliance of Motion Picture and Television Producers (AMPTP). The AMPTP is an enormous bargaining unit that digests the concerns of hundreds of production companies, networks, and studios and then delivers a proposal—representing the united group's interests—to the negotiating table. Whereas in standard bargaining a union tries to garner advantage by playing off one company against another, the AMPTP positions itself so that the three creative guilds must jostle with each other, grabbing for scraps at the table. This tactic, called reverse pattern bargaining, forces each guild into what one member called "a kind of a chess game between the three unions."[28]

GOING GLOBAL: GUILDS IN AN ERA OF INTERNATIONALIZATION

As indicated earlier, an important way a guild might define its work differently than a union is by emphasizing promotion of the profession or craft. This has spatial dimensions that have changed in recent decades. Where once a union would look only for local, regional, or national solidarity, in an era of globalization of the media industries, solidarity for the WGA must be threefold: within their own union, member to member and between East and West; among the WGA, the DGA, SAG-AFTRA, and IATSE; and as we explore in this section, among different countries and communities of professional writers that work for the media industries.

This international dimension is not entirely new. For most of its eighty-year existence as a trade union, the Writers Guild has offered professional support to developing guilds and associations in other countries, guiding media and cultural workers in other countries on how to respond to changes in the industry.

The Writers Guild of America has often called for solidarity not only among its members, but also from aspirants and fellow professional screenwriters across the globe. But in this increasingly globalized era of media production, this aspect has intensified. This was particularly noticeable during the 2007–2008 strike, when the guild made it clear that it would hold accountable any writer who broke the strike. WGA members spoke with film students, instructing them not to take writing jobs with studios as screenwriters. At stake for any writer, locally or globally, was any chance of joining the union. But the guild did not stop at U.S. borders. The WGA asked screenwriters in countries affiliated with the American guild through the International Affiliation of Writers Guilds not to work for American studios during the strike as an act of global solidarity. Having this kind of control of the market on scripts was critical to a successful strike. By including prospective writers and defining them as allies, they increased the chances of unity during the strike.

There is a contradiction in this behavior, however: this unity only confirmed that pathways for international workers into the industry—especially the American industry—are barely open. In this case, solidarity can reaffirm exclusion. And this type of international cooperation is often about leveraging power more than benevolent mutual support. Kevin Sanson argues that global cities offer opportunities for advanced capitalist countries—most notably American but also British and Australian companies—to use their diverse locales, functional technical resources, and skilled practitioners at budget prices.[29] The price of labor is significantly cheaper in part because international production labor is rarely unionized. The easiest way to keep costs low is to film overseas, outsourcing production and postproduction as much as possible to avoid the high costs of unionized labor. The economic and geographic structures of multiplatform global entertainment conglomerates have made transnational production the norm in what are still considered by most national and international audiences to be "Hollywood" productions.[30]

While much of so-called Hollywood production labor is now regularly outsourced across international borders, writing has generally stayed in the United States. There are a few jobs, including screenwriting, that tend to be culturally specific: not all jobs cross borders easily or comfortably. The specificities of language and idiom, trends in narrative structure, and cultural references and social issues make writing for a global audience particularly daunting. Companies might be eager to outsource writing to other Anglophone countries, but the reality is that this still rarely occurs. And yet the WGA seems aware that it is only a matter of time before global competition becomes more fierce. Like many other industries, major media corporations are increasingly prone to outsource work to lower-cost regional media capitals. American visual effects and digital postproduction workers' recent organizing campaigns serve as a legitimate example of

U.S. labor's anxiety about jobs going overseas. Arguably, these developments can provide opportunities for labor in Prague or Budapest or India to earn pay, build skills, build infrastructure, and achieve professional renown. And those jobs could include writing jobs.

The WGA regularly ventures overseas for conversations with other national writers' guilds and related organizations. While part of the mission is solidarity, they also have hopes of professionalizing their international counterparts in the hope of limiting outsourcing. This represents a model of modified inclusion, something WGA West vice president Howard Rodman explained as "we can't give you what we have, but we will help you navigate the waters to get there—in the meantime by helping you secure better wages, we will ensure that our native industry does not see your labor as enticing."[31]

Other writers' guilds exist around the world, primarily in economically developed countries. South Africa, Israel, and Australia have strong screenwriters' guilds. In the United Kingdom, the WGGB is part social club and part professional organization. Greece and Italy are establishing their guilds as social clubs first (with the hope that professionalization will follow).

The WGA has built connections with screenwriters' guilds from around the world and continues to build more, in part through professional organizations like the International Association of Writers Guilds.[32] Granted, the tie with each union, association, or professional organization shifts based on the changing nature of labor relations for each individual country. One example of this is in the case of New Zealand. Though writers in New Zealand have been unionized for over forty years, the Employment Contract Act of 1989 was a terrible blow to creative labor in the country. The act transformed the nature of labor in New Zealand, terminating any chance that media workers would hold rights to residuals. Norelle Scott, a member of the New Zealand Writers Guild, explained how the act decimated the power of creative labor—and it was only writers' affiliation with the International Association of Writers Guilds that kept its membership focused on whatever rights they still controlled.[33] It was through the strength of international partnerships that the New Zealand Writers Guild began to rebuild after this devastating blow. With their ties to the International Association of Writers Guilds, the New Zealand Writers Guild made steps forward, setting agendas and structures for international coproductions and discussing strategies for developing free trade agreements.

Writers in Greece, Italy, and France have over the years developed clear agendas as well—whether or not they are specifically stated. As U.S. formats and sensibilities are exported and transferred around the world, writers who work elsewhere are eager to import professional rights. Many hope in time not only that increased coproductions and transnational industry shifts will lure production dollars but that preproduction will also come to their countries. And with this importation, there is hope that the rights of professional writers will be redefined. American screenwriters see part of that process as making sure local writers protect themselves from their own native industry, no matter what form that native industry assumes.

The WGA has passed on to professional screenwriters across the world their frustration with media production and with the fact that directors, producers, and actors are nearly always paid better. In addition, writers rarely have much control over the way their scripts are used. Spanish screenwriter Agustín Díaz Yanes said, "The worst comment you can ever hear when you go and see a producer is when they say to you: 'The screenplay is essential.' That's when you know they pay peanuts, if they pay at all!"[34] While it is not the sanctity of the screenplay that matters, Yanes's comment about the place of the writer on the lower end of the creative hierarchy speaks to a frustration widely shared among writers working in the global media industries.

In a global media production landscape, the unique dynamics of individual careers can obscure the trends of the media industries. It is not only the power of the major conglomerates at work but also the needs of trade organizations that guide debate and discussion, as well as actions that define patterns of inclusion and exclusion and hierarchies of power. As Bridget Conor observes in her study of labor problems surrounding the *Lord of the Rings* trilogy (filmed in New Zealand), extraordinary displays of "empire in action" demand our attention as we study precarious labor in a global economy.[35] With the expanding frontiers of media production—even within the economy of a single film or film series—there is both a fear of what could happen if unionization is quashed on a global level and hope for what could happen if an alliance across countries were solidified among writers' guilds.

CONCLUSION

The challenges of internationalization are substantial for a national union. The WGA offers one example of how a union has struggled toward regional, national, and global solidarity. But what about those who are yet to be included among the paid workers? Across the globe, professional screenwriters are negotiating the tricky waters of this international production flow. When considering media workers, it is critical to think about the role of national trade organizations and the role these labor groups play as media cross borders. Guilds believe they can ease the processes of production. Many now operate alongside city and regional governments in efforts to attract investment. But access to labor organizations is possible only for people who have established themselves within the industry. And access to the most powerful of these organizations—those in the United States—is limited to people who have already succeeded in selling a script. The aspirants—including international screenwriters trying to make it in their own countries—realize that they are both potential allies and potential competition for those already in coveted A-list writer roles. This further illustrates the tensions and contradictions at work among craft unions and guilds and how their efforts to protect workers can also serve as exclusionary devices. Nevertheless, the WGA offers an example of relatively successful collective worker organization in the media industries. That success now needs to be extended internationally, across different media jobs and social classes. But only by addressing the kinds of tensions and contradictions outlined above can organized labor fulfill its historical mission of protecting media workers.

NOTES

1. Much of the recent critical research on media work has actually been addressed to "cultural work" or "creative labor," and one reason for this choice of terms is the way work has been understood (or neglected) by policymakers and academics interested in the creative industries and the "creative economy." See Mark Banks and David Hesmondhalgh, "Looking for Work in Creative Industries Policy," *International Journal of Cultural Policy* 15.4 (2009): 1–16. For simplicity's sake, and because of the topic of this book, we use the terms *media work* and *media workers* here. For a more detailed discussion of the relations among the concepts *media industries, cultural industries,* and *creative industries,* see Hesmondhalgh, *The Cultural Industries* (Los Angeles: Sage, 2013), 23. On the relations among the concepts of *media work, cultural work,* and *creative labor,* see Hesmondhalgh and Sarah Baker, *Creative Labour: Media Work in Three Cultural Industries* (New York: Routledge, 2011), a source some of this chapter draws on.

2. Among the notable contributions to the "turn to labor" in media and cultural studies discussing or providing evidence of such problematic conditions, see Andrew Ross, *Nice Work If You Can Get It: Life and Labour in Precarious Times* (New York: New York University Press, 2009); Angela McRobbie, "Clubs to Companies; Notes on the Decline of Political Culture in Speeded Up Creative Worlds," *Cultural Studies* 16 (2002); Mark Banks, *The Politics of Cultural Work* (New York: Palgrave Macmillan, 2007); Vicki Mayer, *Below the Line: Producers and Production Studies in the New Television Economy* (Durham, NC: Duke University Press, 2011); Matt Stahl, *Unfree Masters: Recording Artists and the Politics of Work* (Durham, NC: Duke University Press, 2013); and Mark Banks, Rosalind Gill, and Stephanie Taylor, eds., *Theorizing Cultural Work: Labour, Continuity and Change in the Cultural and Creative Industries* (New York: Routledge, 2013). Important research on media labor has by no means been confined to media and cultural studies. A ground-breaking collection from industrial relations studies is Lois Gray and Ronald L. Seeber, eds., *Under the Stars: Essays on Labor Relations in Arts and Entertainment* (Ithaca, NY: ILR Press, 1996); see also Alan McKinlay and Chris Smith, eds., *Creative Labour: Working in the Creative Industries* (Basingstoke: Palgrave Macmillan, 2009). The contributions of geographer Susan Christopherson have been valuable; see below.

3. Michael Denning, *The Cultural Front* (New York: Verso, 1997).

4. Ross, *Nice Work If You Can Get It,* 19.

5. Ibid., 21.

6. Asa Briggs, *The History of Broadcasting in the United Kingdom,* vol. 5 (Oxford: Oxford University Press, 1995), 381.

7. Dave Laing, "Musicians' Unions," *Continuum Encyclopedia of Popular Music of the World,* ed. John Shepherd et al. (London: Continuum, 2003).

8. For a recent analysis of the problems of the U.S. labor movement, see Stanley Aronowitz, *The Death and Life of American Labor: Towards a New Workers' Movement* (New York: Verso, 2014).

9. Alan McKinlay, "Making 'the Bit between the Adverts': Management, Accounting, Collective Bargaining and Work in UK Commercial Television, 1979–2005," in *Creative Labour,* ed. McKinlay and Smith.

10. Meryl Aldridge and Julia Evetts, "Rethinking the Concept of Professionalism: The Case of Journalism," *British Journal of Sociology* 54.4 (2003).

11. Will Herberg, "Bureaucracy and Democracy in Labor Unions," *Antioch Review* 3, cited in Peter Fairbrother and Edward Webster, "Social Movement Unionism: Questions and Possibilities," *Employment Responsibilities and Rights* 20 (2008): 309, who also quote an alternative formulation of the tension: "sword of justice" or "vested interest."

12. Alan Paul and Archie Kleingarter, "The Transformation of Industrial Relations in the Motion Picture and Television Industries: Talent Sector," in *Under the Stars,* ed. Gray and Seeber. Gray and Seeber's collection is the most detailed and valuable study of media labor organizations, but its cases are confined almost entirely to the United States.

13. Vincent Mosco and Catherine McKercher, *The Laboring of Communication: Will Knowledge Workers of the World Unite?* (Lanham, MD: Lexington Books, 2008), 82.

14. Ibid., 104.

15. Ulrich Beck, *The Brave New World of Work* (Cambridge: Polity Press, 2008), 94.

16. Robert Taylor, "The Future of Employment Relations" (Swindon: Economic and Social Research Council, 2001), quoted in Richard Saundry, Valerie Antcliff, and Mark Stuart, "'It's More Than Who You Know'—Networks and Trade Unions in the Audio-Visual Industries," *Human Resource Management Journal* 16.4 (2006): 378.

17. Susan Christopherson, "Beyond the Self-Expressive Creative Worker: An Industry Perspective on Entertainment Media," *Theory, Culture & Society* 25 (2008): 89.

18. Ibid.

19. James Welsh, "WGA Lauds Public Support Polls," *Digital Spy,* November 15, 2007, www.digitalspy.com/tv/ustv/news/a79902/wga-lauds-public-support-polls/.

20. In the United States, different socio-economic groups are often reductively indicated by the clothing they wear to work: formal white collars for professionals, (originally denim) blue collars for manual workers. "No collar" indicates the wearing of T-shirts by those who work from home or in the self-consciously informal IT industries. While the dress code is casual, the workload and working hours are often very demanding.

21. Bob Barbash, interview by the Writers Guild Oral History Project (Los Angeles: Writers Guild Foundation, February 24, 1978), 7, Writers Guild Foundation Archive, Los Angeles, CA.

22. The battle over self-definition is a recurring theme in Miranda J. Banks, *The Writers: A History of American Screenwriters and Their Guild* (New Brunswick, NJ: Rutgers University Press, 2015). This chapter draws upon research for that book and material that appears in it.

23. Barbara Corday, interview with Banks, August 30, 2013.

24. M.W., "Kanter Adds Dimension to Hyphenated Career: Writer-Prod-Dir-Emcee," *WGAw Newsletter,* December 1967, 7, Writers Guild Foundation Shavelson-Webb Library, Los Angeles.

25. John Furia Jr. and David Rintels, interview by the Writers Guild Oral History Project (Los Angeles: Writers Guild Foundation, May 3, 1978), 44.

26. Robert White and Phyllis White, interview by the Writers Guild Oral History Project (Los Angeles: Writers Guild Foundation, spring 1978), 22.

27. On the politics of such distinctions, see Jason Toynbee, "How Special? Cultural Work, Copyright, Politics," in *Theorizing Cultural Work: Labour, Continuity and Change in the Cultural and Creative Industries,* ed. Mark Banks, Rosalind Gil, and Stephanie Taylor (Abingdon: Routledge, 2013); Mayer, *Below the Line;* and especially Stahl, *Unfree Masters.*

28. Marc Norman, interview with Banks, June 2011.

29. Kevin Sanson, "Production Service Firms and the Spatial Dynamics of Global Media Production," paper presented at annual meeting for the Society for Cinema and Media Studies Conference, Seattle, Washington, 2014.

30. Toby Miller, Nitin Govil, John McMurria, Richard Maxwell, and Ting Wang, *Global Hollywood 2* (London: British Film Institute, 2008).

31. Howard Rodman, interview with Banks, February 15, 2011. None of this is really new. In the late 1940s, American writers saw this internationalism as both a boon for business and an encroaching threat. In 1948, Robert Pirosh, who worked with René Clair on a Maurice Chevalier film, referred to American writers who had contracts as part of a postwar invasion of Europe through international coproductions." Yet in 1947, an editorial in the journal *The Screen Writer* portended that "in the years to come, it is not inconceivable that the film industries in India and China may further encroach upon areas which we once held almost exclusively." Editorial, *The Screen Writer*, July 1945, 38.

32. Studies of writers around the world include Eva Novrup Redvall on television screen authorship in Denmark and Bridget Conor on British and New Zealand screenwriters. See Redvall, *Writing and Producing Television Drama in Denmark: From "The Kingdom" to "The Killing"* (New York: Palgrave Macmillan, 2013); Bridget Conor, "Subjects at Work: Investigating the Creative Labour of British Screenwriters," in *Behind the Screen: Inside European Production Cultures,* ed. Petr Szczepanik and Patrick Vonderau (London: Palgrave Macmillan, 2013); and her "Problems in 'Wellywood': Rethinking the Politics of Transnational Cultural Labour," *Flow TV* 13, last modified January 28, 2011, http://flowtv.org/2011/01/problems-in-wellywood/.

33. Norelle Scott, interview with Banks, March 2014.

34. Agustín Díaz Yanes in *Hablan los guionistas,* dir. Alfonso S. Suárez, Sindicato de Guionistas ALMA, 2013.

35. Conor, "Problems in 'Wellywood.'"

REFERENCES

Abirafeh, Lina. *Gender and International Aid in Afghanistan: The Politics and Effects of Intervention.* Jefferson, NC: McFarland, 2009.

Abu-Lughod, Lila. "Do Muslim Women Really Need Saving? Anthropological Reflections on Cultural Relativism and Its Others." *American Anthropologist* 104.3 (2002): 783–790.

Adams, Vincanne. *Markets of Sorrow, Labors of Faith: New Orleans in the Wake of Katrina.* Durham, NC: Duke University Press, 2013.

Adejunmobi, Moradewun. "Evolving Nollywood Templates for Minor Transnational Film." *Black Camera* 5.2 (2014): 74–94.

Aldridge, Meryl, and Julia Evetts. "Rethinking the Concept of Professionalism: The Case of Journalism." *British Journal of Sociology* 54.4 (2003).

Andrejevic, Mark. *Reality TV: The Work of Being Watched.* Lanham, MD: Rowman and Littlefield, 2004.

Appadurai, Arjun. *Modernity at Large: Cultural Dimensions of Globalization.* Minneapolis: University of Minnesota Press, 1996.

Aronowitz, Stanley. *The Death and Life of American Labor: Towards a New Workers' Movement.* New York: Verso, 2014.

Arsenault, Amelia, and Manuel Castells. "The Structure and Dynamics of Global Multimedia Business Networks" *International Journal of Communication* 2 (2008): 707–748.

Babcock, Barbara A. *The Reversible World: Symbolic Inversion in Art and Society.* Ithaca, NY: Cornell University Press, 1978.

Ballantyne, Glenda. *Creativity and Critique: Subjectivity and Agency in Touraine and Ricoeur.* Leiden: Brill, 2007.

Baltruschat, Doris. *Global Media Ecologies: Networked Production in Film and Television.* New York: Routledge, 2010.

Banet-Weiser, Sarah. *Authentic™: The Politics of Ambivalence in a Brand Culture.* New York: New York University Press, 2012.

Banks, John. "The iPhone as Innovation Platform: Reimagining the Videogames Developer." In *Studying Mobile Media: Cultural Technologies, Mobile Communication, and the iPhone*, edited by Larissa Hjorth, Jean Burgess, and Ingrid Richardson, 155–172. New York: Routledge 2012.

Banks, John, and Stuart Cunningham. "Games and Entertainment Software." In *Handbook on the Digital Creative Economy*, edited by Ruth Towse and Christian Handke, 416–427. Cheltenham: Edward Elgar , 2013.

Banks, Mark. "Moral Economies and Cultural Work." *Sociology* 40 (2006): 455–472.

———. *The Politics of Cultural Work*. New York: Palgrave Macmillan, 2007.

Banks, Mark, and David Hesmondhalgh. "Looking for Work in Creative Industries Policy." *International Journal of Cultural Policy* 15.4 (2009): 1–16.

Banks, Mark, Rosalind Gill, and Stephanie Taylor, eds. *Theorising Cultural Work: Labour, Continuity and Change in the Cultural and Creative Industries*. New York: Routledge, 2013.

Banks, Miranda. "How to Study Media and Makers." In *The Sage Handbook of Television Studies*, edited by Manuel Alvarado, Milly Buonanno, Herman Gray, and Toby Miller. London: Sage, 2014.

———. *The Writers: A History of American Screenwriters and Their Guild*. New Brunswick, NJ: Rutgers University Press, 2015.

Barker, Michael J. "Democracy or Polyarchy? US-Funded Media Developments in Afghanistan and Iraq post 9/11." *Media, Culture, and Society* 30.1 (2008): 109–130.

Barnouw, Eric, and S. Krishnaswamy. *Indian Film*. New York: Oxford University Press, 1980.

Beck, Ulrich. *The Brave New World of Work*. Cambridge: Polity Press, 2008.

Berg, Heather. "Labouring Porn Studies." *Porn Studies* 1.1–2 (2014): 75–79.

———. "Sex, Work, Queerly: Identity, Authenticity, and Laboured Performance." In *Queer Sex Work*, edited by Mary Laing, Katy Pilcher, and Nicola Smith. London: Routledge, 2015.

Bhabha, Homi K. *The Location of Culture*. New York: Routledge, 2004.

Bielby, William T., and Denise D. Bielby. "Organizational Mediation of Project-Based Labor Markets: Talent Agencies and the Careers of Screenwriters." *American Sociological Review* 64.1 (1999): 64–85.

Blair, Helen. "'You're Only as Good as Your Last Job': The Labour Process and Labour Market in the British Film Industry." *Work, Employment and Society* 15.1 (2001): 149–169.

Bodroghkozy, Aniko. *Equal Time: Television and the Civil Rights Movement*. Urbana: University of Illinois Press, 2012.

Bose, Derek. *Brand Bollywood: A New Global Entertainment Order*. New Delhi: Sage, 2006.

Bourdieu, Pierre. *Distinction: A Social Critique of the Judgment of Taste*. Cambridge, MA: Harvard University Press, 1984.

———. *The Field of Cultural Production. Essays on Art and Literature*. New York: Columbia University Press. 1993.

Briggs, Asa. *The History of Broadcasting in the United Kingdom*. Vol. 5: *Competition*. Oxford: Oxford University Press, 1995.

Brown, Brian A. "Will Work for Free: The Biopolitics of Unwaged Digital Labour." *TripleC: Communication, Capitalism and Critique* 12.2 (2014): 694–712.

Burton-Jones, Alan. *Knowledge Capitalism: Business, Work, and Learning in the New Economy*. Oxford: Oxford University Press, 1999.

Çakir, Mukadder, ed. *Yeni Medyaya Eleştirel Yaklaşimlar*. İstanbul: Doğu Kitabevi, 2014.

Caldwell, John. "Convergence Television: Aggregating Form and Repurposing Content in the Culture of Conglomeration." In *Television after TV*, edited by Lynn Spigel, 41–74. Durham, NC: Duke University Press, 2004.

———. "Para-Industry." *Cinema Journal* 52.3 (Spring 2013): 157–165.

———. *Production Culture: Industrial Reflexivity and Critical Practice in Film and Television*. Durham, NC: Duke University Press, 2008.

———. *Televisuality: Style, Crisis and Authority in American Television*. New Brunswick, NJ: Rutgers University Press, 1995.

Cammaerts, Bart. "Jamming the Political: Beyond Counter-Hegemonic Practices." *Continuum: Journal of Media and Cultural Studies* 21.1 (2007): 71–90.

Carducci, Vince. "Culture Jamming." *Journal of Consumer Culture* 6.1 (2006): 116–138.

Carey, James. "Historical Pragmatism and the Internet." *New Media & Society* 7.4 (2005) 443–455

Castells, Manuel. *Networks of Outrage and Hope: Social Movements in the Internet Age*. Cambridge: Polity, 2012.

Caves, Richard. *Creative Industries: Contracts between Art and Commerce*. Cambridge, MA: Harvard University Press, 2002.

Chakravarty, Sumita S. *National Identity in Indian Popular Cinema 1947–1987*. Austin: University of Texas Press, 1993.

Christopherson, Susan. "Behind the Scenes: How Transnational Firms Are Constructing a New International Division of Labor in Media Work." *Geoforum* 37 (2006): 739–751.

———. "Beyond the Self-Expressive Creative Worker: An Industry Perspective on Entertainment Media." *Theory, Culture & Society* 25 (2008).

Christopherson, Susan, and Jennifer Clark. *Remaking Regional Economies: Power, Labor, and Firm Strategies in the Knowledge Economy*. New York: Routledge, 2007.

Christopherson, Susan, and Michael Storper. "The City as Studio, the World as Back Lot: The Impact of Vertical Disintegration on the Location of the Motion Picture Industry." *Environment and Planning D: Society and Space* 4.3 (1986): 305–320.

———. "The Effects of Flexible Specialization on Industrial Politics and the Labor Market: The Motion Picture Industry." *Industrial and Labor Relations Review* 42.3 (1989): 331–347.

Chu, Yingchi. "The Politics of Reception: 'Made in China' and Western Critique." *International Journal of Cultural Studies* 17.2 (2014): 159–173.

Chua, Beng-Huat. *Structure, Audience and Soft Power in East Asian Culture*. Hong Kong: Hong Kong University Press, 2012.

Chua, Beng-Huat, and Koichi Iwabuchi. *East Asian Pop Culture: Analysing the Korean Wave*. Hong Kong: Hong Kong University Press, 2008.

Classen, Steven. *Watching Jim Crow: The Struggle over Mississippi TV, 1955–1969*. Durham, NC: Duke University Press, 2004.

Climate Group. *Smart2020: Enabling the Low Carbon Economy in the Information Age*. London: Global Sustainability Initiative, 2008.

Coe, Neil M. "On Location: American Capital and the Local Labour Market in the Vancouver Film Industry." *International Journal of Urban and Regional Research* 24.1 (March 2000): 79–94.

Coe, Neil M., and Jennifer Johns. "Beyond Production Clusters: Towards a Critical Political Economy of Networks in the Film and Television Industries." In *The Cultural Industries and the Production of Culture,* edited by Dominic Power and Allen J. Scott, 188–204. London: Routledge, 2004.

Coe, Neil M., Peter Dicken, and Martin Hess. "Global Production Networks: Realizing the Potential." *Journal of Economic Geography* 8 (2008): 271–295.

Conor, Bridget. "Subjects at Work: Investigating the Creative Labour of British Screenwriters." In *Behind the Screen: Inside European Production Cultures,* edited by Petr Szczepanik and Patrick Vonderau. London: Palgrave Macmillan, 2013.

Cooke, Miriam. *Dissident Syria: Making Oppositional Arts Official.* Durham, NC: Duke University Press, 2007.

Csikszentmihalyi, Mihaly. *Creativity: Flow and the Psychology of Discovery and Invention.* New York: HarperCollins, 1996.

Currid, Elizabeth. *The Warhol Economy: How Fashion, Art, and Music Drive New York City.* Princeton, NJ: Princeton University Press, 2007.

Curtin, Michael. "Media Capitals: Toward the Study of Spatial Flows." *International Journal of Cultural Studies* 6.2 (2003): 202–228.

———. *Playing to the World's Biggest Audience: The Globalization of Chinese Film and TV.* Berkeley: University of California Press, 2007.

Curtin, Michael, Jennifer Holt, and Kevin Sanson, eds. *Distribution Revolution: Conversations about the Digital Future of Film and Television.* Berkeley: University of California Press, 2014.

Curtin, Michael, and John Vanderhoef. "A Vanishing Piece of the Pi: The Globalization of Visual Effects Labor." *Television and New Media* 16.3 (2015): 219–239.

Curtin, Michael, and Kevin Sanson. "The Division of Labor in Television." In *The Sage Handbook of Television Studies,* edited by Manuel Alvarado, Milly Buonanno, Herman Gray, and Toby Miller. Thousand Oaks, CA: Sage, 2015.

Dai, Juncheng, Shengyi Zhou, Michael Keane, and Qian Huang. "Mobility of the Creative Class: A Case Study of Chinese Animation Workers." *Eurasian Geography and Economics* 53.5 (2012): 649–670.

Davier, Lucile. "The Paradoxical Invisibility of Translation in the Highly Multilingual Context of News Agencies." *Global Media and Communication* 10.1 (2014).

Davila, Arlene. *Culture Works: Space, Value and Mobility across the Neoliberal Americas.* New York: New York University Press, 2012.

———. *Latinos, Inc.* Berkeley: University of California Press, 2001.

Denning, Michael. *The Cultural Front.* New York: Verso, 1997.

Deuze, Mark, Chase Bowen Martin, and Christian Allen. "The Professional Identity of Gameworkers." *Convergence* 31 (2007): 335–353.

Donoghue, Courtney Brannon. "Sony and Local-Language Productions: Conglomerate Hollywood's Strategy of Flexible Localization for the Global Film Market." *Cinema Journal* 53.4 (2014).

Downing, John D. H., with Tamara Villarreal Ford, Geneve Gil, and Laura Stein. *Radical Media: Rebellious Communication and Social Movements.* Thousand Oaks: Sage, 2001.

Dudrah, Rajinder, and Amit Rai. "The Haptic Codes of Bollywood Cinema in New York City." *New Cinemas: Journal of Contemporary Film* 3.3 (2005): 143–158.

Eagleton, Terry. "The Revolt of the Reader." *New Literary History* 13.3 (1982): 449–452.

Edgerton, Gary R., and Jeffrey P. Jones. *The Essential HBO Reader.* Lexington: University Press of Kentucky, 2008.

Elmer, Greg, and Mike Gasher. *Contracting Out Hollywood: Runaway Productions and Foreign Location Shooting.* Lanham, MD: Rowman & Littlefield, 2005.

Ernst, Dieter, and Linsu Kim. "Global Production Networks, Knowledge Diffusion, and Local Capability Formation." *Research Policy* 31.8–9 (2002): 1417–1429.

Everett, Anna, and John Caldwell, eds. *New Media: Theories and Practices of Digitextuality.* New York: Routledge, 2003.

Fahmy, Ziad. *Ordinary Egyptians: Creating the Modern Nation through Popular Culture.* Stanford, CA: Stanford University Press, 2011.

Faulkner, Robert R. *Music on Demand: Composers and Careers in the Hollywood Film Industry.* New Brunswick, NJ: Transaction, 1983.

Ferguson, Roderick. *The Reorder of Things: The University and Its Pedagogies of Minority Difference.* Minneapolis: University of Minnesota Press, 2012.

Filiu, Jean-Pierre. *Le révolution arabe: Dix leçons sur le soulèvement démocratique.* Paris: Fayard, 2011.

Flew, Terry. *The Creative Industries: Culture and Policy.* London: Sage, 2012.

———. *Understanding Global Media.* New York: Palgrave Macmillan, 2007.

Flew, Terry, and Stuart Cunningham. "Creative Industries after the First Decade of Debate." *Information Society* 26.2 (2010).

Florida, Richard. *Cities and the Creative Class.* New York: Routledge, 2005.

———. *The Rise of the Creative Class and How It's Transforming Work, Leisure, Community and Everyday Life.* New York: Basic Books, 2002.

———. *The Rise of Creative Class, Revisited.* New York: Basic Books, 2012.

Foucault, Michel. *The Birth of Biopolitics: Lectures at the Collège de France, 1978–79.* Translated by Graham Burchell, edited by Michel Senellart. Houndmills: Palgrave Macmillan, 2008.

Fox, Elizabeth. *Latin American Broadcasting. From Tango to Telenovela.* Bedfordshire: University of Luton and John Libbey Media, 1997.

Fox, Elizabeth, and Silvio Waisbord, eds. *Latin Politics, Global Media.* Austin: University of Texas Press, 2002.

Fuchs, Christian. *Digital Labour and Karl Marx.* London: Routledge, 2014.

———. *Social Media: A Critical Introduction.* Los Angeles: Sage, 2014.

Fung, Anthony, and Vicky Ho. "Cultural Policy, Chinese National Identity and Globalization." In *Global Media and National Policies: The Return of the State,* edited by Terry Flew, Petros Iosifidis, and Jeanette Steemers. New York: Palgrave Macmillan, 2016.

Gall, Gregor. *An Agency of Their Own: Sex Worker Union Organizing.* Washington: Zero Books, 2012.

Gandy, Matthew. "Learning from Lagos." *New Left Review* 33 (2005): 36–52.

Gangadharan, Seeta Peña. "Public Participation and Agency Discretion in Rulemaking at the Federal Communications Commission." *Journal of Communication Inquiry* 33 (2009): 337–353.

Ganti, Tejaswini. *Bollywood: A Guidebook to Popular Hindi Cinema.* New York: Routledge, 2004.

———. "Mumbai vs. Bollywood: The Hindi Film Industry and the Politics of Cultural Heritage in Contemporary India." In *Global Bollywood*, edited by Anandam Kavoori and Aswin Punathambekar. New York: New York University Press, 2008.

———. *Producing Bollywood: Inside the Contemporary Hindi Film Industry.* Durham, NC: Duke University Press, 2012.

———. "Sentiments of Disdain and Practices of Distinction: Boundary-Work, Subjectivity, and Value in the Hindi Film Industry." *Anthropological Quarterly* 85.1 (2012).

García Canclini, Néstor. *El mundo entero como lugar extraño.* Buenos Aires: Gedisa, 2014.

———. "Precarious Creativity: Youth in a Post-Industrial Culture." *Journal of Latin American Cultural Studies: Travesia* 22.4 (2013): 341–352.

Gardner, Howard. *Creating Minds: An Anatomy of Creativity Seen through the Lives of Freud, Einstein, Picasso, Stravinsky, Eliot, Graham, and Gandhi.* New York: Basic Books, 2011.

Garga, Bhagwan Das. *So Many Cinemas: The Motion Picture in India.* Mumbai: Eminence Designs, 1996.

Garritano, Carmela. "Introduction: Nollywood—an Archive of African Worldliness." *Black Camera* 5.2 (2013): 44–52.

Gasher, Mike. *Hollywood North: The Feature Film Industry in British Columbia.* Seattle: University of Washington Press, 2002.

Gelvin, James L. *Divided Loyalties: Nationalism and Mass Politics in Syria at the Close of Empire.* Berkeley: University of California Press, 1998.

Gill, Rosalind. "Cool Creative and Egalitarian? Exploring Gender in Project-based New Media Work in Europe." *Information, Communication and Society* 5.1 (2002): 70–89..

Gitlin, Todd. *Inside Prime Time.* New York: Pantheon Books, 1983.

Goldsmith, Ben, and Tom O'Regan. *The Film Studio: Film Production in the Global Economy.* Lanham, MD: Rowman and Littlefield, 2005.

Goldsmith, Ben, Susan Ward, and Tom O'Regan. *Local Hollywood: Glboal Film Production and the Gold Coast.* Brisbane: University of Queensland Press, 2010.

González, Juan, and Joseph Torres. *News for All the People: The Epic Story of Race and the American Media.* London: Verso, 2012.

Graham, Mark. "Warped Geographies of Development: The Internet and Theories of Economic Development." *Geography Compass* 2.3 (2008): 771–789.

Gray, Herman. "Subject(ed) to Recognition." *American Quarterly* 65.4 (2013): 771–798.

Gray, Lois, and Ronald L. Seeber, eds. *Under the Stars: Essays on Labor Relations in Arts and Entertainment.* Ithaca, NY: ILR Press, 1996.

Gregg, Melissa. *Work's Intimacy.* London: Polity, 2012.

Grimes, Seamus. "Foreign R&D in China: An Evolving Innovation Landscape." In *Innovation and Intellectual Property in China: Strategies, Contexts and Challenges,* edited by Ken Shao and Xiaoqing Feng, 186–205. Cheltenham: Edward Elgar, 2014.

Grindstaff, Laura, and Vicki Mayer. "The Importance of Being Ordinary: Brokering Talent in the New-TV Era." In *Brokerage and Production in the American and French Entertainment Industries: Invisible Hands in Cultural Markets,* edited by Violaine Roussel and Denise Bielby, 131–152. Lanham, MD: Lexington Books, 2015.

Gross, Kenneth. *Puppet: An Essay on Uncanny Life.* Chicago: University of Chicago Press, 2011.

Guback, Thomas H. *The International Film Industry: Western Europe and America since 1945.* Bloomington: Indiana University Press, 1969.

Guimary, Donald. *Citizens' Groups and Broadcasting*. New York: Praeger, 1975.

Habermas, Jurgen. *The Structural Transformation of the Public Sphere: An Inquiry into a Category of Bourgeois Society*. Cambridge, MA: MIT Press, 1991.

Hall, Stuart. "The Spectacle of the Other." In *Representation: Cultural Representations and Signifying Practices*, edited by Stuart Hall. Thousand Oaks, CA: Sage, 2003.

Hariman, Robert. "Parody and Public Culture." *Quarterly Journal of Speech* 94.3 (2008): 247–272.

Harold, Christine. "Pranking Rhetoric: 'Culture Jamming' as Media Activism." *Critical Studies in Media Communication* 21.3 (2004): 189–211.

Harvey, David. *A Brief History of Neoliberalism*. London: Oxford University Press, 2005.

Havens, Timothy. *Black Television Travels: African American Media around the Globe*. New York: New York University Press, 2013.

Haynes, Jonathan. "New Nollywood: Kunle Afolayan." *Black Camera* 5.2 (2013): 53–73.

———. "Nollywood in Lagos, Lagos in Nollywood Films." *Africa Today* 54.2 (2007): 131–150.

Hearn, Greg, Ruth Bridgstock, Ben Goldsmith, and Jess Rodgers. *Creative Work beyond the Creative Industries*. Cheltenham: Edward Elgar, 2014.

Heitner, Devorah. *Black Power TV*. Durham, NC: Duke University Press, 2013.

Henderson, Felicia D. "It's Our Own Fault: How Post-strike Hollywood Continues to Punish Writers for Striking." *Popular Communication* 8.3 (2010): 232–239.

———. "Options and Exclusivity: Economic Pressures on TV Writers' Compensation and the Effects on Writer's Room Culture." In *The Sage Handbook of Television Studies*, edited by Manuel Alvarado, Milly Buonanno, Herman Gray, and Toby Miller. London: Sage, 2014.

Hennessey, Beth. "The Social Psychology of Creativity." *Scandinavian Journal of Educational Research* 47.2 (2003): 253–271.

Hesmondhalgh, David. *The Cultural Industries*. Los Angeles: Sage, 2006.

Hesmondhalgh, David, and Sarah Baker. *Creative Labour: Media Work in Three Cultural Industries*. New York: Routledge, 2011.

Hesmondhalgh, David, and Anamik Saha. "Race, Ethnicity and Cultural Production." *Popular Communication* 11.3 (2013): 179–195.

Hesse, Carla. *Publishing and Cultural Politics in Revolutionary Paris, 1789–1810*. Berkeley: University of California Press, 1991.

Hill, Erin. "Women's Work: Feminized Labor in Hollywood, 1930–1948." PhD diss., UCLA, 2014.

Hjorth, Larissa. "Games: Mobile, Locative and Social." In *The Media and Communications in Australia*, edited by Stuart Cunningham and Sue Turnbull. Crows Nest, NSW: Allen & Unwin, 2014.

Howard, Philip N., and Muzammil M. Hussein. *Democracy's Fourth Wave? Digital Media and the Arab Spring*. Oxford: Oxford University Press, 2013.

Howkins, John. *The Creative Economy*. New York: Penguin, 2001.

Hozic, Aida A. *Hollyworld: Space, Power, and Fantasy in the American Economy*. Ithaca, NY: Cornell University Press, 2001.

Hugo, Victor. *Histoire d'un crime: Déposition d'un témoin*. Paris: Nelson, 1907.

Hull, Gloria T., Patricia Bell Scott, and Barbara Smith, eds. *But Some of Us Are Brave: All the Women Are White, All the Blacks Are Men: Black Women's Studies*. New York: Feminist Press, 1993.

Hunt, Darnell. "Hollywood Story: Diversity, Writing and the End of Television as We Know It." In *The Sage Handbook of Television Studies*, edited by Manuel Alvarado, Milly Buonanno, Herman Gray, and Toby Miller. London: Sage, 2014.

Irvine, Judith T. "When Talk Isn't Cheap: Language and Political Economy." *American Ethnologist* 16.2 (1989): 248–267.

Jacobs, Katrien, Marjie Janssen, and Metteo Pasquinelli. "Introduction." In *C'lickme: A Netporn Studies Reader*, edited by Katrien Jacobs, Marjie Janssen, and Metteo Pasquinelli. Amsterdam: Institute of Network Cultures, 2007.

Jansson, André, and Miyase Christensen, eds. *Media, Surveillance and Identity: Social Perspectives*. New York: Peter Lang, 2014.

Janus, Noreene. "Advertising and the Mass Media in the Era of the Global Corporation." In *Communication and Social Structure: Critical Studies in Mass Media Research*, edited by Emile McAnany, Jorge Schnitman, and Noreene Janus. New York: Praeger, 1981.

Jasper, James M. *The Art of Moral Protest: Culture, Biography and Creativity in Social Movements*. Chicago: University of Chicago Press, 1997.

———. "The Innovation Dilemma: Some Risks of Creativity in Strategic Agency." In *The Dark Side of Creativity*, edited by David H. Cropley, Arthur J. Cropley, James C. Kaufman, and Marc A. Runco. New York: Cambridge University Press, 2010.

Jedlowski, Alessandro. "Nigerian Videos in the Global Arena: The Postcolonial Exotic Revisited." *Global South* 7.1 (2013): 157–178.

Jenkins, Henry. *Convergence Culture*. New York: New York University Press, 2006.

Jenkins, Henry, Sam Ford, and Joshua Green. *Spreadable Media: Creating Value and Meaning in a Networked Culture*. New York: New York University Press, 2013.

Joas, Hans. *The Creativity of Action*. Translated by Jeremy Gaines and Paul Keast. Chicago: University of Chicago Press, 1996.

Jones, Candace. "Careers in Project Networks: The Case of the Film Industry." In *Boundaryless Career: A New Employment Principle for a New Organizational Era*, edited by Michael Bernard Arthur and Denise M. Rousseau. New York: Oxford University Press, 1996.

Jonsson, Stefan. *A Brief History of the Masses: Three Revolutions*. New York: Columbia University Press, 2008.

Kandell, Jonathan. "Americans in Prague: A Second Wave of Expatriates Is Now Playing a Vital Role in the Renaissance of the Czech Capital." *Smithsonian Magazine*, August 2007.

Kantorowicz, Earnst H. *The King's Two Bodies: A Study in Mediaeval Political Theology*. Princeton, NJ: Princeton University Press, 1957.

Karpik, Lucien. *Valuing the Unique: The Economics of Singularities*. Princeton, NJ: Princeton University Press, 2010.

Keane, Michael. *China's New Creative Clusters: Governance, Human Capital and Investment*. London: Routledge, 2011.

———. *China's Television Industry*. London: Palgrave, 2015.

———. *Creative Industries in China: Art, Design and Media*. London: Polity, 2013.

Keane, Michael, and Bonnie Rui Liu. "China's New Creative Strategy: Cultural Soft Power and New Markets." In *Asian Popular Culture: The Global Cultural (Dis)connection*, edited by Anthony Fung. London: Routledge, 2013.

Kenney, Martin, ed. *Understanding Silicon Valley: The Anatomy of an Entrepreneurial Region*. Stanford, CA: Stanford University Press, 2000.

Kesavan, Mukul. "Urdu, Awadh and the Tawaif: The Islamicate Roots of Hindi Cinema." In *Forging Identities: Gender, Communities and the State,* edited by Zoya Hasan. New Delhi: Kali for Women, 1994.

King, Martha. "Protecting and Representing Workers in the New Gig Economy: The Case of the Freelancers Union." In *New Labor in New York: Precarious Workers and the Future of the Labor Movement,* edited by Ruth Milkman and Ed Ott. Ithaca, NY: Cornell University Press, 2014.

Kleinhans, Chuck. "'Creative Industries,' Neoliberal Fantasies, and the Cold, Hard Facts of Global Recession: Some Basic Lessons." *Jump Cut: A Review of Contemporary Media* 53 (2011).

Kokas, Aynne. "Shot in Shanghai: Western Film Co-Production in Post-WTO Mainland China." PhD diss., UCLA, 2012.

Koolhaas, Rem, Harvard Project on the City, Stefano Boeri, Sanford Kwinter, Nadia Tazi, and Hans Ulrich Obrist. *Mutations.* New York: ACTAR, 2000.

Kraidy, Marwan M. "The Body as Medium in the Digital Age: Challenges and Opportunities." *Communication and Critical-Cultural Studies* 10.2–3 (2013): 285–290.

———. "Governance and Hypermedia in Saudi Arabia." *First Monday* 11.9 (2006).

———. *Hybridity: The Cultural Logic of Globalization.* Philadelphia: Temple University Press, 2005.

———. *The Naked Blogger of Cairo: Creative Insurgency in the Arab World.* Cambridge, MA: Harvard University Press, 2016.

———. "The Politics of Revolutionary Celebrity in the Contemporary Arab World." *Public Culture* 27.1 (2015): 161–183.

———. *Reality Television and Arab Politics: Contention in Public Life.* Cambridge: Cambridge University Press, 2010.

———. "The Revolutionary Body Politic: Preliminary Thoughts on a Neglected Medium in the Arab Uprisings." *Middle East Journal of Culture and Communication* 5.1 (2012): 68–76.

Krasnow, Erwin G., Lawrence D. Longley, Herbert A. Terry. *The Politics of Broadcast Regulation.* New York: St. Martin's Press, 1982.

Kumar, Shanti. "Mapping Tollywood: The Cultural Geography of Ramoji Film City in Hyderabad, India." *Quarterly Review of Film and Video* 23 (2006): 129–138.

Lagerkvist, Amanda. "9.11 in Sweden: Commemoration at Electronic Sites of Memory." *Television & New Media* 15 (2014): 350–370.

Laing, Dave. "Musicians' Unions." In *Continuum Encyclopedia of Popular Music of the World,* edited by John Shepherd, David Horn, Dave Laing, Paul Oliver, and Peter Wicke. London: Continuum, 2003.

Larkin, Brian. "Degraded Images, Distorted Sounds: Nigerian Video and the Infrastructure of Piracy." *Public Culture* 16.2 (2004): 289–314.

Latifa. *My Forbidden Face.* London: Virago, 2002.

Lazzarato, Maurizio. "Immaterial Labor." In *Radical Thought in Italy,* edited by Paolo Virno and Michael Hardt. Minneapolis: University of Minnesota Press, 1996.

Lerner, Daniel. *The Passing of Traditional Society: Modernizing the Middle East.* New York: Free Press, 1958.

Levin Russo, Julie. "'The Real Thing': Reframing Queer Pornography for Virtual Spaces." In *C'lickme: A Netporn Studies Reader,* edited by Katrien Jacobs, Marjie Janssen, and Metteo Pasquinelli. Amsterdam: Institute of Network Cultures, 2007.

Li Lanqing. *Breaking Through: The Birth of China's Opening Up Policy.* Translated by Ling Yuan and Zhang Siying. Oxford: Oxford University Press, 2009.

Lobato, Ramon. "Creative Industries and Informal Economies: Lessons from Nollywood." *International Journal of Cultural Studies* 13 (2010): 337–354.

———. *Shadow Economies of Cinema: Mapping Informal Film Distribution.* London: British Film Institute, 2012.

Lotz, Amanda. *The Television Will Be Revolutionized.* New York: New York University Press, 2007.

Lovink, Geert, and Sabine Niederer. *Video Vortex Reader: Responses to YouTube.* Amsterdam: Institute of Network Cultures, 2008.

Lovink, Geert, and Miriam Rasch, eds. *Unlike Us Reader: Social Media Monopolies and Their Alternatives.* Amsterdam: Institute of Network Cultures, 2013.

Lubart, Todd. "Cross-Cultural Perspectives on Creativity." In *The Cambridge Handbook of Creativity,* edited by James C. Kaufman and Robert J. Sternberg. New York: Cambridge University Press, 2010.

MacKinnon, Catharine. *Feminism Unmodified: Discourses on Life and Law.* Cambridge, MA: Harvard University Press, 1988.

Malmberg, Anders, and Peter Maskell. "Localized Learning Revisited." *Growth and Change* 37.1 (March 2006): 1–18.

Mann, Christian. "Christian Mann, General Manager, Evil Angel Productions." In *Distribution Revolution: Conversations about the Digital Future of Film and Television,* edited by Michael Curtin, Jennifer Holt, and Kevin Sanson. Berkeley: University of California Press, 2014.

Marcus, Carmen. *Future of Creative Industries: Implications for Research Policy.* Brussels: European Commission Foresight Working Documents Series, 2005.

Martín-Barbero, Jesús. "Memory and Form in the Latin American Soap Opera." In *The Television Studies Reader,* edited by Robert Allen and Annette Hill. London: Routledge, 2004.

Maskell, Peter, Harald Bathelt, and Anders Malmberg. "Building Global Knowledge Pipelines: The Role of Temporary Clusters." *European Planning Studies* 14.8 (2006): 997–1013.

Mason, Laura. *Singing the French Revolution: Popular Culture and Politics, 1787–1799.* Ithaca, NY: Cornell University Press, 1996.

Maxwell, Richard, and Toby Miller. "'Warm and Stuffy': The Ecological Impact of Electronic Games." In *The Video Game Industry: Formation, Present State, and Future,* edited by Peter Zackariasson and Timothy Wilson. London: Routledge, 2012.

Mayer, Vicki. *Below the Line: Producers and Production Studies in the New Television Economy.* Durham, NC: Duke University Press, 2011.

Mayer, Vicki, Miranda J. Banks, and John Caldwell. *Production Studies: Cultural Studies of Media Industries.* New York: Routledge, 2009.

Mazziotti, Nora. *La industria de la telenovela: La producción de ficción en América Latina.* Buenos Aires: Paidós, 1996.

Mboti, Nyasha. "Nollywood's Aporias Part 1: Gatemen." *Journal of African Cinemas* 6 (2014): 49–70.

McAdam, Doug. "Tactical Interaction and Innovation." In *The Wiley-Blackwell Encyclopedia of Social and Political Movements,* edited by David A. Snow, Donatella della Porta, Bert Klandermans, and Doug McAdam. Hoboken: Wiley-Blackwell, 2013.

McAdam, Doug, Sidney Tarrow, and Charles Tilly. *Dynamics of Contention*. Cambridge: Cambridge University Press, 2001.

McCarthy, Anna. *The Citizen Machine: Governing by Television in 1950s America*. New York: New Press, 2010.

McCrea, Christian. "Australian Video Games: The Collapse and Reconstruction of an Industry." In *Gaming Globally*, edited by Nina Huntemann and Ben Aslinger. Basingstoke: Palgrave Macmillan 2012.

McKelvey, Maureen, and Sharmistha Bachi-Sen, eds. *Innovation Spaces in Asia: Entrepreneurs, Multinational Enterprises and Policy*. Cheltenham: Edward Elgar, 2015.

McKinlay, Alan, and Chris Smith, eds. *Creative Labour: Working in the Creative Industries*. Basingstoke: Palgrave Macmillan, 2009.

McNeil, Legs, Jenniver Osborne, and Peter Pavia. *The Other Hollywood: The Uncensored Oral History of the Porn Film Industry*. 2nd ed. New York: HarperCollins, 2009.

McRobbie, Angela. *British Fashion Design: Rag Trade or Image Industry?* New York: Routledge, 1998.

———. "Clubs to Companies: Notes on the Decline of Political Culture in Speeded Up Creative Worlds." *Cultural Studies* 16 (2002).

———. "From Holloway to Hollywood: Happiness at Work in the New Cultural Economy." In *Cultural Economy*, edited by Paul du Gay and Michael Pryke. New York: Sage, 2002.

Miller, Jade. "Global Nollywood: The Nigerian Movie Industry and Alternative Global Networks in Production and Distribution." *Global Media and Communication* 8 (2012): 117–133.

Miller, James. "NGOs and 'Modernization' and 'Democratization' of Media: Situating Media Assistance." *Global Media and Communication* 5.1 (2009): 9–33.

Miller, Toby. *Cultural Citizenship: Cosmopolitanism, Consumerism, and Television in a Neoliberal Age*. Philadelphia: Temple University Press, 2007.

———. "No More Cybertarians, Please—More Citizens, Thank You." *Television & New Media* 1.2 (2000): 131–134.

———. "A View from a Fossil: The New Economy, Creativity and Consumption—Two or Three Things I Don't Believe In." *International Journal of Cultural Studies* 7.1 (2004): 55–65.

Miller, Toby, Nitin Govil, John McMurria, and Richard Maxwell. *Global Hollywood*. London: British Film Institute, 2001.

Miller, Toby, Nitin Govil, John McMurria, Richard Maxwell, and Ting Wang. *Global Hollywood 2*. London: British Film Institute, 2005.

Miller, Toby, and Marie C. Leger. "Runaway Production, Runaway Consumption, Runaway Citizenship: The New International Division of Cultural Labor." *Emergences* 11.1 (2001): 89–115.

Miller-Young, Mireille. "Putting Hypersexuality to Work: Black Women and Illicit Eroticism in Pornography." *Sexualities* 13.2 (April 2010): 219–235.

———. "Sexy and Smart: Black Women and the Politics of Self-Authorship in Netporn." In *C'lickme: A Netporn Studies Reader*, edited by Katrien Jacobs, Marjie Janssen, and Metteo Pasquinelli. Amsterdam: Institute of Network Cultures, 2007.

———. *A Taste for Brown Sugar: Black Women in Porn*. Durham, NC: Duke University Press, 2014.

Montgomery, Kathryn C. "Special Interest Citizen Groups and the Networks: A Case Study of Pressure and Access." In *Telecommunications Policy Handbook,* edited by Jorge Reina Schement, Felix Gutierrez, and Marvin A. Sirbu, Jr. New York: Praeger, 1982.

Montgomery, Lucy. *China's Creative Industries: Copyright, Social Network Markets and the Business of Culture in a Digital Age.* Cheltenham: Edward Elgar, 2010.

Morini, Cristina. "The Feminization of Labour in Cognitive Capitalism." *Feminist Review* 87.1 (2007): 40–59.

Morley, David, and Kevin Robins. *Spaces of Identity: Global Media, Electronic Landscapes and Cultural Boundaries.* New York: Routledge, 1995.

Morozov, Evgeny. *The Net Delusion: The Dark Side of Internet Freedom.* New York: Public-Affairs, 2011.

———. *To Save Everything, Click Here: The Folly of Technological Solutionism.* New York: PublicAffairs, 2013.

Morris, Meaghan. "The Banality of Cultural Studies." In *Logics of Television: Essays in Cultural Criticism,* edited by Patricia Mellencamp. Bloomington: Indiana University Press, 1990.

Mosco, Vincent. *To the Cloud: Big Data in a Turbulent World.* Boulder, CO: Paradigm, 2014.

Mosco, Vincent, and Catherine McKercher. *The Laboring of Communication: Will Knowledge Workers of the World Unite?* Lanham, MD: Lexington Books, 2008.

Mukherjee, Debashree. "Bombay Modern: A History of Film Production in Late Colonial Bombay (1930–1948)." PhD diss., New York University, 2015.

Murray, Laura, S. Tina Piper, and Kirsty Robertson. *Putting Intellectual Property in Its Place: Rights Discourses, Creative Labor and the Everyday.* New York: Oxford University Press, 2014.

Napoleoni, Loretta. *Maonomics: Why Chinese Communists Make Better Capitalists Than We Do.* Translated by Stephen Twilley. New York: Seven Stories, 2011.

Napoli, Philip. "Public Interest Media Advocacy and Activism as a Social Movement." *Communication Yearbook* 33 (2009): 394–401.

Neff, Gina. *Venture Labor: Work and the Burden of Risk in Innovative Industries.* Cambridge, MA: MIT Press, 2012.

Negri, Antonio. *The Politics of Subversion: A Manifesto for the Twenty-First Century.* Cambridge: Polity, 1989.

Negus, Keith. "The Production of Culture." In *Production of Culture/Cultures of Production.* Thousand Oaks, CA: Sage, 1997.

Newcomb, Horace, and Robert S. Alley. *The Producer's Medium: Conversations with Creators of American TV.* New York: Oxford University Press, 1983.

Noriega, Chon. *Shot in America: Television, the State, and the Rise of Chicano Cinema.* Minneapolis: University of Minnesota Press, 2000.

Oakley, Kate. "Include Us Out—Economic Development and Social Policy in the Creative Industries." *Cultural Trends* 15 (2006): 255–273.

———. "In Its Own Image: New Labour and the Cultural Workforce." *Cultural Trends* 20.3 (2012): 281–289.

Obst, Lynda. *Sleepless in Hollywood: Tales from the New Abnormal in the Movie Business.* New York: Simon & Schuster, 2013.

O'Donnell, Casey. *Developer's Dilemma: The Secret World of Videogame Creators.* Cambridge, MA: MIT Press, 2014.

———. "This Is Not a Software Industry." In *The Video Game Industry: Formation, Present State and Future,* edited by P. Zackariasson and T. L. Wilson. New York: Routledge, 2012.

Ogan, Christine L., Manaf Bashir, Lindita Camaj, Yunjuan Luo, Brian Gaddie, Rosemary Pennington, Sonia Rana, and Mohammed Salih. "Development Communication: The State of Research in an Era of ICTs and Globalization," *Gazette* 71.8 (2009): 655–670.

O'Regan, Tom, and Ben Goldsmith. *The Film Studio: Film Production in the Global Economy.* Lanham, MD: Rowman & Littlefield, 2005.

Orozco, Guillermo, ed. *Historias de la televisión en América Latina.* Barcelona: Gedisa, 2003.

Orozco, Guillermo, and María I. Vasallo, eds. *Transmedia Production Strategies in Television Fiction.* Porto Alegre, Brazil: Globo Comunicação e Participações and Sulina Editora, 2014.

Orsi, Cosma. "Knowledge-Based Society, Peer Production and the Common Good." *Capital & Class* 33 (2009): 31–51.

Osman, Wazhmah. "Program in Media, Culture, and Communication Department of Media, Culture, and Communication." PhD diss., New York University, 2012.

Ouellette, Laurie. *Viewers Like You? How Public TV Failed the People.* New York: Columbia University Press, 2002.

Ouelette, Laurie, and James Hay. *Better Living through Reality TV: Television and Post-Welfare Citizenship.* London: Wiley, 2008.

Outram, Dorinda. *The Body and the French Revolution: Sex, Class and Political Culture.* New Haven, CT: Yale University Press, 1989.

Pang, Laikwan. "The Labor Factor in the Creative Economy: A Marxist Reading." *Social Text* 99 (2009): 55–76.

Parker, Rachel, Stephen Cox, and Paul Thompson. "How Technological Change Affects Power Relations in Global Markets: Remote Developers in the Console and Mobile Games Industry." *Environment and Planning A* 46.1 (2014): 168–185.

Paul, Alan, and Archie Kleingarter. "The Transformation of Industrial Relations in the Motion Picture and Television Industries: Talent Sector." In *Under the Stars: Essays on Labor Relations in Arts and Entertainment,* edited by Lois S. Gray and Ronald L. Seeber. Ithaca, NY: ILR Press, 1996.

Penley, Constance. "Images, Ethics, and Technology: Collision in a Courtroom." In *Images, Ethics, and Technology,* edited by Sharrona Pearl. New York: Routledge, 2015.

Perlman, Allison. *Public Interests: Media Advocacy and the Struggles over U.S. Television.* New Brunswick, NJ: Rutgers University Press, forthcoming.

Peterson, Jennifer. *Murder, the Media, and the Politics of Public Feelings: Remembering Matthew Shepard and James Byrd Jr.* Bloomington: Indiana University Press, 2011.

Pieterse, Nederveen. *Globalization and Culture: Global Mélange.* 2nd ed. Lanham, MD: Rowman & Littlefield, 2009.

Piñón, Juan. "Reglocalization and the Rise of the Network Cities System in Producing Telenovelas for Hemispheric Audiences." *Journal of International Cultural Studies* 17.6 (2014): 655–671.

Pooley, Jefferson. "From Psychological Warfare to Social Justice: Shifts in Foundation Support for Communication Research." In *Media and Social Justice,* edited by Sue Curry Jansen, Jefferson Pooley, and Lora Taub-Pervizpour. New York: Palgrave-MacMillan, 2011.

Pott, Pitman. "Belief in Control: Regulation of Religion in China." *China Quarterly* 174 (2003): 317–337.

Powdermaker, Hortense. *Hollywood: The Dream Factory.* New York: Grosset & Dunlap, 1950.

Pratt, Andy C. "Hot Jobs in Cool Places: The Material Cultures of New Media Production Spaces: The Case of the South of Market, San Francisco." *Information, Communication, and Society* 5.1 (2002): 27–50.

Punathambekar, Aswin. *From Bombay Cinema to Bollywood: The Making of a Global Media Industry.* New York: New York University Press, 2013.

Rai, Amit S. *Untimely Bollywood: India's New Media Assemblage.* Durham, NC: Duke University Press, 2009.

Raina, Maharaj Krishna. *The Creative Passion: E. Paul Torrance's Voyages of Discovering Creativity.* Stamford, CT: Ablex, 2000.

Rajadhyaksha, Ashish. "The Bollywoodization of the Indian Cinema: Cultural Nationalism in a Global Arena." *Inter-Asia Cultural Studies* 4.1 (2003): 25–39.

Rantanen, Terhi. *The Media and Globalization.* Thousand Oaks, CA: Sage, 2005.

Raunig, Gerald. *Art and Revolution: Transversal Activism in the Long Twentieth Century.* Los Angeles: Semiotext(e), 2007.

Redvall, Eva Novrup. *Writing and Producing Television Drama in Denmark: From "The Kingdom" to "The Killing."* New York: Palgrave Macmillan, 2013.

Reichardt, Rolf, and Hubertus Kohle. *Visualizing the Revolution: Politics and Pictorial Arts in Late Eighteenth-Century France.* London: Reaktion, 2008.

Ritzer, George, and Nathan Jurgenson. "Production, Consumption, Prosumption: The Nature of Capitalism in the Age of the Digital 'Prosumer.'" *Journal of Consumer Culture* 10.1 (2010): 13–36.

Rose, Margaret A. *Parody: Ancient, Modern and Post-modern.* Cambridge: Cambridge University Press, 1993.

Ross, Andrew. *Fast Boat to China: Corporate Flight and the Consequences of Free Trade: Lessons from Shanghai.* New York: Pantheon Books, 2006.

———. *Nice Work If You Can Get It: Life and Labor in Precarious Times.* New York: New York University Press, 2009.

———. "Nice Work If You Can Get It: The Mercurial Career of Creative Industries Policy." *Work Organisation, Labour & Globalisation* 1.1 (2006). 1–19.

Rosten, Leo. *Hollywood: The Movie Colony, the Movie Makers.* New York: Harcourt Brace, 1941.

Roussel, Violaine, and Denise Bielby, eds. *Brokerage and Production in the American and French Entertainment Industries: Invisible Hands in Cultural Markets.* Lanham, MD: Lexington Books, 2015.

Ryan, Connor. "Nollywood and the Limits of Informality: A Conversation with Tunde Kelani, Bond Emeruwa, and Emem Isong." *Black Camera* 5.2 (2013): 168–185.

Sandoval, Marisol. *From Corporate to Social Media: Critical Perspectives on Corporate Social Responsibility in Media and Communication Industries.* London: Routledge, 2014.

Saxenian, AnnaLee. *The New Argonauts: Regional Advantage in a Global Economy.* Cambridge, MA: Harvard University Press, 2006.

———. *Regional Advantage: Culture and Competition in Silicon Valley and Route 128.* Cambridge, MA: Harvard University Press, 1996.

Schatz, Thomas. *The Genius of the System: Hollywood Filmmaking in the Studio Era.* New York: Pantheon Books, 1988.

Schiller, Dan. *Digital Depression: Information Technology and Economic Crisis.* Champaign: University of Illinois Press, 2014.

Schiller, Herbert I. *Mass Communication and American Empire.* 2nd ed. Boulder, CO: Westview, 1969.

Schumpeter, Joseph A. *Capitalism, Socialism and Democracy.* New York: Routledge, 2006 (1942).

Schwoch, James. *The American Radio Industry and Its Latin American Activities, 1900–1939.* Urbana: University of Illinois Press, 1990.

Scott, Allen J. *On Hollywood: The Place, the Industry.* Princeton, NJ: Princeton University Press, 2005.

Scott, James C. *Domination and the Arts of Resistance: Hidden Transcripts.* New Haven, CT: Yale University Press, 1990.

Shephard, Benjamin. *Play, Creativity and Social Movement.* New York: Routledge, 2011.

Shim, Doobo. "South Korean Media Industry in the 1990s and the Economic Crisis." *Prometheus* 20.4 (2002): 337–350.

Shin, Chi-Yun, and Julian Stringer, *New Korean Cinema.* Oxford: Oxford University Press, 2005.

Sinclair, John, and Joseph Straubhaar. *Latin American Television Industries.* London: British Film Institute, 2013.

Soloway, Colin, and Abubaker Saddigue. *USAID's Assistance to the Media Sector in Afghanistan.* Washington: USAID, 2005.

Sparks, Erin, and Mary Jo Watts. *Degrees for What Jobs? Raising Expectations for Universities and Colleges in a Global Economy.* Washington: National Governors Association Center for Best Practices, 2011.

Spigel, Lynn. "Entertainment Wars: Television Culture after 9/11." *American Quarterly* 56.2 (2004): 235–270.

———. *Welcome to the Dreamhouse: Popular Media and Postwar Suburbs.* Durham, NC: Duke University Press, 2001.

Sreberny-Mohammadi, Annabelle, and Ali Mohammadi. *Small Media, Big Revolution: Communication, Culture and the Iranian Revolution.* Minneapolis: University of Minnesota Press, 1994.

Stabile, Carol A., and Deepa Kumar. "Unveiling Imperialism: Media, Gender and the War on Afghanistan." *Media, Culture & Society* 27.5 (2005): 765–782.

Stahl, Matt. *Unfree Masters: Recording Artists and the Politics of Work.* Durham, NC: Duke University Press, 2013.

Stallybrass, Peter, and Allon White. *The Politics and Poetics of Transgression.* London: Methuen, 1986.

Standing, Guy. *The Precariat: The New Dangerous Class.* London: Bloomsbury, 2011.

Storper, Michael, and Susan Christopherson. "Flexible Specialization and Regional Industrial Agglomeration: The Case of the U.S. Motion Picture Industry." *Annals of the Association of American Geographers* 77 (1987): 1104–1117.

Straubhaar, Joseph. "Beyond Media Imperialism: Asymmetrical Interdependency and Cultural Proximity." *Critical Studies in Mass Communication* 8 (1991): 39–59.

———. *World Television from Global to Local.* Los Angeles: Sage, 2007.

Szczepanik, Petr. "Globalization through the Eyes of Runners: Student Interns as Ethnographers on Runaway Productions in Prague." *Media Industries Journal* 1.1 (2013).

———. "The State-Socialist Mode of Production and the Political History of Production Culture." In *Behind the Screen: Inside European Production Cultures,* edited by Petr Szczepanik and Patrick Vonderau. New York: Palgrave Macmillan, 2013.

Taormino, Tristan. "Calling the Shots: Feminist Porn in Theory and Practice." In *The Feminist Porn Book: The Politics of Producing Pleasure,* edited by Tristan Taormino, Constance Penley, Celine Parreñas Shimizu, and Mireille Miller-Young. New York: Feminist Press, 2013.

Taormino, Tristan, Constance Penley, Celine Parreñas Shimizu, and Mireille Miller-Young, eds. *The Feminist Porn Book.* New York: Feminist Press, 2013.

Taylor, Clyde R. "Black Silence and the Politics of Representation." In *African-American Filmmaking and Race Cinema of the Silent Era: Oscar Micheaux and His Circle,* edited by Pearl Bowser, Jane Gaines, and Charles Musser. Bloomington: Indiana University Press, 2001.

Terranova, Tiziana. "Free Labor." In *Digital Labor: The Internet as Playground and Factory,* edited by Trebor Scholz. New York: Routledge, 2013.

———. "Free Labor: Producing Culture for the Digital Economy." *Social Text* 18.2 (2000): 33–58.

Thomas, Rosie. *Bombay before Bollywood: Film City Fantasies.* Albany: State University of New York Press, 2013.

Thrift, Nigel. *Non-Representational Theory.* New York: Routledge, 2008.

———. "Understanding the Material Practices of Glamor." In *The Affect Theory Reader,* edited by Melissa Gregg and Gregory J. Seigworth. Durham, NC: Duke University Press, 2010.

Toffler, Alvin. *Powershift: Knowledge, Wealth, and Violence at the Edge of the Twenty-First Century.* New York: Bantam, 1990.

———. *Previews and Premises.* New York: William Morrow, 1983.

———. *The Third Wave.* New York: William Morrow, 1980.

Tomlinson, John. *Globalization and Culture.* Chicago: University of Chicago Press, 1999.

Torres, Sasha. *Black, White, and in Color: Television and Black Civil Rights.* Princeton, NJ: Princeton University Press, 2003.

Toynbee, Jason. "How Special? Cultural Work, Copyright, Politics." In *Theorizing Cultural Work: Labour, Continuity and Change in the Cultural and Creative Industries,* edited by Mark Banks, Rosalind Gil, and Stephanie Taylor. Abingdon: Routledge, 2013.

Trejo, Raúl. "Muchos medios en pocas manos: Concentración televisiva y democracia en América Latina." *Revista Brasileira de ciencias da comunicacao* 33.1 (2010): 17–51.

Vajpeyi, Ananya. "Hindi, Hinglish: Head to Head." *World Policy Journal* 29 (Summer 2012).

Vanderhoef, John, and Michael Curtin. "The Crunch Heard Round the World: The Global Era of Digital Game Labor." In *Production Studies: The Sequel!* edited by Bridget Conor, Miranda Banks, and Vicki Mayer. New York: Routledge, 2015.

Ward, Susan, and Tom O'Regan. "The Film Producer as the Long-Stay Business Tourist: Rethinking Film and Tourism from a Gold Coast Perspective." *Tourism Geographies* 11.2 (May 2009): 214–232.

Warner, Kristen J. *The Cultural Politics of Colorblind TV Casting.* New York: Routledge, 2015.

Warner, Michael. *Publics and Counterpublics.* Cambridge: Zone Books, 2002.

Wasko, Janet. *How Hollywood Works.* London: Sage, 2003.

Wasserman, Herman, and Shakuntala Rao. "The Glocalization of Journalism Ethics." *Journalism* 9.2 (2008): 163–181.

Wedeen, Lisa. *Ambiguities of Domination: Politics, Rhetoric and Symbols in Contemporary Syria.* Chicago: University of Chicago Press, 1999.

Whyte, Martin King. "The Paradox of Rural-Urban Inequality in Contemporary China." In *One Country, Two Societies: Rural-Urban Inequality in Contemporary China,* edited by Martin King Whyte. Cambridge, MA: Harvard University Press, 2010.

Yang, Guobin. *The Power of the Internet in China: Citizen Activism Online.* New York: Columbia University Press, 2009.

Yoon, Hyejin, and Edward J. Malecki "Cartoon Planet: Worlds of Production and Global Production Networks in the Animation Industry." *Industrial and Corporate Change* 19.1 (2010): 239–271.

Yudice, George. *The Expediency of Culture: Uses of Culture in the Global Era.* Durham, NC: Duke University Press, 2003.

Zhao, Yuezhi. *Communication in China: Political Economy, Power and Conflict.* Lanham, MD: Rowman and Littlefield, 2008.

Zhu, Ying. *Two Billion Eyes: The Story of China Central Television.* New York: Free Press, 2012.

Zoya, John Follain, Rita Cristofari, and Rita Wolf. *Zoya's Story: An Afghan Woman's Struggle for Freedom.* New York: HarperCollins, 2002.

Zurayk, Rami. *Food, Farming and Freedom: Sowing the Arab Spring.* Charlottesville, VA: Just World Books, 2011.

NOTES ON CONTRIBUTORS

JOHN BANKS is Associate Professor of Media and Communications in the Creative Industries Faculty, Queensland University of Technology. He researches co-creativity, labor, and social media in the creative industries. He has a special interest in video games developer organizational and studio workplace cultures. His past decade of research on the topic of co-creativity in the video games industry culminated in *Co-creating Videogames* (Bloomsbury Academic, 2013).

MIRANDA BANKS is Associate Professor of Visual and Media Arts at Emerson College and a Research Fellow in the Emerson Engagement Lab. She is author of *The Writers: A History of American Screenwriters and Their Guild* (Rutgers, 2015) and coeditor of *Production Studies: Cultural Studies of Media Industries* (Routledge, 2009) and *Production Studies the Sequel! Cultural Studies of Global Media Industries* (Routledge, 2015). Her work has appeared in *Popular Communication, Television and New Media, Cultural Studies,* and *Montage A/V,* as well as a number of anthologies, including *Gender and Creative Labor* and *How to Watch Television.*

HEATHER BERG, a doctoral candidate at the University of California, Santa Barbara's Department of Feminist Studies, focuses her research on Marxist and queer theory, sex work, and public policy. Her forthcoming dissertation—*Porn Work: Adult Film at the Point of Production*—looks at adult film performance, independent contractor status, worker resistance, and precarity. Heather's writing appears in the journals *Feminist Studies, WSQ, Porn Studies, Social Policy and Society,* and in the anthologies *Queer Sex Work* and *Human Trafficking Reconsidered.*

JOHN CALDWELL is Professor of Cinema and Media Studies at UCLA. His books include *Production Culture: Industrial Reflexivity and Critical Practice in Film and Television* (2008), *Production Studies: Cultural Studies of Media Industries* (2009, coedited with Vicki Mayer and Miranda Banks), *Televisuality: Style, Crisis, and Authority in American Television*

(1995), *Electronic Media and Technoculture* (2000), and *New Media: Theories and Practices of Digitextuality* (2003, coedited with Anna Everett). Caldwell's feature documentaries include *Rancho California* (Sundance premiere, 2002) and *Boron to Buttonwillow* (2016). His awards include German Bauhaus IKKM Fellow (2012), UCLA Distinguished Teaching Award (2010), and National Endowment for the Arts Fellowships (1979, 1985).

STUART CUNNINGHAM is Distinguished Professor of Media and Communications, Queensland University of Technology. His most recent books are *Digital Disruption: Cinema Moves Online* (edited with Dina Iordanova, 2012), *Key Concepts in Creative Industries* (with John Hartley, Jason Potts, Terry Flew, John Banks, and Michael Keane, 2013), *Hidden Innovation: Policy, Industry and the Creative Sector* (2013), *Screen Distribution and the New King Kongs of the Online World* (with Jon Silver, 2013), *The Media and Communications in Australia* (4th ed., with Sue Turnbull, 2014), and *Media Economics* (2015, with Terry Flew and Adam Swift).

MICHAEL CURTIN is the Duncan and Suzanne Mellichamp Professor of Global Studies in the Department of Film and Media Studies and cofounder of the Media Industries Project at the University of California, Santa Barbara. His previous books include *The American Television Industry*; *Reorienting Global Communication: Indian and Chinese Media beyond Borders*; *Playing to the World's Biggest Audience: The Globalization of Chinese Film and TV*; and *Distribution Revolution: Conversations about the Digitial Future of Film and Television.*

ANTHONY Y. H. FUNG is Director and Professor in the School of Journalism and Communication at the Chinese University of Hong Kong. He is also Pearl River Scholar Chair Professor in the School of Journalism and Communication at Jinan University, China. His research interests and teaching focus on popular culture and cultural studies, gender and youth identity, cultural industries and policy, and new media studies. He is currently working on a project on Asian creative and game industries and cultural policy with a focus on China and Hong Kong. He has authored and edited more than ten Chinese and English books. His recent books are *New Television Globalization and East Asian Cultural Imaginations* (Hong Kong University Press, 2007, with Michael Keane and Albert Moran), *Global Capital, Local Culture: Transnational Media Corporations in China* (Peter Lang, 2008), *Riding a Melodic Tide: The Development of Cantopop in Hong Kong* (Subculture Press, 2009, in Chinese), *Policies for the Sustainable Development of the Hong Kong Film Industry* (Chinese University Press, 2009, with Joseph Chan and Ng Chun Hung), *Melodic Memories: The Historical Development of Music Industry in Hong Kong* (Subculture Press, 2010, in Chinese), *Asian Popular Culture: The Global (Dis)continuity* (Routledge, 2013), and *Chinese Youth Culture* (Polity, forthcoming, with Jeroen de Kloet).

TEJASWINI GANTI is Associate Professor in the Department of Anthropology and its Program in Culture and Media at New York University. A visual anthropologist specializing in South Asia, she has been conducting ethnographic research about the social world and filmmaking practices of the Hindi film industry since 1996 and is the author of *Producing Bollywood: Inside the Contemporary Hindi Film Industry* (Duke University Press, 2012) and *Bollywood: A Guidebook to Popular Hindi Cinema* (Routledge, 2004; 2nd edition, 2013).

HERMAN GRAY is Professor of Sociology at University of California Santa Cruz and has published widely in black cultural theory, politics, and media. Gray is the author of *Watching Race* (Minnesota) and *Cultural Moves* (California), and he coedited *Towards a Sociology of the Trace* with Macarena Gomez Barris (Minnesota). Most recently, he coedited *The Sage Handbook of Television Studies* with Manuel Alvarado, Milly Buonanno, and Toby Miller.

DAVID HESMONDHALGH is Professor of Media, Music and Culture in the School of Media and Communication at the University of Leeds. He is the author (with Kate Oakley, David Lee, and Melissa Nisbett) of *Culture, Economy and Politics: The Case of New Labour* (Palgrave, 2015), *Why Music Matters* (Wiley-Blackwell, 2013), *Creative Labour: Media Work in Three Cultural Industries* (Routledge, 2011, with Sarah Baker), and *The Cultural Industries*, now in its third edition (Sage, 2013). He is also editor or coeditor of numerous other books and journal special issues, including *The Media and Social Theory* (with Jason Toynbee, Routledge, 2008) and (with Anamik Saha) a special issue of the journal *Popular Communication*, "Race, Ethnicity and Cultural Production" (2013).

MICHAEL KEANE is Professor of Chinese Media and Cultural Studies at Curtin University, Perth. He is author or editor of fifteen books on China's media, of which his most recent book is *The Chinese Television Industry* (BFI Palgrave, 2015). He previously worked as an ARC Fellow at the Australian Research Council Centre of Excellence for Creative Industries and Innovation, Queensland University of Technology, Brisbane. His specialties include China's cultural and media policy, creative industries in China and East Asia, Chinese and East Asian media, TV formats in Asia, and East Asian cultural exports.

MARWAN M. KRAIDY is the Anthony Shadid Chair in Global Media, Politics and Culture and Director of the Project for Advanced Research in Global Communication, at the Annenberg School, University of Pennsylvania. A recipient of Guggenheim, ACLS, NEH, Woodrow Wilson, and NIAS fellowships, he has published over a hundred essays and six books, including *Hybridity, or the Cultural Logic of Globalization* (Temple, 2005) and *Reality Television and Arab Politics* (Cambridge, 2010), which won three major prizes. Kraidy's *The Naked Blogger of Cairo: Creative Insurgency in the Arab World* is forthcoming from Harvard University Press in 2016. He tweets at @MKraidy.

SHANTI KUMAR is Associate Professor and Graduate Advisor in the Department of Radio-TV-Film and a faculty affiliate in the Department of Asian Studies, the Center for Asian-American Studies, and the South Asia Institute at the University of Texas at Austin. He is the author of *Gandhi Meets Primetime: Globalization and Nationalism in Indian Television* (University of Illinois Press, 2006), and coeditor of *Planet TV: A Global Television Reader* (New York University Press, 2003), *Television at Large in South Asia* (Routledge, 2012), and *Global Communication: New Agendas in Communication* (Routledge, 2013).

VICKI MAYER is Professor of Communication at Tulane University and coeditor of the journal *Television & New Media*. She has authored two books and over thirty journal articles and book chapters about media production and the production of cultural identities and edited two editions of *Production Studies: Cultural Studies of Media Industries* (Routledge 2010 and 2015). This work draws on a current project about local film production and regional tax incentive policies with a focus on New Orleans, Louisiana.

JADE L. MILLER is Assistant Professor in Communication Studies at Wilfrid Laurier Univeristy in Waterloo, Ontario. She received her PhD in communications from the University of Southern California and subsequently held a Mellon Postdoctoral Fellowship at Tulane University before joining the Laurier faculty. Her work on global networks in media industries has been published in a number of journals, including *Global Media and*

Communication and the *International Journal of Communication*. Her first book, entitled *Nollywood Central,* on the southern Nigerian movie industry, is forthcoming from British Film Institute Press in 2016.

TOBY MILLER is Emeritus Distinguished Professor, University of California, Riverside; Sir Walter Murdoch Professor of Cultural Policy Studies, Murdoch University; Profesor Invitado, Escuela de Comunicación Social, Universidad del Norte; Professor of Journalism, Media and Cultural Studies, Cardiff University/Prifysgol Caerdydd; and Director of the Institute of Media and Creative Industries, Loughborough University London. The author and editor of over forty books, his work has appeared in Spanish, Chinese, Portuguese, Japanese, Turkish, German, Italian, Farsi, and Swedish. His most recent volumes are *The Sage Companion to Television Studies, The Routledge Companion to Global Popular Culture, Greening the Media,* and *Blow Up the Humanities.*

CONSTANCE PENLEY is Professor of Film and Media Studies and founding Director and Co-Director Emerita of the Carsey-Wolf Center at the University of California, Santa Barbara. A founding editor of *Camera Obscura: Feminism, Culture, and Media Studies,* she is the author of *The Future of an Illusion: Film, Feminism, and Psychoanalysis; NASA/TREK: Popular Science and Sex in America;* and the forthcoming *Teaching Pornography.* She is the editor or coeditor of many influential anthologies, including *Feminism and Film Theory; Technoculture; Male Trouble; The Visible Woman: Imaging Technologies, Gender, and Science;* and *The Feminist Porn Book: The Politics of Producing Pleasure.*

ALLISON PERLMAN is Assistant Professor in the Department of Film and Media Studies and the Department of History at the University of California, Irvine. She is the author of *Public Interests: Media Advocacy and Struggles over U.S. Television,* forthcoming from Rutgers University Press. She also is the coeditor of *Flow TV: Television in the Age of Media Convergence* (New York: Routledge, 2010).

JUAN PIÑÓN is Associate Professor at the Department of Media, Culture, and Communication at New York University. He has a PhD in media studies from the University of Texas at Austin and an MA from Universidad Iberoamericana in Mexico City. Dr. Piñón is interested in the intersection of Latin American transnational media corporate dynamics with the established mode of production of U.S. Latino media. He is the U.S. coordinator of the Ibero-American Observatory of Television Fiction (Obitel), an international academic research project on television fiction. His work has been published in *Communication Theory, Global Media and Communication, Television and New Media,* and *International Journal of Cultural Studies,* among the most salient.

VIOLAINE ROUSSEL is Professor of Sociology at the University of Paris VIII and Research Fellow at the CRESPPA-CNRS (Centre de Recherches Sociologiques et Politiques de Paris) in France, as well as Adjunct Professor at the University of Southern California. A former Fulbright Scholar, she started exploring the entertainment industries with extended work on arts and politics, published in three volumes: *Voicing Dissent* (Routledge, 2010); "Arts and Politics: A French-American Perspective" (Springer, 2010); and *Art vs War: Les artistes américains contre la guerre en Irak* (Presses de Sciences Po, 2011). She was recently awarded a Marie Curie International Outgoing Fellowship by the European Commission to study the role of talent agents in Hollywood, and she is currently preparing a book on that topic.

In 2015, she coedited *Brokerage and Production in the American and French Entertainment Industries* (Lexington Books, with Denise Bielby).

KEVIN SANSON is Lecturer of Entertainment Industries at Queensland University of Technology in Australia. His research examines the spatial dynamics of international film and television production, focusing especially on shifting working conditions and practices in global production hubs. He is coeditor of *Distribution Revolution: Conversations about the Digital Future of Film and Television* and *Connected Viewing: Selling, Streaming, and Sharing Media in the Digital Era* and is part of the founding editorial collective of *Media Industries,* the first peer-reviewed open-access journal for media industries research.

MATT SIENKIEWICZ is Assistant Professor of Communication and International Studies at Boston College. His research has been published in *Critical Studies in Media Communication, Communication and Critical/Cultural Studies, Media, Culture and Society,* and *The International Journal of Cultural Studies.* He is the coeditor of *Saturday Night Live and American TV,* the codirector of the documentary *Live From Bethlehem,* and the author of the forthcoming book *The Other Air Force.*

PETR SZCZEPANIK is Associate Professor at Masaryk University, Brno, and editor of the Czech film journal *Iluminace.* His current research focuses on the Czech (post)socialist production system, some of the results of which were published in *Behind the Screen: Inside European Production Culture* (Palgrave, 2013, coedited with Patrick Vonderau). He was also the main coordinator of an EU-funded project, "FIND" (www.projectfind.cz), which used student internships in production companies to combine job shadowing with ethnographic research on production cultures.

KRISTEN J. WARNER is Assistant Professor of Telecommunication and Film at the University of Alabama. Her research interests are centered at the juxtaposition of televisual racial representation and its place within the media industries, particularly within the practice of casting. Warner's work can be found in *Television and New Media* and *Camera Obscura.* She is also the author of *The Cultural Politics of Colorblind TV Casting* (Routledge, 2015).

INDEX